Lives in Spirit

*SUNY series in Transpersonal
and Humanistic Psychology*

Richard D. Mann, Editor

Lives in Spirit

Precursors and Dilemmas of a Secular Western Mysticism

Harry T. Hunt

STATE UNIVERSITY OF NEW YORK PRESS

Published by
State University of New York Press, Albany

For information, address State University of New York Press,
90 State Street, Suite 700, Albany, N. Y. 12207

Production by Diane Ganeles
Marketing by Fran Keneston

Library of Congress Cataloguing-in-Publication Data

Hunt, Harry T., 1943–
    Lives in spirit : precursors and dilemmas of a secular Western mysticism /
Harry T. Hunt.
        p. cm. — (SUNY series in transpersonal and humanistic psychology)
    Includes bibliographical references and index.
    ISBN 0-7914-5803-2 (alk. paper) — ISBN 0-7914-5804-0 (pbk. : alk. paper)
        1. Mysticism—Psychology—Case studies.   2. Secularism—Psychology—
Case studies.   3. Spirituality—Psychology—Case studies.   4. Transpersonal
psychology—Case studies.   I. Title.   II. Series.

BL625.H85 2003
291.4'2—dc21
                                                                            2002045266
10   9   8   7   6   5   4   3   2   1

Contents

Acknowledgments

This book completes the plan, apparently begun well before I knew there was one. My undergraduate honors thesis at Harvard was an integration, foreshadowing the one herein, of Jung, psychoanalytic object-relations theory, and Max Weber on the sociology of mysticism, all applied to the life and system of Gurdjieff. I was left with the issue of how to decide between psychoanalytic views of spirituality as regression and transpersonal intuitions of its higher cognitive development. Beginning in graduate school at Brandeis, and to address this question, I sought a cognitive psychology appropriate to a detailed phenomenology of altered states of consciousness, and still later applied both, in papers and in two books, to research and to theory on meditation, introspective consciousness, metaphor and imaginative absorption, dreaming and transpersonal states, and consciousness itself.

All along I continued to teach on the personality and sociological sides of these issues, gradually including some of the life histories found herein and to which I now finally return, adding in the precise synthesis of spirituality and psychodynamics developed in recent years by A.H. Almaas, along with my own cognitive-developmental understanding of these states. Of course, the personal side of this had begun still earlier, with the death of my father in childhood. My intense reaction therefrom against all things religious, and my satisfaction in my high school atheism, were as abruptly set aside in beginning to read Jung and Nietzsche, and still later William James and Rudolf Otto, which convinced me that the core of religion had never been about belief (or failed prayer) but rather individual experiences directly undergone. These could be studied empirically. That

xi

was the revelation, and from it, along with my own later meditative and consciousness explorations, everything followed. I am apparently one of those academics who spend their thirty-year career on the currents and cross-currents of one problem.

So this time around perhaps I should first thank myself, immodestly perhaps, but still with gratitude and some surprise for seeing it through to the point where the questions that troubled me have been addressed, at least to my own limits and satisfaction, and with a sense of something completed.

I very much appreciate the understanding and guidance of Carol Munschauer, Scott Layton, Alia Johnson, and Hameed Ali. I am grateful to Ali, Frank Rocchio, and Laurie Hollis-Walker for reading and commenting on the manuscript, and to the latter for her kind help in its final preparation. I am also grateful for the friendship of Charlotte Swick throughout, and I thank my children Amanda and Nathan for their encouragement and support. I deeply appreciate the invaluable secretarial assistance of Linda Pidduck, who so expedited and smoothed this effort. My gratitude also goes to Diane Shephard, Archivist of the Lynn Historical Society.

Both now gone, I thank my parents, Margaret and Arthur Hunt.

Introduction

The concern of this work is with the lives of a number of figures, who, collectively and at least in hindsight, can be seen as precursors of a contemporary transpersonal psychology of spiritual development and as exemplars of what the sociologists of religion, Max Weber and Ernst Troeltsch, saw as a western this-worldly mysticism—predictably characteristic of modernity and culminating in contemporary "New Age" spirituality. We will focus on the spontaneous openings of consciousness and attendant personal and social struggles found in Nietzsche, Emerson, Thoreau, and later Jung, Heidegger, Gurdjieff, Crowley, and Blavatsky, as well as more contemporary figures such as Maslow, Jean Houston, and the counterculture figure Jerry Garcia. Their lives will prove directly relevant to all those today who are also in search of "higher states of consciousness" in the context of our hyper-individualized, sensate, and materialist society. The strengths and vulnerabilities of much contemporary spirituality do seem best understood by seeing their more exaggerated forms in these paradigmatic precursor figures.

Several different levels of analysis are intertwined in this attempt to understand the birth of a modern this-worldly spirituality through these figures. First, there is the descriptive phenomenology of mystical or numinous experience that allows us to approach these states as empirical phenomena open to a nonreductive, but broadly "naturalistic" study. The basics of the descriptive phenomenology of an experiential core of human spirituality were developed by William James and Rudolf Otto, and extended in very different ways by Martin Heidegger, Marghanita Laski, Abraham Maslow, Carl Jung, and most recently by A.H. Almaas. The transpersonal psychology of Almaas and

1

others, focused on the unfolding of numinous experience in self-actualizing individuals, becomes the second major level of inquiry. It is the understanding of Almaas that experiential openings of the kind undergone by our paradigmatic figures, must, to some degree, both stir up and be distorted by underlying conflicts of a narcissistic and schizoid nature. Such conflicts seem endemic to our modern hyper-individualized society and are the special province of British psycho-analytic object-relations theory and Kohut's related self-psychology. Our third strand of analysis, then, will be the psychodynamic approaches of D.W. Winnicott, Melanie Klein, W.R.D. Fairbairn, and Heinz Kohut, which can be seen as illuminating the inevitable underside and challenge of spiritual awakening. The final level of analysis is the comparative sociology of "radical salvation movements" developed by Max Weber and Ernst Troeltsch. They understand the struggles toward an "inner-worldly" mysticism as the potential response of an alienated, educated, and middle-class modernity to the historical secularization of the Judeo-Christian tradition first announced by Nietzsche's "God is dead."

While my overall perspective could best be termed "transpersonal," it should also be clear that the present work is based on a specific bridging of a series of divisions that have grown up, detrimentally in my view, between current transpersonal approaches and the more mainstream human sciences. First, there is the split between transpersonal intuitions about "higher states of consciousness" and the contemporary cognitive psychology of consciousness. It has been the burden of some of my previous work (Hunt 1989, 1995a, 1999) to show the mutual relevance of studies of meditative or related psychedelic states and a holistic cognitive and neuropsychology. Second, and more developed herein, there has been the unfortunate tendency to separate transpersonal studies of self-realization from the supposedly "lower" psychodynamic psychologies of conflict. While the reductionism of Freud and many of his successors with regard to spirituality seems deeply misguided, Maslow himself came to see that transpersonal development could entail characteristic spiritual or "meta" pathologies. What he did not see is how similar these patterns of grandiosity, despair, or withdrawal are to the personal and clinical difficulties that became central to the expansion of psychoanalysis brought about by Winnicott and Kohut. The latter offer the transpersonalists a ready-made and detailed understanding of the difficulties that can intrude on a spiritual path.

A closely related split between transpersonal approaches and the rest of psychology comes from the failure of the transpersonalists to utilize the life-history methodologies developed by psychodynamic theorists of life-span development such as Erik Erikson (1963, 1969), and Robert W. White (1975), and later applied so effectively to midlife crisis by Levinson (1978), counter-cultural youth by Keniston (1966), and the psychohistory of creative innovation by Gardner (1993). It is one of the ironies of the development of transpersonal and humanistic psychology, with its alienation from what was seen as the sterility of mainstream universities, that Maslow and others ignored the one methodology, ironically also overlooked by academic personality psychology, most suitable to validate their observations. It was the psychobiographical life history, first developed by Henry Murray (1938) and extended by R.W. White and others, that was best suited to explore Maslow's observations of a spontaneous spirituality in mid and late-life "self-actualization." Since self-actualization was a potential development in the lives of relatively creative and autonomous individuals, any logic of validation must ultimately rest with these detailed methodologies for the empirical study of individual lives.

Finally, there is the tendency among some transpersonalists to leap to speculative versions of a linear-historical or even biological evolution of consciousness to understand the contemporary development of a "new age" spirituality, ignoring the more plausible empirical contributions of the anthropology and sociology of ecstatic states. Max Weber, Ernst Troeltsch, and others have provided a template for understanding the intersection of social change and revolutionary religiosity in a way that makes the modern tendency toward an inner-worldly, experiential spirituality comprehensible in purely sociocultural terms.

A full understanding of the precursors of this modern spirituality will necessitate an undoing of these misleading divisions between transpersonal psychology and the comparative sociology and anthropology of religion, psychodynamics and life history methodology, and the cognitive psychology of consciousness. Put otherwise, these precursor figures will be most fully illuminated when we bring all these levels of analysis together, understanding them not as some "explaining away" of human spirituality, which is after all a basic capacity of our symbolic species, but as showing the complex matrices through which it will be expressed.

The first three chapters introduce this multi-disciplinary framework of understanding. They are the equivalent of setting out the pieces of a board game, thence opening into subsequent movement and combination. In turn, the successive life histories to be considered will illuminate and develop the fuller implications of this guiding theoretical perspective. Chapter one outlines the descriptive phenomenology of transpersonal or numinous experience, considered as the cross cultural experiential core of human religiosity, and begins an exploration of psychoanalytic object relations theory as best describing the conflicts and derailments that can also occur with these states. Chapter two is an overview of the transpersonal psychology of numinous or "essential" development of A.H. Almaas. Then in chapter three the sociocultural approach of the sociologists Max Weber and Ernst Troeltsch will be introduced, along with Erika Bourguignon's supportive work from the anthropology of shamanism, in order to better understand how it is that the contemporary interest in altered states of consciousness and "new age" mysticism have become predictable twentieth-century developments—and also why this contemporary reorganization of spirituality is so often conflicted and imbalanced. In particular, Weber and Troeltsch saw, in the wake of a secularization of the more prophetical tradition of Christianity, the advent of an inner-worldly mysticism emerging within the educated middle classes. This form of spirituality seeks an expansion of consciousness while staying within the world, within daily life, rather than withdrawing to caves and monasteries in the manner of the more traditional "other-worldly" mysticisms. A this-worldly experiential spirituality, must, for Weber, run into characteristic difficulties through its very openness and sensitivity amidst a complexly demanding secular society—as we will see in detail in the figures initiating this cultural turn.

Chapters four and five continue to unfold this multi-layered framework of understanding by setting out something of its historical context. The history of a characteristically western inner-worldly mysticism begins in the Hellenistic era of Roman hegemony, wherein we can locate the basic template of its contemporary manifestations, as well as the spiritual pathologies and distortions to which it can give rise. In chapter four, anticipations of the full range of a contemporary "this-worldly" mysticism can be found in the more personal development of the Stoic and Socratic philosophers on the one hand, and, on the other, in the "formless" mysticism of Plotinus, the neo-Platonist philosopher of the third century A.D. Chapter five will consider those competitors of Plotinus, the so-called Gnostics, whom he attacks for the very narcissism and withdrawal that are the meta-pathologies of contemporary spirituality. The Gnostics show how the cultivation of a radical openness of consciousness, in the complex and pressured society of the Roman provinces, faced the dilemmas of defensive narcissism, dualistic splitting, and hatred that became directly enshrined in their often bizarre cosmologies. If the present treatment were purely historical we could then proceed to heretical Christian movements like the Bogomils and Cathars, Jewish Kabbalistic mysticism, and later Renaissance visionary magic, and finally to Swedenbourg and the later romanticism of Goethe, Blake, and Coleridge—all as variants of a characteristically Western inner-worldly mysticism and already effectively traced by Hanagraaff (1998). Instead, our principle concern is with the figures of modernity whose struggles and neo-Gnostic dilemmas initiate the contemporary shape of a "naturalistic" spirituality.

Chapter six, then, begins our focus on these paradigmatic figures of spiritual modernity with the life and philosophy of Nietzsche, who confronted a very contemporary nihilism with his own notion of a higher, experience-based "self actualization." His early personal history and characterological dynamics were such, and potentially apart from his final neurological breakdown, that his own ecstatic opening was doomed to major conflict—much as was later also the case with Abraham Maslow. In chapter seven, we will consider the American anticipation of this Nietzschean revolution, in the this-worldly transcendentalism of Emerson and Thoreau, also to be contrasted with Hiram Marble, a spiritualist of their times. Thoreau is a perfect exemplar of historical tendencies toward a new understanding of spirituality, here as a creative nature mysticism. Thoreau, as with Nietzsche, founders around his inability to fully assimilate the wounded hatred and destructiveness running through his personal life. Emerson by contrast is perhaps the unambiguous spiritual "good news" among our precursor figures.

Chapters eight and nine consider the temptations and distortions that can ensue when a this-worldly spirituality becomes linked to political movements and ideologies. In this context, we consider the unfortunate fascination with National Socialism in the early 1930s shared by Carl Jung and Martin Heidegger. Drawn in by their own personal grandiosity and regressive romanticism, both gradually saw their error and extricated themselves and their systems from these upsetting implications.

Chapters ten, eleven, and twelve concentrate on figures whose inner-worldly mystical movements have directly or indirectly affected modern transpersonalism. Chapter ten considers the life and system of George Gurdjieff, the widely influential Russian spiritual teacher, again both in terms of his genuine success in integrating classical Sufism and western psychology, very much anticipating Almaas, and in the conflicts apparent through much of Gurdjieff's life.

In chapter eleven, and more on the dark side, we will examine the tortured life of Aleister Crowley, with his compulsive use of sexual ritual and magical methods of consciousness transformation, including his enthusiastic advocation of not just psychedelic drug use, but heroin and cocaine. He will offer an interesting contrast to the more recent life of Jerry Garcia, a deeply reluctant guru of psychedelic exploration. In the early Jung and Heidegger, and in Crowley, we find a false will and control that distorts spiritual development in certain characteristic ways, temporarily with Jung and Heidegger, but permanently with Crowley, who emerges in his own right as an example of a post-Nietzschean mystic who goes horribly, disastrously wrong.

In chapter twelve, the focus will shift to the development of a specifically feminist spirituality, in which these same inner-worldly mystical tendencies have made use of mother and goddess imageries as symbols for a spiritual absolute. Again, this can appear as a valuable spiritual opening for many women, while also potentially limited by the unresolved psychodynamic issues which it can also raise. Here we will examine the life of the theosophist Madame Blavatsky and the recent autobiography of Jean Houston, one of the major developers of a post-Jungian mythological psychology very much centered around goddess imagery.

The concluding chapter offers an overview of some common patterns in the lives of these pioneering spiritual individuals and explores the implications of their personal struggles for a current "new age" spirituality and transpersonal psychology. This includes linkages to "deep ecology" and popular but speculative theories of an "evolution" of consciousness. Our concern throughout is how best to understand the psychological, social, and historical forces that seem to push and encourage some among the educated and middle classes to develop this interest in a direct experiential spirituality, often understood in naturalistic or "scientific" terms. Their remaining within the complexities of everyday society must then bring out certain tensions and conflicts that will distort spiritual development in ways that can also be compensated, even transformed, to varying degrees.

The range of transpersonal thought and "New Age" spirituality constitutes a movement that seeks to address modern emotional and intellectual needs for a sense of purpose and meaning in life. In more classical societies and cultures, this sense of an encompassing and supporting meaning was self-referentially read off an ordered and supporting cosmos. The resulting sense of groundedness was reinforced and ratified by spontaneous and induced numinous experience, as reflected back to the group by its spiritual virtuosos. The reading of our core sense of identity from a mirroring and surrounding array begins, in the accounts of Winnicott and Kohut, in infancy. The infant gains its first sense of being real and alive by seeing its own expressiveness reflected back by an engaged and spontaneous mothering one. This same principle is then carried forward on a more abstract level as a culture's spiritual/metaphysical definition of reality. When that sense of an encompassing order is lost, in the eras of alienation that Weber found to be periodically inevitable in the histories of the great world civilizations, then the core of adult identity is also deleted in a manner formally reminiscent of the infant or young child whose aliveness is not sufficiently mirrored back. On both levels, there is a profound loss of sensed support and holding. The same dynamic conflicts become endemic, and, on both concrete childhood and abstract cultural levels, individuals face dilemmas that modern psychoanalysis understands as narcissistic and paranoid-schizoid.

It was Nietzsche, a bit over a hundred years ago, who announced this level of spiritual crisis in the modern west. Nietzsche and the other figures we will consider attempted to throw out around us once again an experientially sensed unity and purpose. Largely without traditional spiritual supports, they explored transformations of consciousness that might carry such a renewal. In so doing they had to face, very much alone, dilemmas and fears of "psychotic" proportions—adult versions of the "primitive agonies" Winnicott locates in children deprived of essential emotional support. In this regard, the pioneering figures we are studying, re-creating on their own the rudiments of a this-worldly spirituality in terms consistent with modernity, were astonishingly courageous. Only fully understandable in hindsight, the inevitable failures and miscarriages in such an endeavor attest to courageous acts undertaken without a net.

PART I

Psychological and Cultural Bases of Inner-Worldly Mysticism in Modern Western Society

CHAPTER 1

Phenomenology and Psychodynamics of
Transpersonal Experience

We begin with the development of phenomenologies and descriptive psychologies of mystical experience. The historical and cultural context for these concerns starts in the nineteenth century, where there appears a strong interest in a naturalistic philosophical understanding (Schleiermacher, Nietzsche) and social science (Tylor) of mystical and religious experience. All the great pioneers in the history of the social sciences, from James and Jung, early developmentalists like Hall and Baldwin, to Weber and Durkheim, were similarly preoccupied at the turn of the twentieth century with trying to define a spontaneous core of religiosity—and this as a fundamental task for the emerging human sciences. What we have, then, is a developing interest in the idea that there might be, quite apart from dogma and social custom, a felt experiential core to religion. This would be a cross-cultural universal of humanity, reappearing in every society and every era as the direct sense of something sacred or holy. Dogma would come in later, draped over this potentially renewable experiential core and sometimes almost erasing it.

A key to these approaches is that this experiential core, whatever else it may involve, is a thoroughly human phenomenon and open to investigation as such. After all, this was the opening era of the new human sciences and the naturalistic phenomenology that was their accompaniment, and pursued by psychologists, anthropologists, and sociologists, not theologians. If there is an experiential core to religious experience as a human phenomenon, this allows putting to one side, or "bracketing," the more traditional metaphysical questions of truth or falsity, as well as all those debates of science *versus* religion.

11

Alternatively, these questions can be asked over again in a radically new, pragmatic spirit. We can then ask of this human phenomenon, what is the function of religious or mystical experience? What is it like? What does it do? These questions became especially significant if, with William James, Carl Jung, or Max Weber, we also see that this experiential core is fundamental to any sense of overall significance or purpose in human life. So what we are studying here is the ground of a potentially fragile sense that our lives have an overall meaning.

The continuing relevance of this issue comes not only from the periodic resurgences of evangelical and "new age" spirituality, but also from various questionnaires showing that between 30 and 50 percent of adults in North American society claim to have had a classical mystical-like experience (Spilka et al. 1985)—with rates almost as high for related phenomena like out-of-body experience, near-death experience, lucid dreams, and other "altered states of consciousness." While all these states show minor cross-cultural differences, there is a still more striking overlap, and they can be experienced entirely independent of prior knowledge or suggestion (Hunt 2000). So we are dealing with something that potentially one out of two people eventually undergoes and comes to regard as among their more personally significant life experiences.

Of course, it is also true that the human science of an experiential core of spirituality can approach that core either reductionistically or from a more holistic point of view. Sigmund Freud, and the sociologist Emile Durkheim, took the more reductionistic approach. For them, an experiential core, while admittedly a powerful force in human life, is a kind of illusion, and derives from something more fundamental. Freud, in his *Civilization and Its Discontents* (1930), sees mystical experience as a regression to the state of mind of the newborn infant, to what he regarded as the "oceanic feeling" of a primary undifferentiated narcissism. This leaves a God image as the projection of an early all-powerful parent relation. For Durkheim, in *The Elementary Forms of Religious Life* (1912), such primordial feelings are the unwitting projection of the actual energy of the social group itself, the directly sensed basis of its cohesion, projected onto an all encompassing supernatural realm. Meanwhile, neuro-cognitivists from Hebb (1980) to Persinger (1987) have posited epileptoid physiological discharge as the ultimate explanation.

On the other hand, there are the figures to be considered below in more detail, including William James, Jung, Weber and Troeltsch, Rudolf Otto, and Martin Heidegger, who saw in this experiential core a higher cognitive and feeling capacity. James termed it "noetic"—a potential development open to adulthood and the very opposite of something regressive or primitive. That debate runs all through the history of the human sciences of mystical experience, and I have addressed it at much length elsewhere (Hunt 1984, 1985, 1995a, 2000). So it is to these more positive understandings of an experiential source of spirituality, and its relevance to a series of this-worldly or naturalistic mysticisms appearing and disappearing over the past 150 years, that we now turn.

Descriptive Phenomenologies

The foundation of a phenomenology or radical naturalistic description of spiritual experience begins, at least in its more personal and deeply felt forms, with Friedrich Nietzsche (1844-1900). Nietzsche, in his major writings of the 1880s, beginning with *The Joyful Wisdom* and *Thus Spake Zarathustra*, provides the first sustained argument for a radically relativistic, even nihilistic, understanding of human knowledge: "God is dead"; there are no conceptual absolutes; no ground under humanity, no fixed conceptual reality. Nietzsche's proposed solution is the overman, the creative person of the future. This new form of creativity, which Nietzsche partly imagines and partly tries to attain in his own life, will have the strength and capacity to say yes to life and yes to the universe—in the very face of its ostensible meaninglessness.

At times in his writings, as in *Zarathustra* and *The Antichrist*, Nietzsche envisions this yea-saying as possible because his creative person of the future will be in a new kind of direct contact with the same capacity for ecstasy and rapture that had been the traditional core of religious experience and personal sainthood. But the creative person of the future, and Nietzsche is obviously in part envisioning this past century, will understand this ecstatic experiential core as a human phenomenon. It is the human intensification of the life force within us, and not something supernatural to be projected onto a metaphysical or political absolute. In the notes collected posthumously as *The Will to Power*, Nietzsche actually calls for the development of a natural physiology of ecstasy, again as something human and biological. Presumably he would have found the experimental mysticism of psychedelic drug research of the 1960s especially interesting.

A question, however, and one Nietzsche may not be alone in foundering over, is whether, given the phenomenology of these experiences as coming from a place that *feels* utterly objective and all encompassing, it is finally possible to experience them as somehow also "ourselves"—at least without a dangerous and destabilizing grandiosity. If, as we will see later, the fully felt impact of these states automatically and inherently points to some sensed "wholly other," then it may not even be possible to make full contact with this experiential core and still understand it as an expression of our own human mind and being. Quite apart from the question as to whether any such naturalistic understanding, however emergently and holistically stated, may itself be subtly reductionistic, is it even possible for the person or group actually undergoing these states? Indeed, the phenomenology of these experiences is always beyond language, beyond ordinary conceptualization, as Nietzsche also saw.

Nietzsche has had a tremendous and often tacit influence on twentieth-century approaches to this issue—one that will reappear in the personal crises of Heidegger, Jung, Maslow, Crowley, and Gurdjieff. From Nietzsche we can trace two major lines of descent, one specifically phenomenological and the other more within psychology. The phenomenological side needs consideration first because it provides the vocabulary to describe these experiences empirically, while rigorously setting aside all questions of metaphysical truth or illusion.

A major development of Nietzsche's questioning on the human capacity for a sense of transcendence appears with Martin Heidegger, beginning with his lectures in the 1920s (Van Buren 1994) and culminating in his final more mystical writings after World War II *(The Question of Being, Time and Being).* Heidegger began as a student of Edmund Husserl, and Husserl, as the originator of philosophical phenomenology, was calling for a new qualitative science of consciousness. Consciousness was the necessary medium and context for all human inquiry, and phenomenology would be based on its direct description—bracketing or putting aside all assumptions of a theoretical or commonsense sort, and describing the resulting structure of experience as it is immediately given. One of the projects that comes out of Husserlian phenomenology was the attempt at a phenomenology of the felt core of the religious. Both Heidegger and Rudolph Otto, who is considered below, were encouraged by Husserl in this attempt at a radical description of the felt sense of the sacred and its foundation in human life.

For Heidegger, very much like William James, the core of mystical experience is cognitive or noetic. It is not merely an emotional or affective discharge, but always and of necessity *about* some-

thing, and what it is about, although ineffable, is something ultimately abstract—the felt meaning of existence or Being itself. In
his master work *Being and Time* (1927), Heidegger sees the source
of the human possibility for a sense of felt transcendence, that is,
to sense a "something" that encompasses and grounds us, in our
unique capacity to be aware of the openness of time—the temporality of human existence. Human beings have an open sense of a
future ahead as inherently unknown and unknowable, except that
it ends in the non being we term "death." Yet, if we are really strict
about it, we do not know death at all in any first person sense. At
most we have *near* death experiences. For Heidegger then, it is this
openness or unknownness of the future ahead, felt initially within
the existential anxiety it can evoke, that is the immediate source of
what he calls the sense of being or presence. This sense of sheer
"isness" is akin to what James (1912) termed the "thatness" of
"pure experience." It is the basis of direct mystical or religious
experience, and the source of its inner possibility.

It would be the underlying felt sense of Being that the various
traditional religions represent, and as inevitably obscure, with doctrines of God, Void, Brahman, or Tao, as well as the abstract categories of Western metaphysics. Within all of these concepts and
dogmas, if appropriately deconstructed or "liquified," Heidegger locates this potential for attunement to the sheer immediacy and
nowness of Being. The felt core of all spiritual experience, then, is in
our human capacity for awe and wonder at the sheer facticity of
things—an awe and wonder that anything is at all, however occasionally we may come to experience this without the cultural support of spiritual traditions. Again, Being as presencing is not a
concept but a potential felt sense or "primordial experience." For
Heidegger, we in the modern West have lost our access to this immediate sense of isness through the secularization and decline of
both traditional Christianity and classical metaphysics—a view
also variously reflected in Nietzsche, Weber, Jung, and Otto. Heidegger's own enterprise was to be the recovery of this experience of
beingness, directly within nature and art and more indirectly
through the re-opening of its underlying felt sense within the frozen
concepts of speculative metaphysics and theology.

Heidegger's highly abstract phenomenology of the primordial
experience of Being offers a broader context for the more specific experiential dimensions located by Rudolf Otto in his 1917 book translated into English as *The Idea of the Holy*. Otto coins a special term
for this felt sense of the sacred, which he calls the *numinous*. This

special usage is intended to separate a central felt core from religious conceptualization or dogma, which he refers to as the "schematization" of the numinous. Cognitive schematization of this felt sense allows us the representation of something both ineffable and all encompassing, but at the price of freezing its openness and immediate impact. Otto's description of the more specific dimensions of the numinous, below, is derived predominantly from Judeo-Christian religious writings and mysticism, but he also includes the Indian Vedic tradition, which he developed further in an influential work comparing Meister Eckhart and the Indian mystic Sankara (Otto 1932). Otto's terminology was later used by the American psychiatrist Harry Stack Sullivan (1953) to represent the more overtly uncanny and negative experiences of psychotic onset, by Jung in his phenomenology of positive spiritual development and its potential vicissitudes, and it indirectly informed some of Heidegger's own later analyses (*Basic Questions of Philosophy*).

Otto's first dimension or aspect of the numinous he calls "creature feeling." This is the felt sense of total dependency or helplessness in the face of an experience that feels potentially so powerful and outside everyday life that it is more like "it has you" rather than "you have it"—an aspect first described by Schleiermacher (1821). Often in the writings of the mystics, especially in the first dawning of their experiences, and as well in modern secular people who may not even see their experiences as specifically religious, we find descriptions of a deeply felt humility, sense of finiteness, radical incompleteness, or personal unworthiness—a hollowness of one's life or one's sense of self. This sense of creature feeling becomes schematized in theology by concepts like sin, fate, karma, all of which from Otto's point of view are historical and cultural attempts to capture and express this more spontaneous and primary felt aspect. We will see below how this creature feeling is reflected in the still more specific phenomenologies of Laski (1961) and Almaas (1988) as feelings of inherent existential inadequacy, felt deficits, or "holes" in one's personal being.

Otto then divides his account between two further aspects, each with still more specific subdivisions. The first aspect he calls the sense of the *tremendum*, again using the Latin to distance his phenomenology from our more usual conceptual associations. *Tremendum* describes the felt power or energy aspect of the numinous, and it has three subdivisions. First, there is the emotion of awe—an overwhelming sense of amazement, strangeness, or uncanniness, which can range between bliss and horror. The numinous includes an aesthetics of the demonic as well as the angelic. When this dimension is schematized in various religious traditions, we find ideas of the incomprehensibleness and mystery of God, which is also central to the attitude of "not knowing" in many mystical traditions.

Second within the *tremendum*, there is a sense of being in contact with something overpowering, massive, and august. When this becomes schematized, it tends to appear as ideas of the omnipotence of God. Here, Almaas will speak of an essential spiritual will and strength. Finally within this division, there is the sense of urgency and excitement. This becomes schematized in notions of an absolute force and energy. Already we can see that some mystical experiences may involve more creature feeling, while others will be primarily centered on awe, or force and energy, etc. This potential for differential unfolding will become important for understanding one-sided and partial developments of the numinous in contemporary spirituality.

The third major aspect of the numinous Otto terms the sense of *mysterium*. This is the more cognitive, or what James (1902) called noetic, sense of an Absolute—whether as God, Void, Brahman, Tao, or in Heidegger's sense, Being itself. It is first subdivided into a sense of fascination and wonder, usually entailed by the sense of inherent goodness and perfection, or occasionally total evil, felt in these states. In its positive side it is associated with feelings of love and compassion, which again may be dominant in some spiritual experiences and not others. Otto describes the second dimension of *mysterium* as the sense of something "wholly other." This is the experience of the object of mystical experience as ineffable and utterly outside language and conceptualization. It is this sense that has pushed mystics, East and West, to a language of paradox and in the extreme towards a view of the Absolute as a pure nothingness or emptiness, since anything more definite must falsify to some degree. Meister Eckhart came to experience "the godhead" as a nothingness and shining emptiness, and so was regarded as a heretic by the medieval Church. The Buddhist void, as the paradoxically full emptiness that is simultaneously the sense of everything, is perhaps the fullest schematization of this dimension. For Almaas, following Plotinus, the predominance of this sense marks the more "formless" dimensions of spiritual realization, also central to the later Heidegger.

Not only can some of these dimensions be felt and developed without the others, but some of the resulting experiences, while clearly part of Otto's phenomenology of a numinous core of human spirituality, may fall well outside our modern, already secularized and narrowed sense of what is "religious." The numinous is not only the primary but the broader category, including a range of experience that more traditional cultures have often seen as involving the sacred, such as creative ecstasy, intense sexuality, and ritualized physical pain and torture. Today a sensed numinosity also appears in the response of some scientists to the universe itself, as well as in peak experiences in athletics, drugs, and thrill seeking. If the numinous is at the center of a sense of overall purpose and meaning in human life, reconnecting to that core in our "new age" may also entail varying degrees of potential imbalance and even danger.

A still further level of specification of Otto's numinous is found in a remarkable book by Marghanita Laski entitled *Ecstasy* (1961). She offers probably the most complete phenomenology of these experiences prior to Almaas (chapter 2), culling through accounts of ecstasy and aesthetic states from average people and from classical mystical experience to locate common dimensions. Reminiscent of Otto on creature feeling, she describes an initial dimension of loss— the sense of a falling away of the ordinary sense of time, desires and values, and sense of self or individuality. When these senses of felt limitation are experienced with intensity, Laski speaks of "desolation experiences." These include strong feelings of loneliness and abandonment, loss of felt meaning or significance in everyday reality, and a sense of personal futility, deficiency, inadequacy, or sin. Heidegger described this dimension of loss in terms of the inherent or existential limitations in human life that we ordinarily avoid but occasionally must face. Laski's second dimension, the more positive side of these experiences, involves that sense of deficiency or loss now replaced or "filled" with ecstatic feelings of gain, as the specific sense of answer and resolution to such existential dilemmas. These "gains" refer to the classic claims about mystical experience, with its felt sense of unity or oneness in all things, eternity, freedom and release, certain knowledge, love, and a sense of new life and/or of a new or reborn self.

Finally, and most originally, she adds a dimension describing the cognitive forms taken by these feelings of gain in terms of the "quasi physical sensations" of ecstatic experience. Quasi physical sensations range from a clearly metaphorical usage, as in someone saying they felt an "upsurge of faith," to something more directly imagistic and even hallucinatory, as in someone describing a literal sense of floating or levitation—with a midrange of something more ephemeral and subtle. Laski distinguishes a number of such quasi sensory words or phrases that are used to describe what seem to be the metaphoric bases of ecstatic states—the imagistic roots of the cognitive or noetic component of mystical experience. Specifically, Laski locates six dimensions of primary metaphor or physiognomy: 1) "up" words, describing floating sensations, buoyancy, lightness, and levitation, 2) "inside" words or phrases, as in "an enormous bubble swelling inside one's chest," 3) "luminosity," fire, and heat words, as in flashing, brilliant lights or "burning with love," 4) "darkness" words, as in "a shining velvety darkness" or accounts of an infinite black emptiness into which the person might dissolve, 5) "enlargement" words, as in a sense of expanding, or even bursting, and finally, 6) the use of what she calls "liquidity" or "flow" words, as in bubbling, melting, dissolving, and flowing.

There are many examples of the ways that these quasi physical dimensions are not only used to represent the nonverbal realizations of numinous experience but seem to be directly embodied as part of the felt meanings of the state itself. This first account is from Richard Bucke's early collection in *Cosmic Consciousness* (1901). He was a close friend to Walt Whitman, and this is his own experience, described in the third person:

> He found himself wrapped around as it were by a flame-colored cloud. For an instant he thought of fire, . . . the next he knew that the light was within himself. Directly afterwards came upon him a sense of exultation, of immense joyousness, accompanied immediately by an intellectual illumination impossible to describe. He saw and knew the foundation principle of the world as what we call love and that the happiness of everyone is in the long run absolutely certain. (Bucke, *Cosmic Consciousness*, 8)

The second example is from one of my own subjects, a young woman describing a meditation session in an experimental study:

> I was unaware of which parts of my body were where. It was as if it was all mixed up. It was as if it didn't matter which part was where, as if I was floating. It felt extremely good, floating and moving very calmly, nothing mattered at all. Physiologically I felt a tingling all over. I stopped thinking and started floating. That is, I did feel the pressure of the chair—it was an "inner" floating, like I was a shell with all these things floating around inside. It felt good. There was a feeling of a rolling—not me, but in my body, a feeling of not knowing where my body ended and began, a rolling feeling. I

can't get hold of it. I don't know the words. It was just a sense of being a blob, rather than having legs or arms. It seemed to last a long time. At the end I was floating and then I had an intense feeling of exploding. It was an extremely strong feeling, as though I let go and exploded. Then I floated a bit more and 'came down.' It was a climactic point, like a nonlocalized orgasm . . . but there was a more detached feeling than in sex. There was just awe.

The prominence of quasi-physical metaphors and physiognomies in such accounts is consistent with the view that these states are in part based on the felt embodiment of abstract images of light, color, force, expansion, and spaciousness, in contrast to the more concrete metaphors, for instance, of ordinary dream content. The cognitive psychologists Lakoff and Johnson (1999) and Arnheim (1969) have attempted to show that abstract thought, verbal and nonverbal, is impossible without the use of such abstract "image schemas." I have argued at length elsewhere (Hunt 1995a) that these states of consciousness can be regarded as forms of heightened self-awareness based not on the applied symbolic operations of everyday consciousness but on the forms of consciousness itself. These became visible via an embodying of synesthetic metaphors derived from the more abstract properties of nature, which are more suitable to represent the basic features of our experience than is ordinary pragmatic language.

We could say that this is why there can be such a thing as "nature mysticism," with the contemplation of light, wind, fire, and flowing water, the heights and depths of ravines and mountains, etc., inducing ecstatic states in those suitably open to their kinesthetic embodiment and resonance. Emerson, Thoreau, Jung, and Heidegger all precede the above cognitivists in the view that our capacity for deeper self-awareness rests on our ability to sense our consciousness as a "stream" and our passions as "fiery," or Being itself as the shining forth of "light." Accordingly, all mysticism is ultimately rooted in a kind of nature mysticism—whether its luminous, expansive spaces, infinite energies, and dissolving blacknesses are "triggered" by perceptions from "without," as Otto and Laski both describe, or emerge spontaneously from abstract imagery "within."

The two preceding accounts illustrate what Laski calls "intensity ecstasy," its most prototypical and common form. With more development, intensity ecstasy will tend to separate more into the three forms of classical mysticism: knowledge, love and compassion, or strength, will, and power. Intensity ecstasies also fall between two contrasting poles of numinous experience. The first pole involves realizations of felt presence that seem more personal, and related to what Maslow (1962) saw as the "I am" experience at the core of his accounts of peak experience. Rather than losing oneself in a sense of something vast and encompassing, there is instead a felt enhancement of individuality, and sometimes of personalness, but purified and renewed, with deep feelings of joy and self-acceptance. Sometimes people will describe this as a sense of "becoming who one really is," as the realization of an inner, true self.

Laski's term here is "Adamic ecstasy," since the more orthodoxly religious will often state that they feel as though they are in the condition of Adam and Eve before the fall—with a kind of innocence, purity, and newness in their feeling of themselves as persons. Others may use words like noble savage or innocent child, primal man or primal woman, or, most commonly, true self. Almaas in this context speaks of a realization of "essential self," and of "personal essence" for its more personally contactful aspect. There is the sense that the ego has been re-formed and purified, that one is personally redeemed in some fundamental way. Here again is an example from Bucke:

> I went out in a happy tranquil mood to look at the flowers.
> . . . The pleasure I felt deepened into rapture. . . . There was
> and is still a very decided and peculiar feeling across the
> brow above the eyes, as of a tension gone, a feeling of more
> room. . . . Another effect is that of being *centered* or of being *a*
> center. . . . The consciousness of completeness and perma-
> nence in myself is one with the completeness and perma-
> nence of nature. . . . I often ponder on it and wonder what has
> happened—what change can have taken place to so poise and
> individualize me. (Bucke, *Cosmic Consciousness*, 272)

At the other pole, again with intensity ecstasies in the middle, there are the more impersonal and classical mystical experiences of a dissolving or disappearing of the sense of self into a felt oneness or totality, whether that is termed God, void, or the infinite. For Laski this is "withdrawal ecstasy," for Almaas the "boundless dimensions." In its transcendence of individuality and dissolution of self, it is almost the very opposite of the experience of "personal essence," and is, of course, the special preoccupation of the Buddhist, Yogic, and Vedic meditational paths. Here is a compendium description from several different Western subjects engaged in such deep meditational practices:

These subjects describe a sense of transcendence beyond the normal boundaries of self in terms such as "the duality between subject and object was overcome," "forgetting about my individuality . . . forgetting who I was," and "I didn't even know that I was a human being . . . there was complete merging where one loses body consciousness . . . there was no personality left." A different sense of reality, involving an expansion in the sense of space and/or time is combined with a sense of calm, serenity, and stillness: "A field of awareness that is cosmic . . . there was no sense of limitation, there was awareness, endless, boundless, oceanic." "Although there is nothing, now I am experiencing that nothing as enormous . . . like out of all space . . . the longer I can stay in it . . . the more I see how *vast* it is . . . There's no form, it's blackness, and what I find is that it's getting bigger." (Gifford-May and Thompson, *"Deep states" of meditation*, 124–27)

We will see below how for Almaas these experiences of formlessness, while the ultimate goal of mystical and meditational movements, may not initially be fully safe for contemporary Western seekers, given our uncertain issues around self-esteem, unless one has first experienced a more personal kind of presence. The formless dimensions may be too dislocating without the strengthening and renewal of a basic sense of self that is at the core of peak experience and Adamic ecstasy.

Personal Development, Psychodynamics, and Metapathology

The main contribution on the psychology side of the post-Nietzschian interest in numinous experience, now formalized within contemporary transpersonal psychology, has been to the relation of these experiences to personality and character. Although William James, in his seminal *The Varieties of Religious Experience* (1902), was not directly influenced by Nietzsche, both Jung and Maslow understood what they were doing as very much within a Nietzschean heritage. In the *Varieties*, James presents his own phenomenology of mystical experience as an abstract felt meaning, with features of ineffability, noetic character, and felt unity, but he concentrates on its potentially positive effects on character. While James concedes the thin line between some religious experiences and psychosis, he demonstrates how the potentially positive effects of mystical states can include an enhancement of compassion and personal autonomy, which he terms "strength of soul." He also describes feelings of personal freedom and spontaneity, and an increased capacity for empathy.

William James had a direct influence on Carl Jung (Shamdasani 1995), who in his early *Two Essays on Analytical Psychology* was developing his own psychology of what he called the individuation of Self, involving progressive numinous or "archetypal" experiences considered as a natural process of personal growth. Jungian individuation tended to begin in midlife and beyond, but it could also start earlier in adolescence in spiritual virtuosos. It begins as the person comes more and more to contemplate the inevitability of their own death—as also with Heidegger in *Being and Time*. Jung believed he was observing in his clients a spontaneous version of what the great mystics have described, which he sought to guide and balance by techniques of "active imagination" that encourage a dialogue between the ordinary ego and the imageries thereby unleashed. If archetypal experiences do not overwhelm or overly inflate the person, which Jung saw as an invariable risk given their potential intensity, then they gradually move toward a greater integration and balance of personality—of the inner identities of male and female, the "shadow" side of evil, the high and the low.

Beginning in the 1950s, Abraham Maslow covered a very similar ground, which he saw as the potential for a midlife "self actualization," a spontaneous unfolding similar to the classical mysticisms, and guided by "peak experiences," which Maslow described in ways similar to Laski's Adamic ecstasy. Maslow's work initiated what is now called transpersonal psychology, of which Ken Wilber (1995) is the best known contemporary representative. For Maslow self-actualization is a selective potentiality related to creativity. It can also be understood in terms of more recent research in the basic personality trait of imaginative absorption or openness to experience (Hunt 2000). Self actualization involves a shift away from what Maslow somewhat pejoratively calls the "deficit motivations" of basic self-esteem, family involvements, interpersonal needs, and worldly success, toward "being values." These being values of the second half of life are indeed very similar to Erik Erikson's view of the developmental task of old age as seeking the maximum wisdom and integrity possible in the face of potential despair (Erikson et al. 1986). For both Erikson and Maslow this development is marked by an increased acceptance and detachment, orientation to the here and now, nurturance and compassion, and an increased openness and spontaneity. Self-actualization for Maslow is a natural or inherent growth potential that is most directly cultivated in the mystical religions, but can appear in all societies in the second half of life.

My own contribution to the cognitive-developmental side of such a "spiritual intelligence," as the higher unfolding of what Howard Gardner (1983) identifies as the intra-personal frame of symbolic intelligence, has been to suggest that self-actualization involves a shift toward what Piaget termed the "formal operations" of thought—specifically in the sphere of feeling and the "affective schemata" (Hunt 1995a, 1995b, 2000). Piaget (1962) had concluded that formal operations could not be attained in affect or in the images of feeling, because, unlike the stability offered by the external world for the intellectual or logical schemata, there was no point of fixed and necessary accommodation to push the development of emotional intelligence. Piaget missed, however, the analogous role of concentrative meditation, the proximity of death, and/or the passionate concern for a sense of meaning and purpose in life, in providing just such a fixed point for the abstract development of affect, however difficult and selective that may be. Spontaneous imagistic metaphors of light, flow, expansion, and spaciousness that are themselves abstract and mediate ecstatic states attest to this further development of our self-reflective capacity, corresponding to the more existential and encompassing concerns of later adulthood.

Erikson (1962) had suggested that those who become religious-mystical virtuosos earlier in adulthood have precociously engaged the more inherently spiritual issues of the integrity-despair crisis of older age. For Erikson such earlier spirituality casts forward developmentally toward a view of the totality, value, and meaning of a person's life. Adolescent issues of personal identity are thereby transformed into a general existential or human identity, and residues of the trust-mistrust issues of early childhood into a more abstract dimension of faith. Edwin Starbuck (1899), influenced by James, had earlier concluded that the adolescent conversion experiences he collected constitute an accelerated maturation, or process of "unselfing," not normally completed until at least midlife. Such experiences lead to the foundation of a "new center" of the self, overcoming ordinary egocentricism and oriented to issues of "universal being and . . . oneness with the larger life outside" (1899:147).

Certainly for Maslow self-actualization is a higher cognitive and emotional stage, only appearing after the earlier deficit conflicts of such importance to classical psychoanalysis have been resolved. In his view, psychoanalysis, and he only knew the Freudian form as it had developed up to the 1950s, was perfectly suited to dealing with such lower "oedipal" childhood conflicts. Whereas self-actualization described a positive mental health largely opposed to the concerns of psychoanalysis. Of course, it is true that Freud saw mystical experience as a primitive regressive state, a return to early infancy. This Maslow rejects, and rightly so, given the indicators of abstract metaphoric cognition in the very fabric of ecstatic states.

Yet for Maslow, and for much of what is now called transpersonal psychology, this opposition to psychoanalysis as something "lower" has also tended to de-emphasize the inherent role of suffering in spiritual development, which had been so clear to James and Jung. Indeed, the phenomenologies of Otto and Laski, as also the classical descriptions of Christian mysticism by Underhill (1955), are full of descriptions of deep, even overwhelming conflict and emotional pain in these states, both in their early and later more subtle stages. Yet Maslow, and more recently Wilber, tend to view the presence of intense suffering and dynamic conflict in accounts of spiritual development as showing unresolved holdovers from earlier stages of childhood that have not been fully assimilated—for Wilber (1984) necessitating a cessation of meditative and spiritual practice until these issues can be addressed by more traditional psychotherapy.

Anticipating the currently emerging sense that transpersonal psychology needs to include psychodynamic conflict as inherent to any higher self-actualization, Maslow himself, near the end of his life, in his *Farther Reaches of Human Nature* (1971), identified what he called spiritual illnesses or "metapathologies" (James had earlier termed them "theopathies") that emerge in the lives of people going through this self-actualization process and which can distort or derail it. He finally conceded, as perhaps also more consistent with what we will see of his own life (chapter 6), that the unfolding of Being-values was not a conflict-free transcendence.

Manifestations of metapathology during spiritual development include feelings and attitudes of narcissistic grandiosity, since the power and beauty of such states can easily lead to a falsely inflated sense of identity. Or, the detachment from everyday reality inherent to these experiences can turn into a more destructive social withdrawal, loss of feeling, and apathy. Finally, there can be intense states of despair, deficiency, and emptiness, often referred to in classical mysticism as a "dark night of the soul" and seen as a vulnerability within the more "formless" phases of spiritual development. As we will see in the life histories to follow, the dark night can also come in many shades of grey as well, all painful in their felt loss of meaning, purpose, and direction. Wilber (1984) later developed a specific classification of subtle pathologies associated with the formless levels of mystical experience, but he also kept them completely separate from "lower" psychodynamic conflicts.

Maslow himself had stopped reading psychoanalysis fairly early in his career, so his understanding was largely based on Freud's almost exclusive preoccupation with the middle, "oedipal" years of childhood. During the very years Maslow was developing his psychology of self-actualization and Being values, psychoanalysis itself was undergoing its major creative expansion. In particular, in the 1950s and 60s the British object-relations theorists D.W. Winnicott, W.R. D. Fairbairn, and W. R. Bion, all strongly influenced by Melanie Klein, and in the 1970s Heinz Kohut's self-psychology, all expanded classical psychoanalysis to deal with the character problems related to narcissism, schizoid personality, and borderline personality. These were increasingly the problems presented by psychotherapeutic clients and are widely regarded as endemic in our postmodern culture of alienation and valuative crisis. Presenting issues include grandiosity, withdrawal, feelings of deep deficiency in sense of self, and/or feelings of futility and meaninglessness in life—which for these psychoanalysts were to be conceptualized in terms of the pre-oedipal patterns of relationship with the mothering one in the first two or three years of life.

It is especially interesting that the broadly narcissistic and schizoid dilemmas of contemporary clients in psychotherapy are so reminiscent of Maslow's descriptions of metapathologies: false grandiosity, isolation, despair over felt deficiency and low self-esteem, and feelings of futility and emptiness. Clearly the clients of the object-relations analysts were often paralyzed in terms of capacities for work and relationship. They are very different people than Maslow's self-actualizers, who are often older and have been largely successful in these more specific developmental concerns. But the emotions and inner themes are very similar.

Meanwhile, for Winnicott (1963a) and his follower Masud R. Khan (1974, 1979), there is already an existential and spiritual dimension in many narcissistic character difficulties, so that feelings of unreality and futility, defensive grandiosity, isolation and detachment, and a tendency to split experience between idealization and paranoid suspiciousness are linked to a longing for a kind of oblivion and nothingness—and for a total dependency that no ordinary human person or therapist could meet. As Jung had earlier said, only a god could satisfy such passion. Khan described a search for special "happenings" in such clients that are felt to be potentially healing and redeeming, and can involve destructive sexual perversions and encounters, overuse of drugs or alcohol, and dangerous thrill seeking—all in the hope that something transformative will happen and give the sense of meaning so lacking in their lives. Indeed, this almost sounds like a lower or inferior mysticism, which had been earlier suggested by James in regard to alcoholism. These clients are looking for a radical renewal of some kind, with the sense that this would rest on some all-powerful, transformative experience or state. Again, these clients are not the people Maslow was studying, but the themes and vulnerabilities overlap.

Maslow and Wilber appear to have been over-optimistic in their separation of the transpersonal and psychodynamic, and that is also the conclusion of a growing number of contemporary transpersonal psychologists, who acknowledge an overlap between the pursuit of a spiritual path and the psychodynamic conflicts that will, at various points, be specifically stirred up by that very quest (Rothberg 1996; Feuerstein 1990). In particular, Jack Engler (1984) has described how many Western meditation practitioners often seem to mistake their own self-pathology and narcissistic difficulties for the higher states of consciousness being sought in the Eastern traditions. Since from the perspective of object-relations psychoanalysis, there are very few people in contemporary Western culture with a stable and healthy sense of self-esteem, most of us being pretty insecure, then a person deeply committed to a yoga practice might easily mistake their own rather ordinary defensive grandiosity for the higher Self or *purusha* being sought—whereas they are actually blocked from inner realization by such a false sense of themselves. Or, a very withdrawn, private person, with strong feelings of deficiency and inadequacy, may encounter Buddhist practices based on the notion that the self is an empty voidness, with no reality or core, and so confuse Buddhist emptiness, with its paradoxical fullness, spontaneity, and humility, with their own sense of deficient emptiness.

Along these lines, psychoanalyst and meditator Mark Epstein (1998) has pointed out that any search for states that are intuitively sensed as "higher" and "perfect" must stir up feelings of one's own inadequacy and falseness by sheer contrast alone. These painful feelings, akin to Maslow's metapathologies, will be especially exacerbated where earlier development has left a more extreme vulnerability in regard to basic self-esteem and sense of identity. Epstein concludes that for many advanced meditators, and those undergoing spontaneous processes of self-actualization, the only path to fuller realization may require accepting the feelings of deficient emptiness and futility that also underlie the more extreme narcissistic disorders. We will see below how Almaas makes such links between psychodynamics and the transpersonal into a systematic principle of spiritual practice.

It is this ordinary sense of self and self-esteem that traditional societies seem to have been able to instill in their children far better than the modern west, with our specific valuation of independence and autonomy that many parents begin to impose on even very young toddlers and infants in ways, curiously enough, that they would immediately understand as traumatizing and distorting if applied to puppies or kittens. So we arrive at the view, happily less prevalent today, that spending the night alone in the dark in one's very own room as soon as possible after birth, however obviously distressing, will somehow build character. "Crying it out" will help babies attain the later independence they are supposed to have, and the stupors that supervene periodically (Ribble 1943) will be needed rest for all. It is of interest that most traditional peoples, who are never separate from a mothering presence until three or four, have looked with horror on western childbearing practices with the very young. Perhaps it is not accidental that it is our culture that invented psychotherapy, whose theories of psychodynamics have come increasingly to concentrate on the first three or four years of life and its role in establishing a basic sense of self. Whatever else, chronic vulnerabilities in self-esteem, with an increasingly rampant compensatory narcissism, will surely exacerbate the thematically related metapathologies of spiritual development.

A caveat, before proceeding further with these contemporary psychoanalytic theories of the narcissistic and schizoid dilemmas of modern living and their relation to spirituality: it is important to stress that we do not have to follow object-relations and self-psychology in their focus on the first years of life as by themselves "causing" later adult personality difficulties. Not only have such hypotheses been difficult to test, but themes of exaggerated autonomy, isolation, and mistrust can be reinforced throughout later childhood and through the culture itself. Instead, these theories might better be taken as descriptive Platonic psychologies of the basic forms of human relationship, whose inner dynamics may simply be most easily understood in terms of their first manifestations in development. From this perspective, psychoanalysis is our most developed applied phenomenology of the inner life, couched in terms of deep patterns that are in themselves more important and useful for understanding than the often distracting debates about early childhood "causation."

Despite the best corrective efforts to develop independent dynamic psychologies of adulthood by Jung, Erikson, and existential psychiatry, the influence of Freud has meant that our "topography" for emotional suffering has been cast into the pathologicized language of clinical diagnostics and located in terms of potential childhood origins. Yet whatever else the relation between psychopathology and "normality," the former does exaggerate the latter, and so reveals its less accessible and deeper structures. Suffering that once would have been "schematized" in terms of sin and redemption, is today understood psychologically in terms of its first manifestations in childhood. It is here, once we put aside debates about explanatory science in favor of structural description, that psychoanalysis excels—a point also made by Maslow (1966). Certainly the deepest emotional issues in our lives start somewhere, and the first manifestations of anything can cast an especially clarifying light on its most basic forms.

The use of these psychoanalytic psychologies of early development in all that follows can also be taken in the sense of the Jungian psychologist James Hillman in *The Soul's Code*, namely that patterns of experience in early childhood, including traumatic incidents, may show not so much the "causation" of later character, as the first manifestations or seeds of the individual's destiny and/or basic temperament. Long remembered early events stand out in part because they do highlight the basic patterns of someone's life, often so hard to detect amidst the differentiated complexity of adult experience. Going further, I would suggest that the first manifestation of any basic dimension of experience is "form near," in contrast to its later, more differentiated expressions—much in the way that pathological exaggerations in adulthood similarly reveal basic forms less directly visible in more balanced living. Along these lines the more extreme early traumata and distortions of such interest to object-relations theory may actually fixate experience at these earlier "form-near" levels and so show them more clearly. Whatever early trauma does or doesn't "cause," the way it is later recalled may help to reveal the basic patterning of a life.

For Winnicott (1971), Kohut (1977, 1984), and the more detailed developmental psychoanalysis of Margaret Mahler (Mahler et al. 1975), the narcissistic vulnerabilities in sense of self found in modern therapy clients, and we can add, in spiritual metapathologies, do have their first manifestations in deficiencies in the primary caretaking of the first years of life, also intersecting with innate differences in early-infant sensitivities. Winnicott and Kohut place the origin of a sense of self in the complexities and inevitable miscarriages of the "mirroring relationship" between infant and primary parent. Their concept of "mirroring" is the generic principle behind the infant's early fascination with having its facial expressions and gestures imitated, and imitating in turn. Very simple forms of mirroring, with opening the mouth and tongue protrusion, are present from birth. I have argued elsewhere (Hunt 1995a) that these constitute the first manifestations of a capacity for the cross-translation of the perceptual modalities that is basic to all human symbolism. The human mind itself first appears in the infant's matching of its kinesthetic facial expression to the face seen gazing into its own.

For Winnicott (1971) the infant comes to learn who it is, and ultimately what it does and does not feel, through seeing this mirrored back by its primary caretakers. The gradual internalization of this developing relation forms the core of a self-awareness and sense of self, and so determines the degree to which the young child comes to feel fully embodied and in the world—with a sense of feeling real and alive. Winnicott (1964) even calls this the dimension of *being*, in contrast to the more extraverted *use* of a later sense of self. It was this use of self that was also Freud's predominant concern in his conjoined psychology of middle childhood and the classical psychoneuroses.

Mahler's concept of "symbiosis" is similar to Winnicott's mirroring, but couched more in terms of the infant's hypothetical inner feeling of fusion or oneness with the mother—reflected, when all goes well and no one is in too much of a hurry, in a primary attunement with the mother. For Kohut (1977) this also allows a developing containment or modulation of the extremes of the infant's arousal and states of tension. Again, it would be the internalization of this symbiotic fusion relation that becomes the core of the sense of self in later childhood. All kinds of awful things may happen afterwards, but they will not shake that core of self-esteem, while without it there may be a vulnerability in sense of self that is potentially life long. We must again add, however, a point largely missed by these analysts, that our highly competitive society, with the most extreme valuation of individual autonomy and separateness of any culture in known human history, might well continue to test and push that inner sense of self in such a way that it could later be destabilized and/or rendered narcissistic whatever its initial foundations.

Winnicott provides this evocative picture of the first manifestations of what would be our life-long capacity for mirroring and "taking the role of the other":

> What does the baby see when he or she looks at the mother's face? I am suggesting that, ordinarily, what the baby sees is

himself or herself. In other words the mother is looking at the baby and *what she looks like is related to what she sees there*. . . . I am asking that this which is naturally done well by mothers who are caring for their babies shall not be taken for granted. I can make my point by going straight over to the case of the baby whose mother reflects her own mood or, worse still, the rigidity of her own defences. In such a case what does the baby see? Of course nothing can be said about the single occasions on which a mother could not respond. Many babies, however, do have to have a long experience of not getting back what they are giving. They look and they do not see themselves. There are consequences. First, their own creative capacity begins to atrophy, and in some way or other they look around for other ways of getting something of themselves back from the environment. . . . Some babies do not quite give up hope and they study the object and do all that is possible to see in the object some meaning that ought to be there if only it could be felt. Some babies, tantalized by this type of relative maternal failure, study the variable maternal visage in an attempt to predict the mother's mood, just exactly as we all study the weather. (Winnicott, *Playing and Reality*, 112–13)

What are the deeper implications when this early mirroring fails in its full development? Exposed to chronically insufficient empathy, the infant may develop a premature sense of compliance, what Winnicott calls the false-self orientation, with its tacit background of despair and futility. Indeed, one of the paradoxical concomitants of early isolation will be an exaggerated impact of the parents when they are present. The infant may come to learn that its needs and states are secondary to parental concerns, and when such things are learned too early, only an extreme and precocious accommodation can produce what feelings of safety and security are still possible. Along with such mechanical and soulless compliance, there may also be a relative withdrawal, to the point of a schizoid isolation and rejection of feeling. The infant never becomes fully engaged by the world. Again, such patterns can appear at any time of life when our inwardness finds no outer reflection.

Alternatively, and rounding out the issues that clinicians term narcissistic in adulthood, there may develop a kind of a secret omnipotence, a sense of having a hidden "true self" that should never be revealed, or which must be continuously sought in states of emotional intensity. Fairbairn (1954) suggested that the parent's failure to show love for the infant in its own right, and to reflect back the infant's own nascent love, gets associated in the child with the sense that love itself is deficient and dangerous. This leaves the young child and later adult with a deep shame and inadequacy, and caught in a pattern of splitting between an overly idealized sense of lost goodness and feelings of malevolence and hatred. Keeping in mind that the object-relations theorists may primarily be describing the extremes of pervasive dilemmas of value and meaning throughout modern society, we can see how these issues of false and true self could become associated with the search for new forms of spirituality.

There is a continuing debate over spirituality among contemporary psychoanalysts. On the one hand, Winnicott, Bion, and Kohut, and their successors Eigen (1998) and Swartz-Salint (1989), see spirituality, with Jung, as a *sui generis* dimension of human experience. It may develop out of early mirroring issues but is not reducible to them. On the other hand, for Rizzuto (1979) any experience of transcendence is an adult re-experience and projection of the similarly all-encompassing infant imagos of the primal parents. Jung (1928) himself had agreed that these parental imagos provide the raw material for a later archetypal or numinous imagination, which is nonetheless its own sphere of human intelligence and not to be reduced or explained away through its developmental roots.

W. R. Bion (1970) goes further, concluding that not only is an openness to the "formless infinite" an inherent human capacity, but that an early sense of "catastrophe"—marked by Winnicott's traumatized infant agonies of disintegration anxiety, falling forever, and exploding/imploding—may later falsely fill and block that openness to the numinous, and so become experientially fused and confused with it. Rizzuto's detailed case demonstrations in *The Birth of the Living God*, very much in the tradition of Freud himself, of the origins of adult images of God in early family relations, would be, for Bion, an illustration of a specific developmental blockage and failure within an inherent spiritual dimension—a blockage that the classical mystics have surmounted. Bion describes how in therapy with such clients, where this sense of an all-pervasive catastrophe and dread is allowed to come forward, it may finally transmute into an openness to Being as such.

Winnicott (1963a) also captures the relation of spiritual experience to early trauma in sense of self, while yet conceiving of spirituality itself as an inherent human capacity not thereby to be explained away:

> I suggest that in health there is a core to the personality that corresponds to the true self of the split personality . . . and that the individual person knows that it must never be communicated with or be influenced by external reality. . . . Although healthy persons . . . enjoy communicating . . . each individual is [also] an isolate, permanently noncommunicating, permanently unknown, in fact unfound . . . and this is sacred and most worthy of preservation. . . . Perhaps not enough attention has been paid to the mystic's retreat to a position in which . . . the loss of contact with the world of shared reality [is] counter balanced by a gain in terms of feeling real. (Winnicott, Communicating and not communicating, 185–87)

While adult spiritual development may be in part driven by unresolved early issues in sense of self and feeling real—which for Winnicott is the earliest developmental stage of what becomes our capacity for attunement to Being—it is not reducible to early traumatization. At the same time, powerful numinous experiences may stir up later versions of these same dilemmas as metapathologies. If so, the transpersonal psychologies will be in double need of a sophisticated psychodynamics, the view most developed by Almaas.

We are left with a complex picture of the relation between "higher" self-actualization and "lower" dynamics. For if mystical and peak experiences do reflect abstract cognitive metaphors of heightened self-awareness, how is it that these states are so pervaded by early object-relational themes of nurturance and compassion, holding, and idealization? The answer would be that the heightened self-awareness afforded by the abstract metaphors of luminosity, expansion, and spaciousness allows us a view of the very structure and nature of consciousness itself. We have seen that adult self-referential consciousness is based on an internalization of the early mirroring relation with the mother, which is also the first developmental manifestation of our capacity to "take the role of the other," in the terms of George Herbert Mead (1934). Accordingly, the themes of early mirroring and holding, and its traumas, will reappear in numinous states of consciousness, not because the latter are developmental regressions or blockages, but because this is the inner structure of our human consciousness—the very source of its reflexivity, self-awareness, and symbolic capacity. It is, after all, the perennial claim of the meditative traditions to show us "pure consciousness" (Forman 1999).

The direct experience of the inner dyadic and dialogic structure of human self-awareness in higher states of "pure consciousness," whether occurring spontaneously or encouraged by techniques of sustained meditation, must then also stir up and exteriorize any major unresolved vulnerabilities in early relating and sense of self. It must stir up the schizoid, narcissistic, and borderline dilemmas already part of the person's ongoing life. In addition, these states of consciousness will also create "higher" or "meta" forms of these same conflicts whenever the release of "intensity ecstasies" threatens to overwhelm the person's current cognitive capacity and sense of self, since that will re-create an entirely new version of the early vulnerabilities of holding and mirroring.

This relation between the spiritual enhancement of self-awareness in adulthood and this basic mirroring structure can be seen in the way that the radically open attitude of deep meditation comes to release deeper and deeper forms of experience, until its "intensities" temporarily may exceed what can be safely allowed without destabilization and anxiety. That will re-create the form of the early situation of such interest to Winnicott and Kohut, where the mothering one cannot always modulate and contain within safe limits the extremes of arousal and stress in very young infants. In long-term meditation, as with more spontaneous transpersonal development, the results will be the release of major unresolved narcissistic vulnerabilities, where they are already present, and/or the creation of new "meta" levels of these same issues. As with the calming of the infant with maternal holding, still deeper meditation, and other forms of spiritual guidance and support, can gradually stabilize and contain these forms of enhanced self-awareness—a process well illustrated in accounts of long-term meditative practice (Walsh 1977).

To the skeptic who would find this whole process in itself utterly and merely "narcissistic," one can only appeal to some of the paradigmatic figures to follow. While narcissistic and schizoid complications appear and reappear as blockages to their individual spiritual developments, it will also emerge that the deeper self thereby embodied can also move toward a genuine opening—an embodiment of the potential of the human being to experience a sense of encompassing meaning and purpose that connects the individual with all others and with Being itself.

CHAPTER 2

A. H. Almaas and the Synthesis of Spiritual
Development and Psychoanalytic
Object-Relations Theory

Almaas, Transpersonal Psychology, and
Psychodynamic Perspectives

A. H. Almaas and his Diamond-Heart perspective offer the most
complex system within contemporary transpersonal psychology for
the understanding and guidance of individual spiritual development. Almaas outlines multiple aspects and dimensions of numinous experience and relates them to the specific psychodynamic
conflicts and dilemmas that can both block and be stirred up by numinous, or what he calls "essential" experience. We will see later
how valuable this perspective can be for understanding our major
precursor figures of contemporary inner-worldly mysticism, and the
way in which psychological blockages could distort their spiritual
realizations—and almost inevitably so, given their pioneering status in facing the deeper cultural crises of meaning and its loss. It
will be most useful to view Almaas against a background debate
within the contemporary transpersonal psychology of higher states
of consciousness between two of its major exponents, Ken Wilber
and Michael Washburn, with Almaas offering the needed synthesis
between the two extremes.

Wilber (1995, 1997, 2000), who is probably the best known of the
modern transpersonal psychologists, sees spiritual states of consciousness as higher forms of abstract cognition. In contrast to the

above suggestion that these states involve a gradual progression into formal operations within what Piaget termed the affective schemata, Wilber posits *post* formal stages within the intellectual schemata as the basis of spirituality. At its core, Wilber's system is based on a linear or ladder model for all forms of human intelligence, with the capacity for experiences of transcendence at its integrative apex. This contrasts with my own consideration of spirituality as one form or frame of symbolic intelligence, based on an intuitive, imagistic self-awareness (Hunt 1995a, 1995b), albeit one that can contextualize and balance the others. For Wilber, under optimal circumstances and maximum cultural support, the capacity for a witnessing consciousness would unfold into a post formal cognition, best illustrated by the higher "nondual" stages of Vedantic and Buddhist meditation.[1]

Wilber has long argued that the major source of error in the psychological understanding of numinous experience is the "pre-trans fallacy," found in such different ways in both Freud and Jung. This fallacy is the tendency to confuse regressive or primitive states of consciousness that are "pre-ego" (which might be theoretically posited within the first two years of life before the development of a central self-image) with spiritual states that are "trans-ego"—reflecting a higher post formal development beyond the fixed, egocentric sense of self. He thinks that Jung, in his own life and work on archetypal imagination, confused what were really unresolved pre-egoic childhood states of the kind best understood by object-relations theory with higher states of consciousness. Correspondingly, Freud confused genuinely higher, integrative states of consciousness, which he described in terms of "oceanic feeling" and a "nirvana principle," with regressive pre-egoic primitive states. In the case of Freud, a genuinely higher stage is confused with something lower, while with Jung it is the other way around, since Jung's archetypal experiences can be difficult to separate at times from the paranoid-schizoid themes of Klein and Winnicott. Indeed, Michael Fordham (1957) created the London School of Jungian psychology based on the use of Melanie Klein's (Klein et al. 1952) elaborate inner iconographies of the first year of life, as the perspective on early development missing in Jung. Here infancy is seen as the deintegration of the very same archetypal identities later reintegrated in self-realization.

For Wilber, the conflicts of self pathology and narcissism, which can be so exacerbated in spiritual development and/or appear as "higher" metapathologies with the same inner dynamics, are disruptive distortions of higher meditative practice and should lead to its temporary cessation in order to do what is essentially a lower, remedial psychotherapeutic work. These kinds of conflicts for Wilber are unfortunate, potentially unnecessary, and certainly undesirable disruptions of a higher-growth phase.

The position of Michael Washburn (1988, 1994), actually quite close to that of Fordham, stands in contrast to the various higher cognitive-affective views of transpersonal development—formal and post formal. For Washburn, transpersonal experience is also a process of self-actualization, a spontaneous unfoldment in midlife, but developmentally it is a "u-turn" that turns back around on what Washburn calls the "dynamic ground" of early childhood. It is the experiential reintegration of Freud's Id, leading to a corresponding expansion of an essential identity or true self. Sometimes Washburn writes as though he thinks spiritual experience is nothing other than the mature ego of midlife reencountering and re-assimilating split-off conflicts from very early childhood. At other times he seems more in line with Almaas, this u-turn being less a regression than a return to an interrupted line of development. Either way, self-pathology and narcissism, dilemmas in self-esteem, and paranoid-schizoid conflicts will be inherent to the spiritual path, rather than the unfortunate errors and fixations they are for Wilber.

Part of the contribution of Almaas (1986b), in this context, is that he combines both an "uncovering" and a "higher development" model of spiritual experience. He agrees with Washburn that essential experiences will necessarily involve the uncovering of early experiences from childhood, but also with Wilber that adult realization of essence requires the development of heightened degrees of self-reflective awareness. For Almaas, preliminary forms of essence are the deep or Platonic structures of human experience that will be sensed directly in numinous experience. These are present in an early developmental form in young children. They do not appear as numinous experiences per se, which as above may depend on mediation by abstract cognitive metaphor, but are reflected in what we tend to see as the purity, wholeness, and spontaneity of young children, their joy, energy, and love.

These form-near levels of experience will be elaborated and developed in later, more abstract, spiritual experience, but they become gradually lost in childhood, not only due to possible trauma in the extremely impressionable infant and toddler, but ultimately because of an almost inevitable lack of mirroring recognition and support from adults who have themselves not developed spiritually in a secularized, material culture. These early forms of spontaneous love, joy, strength, will, and power, that we may appreciate but often not understand in the very young child, will, by the ages of five or six, become replaced by defensive ego- and object-relational patterns. The heightened self-awareness typical of, but not unique to, advanced meditational practices has the potential to unblock these lost potentials, so that these early attunements to Being can then develop further into a more explicit and genuinely abstract spirituality. What the child's versions of essence lacked was precisely the transforming self-awareness of a detached witnessing consciousness and the abstract metaphors that develop them into specific states.

Again, we find here both Wilber's insight that essential states must entail a higher cognitive development, and so are not regressions, however romantically conceived, along with Washburn's view that the child has had its own developmental start in this direction, which has inevitably been interrupted. So higher spiritual development is *also* a return to an interrupted form of awareness that can be continued and developed into a radical openness to the immediate sense of Being, which Almaas, like Heidegger, sees as the core of the spiritual traditions.

Almaas's Diamond-Heart system is itself a synthesis of a number of very different currents in transpersonal and existential psychology, psychoanalytic object-relations theories of narcissism and self-pathology, and Eastern meditative practices most reminiscent of Buddhism, Taoism, and Sufism. Conceptually, Almaas's system is built around the Sufi influenced, Gurdjieff-Ouspensky school of this-worldly meditative practice called "self-remembering," which seeks to cultivate an ongoing sense of here and now presence in the midst of everyday activities. Almaas adds to a Gurdjieffian core of self-awareness practices (as also discussed by Tart 1994), teachings and practices on the formless dimensions of mystical experiences, quite similar to Plotinus, and the contemporary developments in psychoanalysis reviewed in chapter 1. On the practical side of work and guidance with students, the system combines Reichian bioenergetic body and breath work, with Eastern meditations on chakra and subtle body energies, group and individual therapy, and guided imagery. The basic course of instruction takes about seven years, while to become a teacher of the system is another seven or eight years, making this training, first developed in the late 1970s, more extensive than that of psychoanalytic training institutes.

For Almaas, and in complete contrast to Wilber (1984, 1997), there is no inherent separation between working on psychodynamic conflicts and spiritual realization. Rather, they are two sides of the same potential experience. Step by step work on so-called lower emotional conflicts, if it is done while cultivating a sense of presence, can release facets of what Maslow would call peak or Being experiences. This potential for essential or numinous experience is inhibited by specific tensions in the body image and muscles that are based on chronic emotional conflicts and are the focus of the bioenergetic therapies pioneered by Wilhelm Reich (1949). Almaas found that fully accepting these body-centered experiences of anxiety, despair, and rage, without resisting and so allowing them fully into awareness, can lead to a transmuting of these sensed deficits into direct experiences of presence. Such sequences of felt suffering and subsequent opening to the numinous are consistent with Otto on the preliminary role of creature feeling, and with Laski on desolation experiences, although Almaas's sequence usually occurs in smaller, more partial steps. As these felt deficits open into experiences of Being, Almaas describes the same feelings of spaciousness, flowing energy, luminosity, and increased spontaneity and vitality that also figure in Laski's "quasi physical" sensations of ecstasy.

Presence or essence is Almaas's primary term for what Heidegger calls primordial Being experience. The sense of presence is our unique potential as self-aware beings:

> Presence can be sensed at times of intense and deep emotion, when a person is fully feeling an emotional state, not controlling or inhibiting it, when he is involved wholeheartedly in the feeling, totally immersed in it in a free and spontaneous way without judgment or holding back. This usually happens only when the person feels totally justified in feeling the emotions. For example an individual might experience a great loss like the death of a loved one, and so feels justified in feeling the grief and sadness. A person might get so involved in the sadness, so immersed in it, that the feeling deepens as if it were miles deep, going to greater depths and profundity. This state might become so deep and profound that it feels thicker and denser as he gets more deeply immersed in it, so deep and profound that he experiences himself permeated by a kind of presence. It is as if the profundity and the depth *are* an actual presence, palpable and quite clearly there. (Almaas, *Essence*, 3)

Essence is Almaas's more generic term for presence, whose core is this sense of "I am," but which can appear with different aspects or facets:

Essence is the direct experience of existence. Of course, essence can be experienced as other things, such as love, truth, peace, and the like. But the sense of existence or being-ness is its most basic characteristic. (Almaas, *Essence*, 11)

Some discussion is needed of what seems to be one of Almaas's most unusual notions, namely that when fully sensed and witnessed, the sensed deficits and chronic muscle tensions and numbness that hold emotional pain can be experienced as holes, cavities, or gaps in the body image. It is these "holes" that transmute into the spacious-ness of essential states. The underlying principle, although here lit-eralized in body image and sensation, is similar to the British psychoanalyst Michael Balint's (1968) view that the deepest trans-formations in psychotherapy come with finally accepting the idea of a "basic fault" in oneself. For Balint this initiates a natural mourning that signals the end of therapy. The difference is that for Almaas the full acceptance of a sense of deficiency in oneself, based on the direct experience of one's character flaws as inevitable and unavoidable, re-sults in at least their partial transformation. Accepting the sense of basic fault while maintaining the witnessing attitude of meditation, or the simpler approximation of simultaneously sensing one's arms and legs as a kind of frame for experience that would otherwise be overwhelming, actually allows it to transform. Facets of the emo-tional pain are replaced with corresponding facets of numinous or essential states.

That these deepest senses of personal deficiency would be expe-rienced as "holes" in the body image requires more explanation. Bioenergetic therapies are based on the observation that chronic emotional conflicts become held or frozen in unconscious patterns of muscle tension. Reich located typical centers of tension in the eyes, the mouth, tongue and throat, the chest and upper back, solar plexus, abdomen, and pelvis. Techniques for de-blocking these con-tractions include changing one's pattern of breathing, deliberate tensing and relaxation, and the use of pressure and massage. When these areas of tensions are dissolved, Reich (1949) described feelings or sensations of streaming, melting, and flow inside the body. While we might wish to explain these effects in terms of deep muscle re-laxation, they can be experienced phenomenologically as actual pat-terns of liquid or energetic flow within the body, with blockages and sudden expansions potentially felt as frightening sensations of im-ploding or exploding. Again, Laski describes such sensations as part of her quasi physical aspects of ecstasy, while Reich described feelings of spontaneity, energy, and vitality reminiscent of Maslow on peak experience.

On the more conflicted and negative side, it is also of interest that body hallucinations in schizophrenia often involve specific complaints of gaps or holes in the body, and strange energies and forces moving within them (Angyal 1936). Often these seem like more literal and extreme (i.e., hallucinated) versions of the body metaphors used ordinarily to describe deeply felt emotions—such as one's heart as broken or missing, anxiety as a disintegration, fear as a sinking sensation, and confusion as being dizzy or empty headed. There seems to be a continuum between such descriptions as obviously metaphoric and purely verbal usages, to kinesthetic images that are directly felt with intense emotion, to the hallucinatory elaborations of these patterns in psychoses.

Meanwhile, there is now some agreement among transpersonal psychologists that there is a close correspondence between the typical foci of chronic contraction in bioenergetic therapy and the sort of body energy centers that Buddhist and Hindu meditative traditions describe as chakras, as well as with the more subtle Sufi lataif system (Hunt 1995a). Interestingly, the Chinese Taoist term for these centers literally means cavities or indentations. Activation of these areas of the body image spontaneously or in deep meditation is associated with intense emotion, feelings of energetic flow and release, and the experiences of luminosity, colors, and the quasi physical sensations of Laski. I have argued elsewhere (Hunt 1995a) that in cognitive terms these states constitute complex or abstract synesthesias. Our self-referential symbolic capacity, common to both language and the arts, would be based on cross modal translations between patterns of vision, kinesthesis, and sound. In chakra activations these synesthesias are manifested for their own sake as abstract felt meanings, independent of the usual subordination of mind to the more practical tasks at hand.

Almaas's own approach is also reminiscent of Eugene Gendlin's (1978) method of experiential transformation in psychotherapy, which he calls focusing. For Gendlin, if we observe our more painful and intense emotions we will find them to be felt more in some areas of the body than others. In a particular conflict, you may feel as though your chest is going to burst or your head is going to explode or your stomach is going to fall out, etc. We can find much the same with more subtle feelings and background moods. Focusing involves centering on an area in the body specific to a particular state, fully sensing it, and then letting it translate into a color or an image that expresses both the feeling and the body sensation, and eventually allowing a word or phrase to appear that expresses the entire sense of the emerging felt meaning. Such an amplification of painful emotion can bring about an experience of opening, or "felt shift," in which the emotion reconfigures. The pain and density of one's sadness might become lighter, with the feeling of understanding and a new clarity, or it might transmute into a very different, more positive feeling. Again, an Eastern meditator reading this might see Gendlin's method as a very brief and focused chakra meditation.

We are now in a better position to understand the basis of what Almaas (1986b, 1988) terms his "theory of holes." Since essential experiences are commonly mediated by metaphoric experiences of open spaciousness and expansive glowing light, then it makes sense that if we are to make a transition experientially from the background bodily tensions, which support our ordinary sense of self, to the direct experience of space, then the beginning of this process might first appear in awareness as a gap or a hole—as the metaphoric embodiment of feelings of deficiency. These holes, when fully accepted, would be experienced as "filled" by and transmuted into Laski's "feelings of gain," and mediated by her quasi physical sensations of ecstatic release. If we are to move from ordinary emotional conflicts, which we resist looking at because of the pain involved, to the expanded spaciousness of essential states, the transition would begin with the metaphoric translation of these conflicts into Almaas's holes as the liminal beginning of the direct experience of space.

Almaas shares with both Winnicott and Bion the view that presence and sense of being, or what Winnicott calls "feeling real," is the opposite of the ordinary sense of self based on identifications with others. For all three, and illustrating this coming together of the transpersonal and psychoanalytic, all self-representations, all constructed representations of ourselves, are partial and necessarily falsified—in that they are based on the internalization of early relationships with parental figures, rather than being centered on a more immediate sense of isness or presence. This direct conflict between experiences of essence and the existence of ordinary self-images and identifications, means for Almaas that when the person's self-image is seen through as necessarily false or incomplete, and so is dissolved, it is replaced by the direct awareness of presence.

It is of course a fairly radical perspective to see all self-images as partially defensive, incipiently schizoid structures that replace a more primary awareness of the ongoing immediacy and spontaneity of experience. Along with most traditional mystical teachings, it implies that what we ordinarily call "personality" already reflects a deep occlusion of our most basic experiential potentialities:

> Essence . . . has nothing to do with identification. It exists purely as itself. There is no identification with past experience or any self-image at all. In fact, its presence is concomitant to the absence of identification with any self-image or psychic structure. When we are identified with a self-image we acquired in the past, we are not being our true nature. This means that for the realization of essence the first step is to disidentify. . . . (Almaas, *Essence*, 46)

For Almaas our true nature rests on our capacity for the immediate awareness of Being, a view close to both Heidegger on "authenticity" and W. R. Bion on the difference between self-image and truly being oneself:

> The belief that reality is or could be known is mistaken because reality is not something which lends itself to being known. It is impossible to know reality for the same reason that makes it impossible to sing potatoes; they may be grown, or pulled, or eaten, but not sung. Reality has to be "been." . . . Is it possible . . . to affect a transition from knowing the phenomena of the real self to being the real self? (Bion, *Transformations*, 148)

Almaas also agrees with Fairbairn (1954) and Harry Stack Sullivan (1953) that our identifications and self-images, however normal and inevitable we may take them to be, are also residues of impactful experiences from childhood, both positive and negative, that could not be fully assimilated or digested, or the term preferred by Almaas, "metabolized." Owing to the intensity of early experience and the child's inherent vulnerability, it becomes safer to create a self-image as a defense against anxiety, rather than feel the pain of an experience in which the child's spontaneity or aliveness or power or love is not accurately recognized and mirrored by the all-important parents. The disidentifications finally allowed by the development of a detached witnessing capacity entail a dissolving of self-image. When the self-image is dissolved, the person will experience a loss of physical and self-boundaries, leading to what Almaas terms the direct experience of space—the basis of classical mystical experience and close to Laski on the quasi physical sensations of light, expansion, and dissolution. For Almaas, these shifts from self-image to experiences of space typically happen in increments. This separates him from Eastern meditational traditions that teach sudden enlightenment. The implication would be that at least in the modern West, with our extreme and early emphasis on autonomy and identity, it may be a lot safer to attempt a piecemeal dissolution of ordinary self-identity.

Multiple Forms of Essence: A Cartography of the Numinous

Almaas distinguishes multiple aspects and dimensions of essential experience, reminiscent of Laski but more detailed. Like Laski, the more common access experiences center on features of her "intensity ecstasy," which can then develop toward personal essence or toward the more abstract formless dimensions. Each aspect has its characteristic hole or deficit that can either block its development or be stirred up in its aftermath, and which can be understood in terms of its own object-relational dynamics. Each aspect also has a characteristic false form that can appear when its specific feelings of pain and deficiency are not fully accepted. Whereas all mystical traditions stress the paradoxical and ineffable qualities of these experiences, the false forms lack this metaphoric complexity and poetic expression. They are mainly states of pure intensity, but without the sense of awe and sacredness associated with the numinous. These false forms of essence are distortions of spiritual experience. So there are true and false aspects of essence, and it is the full experience of holes or felt deficiencies that is required to release the true aspects.

The dangers of numinous experience for Almaas include not only these false forms or distortions, and the dynamic conflicts that they can exacerbate, but also the inevitability that spontaneous transpersonal experience will tend to center more on some experiential aspects than others, and so move into states of relative one-sidedness and imbalance. Accordingly, different spiritual groups can become one-sided in their articulation of essential states, especially so in the contemporary development of inner-worldly mystical schools and cults. However inevitable these groups may be in social-historical terms (chapter 3), they will tend to lack the more balanced development of the traditional mysticisms. This will be especially so in the major precursor individuals to be discussed below. The true, complexly paradoxical forms of essence are obviously experiences of deep value and meaning for those who undergo them, but for Almaas

(1984) positive development in one or two aspects and not the others can still lead to long-term imbalance.

As we will see in some detail, each true or genuine aspect of essence has its own characteristic felt qualities or cross-modality physiognomies, akin to Laski on quasi physical sensations. We will consider seven major aspects of essence, again roughly related to what Laski terms "intensity ecstasy." These arise with specific imageries and metaphors that mediate the numinous experience and its self-aware recognition. Each has its characteristic physiognomic or synesthetic expression, often appearing as a specific color, density, texture, spaciousness, and/or shape. These are similar to the synesthetic qualities of Eastern chakras, although Almaas (1986a) prefers the more subtle Sufi system of lataif. Accordingly, as part of their kinesthetic mode of expression, but with large individual differences, each aspect will tend to be felt in particular regions of the body—or more properly, the body image or experienced sense of the body.

To proceed through these physiognomic characteristics of the major aspects, essential or true strength includes, for Almaas, a paradoxical quality of vulnerability. Qualities of the strength aspect are a sense of expansion, and a capacity for separation related to autonomy. Its physiognomy can include a feeling of aliveness, passion, heat, and the color red, and with a sense of bodily fullness. It is often felt more on the right side of the body. It can also bring with it an expansion and clarification of insight and a sense of beauty. The false form of strength comes out as anger and hardness. In Nietzsche's writings and life we will find evidence of both true and false aspects of states of essential strength. As the form of creature feeling or desolation specific to this dimension, that through which it can emerge, the hole or deficit of true strength is the full sensing and accepting of the fear, terror, and weakness typical of the young child feeling its lack or loss of basic autonomy. The childhood roots of the early sense of an autonomous self between two and four years of age have been the preoccupation in different ways of Margaret Mahler et al. (1975) and Heinz Kohut (1977). Almaas provides this vignette of a dawning of the strength, or red aspect, from a married man in his middle years, whose dynamic issues center around residues of early separation from his mother. Again, the notion is that the full re-experiencing and acceptance of the pain of these feelings has the potential for a direct transmuting into a specific essential state:

> I saw the problems associated with my mother as a pile on the floor, and I burned them all up. . . . I felt a very warm

feeling in my solar plexus and in my back. I've been able to
experience this heat many times before. I also remember
that at first I thought I had some sort of fever as my whole
body became hot. As I discussed with you on Friday, I felt I
had a blackish kind of lump or ball in my solar plexus, as big
as a basketball. I felt this blackness peeling or dissolving to
reveal some kind of beautifully translucent presence in the
belly. As I talked with you this presence grew very quickly
and filled me up enough to give me a sense of having a full
belly. When it went into my chest it strengthened my shoulders. I felt very pleased with myself, very happy. . . . I feel
stronger, more accepting of myself and more aware of liking
me. (Almaas, *The Pearl Beyond Price*, 207–8)

Essential joy includes a softness and poignancy. Its quality is
yellow, and delicate, expansive, light, and curious. False joy is manic
intensity, and having one's joy lost in external goals or objects rather
than feeling it in its own right and sufficient unto itself. There is a
desperate controlling quality that comes into false joy. One must
have this thing that makes one happy. It is this false joy that becomes central in certain drugs and alcohol. There is also Nietzsche's
later frenetic joy before his breakdown, a false forced bliss that
makes most readers of his final *Ecce Homo* uneasy. The hole of essential joy is the loss of the young child's spontaneity and expressiveness, and when kinesthetically embodied Almaas suggests it is
localized more on the left side, opposite strength.

The third basic aspect Almaas calls essential will. This is a steadfastness, with a paradoxical quality of letting be and allowing things
to unfold. The person feels steadfast in accepting whatever happens,
so an attitude of letting be does not contradict the simultaneous presence of will and intention. The physiognomy of true will is a sense of
openness, with a kinesthetic softness and a color of white or silver,
and a purity and transparency. It tends to be located in the solar
plexus. For Almaas it is essential will that is also experienced as a
central column going up the interior of the body image and which in
yoga is associated with the kundalini experience. False will is will in
the sense of control. It is the kind of worship of the will found in
Hitler, and which Heidegger extolled during his year as Nazi rector of
Freiburg during the early Hitler years. Jung was similarly fascinated
by this frenetic intoxication. The driven intensity highs of cocaine
could also be taken as direct manifestations of false will. The specific
hole of essential will is the lack of any sense of holding or contain-

ment, a lack of support in Winnicott's sense, potentially beginning from early infancy. The way the mothering figure holds the baby is both a physical protection and a holding or containing of its emotions. It is a primary empathic attunement. For Winnicott, manifestations of a chronic lack of support appear as fundamental anxieties about dissolving or falling forever. Later in life this lack of support is associated with feelings of personal inadequacy and worthlessness, since the internalization of early levels of support is fundamental to our sense of self.

Essential power is the energy and force central to Otto's description of the numinous, yet including within it a paradoxical peace and stillness. The physiognomy here is a blackness, silence, and stillness, with a substantiveness and sense of majesty. The false form is hatred, a sense of the malign and ominous, and the drive for simple domination as a potential result. Kinesthetically Almaas localizes power in the forehead, with hatred often being held in contractions of the eye muscles. We will see later the importance in some of our exemplars of separating hatred as false power from anger as false strength. The hole of power is a hopelessness and sense of futility, either with an apathy or a quality of desperate inner agitation. False power comes out in all things satanic and demonic, which will be most obvious in the negative mysticism of Crowley, and in his long-term use of heroin—the bringer of false peace. The dynamic roots of the felt deficiency of power lie in what Almaas and some object-relations theorists refer to as "negative merging."

The origins of this view of a negative side of the early mirroring situation are found in Melanie Klein et al. (1952), Otto Kernberg (1984), and especially in Harry Stack Sullivan (1953), who was one of the first to posit a primary empathy shared between infant and mothering one in the first year of life, by which the infant comes to feel the mother's emotional state and vice versa. Its positive form is symbiosis or mirroring, but if the infant is being taken care of by a mothering one who is in a state of chronic apathy, depression, terror, or rage, then the infant must share these states as well. There may then be the deeply frustrating sense that the same mother who is so desperately needed for a basic sense of support and self-recognition is also somehow the source of these awful feelings. Accordingly, both empathic intimacy and true autonomy become impossible.

When negative merging becomes extreme, it tends to produce a premature separateness and a precocious pseudo-autonomy, which is really more of an isolation and escape. Schizoid withdrawal is associated with deep feelings of hatred, which has a colder, more sustained sense than explosive anger, and which may or may not be split off from consciousness. For Fairbairn (1954) relating based on hate is thus substituted for a love that is not mirrored back by the mother and so becomes instead a source of shame and inadequacy. This becomes one of the earliest and deepest blockages in the development of a sense of fully embodied beingness and feeling real. We will see how this negative side of merging is linked to the implicit dualism and lack of full experiential integration in the inner development of Crowley, certainly, but also in Nietzsche, Thoreau, Jung, Heidegger, and Gurdjieff.

Whereas strength, joy, will, and power are all related to Otto's discussion of the numinous *tremendum*, the aspects of love, compassion, and essential intelligence are closer to Otto's *mysterium*.

Essential love, or what Almaas also refers to as "merging essence," has a paradoxical self-sufficiency, in that when it is truly felt, nothing further outward is needed. On the level of essence one cannot pine away from essential or true love, because the state itself directly answers the longing. The physiognomy is a sense of sweetness, honey-like flow, melting, and a golden color, often located in the chest at the sternum. This state has its developmental origin in the positive symbiosis or felt union between infant and mothering one in the first six months of life—the infant entering into periodic oneness states whose form becomes the heart of adult love and, on a more abstract level, of unity experiences in the formless dimensions of mysticism. The false form of love is fixated, controlling, and obsessional. The hole of merging essence is the aloneness and painful isolation side of the schizoid dilemma. The following account of the emergence of a sense of essential love comes from a professional woman in her 30s working on the issue of her identification as a woman in relation to her mother:

> I felt a large gaping wound around my heart and lungs as you spoke. I kept trying to fill it in various ways, one of which is trying to be my mom. When she is sick and upset I get sick. I worked on the hole in a private teaching session before. I have a gigantic wound where my mother continued to emotionally stab me as an infant every time my strength and love came out to her. I believe subconsciously that I am her and she I. I believe that she has the love and warmth and I am nothing without her. As we worked Saturday night I felt at some point a juicy honey-like feeling or presence in my chest where the wound is. It was sweet and warm and like nectar. (Almaas, *The Pearl Beyond Price*, 230)

The sixth aspect is essential compassion, and for Almaas compassion for oneself is crucial for any assimilation of the painful inner dynamics that are part of spiritual self-realization. The predominant color for compassion is green, and it can be kinesthetically embodied in the center of the chest as a sense of flowing, lightness, and tenderness. The false form appears as the compulsion to help, to give oneself up for others and offer a reassurance intended to make someone else's pain go away, rather than respecting the fact of another's pain and offering the deeper holding of staying present with them. Jean Houston's autobiography will offer an example, common among those who work with others, of this helping others at the expense of oneself. Nietzsche's famous attack on Christianity is primarily against what Almaas would regard as false compassion. The hole or pain of the absence of essential compassion is a harshness and insensitivity, ultimately a lack of understanding and genuine support for oneself and/or others. The utter absence of compassion and empathy will be striking in the example of Crowley.

The final aspect relevant to our later analyses is essential intelligence or "brilliancy." Here Almaas approximates the classic distinction between mysticisms of knowledge and those centered more on love—Meister Eckhart and Plotinus and their ecstasies of noetic insight vs. the ecstasy of divine love in St. Teresa. Brilliancy is often associated with an openness to an inherent sense of mystery and "not knowing," which is especially important for the full development of these states. The physiognomy of brilliancy is a white shining radiance, and sense of elegance, and perfection. There is a spontaneous synthesizing quality here of all essential aspects and it does not have a bodily center in the sense of the other aspects. Its false form is certainty, static knowledge, dogma, and thinking one knows final truth. Its hole is the confusion and perplexity of the young child, where what is happening in the early family surroundings is contradictory or chaotic, in contrast to the child's implicit sense of clarity and coherence in more benign circumstances. Confusional features of early experience are central to the Kleinian analyst Herbert Rosenfeld (1965) and to W. R. Bion (1962). As with all the other aspects, the fullest manifestations of brilliancy would come from fully accepting the confusional states that are actually present. The most striking manifestations of the brilliancy aspect in our paradigmatic figures will be in Plotinus, Emerson, Nietzsche, and of course, Heidegger.[2]

To complete this overview of Almaas's synthesis, he sees, as with Laski, two poles or extremes of development for the qualities we have just discussed. The first one is the end point of classical mysticism in purely transcendent, formless experiences in which the sense of self is felt to dissolve into all-encompassing unity. In Weber's typology of religious experience to be dealt with in the next chapter, these experiences are the speciality of the classical "otherworldly" mysticisms. Here the more formed qualities of numinous strength, joy, will, power, compassion, love, and intelligence expand into a pure spaciousness beyond the embodied sense of self and into a boundless sense of infinity and timelessness. Personal love and contact for instance, expand into a sense of boundless cosmic love that gradually becomes inseparable from similar expansions of the other essential aspects. These are the classical realizations of Void, Brahman, Godhead, Being, or Absolute, depending on the tradition involved. They are nameless, ineffable, and ultimately nonconceptual. Since Almaas's account is close to Plotinus here, we will deal with the levels within these formless dimensions, and the cognitive processes mediating such experience, in chapter four on Plotinus. There is a danger for Almaas in the premature experience of the formless dimensions, especially in the hyper-competitive and egoistic modern West, with our unique emphasis on autonomy and resultant dilemmas of self-esteem. The formless dimensions can be used as an escape and even dissociation from the pressures of ordinary relating. As Almaas says, "transcending a situation is not necessarily the same as resolving it" (Almaas 1988:15).

In regard to the opposite pole of potential development, Almaas sees the ordinary ego as a distortion of a more personal form of spiritual truth. This personal spiritual realization needs to be present before it is fully safe psychologically to dissolve into formlessness. This development of sense of self comes in two aspects, which he terms personal essence and essential identity. Traditionally, these have been more the concern of what Weber calls the "inner-worldly" mysticisms of Sufism and Taoism, and the Christian understanding of soul and spirit. To varying degrees, these experiences of an enhanced sense of self are also found in Laski's Adamic ecstasy, as a feeling of pure "I amness," and in the sense of one's identity as pure Being. They are also related to Heidegger's notion of individual "authenticity" in moments of self-awareness of our own existence, and to Maslow on peak or Being experiences as experiences of primary identity.

Personal essence is the side of these self-realization experiences that feels more like a specifically and uniquely personal sense of one's own being (Almaas 1988). The experience of personal essence, or what Almaas, reminiscent of Sufism and Hermeticism, calls "the pearl," involves a sense of genuine autonomy, with qualities of personalness itself, personal strength, maturity and integrity, and a capacity for genuine contact with others. So a capacity for personal intimacy is part of personal essence. Almaas is describing here in spiritual language various theorists' notions of optimal personality development, including not only Maslow, but Sullivan, Erikson, and Kohut. Essential identity, or what Almaas calls "the point," differs from personal essence in being less specifically personal and more centered on a fully felt realization of oneself as a pure manifestation or expression of Being itself (Almaas 1996). It is especially important as a gateway into the more formless dimensions and is closer to Heidegger's authenticity, Jung's Self, Gurdjieff's Essence, and Winnicott's true self, than to Maslow, Erikson, Sullivan, or Kohut.

Without the development of personal essence and essential identity, the formless dimensions can be a real danger to the person because a fundamental sense of identity is dissolving before it has really been developed in its own right. Here, Almaas goes beyond Engler's view of how Western students of Eastern practices can go awry because they need to have a stable ordinary sense of self before they can safely lose it. For Almaas, as with Sufism, Gurdjieff, and Jung, there are actual spiritual developments of that ordinary sense of self that are also needed.

To deal briefly with the developmental prototypes of the inner forms of these adult realizations, the symbiotic or mirroring stage, with its dissolution of boundaries, is the pattern whose re-experience, not as regressive content but as form or template of experience, opens out into the formless dimensions. Personal essence is based on the form of early autonomy and sense of self discussed by Mahler et al. (1975) in terms of the "rapprochement" phase, in which an earlier sense of pure individuation around the age of two, gradually becomes balanced with the equally powerful need of the child for a more realistic autonomy and emotional contact. This progressive balancing becomes the unique spontaneous personalness of the child by around three and four. Essential identity, on the other hand, has as its initial pattern in the more purely individuating and often reckless independence of the exploring two-year-old, which Mahler called the "practicing" subphase of separation/individuation. Its pathology appears as the narcissistic grandiosity of such interest to Kohut and his self-psychology.

Without some initial experiences of personal essence and one's essential identity as Being, the formless dimensions can stir up intolerable experiences of terror, deficiency, and loneliness, which will either block the more abstract formless states, or lead to the various spiritual metapathologies. For Almaas, these include narcissistic grandiosity, which we will see in Nietzsche, just before his final breakdown into organic dementia, Crowley, and Heidegger and Jung in their brief period of fascination with National Socialism. Almaas also mentions spiritual forms of negative merging, in that the person may become defensively embroiled in a negative group or relationship, as in Thoreau's bitter personal struggle with his mentor, Emerson, or Heidegger's joining of the Nazi party. There can also be a schizoid isolation and withdrawal, as an extreme separateness defending against hatred and shame, which will be very visible in Thoreau and Crowley, and in the later Nietzsche. We should probably add a category of metapathology that involves a manipulative sociopathy. Here we have the so-called "wild gurus," acting out emotionally and sexually, and generally abusing their followers (Storr 1996). Certainly Crowley manifested such tendencies with his immediate followers, and we find them in somewhat more benign forms in Madame Blavatsky and Gurdjieff.

Essential or numinous states may move ultimately towards integration, but they can also have a powerfully dislocating impact, stirring up new or old forms of what amount to psychotic levels of anxiety. The result is that outside long-established spiritual traditions and especially in the re-invention of inner-worldly mysticism in the modern West, individual spiritual development involving direct experiences of the numinous will also entail various forms of one-sided or imbalanced development, false distortions of essential aspects, and metapathological and characterological conflicts. These dilemmas do not detract from the importance of the development of these new cultural forms, but we will see in our prototypical life histories some of the very real difficulties to be faced.

Issues and Controversies

The phenomenology of essential states developed by Almaas describes experiences of being in contact with something inherently objective and real. Yet these states are mediated by the above sensory metaphors and physiognomies—such as luminous space or infinite darkness—and seem not describable at all, or maybe even experiencable, without them. This opens up the question of whether these experiences are in some sense constructed by means of this kind of metaphoric self-awareness. Does spirituality describe something ontologically primary or is it a cognitive construction, even a projection out of whole cloth, as Freud himself thought? For Almaas, essence is not primarily a state, and certainly not a psychological process, but a reality of Being. Whereas the early Jung was content to see the numinous as "psychic reality," Almaas, with Heidegger, understands Being as a truth, which our human self-awareness allows us to experience as presence. It does seem true that we do exist. We really are present in our lives and in the world. In numinous experience, whatever else it is, we are directly aware of that Being—immediately and primarily.

Indeed, the developmental templates of the essential states located by Almaas are not only found in the object-relational patterns of infancy, but seem nascently present in the basic flow of perception in all moving animals (Hunt 1995a, 1999). Thus we see the expansive form of strength in the continuous expansion out and ahead into horizonal openness, in Gibson's (1979) account of ambient perception in the locomoting animal. Essential or inherent will appears in the directionality and intent of perceptual flow, and essential power in the energy of creaturely movement. We might also locate the form of an essential joy in the spontaneity and aliveness of physical movement, and compassion in the way that Gibson pictures the organism as contained, guided, and "afforded" by its surroundings. One possibility then is that it is the abstract synesthesias and physiognomies of essential states, based on our capacity for symbolic self-awareness, that moves these forms from the concrete activity they guide into direct experience as such. If so, these imageries allow us to *recognize* and *bring forward* what is most fundamentally real and true about our lives. The result would be numinous experience.

Presence as a felt realization is accordingly more than a metaphor. Yet it would be the cross-modal, synesthetic bases of all metaphor, which, felt as such rather than being more ordinarily subordinated to symbolic reference, will mediate that realization (Hunt 1995a). For Almaas the fully felt kinesthetic embodiment of essence can be actually sensed as a fluid substance or force flowing within the body—a state which for him, as well, seems to involve what could be described as a cross-modal, abstract synesthesia:

> Essence, when experienced directly, is seen to be some kind of substance, like water or gold, but it is not physical substance like physical water or gold. . . . Imagine that this water is self-aware . . . of its own energy and excitation. Imagine now that you are this aware substance, the water. This is close to an experience of essential substance.

Essence is self-aware. It knows itself, intuits itself, sees itself, hears itself, smells itself, tastes itself, touches itself. But all this is one act, one unified perception.

Connecting the various capacities [for subtle perception] with different energetic centers does not mean that it is only in those locations that the capacities are exercised. In fact, such capacities can be exercised, when developed, at any location in the body; indeed they overlap. Texture [belly] can be discriminated by taste [heart], even by seeing [head], as can density and viscosity. . . . This phenomenon points to a very deep truth, that of the unity of senses. . . . (Almaas *Essence* 50, 80, 132–33)

This account may still seem puzzling in terms of cognitive process, until we recall that from Vico, Goethe, and Emerson, to Jung, and most recently Lakoff and Johnson, our capacity for abstract self-awareness depends on the reuse of physical phenomena as metaphors. Thus, with William James, we speak of and think in terms of a "stream" of consciousness when we seek to represent the moment by moment transformation and "flow" of subjective awareness. The more vividly embodied and felt this metaphor becomes, the more it will approach Laski's direct quasi physical experience of a flowing liquid.

To return now to a developmental perspective, consider the most abstract form of essential states: the cross-modal translation of bodily kinesthesis into the pure luminosity or shining blackness of visual space, as the basis for the dissolution of self in classical mysticism (Hunt 1984, 1995a). It would be the translation of body image into the open spaciousness of vision, and thus its dissolution, that makes psychological sense of descriptions of such experience as an "annihilation" or "dying." It does not seem that these states would be part of the experience of the neonate. So the regression or primitivization model of essential states cannot be correct. The mirroring capacity of the infant seems clearly to be a cross-modal translation, but it is limited to the concrete specifics of facial expression, gesture, and vocalization. Apart from childhood precosities in the realm of spiritual experience, much as with any other basic frame of intelligence (Hunt 1995b), the infant precursors of essential (and aesthetic) states would consist in periods of self-exploration of sensations and surroundings in quietly engaged "alone time" as described by Buchholtz (1999). Yet these behaviors hardly show the tonic immobility, emotion, and sustained focus of later essential states. Thus, with Almaas, while essential states do "uncover" and "abstract" the primordial inner forms of experiencing and relating, they are, as such, also "developments" that reflect our symbolic intelligence and its potential for a transforming reflexivity. In spiritual development, a directly sensed turning around on the inner forms of our experience brings our very beingness into a directly felt realization.

Although these states are clearly not regressive, their bringing into consciousness of its organizing forms will also entail the reemergence of the initial experiences and blockages of childhood development, during which these forms were specified. Thus, in the debates between Jung and Freud, and now Wilber and Washburn, both sides are correct—at least within the broader context of the abstract nature of essential states and the correspondingly "metaphysical" level of their felt meanings. As we have seen in the previous chapter, the "regressive" nature of the suffering involved in spiritual development will seem even more striking in an era where our phenomenologies of conflict and emotional pain come, for good or ill, from the extremes of clinical psychiatry, and our attempts, starting with Freud, to locate their precursors in early childhood. Other cultures have had a language for suffering that is more mythological, existential, or directly spiritual. It may be that in our era, one of the reasons that Almaas's system is possible, even inevitable, is that our language for suffering has changed and become centered on childhood origins and precursors.

An age that rejected this understanding of emotional conflict in terms of its developmental manifestations, whether taken on Freud's "causal" model or on Hillman's view of early indicators of temperamental destiny, might well find Almaas's synthesis of spirituality and psychology puzzling, or less helpful. At present, however, it does uniquely integrate the multiple conflicting discourses on the nature of spirituality in our own time. And of course it may also be objectively true that childhood in our complex and confusing times, in contrast to more traditional societies, has actually become more anxiety provoking. That, of necessity, would be an added burden for spiritual realization in our era. As much as many today question Freud and wonder how best to understand his classical psychoanalysis, it may be no accident that we ended up with him.

CHAPTER **3**

The Sociology of Inner-Worldly Mysticism in
Max Weber and Ernst Troeltsch

There are three strands of analysis to be combined and applied to our multiple precursors of the this-worldly or New Age spirituality that has increasingly come to characterize religiosity among the educated classes of nineteenth- and twentieth-century Western societies. The first strand is the transpersonal psychology of higher states of consciousness, as most inclusively articulated by Almaas. The second strand is the contemporary psychoanalytic approaches to object-relations and self-psychology, also addressed by Almaas, since transpersonal states of consciousness will inevitably stir up exactly the personal issues that have been the speciality of these dynamic psychologies. The third strand is the socio-cultural level of analysis that will help to explain how and why a this-worldly mysticism would become so predominant in the modern West. In particular, the sociology of religion of Max Weber (1864–1920) and Ernst Troeltsch (1865–1923) can be used to approach this characteristic "new spirituality" as both a paradigmatic societal organization of the numinous and yet unique in its particular manifestations within modern industrialization and increasing globalization.

Max Weber on Radical Salvation Movements

In a series of writings, mostly unpublished during his lifetime, Weber investigated the relation between revolutionary change in complex societies and the appearance of what he called "radical salvation movements," which emerge at times of widespread alienation

(Weber 1915, 1922). His history of the classic civilizations traces the conflict between inherent pressures toward "bureaucratization," or "rationalization," and a more revolutionary and personal creativity. The capitalist economy and power of science in the modern West thus represents a historically unique and increasingly global triumph of such organization over our similarly heightened emphasis on the individual. Based on his detailed cross-cultural analyses of the religious histories of India (1967), China (1964), and Judaism (1952), as well as Hellenistic Rome and Islam (1922b), and his key focus on the Protestant Reformation (1905), Weber traced these alternating eras of secularization and "re-enchantment" into the present crisis of Western values.

Periodically in the history of complex civilizations, as social conditions change, the dominant religion no longer reconciles individual life circumstances. Accordingly, there follow attempts at a renewal of the lost connection to a more immediate sense of the numinous, or what Weber himself called "charisma," thereby emphasizing both its revolutionary social impact and the power of its personal inspiration. What begins as small groups centered around a few religious "virtuosos" capable of an original experience of charisma can lead to new schematizations of the numinous more in keeping with dilemmas of the time. If these ecstatic groups resonate widely enough, they may become new establishment religions, thereby renewing a sense of purpose and meaning in everyday activities.

Put otherwise, if numinous experience is a noetic felt meaning so abstract as to provide an all-inclusive sense of coherence for a culture, there could correspondingly be eras of a diffuse loss of significance— a kind of culture-wide semantic satiation, marked by relative indifference, boredom, and sense of futility. Jung, Heidegger, and Gurdjieff all wrestle with these feelings, while Nietzsche and Emerson had earlier foreshadowed the crisis. Weber is locating a long cycle in all world civilizations that alternates between times of secularization, with their alienation and disenchantment, and the periodic re-enchantments afforded by new sects, cults, and visionary individuals. This process may at times spark new mass religions that can spread rapidly across multiple societies, as in early Christianity, Buddhism, Islam, and the Protestant Reformation.

Weber himself is a complex and much debated figure (Bendix 1960; Käsler 1988). In many ways his combined legacy and controversy in sociology are analogous to those of Freud in psychology. Somewhat like Freud, he was deeply ambivalent about what he took to be the unique history of the modern West. European civilization, with its increasingly internationalized economy, represented a unique socio-economic development in human history, with an unprecedented and inexorably progressive rationalization of experience and behavior. This Weber saw as both constructive and destructive. Indeed, as a founding figure of modern sociology, he can be read very differently. On the one hand, he clearly values science and its complex interdependence with the organizational powers of modern economies. On the other, and deeply influenced by both Nietzsche and Marx, he also speaks of capitalism as a "masterless slavery" (Hennis 1988; Albrow 1990). He saw the triumph of an unfettered capitalism as creating an "iron cage" or "shell hard as steel" (Baehr 2001), with the technological potential of so organizing and rationalizing everyday life as to stop the possibility of any major spiritual re-enchantment that might address the anxieties and alienation of modern times. His source for the cage/shell metaphor may have been Bunyan's *Pilgrim's Progress*, where a willful loss of faith is the "iron cage of despair" (Tiryakian 1981). In this regard, we could say that Nietzsche's "God is dead" prophesizes our uniquely materialistic, and increasingly global, secularized civilization, while contemporary psychoanalytic accounts of an endemic sense of schizoid futility and defensive narcissism take its pulse on the level of our hyper-autonomous individualism. In Weber's own tragic view, the forces of rationalization and re-enchantment were ultimately "irreconcilable" (Bendix 1960).

We can compare Weber's thought on the periodicity between secularization and re-enchantment in world civilization, and the possibility that the modern West both follows and irrevocably alters this pattern, to another macro-sociologist of the mid-twentieth century, Pitirim Sorokin. In his immense work *Social and Cultural Dynamics* (1957), Sorokin put forward a similar notion of broad cycles within the major world civilizations, starting in Egypt, India, and China, and continuing through Greece and Rome, and into Medieval and Renaissance Europe. He locates a general alternation between sacred or "ideational" eras and "sensate" ones, as starkly disparate ways of organizing economy and culture—and with periods of "classicism" occasionally mediating between the two.

Ideational eras are those foundational times where cultural reality is defined in terms that are ultimately religious or spiritual. Here there is a consensus, as found for instance in the old kingdom of Egypt, early Islam, or early Christianity, that amounts to a vision of the sacred that unifies and integrates the society and is reflected in spiritual and nonmaterial values. There is a corresponding non naturalistic sacred art that tends to be geometrically schematic, abstract, and symmetrical. Sensate eras emerge out of the gradual loss of these unifying ideational visions, which can begin in some spheres of society before others. The values of sensate eras are more materialist and pragmatic, with an accent on the secular individual, and a relativism of values that verges on or can pass into cynicism and nihilism. All of which might sound very familiar. Examples of classical eras, as a temporary and precarious balance between the ideational and sensate, would include Athenian Greece and the Renaissance. It should be clear that Sorokin's and Weber's cross-cultural periodicities of history stand in marked contrast to linear models of the development of civilization, as found in Hegel, and more recently Jean Gebser and Ken Wilber (see chapter 13).

However, Sorokin, like Weber, also found something unique in the situation of the modern technological west. Sorokin's original four-volume version of *Social and Cultural Dynamics* (1937–41) presents a vast statistics to document these cycles in terms of typical changes in art, organization of the economy, kinds of wars, dominant social groups, and modes of social organization. On the basis of these comparative analyses he would have predicted the end of the modern sensate era in the late 1800s, to be replaced by a renewed ideational world-view, which of course did not happen. Instead we became more and more radically sensate, individualistic, and materialistic, culminating in the modern era. A question that comes out of Sorokin's work is whether there is something about the self-perpetuating, rationalizing, controlling nature of a world-wide corporate economy, with ever-increasing degrees of bureaucratization and organization, and an all-pervasive mass media of sensate entertainment, that would block or impede any radical spiritual reorganization. In terms of the potentially irreversible impact of an unrestrained capitalist economy on the environment, the dominating metaphor may have become less "iron cage" than "run-away train."

Certainly there has never been such a monolithically driven materialist culture in world history. The closest competitor would be Rome, but all during its middle and later phases, Rome was rife with the radical religious movements of potential renewal. Often these had a wide membership, and some, as we will see, were historical precursors to the much more restricted scope of contemporary "New Age" spirituality. Rome, of course, initially persecuted the group around Jesus, the radical salvation movement that culminated in the Christian hegemony. The issue emerging from Sorokin and Weber is whether any comparable spiritual renewal is possible in a rationalized globalized economy, and more specifically what form its initial manifestations might take.

To return to Weber (1915, 1922b), he actually locates two "ideal types" of radical salvation movement, each with its respective form of charismatic experience, a typically different economic class of social origin, and a different kind of impact on society. He terms these forms "mystical contemplation" and "active ascetic conduct," although we will see from the phenomenology of the latter that it might better be termed "propheticism." Mysticism tends to focus on an individualized development of numinous experience for its own sake, usually based on specific techniques of consciousness transformation, most often the wide variety of meditational practices more or less common to Indian yoga, Buddhism, Taoism, Sufism, and medieval Christianity. Mystical movements tend to originate from the aristocratic, artistic, and intellectual circles of societies. The stereotype would be Buddha the prince. Periodic cultural alienations in these circles will be experienced as a primarily personal and internal matter. Because these classes are already more individually centered and their outer economic circumstances more secure, they are not tempted by the view that a fundamental alteration in their outward socio-economic circumstances would resolve the pain they feel.

Accordingly, the solutions sought to this more personal alienation and loss of meaning will be an *inward* transformation, an "introverted ecstacy," which Weber sees as an "individualistic flight from the world." The individual mystic is seeking a purely experiential union with, or dissolution into, an Absolute or all-inclusive oneness. Accordingly, Weber believes that the impact of mystical movements on reorganizing the socio-economic fabric of society has always been minimal. Here is Weber on prototypical mystical experience:

> The inexpressible contents of such experience remain the only possible "beyond" . . . an incorporeal and metaphysical realm in which individuals intimately possess the holy. Where this conclusion has been drawn without any residue, the individual can pursue his quest for salvation only as an individual. . . . This was the case with Asiatic and, above all, Indian world religions. For all of them, contemplation became the supreme and ultimate religious value accessible to man. Contemplation offered them entrance into the profound and blissful tranquility and immobility of the All-one. (Weber, *The Social Psychology of the World Religions*, 282)

Asceticism/propheticism is Weber's opposite ideal type. Its paradigmatic figure is the ethical prophet. Here the phenomenology of the charismatic experience is not a dissolving into or merging with an impersonal Absolute, but rather one of being inspired, filled, or possessed by a theistic spirit. This usually also involves some sort of ethical or social message, either heard within or dissociatively spoken without. It centers on audition, rather than vision. In the prophetical religions of ancient Judaism, early Christianity, and Islam, and in the more rationalized ethicalities of Confucianism and the Protestant reformation, it is the person's conduct in the world that becomes the primary mark of salvation. The emphasis is predominantly ethical rather than aesthetic and experiential. Directly felt inspiration is to be manifested socially in a moral message or as specifically ethical conduct. There is often an escatology, a doctrine of final time or salvation in terms of a day of judgment, and a preoccupation with future utopias that may either be conceived as an afterlife in heaven, or something to be enacted ahead of time by righteous conduct in daily life, or actual utopian communities of the elect.

Weber outlines an experiential phenomenology for the "auditive prophet" very different from that for the mystic:

> Things have been quite different where the religiously qualified virtuosos have combined into an ascetic sect, striving to mold life in this world according to the will of a god. . . . The path to salvation is turned away from a contemplative "flight from the world" and towards an active ascetic "work in this world." . . . The religious virtuoso can be placed in the world as the instrument of a God and cut off from all magical means of salvation. At the same time it is imperative for the virtuoso that he prove himself before God, as being called *solely* through the ethical quality of his conduct in this world. . . . Asceticism has wished to rationalize the world ethically in accordance with God's commandments. (Weber, *The Social Psychology of the World Religions*, 290–91)

We might think here of the early Christians prepared to die for their beliefs, in contrast to the mystery school of Plotinus, where one withdraws in order to contemplate the Absolute and then returns the next day to an ordinary middle- or upper-class Roman life.

Prophetical movements tend to originate in the lower middle classes, or among oppressed peoples like the ancient Hebrews, or in colonized peoples in modern times (Lanternari 1963). The stereotype here is Christ the carpenter. The alienation experienced by the lower middle classes or specifically oppressed groups tends to be socially shared and more obviously based on historical and economic persecution. The result is that prophetical inspiration tends to involve a more active attempt at the mastery of social problems. So the impact of prophetical movements on society tends to be more direct and revolutionary than mystical movements. Prophetical movements are already the response of a people who see themselves as a group rather than as the individuals of the more artistic and educated classes. Examples of this revolutionary impact on society can be found in the Protestant Reformation, early Christianity and Islam, and contemporary Evangelical Christianity and Islamic fundamentalism.

Weber further subdivides his classifications. In addition to distinguishing between mysticism and asceticism as radical salvation movements, he makes an additional distinction between "inner-worldly" and "other-worldly" forms within both these general types. This becomes central for understanding his key postulate of a confluence between the inner-worldly asceticism of the Protestant Reformation and the development of capitalism—and for our present approach to the congruence between contemporary socio-economic conditions and an inner-worldly mysticism. As with any classification there will be mixed groups, but no one has gone further than Weber in identifying the social forms of spirituality.[1]

Inner-worldly mysticism cultivates an experiential sensitivity and openness in the midst of everyday social reality. Historically this is the attitude of much Sufi and Taoist practice, and the Western esoteric and occult tradition. Inner-worldly mysticism can be contrasted with the better known forms of other-worldly or classical mysticism, where adepts withdraw into monasteries, caves, or special societies separate from mainstream social reality and cultivate a more impersonal transcendent experience of oneness—as in traditional Indian yoga, monastic Buddhism, and medieval Catholic monasticism.

Meanwhile, other-worldly propheticism describes those special groups who withdraw into relatively isolated communities in order to live a godly or ethical life, apart from the mainstream. We see this in the desert communes around the ancient Hebrew prophets, Essenes, and early Christians, as well as in some of the Protestant sects, later Puritan groups coming to the New World, and in the various experimental Utopian communities of the nineteenth and twentieth centuries.

The most important category for Weber, in the sense of providing the greatest potential leverage for social transformation, is inner-worldly asceticism and its ethical prophets. Here the group stays within the larger community, and proof of salvation or grace comes through one's ethical conduct from inside the mainstream social order, as in early Calvinism where actual vocational dedication and success in the world became the mark of God's grace. Contemporary revivalist Pentecostalism, with its primary appeal to the lower-middle and working classes, carries forward this expectation of material reward for faith and ethical conduct. Confucianism and much of Islam are also examples of inner-worldly asceticism, but Weber concentrates, in his most controversial and widely studied work, *The Protestant Ethic and the Spirit of Capitalism* (1905), on the Protestant Reformation. He holds this to be unique in world history in perfecting and exaggerating the features of inner-worldly asceticism in a way that paved the way for a modern capitalist economy.

Weber argued that the early development of capitalism, as a systematic cycling of capital and investment beyond the level of mercantile trade, needed the sanctified ethic of vocation and "calling" that was the special prescription of the early Protestant sects. Quite literally one's vocational calling was considered sacred. People with this level of "vocation" were necessary to ensure individual responsibility for the integrity of business dealings spread over thousands of miles. It was the growing secularization of this attitude that became a crucial element in the growth of a capitalist economy, and carries forward today in the "professionalism" of many lawyers, doctors, teachers, scientists, and business persons for whom nothing on the face of the earth matters more than "career." In Weber's view, the Protestant Reformation was the first crucible for the ethical autonomy and individualism needed to create and support an extended capitalist economy.

Weber actually undertook his immense project of comparison with other charismatic traditions to test this hypothesis. The closest parallel to the "ethic of vocation" in Protestantism is Confucianism, whose "exemplary" adapation to the social order he contrasts with the potentially causal "active mastery" of the Protestant ethic. To further support his thesis, Weber toured Protestant communities in the United States and studied the importance of church affiliation as a badge of authenticity in doing business over great distances, with small churches literally making good on dishonest business practices of their soon to be ex-members (Weber 1906). He saw such religious sanction for business ethics as a microcosm for the broader workings of a new world economy of such complexity that it only could emerge on the basis of this widely shared ethic of vocation, personal autonomy, and unprecedented rationalization of daily life. Once so created, the "mechanical foundations" of modern capitalism would no longer require such continued support. Our contemporary exaggerated emphasis on autonomy and individuality, however, is for Weber the *secularization* of the active ethic of vocation of the Protestant Reformation. Unique to the West, it supported the super rationalization and hyper-organization of modern economic structure, although there has been much debate as to whether this relation was truly causal or more secondary and concomitant.

Inner-Worldly Mysticism as the "Secret Religion of the Educated Classes"

It was Ernst Troeltsch, in his two-volume master work *The Social Teaching of the Christian Churches* (1931), who used Weber's basic typology to suggest that what Weber had termed "inner-worldly" forms of mysticism offered the only possible move towards contemporary spiritual renewal in the face of our own materialist, sensate, radically individualist society—itself the final secularization of the Protestant Reformation. Troeltsch had a more favorable, if ambivalent view of this renewed potential for mysticism than Weber (1918b), who saw the "transcendental realm of mystic life" as the mere recourse of a marginalized privacy. Troeltsch utilizes a slightly different vocabulary for Weber's distinctions, and it is these modifications that have been largely taken over by contemporary sociology.

Troeltsch substitutes "sect" for asceticism, by which he means primarily radical revivals of traditional prophetical movements, as in Pentecostalism. Whereas he keeps the term "mysticism" for newer nontraditional groups, mostly "inner-worldly," and centered on the direct experience of the numinous for its own sake. These are often termed "cults," "New Age," or "new religious movements" in contemporary studies. Again, the emphasis in mysticism is more aesthetic and experiential than ethical. Ethics is certainly important in the classical Eastern mysticisms, but rather as something preliminary, in that it is not considered safe to do advanced meditation or yoga without following certain ethical precepts. But the point of these practices goes beyond those precepts, so that the higher stages of the meditational path are in some sense "beyond good and evil." Preliminary ethical precepts are a means to help the individual to be more fully open in a containable way to powerful higher states of consciousness. Their realization is the point of the practices and will produce their own inner transformations of character.

Why then in terms of Weber's typology, and its associations with background socio-economic conditions, would we expect such a turn to mysticism, and why would it be predominantly inner-worldly? On the one hand, if we are in the aftermath of a secularization of the Protestant Reformation, as an inner-worldly prophetical orientation, that would suggest that charismatic renewal, especially in the educated classes, would shift toward the mystical. The secularization of the Protestant ethic has already left us with the values of radical individualism, which, with patterns of education also more traditionally associated with aristocracies, means that where the contemporary middle and upper-middle classes increasingly predominate in the industrial West, they will understand their alienation inwardly, rather than in outward political-economic terms, and so seek a more directly experiential solution.

On the other hand, the fact that our values are now so predominantly secular and material will tend to keep any spiritual renewal within an inner-worldly form. While there is a widespread contemporary interest in Eastern meditational practices, comparatively few go to India and live in ashrams. Most meditational groups and New Age "cults" are based on living an outwardly ordinary life in society and pursuing one's vocation, while turning inward through daily individual meditative practice and periodic group retreats. We could go still further and suggest that whereas a traditional prophetical Christianity centered on love and compassion, and subordinated other essential aspects to them, a shift to an inner-worldly mysticism would center more on the aspects of what Almaas terms strength, joy, will, and power, thus reflecting the contemporary values and dilemmas of individual autonomy.

To extend Weber's analysis of the Protestant ethic into a parallel account for the development of inner-worldly mysticism in the twentieth century, we could say that just as capitalism needed an inner-worldly ascetic and ethical attitude of vocation in order to develop fully, our society of autonomous individuals, separate to the point of isolation, social fragmentation, and extreme loneliness, may not be fully livable or bearable without some renewed access to a direct experiential sense of presence or "I amness"—as the more personal, identity-centered aspect of the numinous. In other words, without some sense of our inherent beingness as a lived and shared foundation for being an individual in the modern world, it is not clear what society can offer us in order to sustain our historically unique emphasis on autonomy and radical independence. It is otherwise not clear where we are to find the sense of immediately felt meaning and purpose, which can become so important during periods of life crisis in early-adult identity, midlife transition, and old age. In an era of increasing globalization, with a relative weakening of a traditional identity based on nation and extended family, a more inner spiritual rootedness emerges as one alternative—also consistent with the increasing separation and isolation of private life from vocational life as discussed by Stone (1978).

Considerable support for Troeltsch's basic distinctions and the place of a this-worldly mysticism in contemporary Western society comes from more recent research on the differences between revivalistic "sects" and "new religious movements." Stark and Bainbridge (1985), studying "sect" and "cult" locations throughout the United States, found that in regions higher in traditional churches and sects, the newer, more mystical groups, such as scientology, Rajneesh, and Buddhist, Taoist, or Yogic meditation societies, were rare. Churches and sects tended to coexist, as in the deep south and midwest, whereas "cults" emerged in regions where church membership had more permanently weakened, as in the West Coast, Arizona, and New Mexico. "Sects" and "new religious movements" appeared to appeal to very different people and regions.[2] Dawson (1998) summarized evidence showing that members of the newer mystical groups, the vast majority fitting Weber's "inner-worldly" criteria, tend to be younger, better educated, more often from middle and upper-middle class backgrounds, and more predominantly female, in comparison to sect and church groups. We could add that it is those higher on the basic personality trait of absorption/openness to experience, also more common among women, who are more likely to report the spontaneous alterations of consciousness associated with these spiritual interests, such as classical mystical experience, lucid dreaming, out-of-body experience, and states of vivid imagery and synesthesias (Hunt 2000).

To return more specifically to Troeltsch and his explicators (Campbell 1978; Garrett 1975), it was his view that the atomistic individualism of modern society makes a diversely manifested inner-worldly mysticism the "secret religion of the educated classes," an emerging "invisible church"—socially invisible because its expression can be so individualistic. To put this in more contemporary terms, a particular person with a proclivity to lucid dreaming or out-of-body experience, and perhaps understanding these phenomena in terms of a private sense of something "beyond" or "transcendent," may or may not group together with similar individuals in pursuit of these interests.

Troeltsch sees a tendency in inner-worldly mysticism towards an "antinomian" attitude, referring to its felt transcendence and/or disregard of orthodox moral values. This can reach the extremes of a "libertinism" in which new cults and searching individuals may explore orgiastic experiences or drugs as avenues for the further opening of direct experience. Indeed, the experiential emphasis of mysticism, combined with an inner-worldly orientation, creates a potential dilemma in the search for a radical solution to felt alienation with regard to sexuality in particular. There can be the sense that sexuality has its own potentially transcendent aspect, certainly, along with drug use, a major preoccupation of Crowley and many others. Or, what of certain kinds of political power, which proved so tempting to Jung and Heidegger in their periods of personal grandiosity? For the other-worldly mystic, these are less often issues, since one jettisons everything in the retreat to the monastery or ashram. But for the inner-worldly mystic, who is experientially and aesthetically oriented, how the energies of sex and power are to be handled, whether as temptation or conduit, can become a confusing and painful issue.

Troeltsch (1931) also characterizes the inner-worldly mystical attitude as tending toward a cultural "syncretism" in its easy combination of diverse sources and practices. We have already seen this tendency in Almaas, where Sufism is mixed with Buddhism and Gurdjieff, and in turn fused with psychodynamic theory and bioenergetic therapy. Such syncretism also means that there is not the same tension between inner-worldly mystical movements and science as with the more traditional theistic religions. This is especially clear in much New Age spirituality and hands-on-healing, where the language of primary description overlaps into physiological and psychological "energies" and "fields." Hanegraaff (1998) calls attention to the complex ways in which the earlier successive waves of Renaissance magic, mesmerism, romanticism, and even mediumistic spiritualism were linked to the "nature philosophy" of their times and/or to claims of physical evidence.

Most of the modern precursor figures we will be examining are both *examples* of a this-worldly mysticism *and* offered their own broadly empirical *theories* on the nature of spirituality. From a social-cultural perspective even the modern interest in a science of consciousness and a human science of transpersonal states can be seen as itself part of this tendency toward an inner-worldly mysticism, because literally we are trying to understand the mystical as something human (i.e., as something neuro-cognitive) and so as *this*-worldly. Our modern attempts at a science of spirituality then become a new culturally acceptable form for what is *also* a new culturally based spiritual orientation. We will discuss the widespread, but questionable linkage of New Age spirituality and evolution in the concluding chapter.

Finally, and on the more negative side for Troeltsch, he agrees with Weber that inner-worldly mysticism tends to lack a community bond, both with society at large and in terms of its own historical continuity. All mysticism is individualistic, but its other-worldly forms can preserve the unbroken transmission of a teaching lineage precisely through their removal from mainstream society. Inner-worldly mysticisms, however, are by definition more open to the changing social conditions in which they emerge, without seeking to transform these as in prophetical movements. Historically in the West, esoteric and occult movements have come and gone rapidly, with little direct influence on their successors. Different eras in Western history have seen a characteristic inner-worldly mysticism appearing in largely separated and noninteracting forms. These traditions tend to be unstable, and Troeltsch wondered if they actually made the community bond weaker. This is a controversy to which we will return below in terms of some current questioning as to whether all contemporary New Age spiritualities and transpersonal states are inherently narcissistic.

It will help orient us further in regard to the fundamental controversy about the social and personal instabilities of a characteristically Western inner-worldly mysticism, to review its higher cultural expressions in some of our key paradigmatic figures. The struggle emerging will be clear enough. How *is* the deep humility and sensed deficiency of "creature feeling," inherent to the numinous, to be reconciled with the modern Western emphasis on autonomy and individuality? Is this an irreconcilable collision, necessarily ending in withdrawal and/or grandiosity, or is something more balanced and reconciling possible within a modern this-worldly spirituality, alongside its often more obvious instabilities and metapathologies? Certainly Nietzsche, Maslow, Jung, Heidegger, and Gurdjieff reflect a spiritualization of individuality, as a direct response to "mass" society and culture. The deeper question is whether this emphasis on the individual is necessarily a marginalization or a potentially constructive response to contemporary dilemmas.

Jung and much of the Jungian psychological movement can be considered from a societal perspective as a syncretic inner-worldly mysticism, albeit with some controversy as to whether its origins were more "science" or "visionary" (Noll 1994, 1997, Shamdasani 1998). Active imagination techniques of archetypal imagery induction were developed by Jung to focus and balance an "individuation" of the Self, a process he saw as a naturalistic, empirical version of the traditional mysticisms. Jung (1944) studied Renaissance alchemy as a metaphoric anticipation of his own psychology. In that regard the inner-worldly orientation of alchemy seems clear, since its goal in the philosopher's stone is "the red" (rubedo) of essential strength. This contrasts with the white light (albedo) of classical mysticism, which for the alchemist was only preliminary to the fuller personal integration sought. It was the vitalist Self that was sought, not a withdrawn monastic one.

Jung (1959) compares his Self to the Gnostic and alchemical idea of the Anthropos, in that these practices had as their goal the re-creation of the primal human being—of the angelic condition of Adam and Eve before the fall. Jung's Self is far closer to Almaas on personal essence, with its autonomy and vital fullness, than it is to the formless dimensions. Jung's archetypal realizations do not involve dissolving into shining darkness, but a balancing and progressive integration of personal identity with the images of shadow, anima or animus, old wise man or woman, and divine child—all forms of normally unconscious collective identities to be synthesized into a fully individuated personhood. The self-realization Jung describes is a sacralization of the individual *within* the social world.

Heidegger's (1927) analysis of human existence (Dasein) can also be seen as both an exemplification and its own understanding of Weber's inner-worldly mysticism. Again, for Heidegger what has been lost is our immediate sense of Being, the noetic core of our potentiality for a felt transcendence and sense of inclusive significance. How brilliant to suggest, in our sensate, material culture, that the core of the sacred is sheer isness. What could be more empirical and concrete and undeniably real in our era of scientific fascination with "fact" than the immediate nowness and "facticity" of Being? Here is a truly this-worldly core for the numinous. Dasein, or human being-there, is the full sensing of one's felt presence or I amnooo, which for Heidegger reflects our potentiality for "authenticity" as a personal attunement to Being as such, and which is related to Almaas on both personal essence and essential identity. The later Heidegger, of course, is much more of a classical mystic, but his earlier discussions of authenticity are reminiscent of Maslow on self-actualization, which itself can be taken as a psychologizing of inner-worldly spirituality. The individual, still very much within the world for Maslow, develops Being-values of nurturance and nowness through the spontaneous "peak experiences" which he also calls identity experiences and direct experiences of Being.

A final example of inner-worldly mysticism in its higher, less cultish forms, is Gurdjieff's (1975) and Ouspensky's (1949) "fourth way" practice—a "self-remembering" meditative practice to be done in the midst of everyday life. Gurdjieff portrays the average modern person as lost within what Fairbairn later termed the schizoid position—split, inwardly withdrawn and asleep, with no central "I am-ness" or essence, and lost in the imaginative daydreams he terms "identifying." "Self-remembering" is literally an extraverted meditation aiming to develop an ongoing witness capacity in the midst of daily social life. Self-remembering is the cultivation in the midst of social participation of a nonverbal and immediate sense of presence that could be paraphrased, "I am here now, in this place, doing and feeling what is happening." A simpler form would be to try to be aware of the sensations from one's arms and legs while one is fully engaged in everyday situations, without losing either the participatory or witnessing aspect. Awareness of one's arms and legs functions here as a sort of meditative "holding" of one's ongoing state. This practice is also at the core of Almaas's Diamond-Heart work, which is itself a neo-Gurdjieffian system, Gurdjieff having adapted much of his teachings from inner-worldly Sufism.

Dilemmas and Societal Implications of Contemporary Inner-Worldly Mysticism

Weber and Troeltsch were both concerned that the shift to inner-worldly mysticism among the educated classes, with its attendant individualism, would be associated with a relative withdrawal from community and social action. Indeed, the above figures all sought a specifically spiritual development of the autonomous individual. More recently, both the sociologist Robert Bellah, in *Habits of the Heart* (Bellah et al. 1985) and the Jungian psychologist James Hillman, in *We've Had a Hundred Years of Psychotherapy and Everything's Getting Worse* (Hillman and Ventura 1992), have similarly pointed to a seeming exacerbation of narcissism and personal isolation in New Age spirituality. The situation, however, seems more complex.

First, it is of interest that Weber's mysticism-propheticism typology for complex civilizations has its social precursor in the classification for types of trance experience developed by the anthropologist Erika Bourguignon (1973) for non literate, native societies. Through detailed cross-cultural comparisons, she distinguished between the "vision trance," or "shamanic," organization of spirituality found in the "single-class" societies of hunter-gatherers, and the more conflicted

Lives in Spirit

"possession trance" of the multi-class, often polygamous, agricultural peoples, whose "primitive prophecy" states are more directly reflective of social tensions. Bourguignon's relatively dichotomous clusters have been statistically confirmed by Shaara and Strathern (1992).

Inner-worldly mysticism is obviously closer to shamanism as practised in hunter-gatherer societies than it is to possession trance, whose more abstract development would turn into ethical prophecy. Hunter-gatherer societies tend to have practices that involve taking hallucinogens, seeking sacred dreams and out-of-body experiences, and trance induction. A direct experience of the numinous is often sought by an individual shaman or initiate in solitary retreats, with its implications only later shared with the group. Even when trance states are communally induced, each participant turns initially inward (Winkelman 2000). The possession trance of agricultural societies, on the other hand, with their greater social stresses largely associated with class distinctions, slavery, and personal property, takes the form of being possessed by a spirit, often with glossolalia and later amnesia. The often intense experiential core is less central than the resulting ethical message, later interpreted by the group in terms of its social meaning. In Almaas's terms, we could say that possession trance, with its phenomenology of intrusion and inescapable social conflict, involves a "negative merging." Meanwhile shamanic trance, at least once an introverted death-rebirth crisis is accepted, moves more toward the positive mergence states of mysticism. The paroxysmal and "class struggle" features of possession trance have a quality of "identification with the aggressor."[3] We can see why any communal sharing of the direct experience of the numinous comes to be minimized in possession and primitive prophecy. Increasingly it becomes the *price* for the authenticity of message rather than the *goal*.

Going further in terms of Weber's language of classification, shamanism or "vision trance" literally *is* a form of inner-worldly mysticism, since it is a directly experiential, contemplative spirituality that stays within and deeply impacts the everyday social order. Yet, contrary to contemporary critics of Western inner-worldly mysticism, the visionary religions of hunter-gatherer people actually bind their societies together and create a relative stability and social cohesion, in contrast to the continuous dissensions that possession trances address but do not resolve. Although shamans are usually selected on the basis of a natural openness to intense dreams and states of consciousness, anyone in the group may have their own direct experience of the numinous in trance or sacred dreams, and all such experiences are treated as potentially of equal importance.

So here a directly contemplative attitude, also a key feature of the world mysticisms, is open to all members of the group, creates a powerful social cohesion, and commonly guides group decisions. The implication is that the relative social withdrawal and marginalized privacy of contemporary inner-worldly mysticism may not be inherent to its phenomenology, but more associated with its appearance in the form of alienated radical salvation movements in a highly complex socio-economic context—one already characterized by a conflicted hyper-autonomy and a growing "culture of narcissism" (Lasch 1978). Yet if the twentieth century's turn to inner-worldly mysticism is both a reconstitution and development of shamanism as the originary form of human spiritual organization, how does it happen that its effects can at times seem so specifically isolating?

Weber (1922b) himself comments that inner-worldly mysticism has what he calls a characteristically "broken" quality, in contrast to both the propheticisms and other-worldly mysticisms. For Weber this quality of "broken humility" is inherent to inner-worldly mysticism and found across very different cultures. The cultivation of a here and now experiential openness, while remaining within everyday social life and not withdrawing into a special community, will also entail an openness and heightened sensitivity to all the pain and frustration of ordinary living. Other-worldly mystics also cultivate a radical acceptance of direct experience but they have removed themselves from much social complexity, and the more concentrative methods associated with yoga may actually suppress emotional conflict, in marked contrast to the mindfulness methods associated with Zen Buddhism and Sufism. Both inner- and other-worldly prophets will use these same social and personal conflicts to energize their passion for ethical conduct, leading directly or indirectly to actual social change. The inner-worldly mystic, however, cultivating self-remembering, the increased sensitivity of psychedelic drugs, or the experiential openness of mindfulness meditation, is going to encounter the conflicts and anguish of everyday life immediately and unbuffered. This means that for all practical purposes, and here like the propheticisms, the inner-worldly mystic often remains caught within a dualism, since his/her conflictedness with the world, while quieter, is equally unavoidable—if also at least potentially dissolvable with time, distance, and reconciliation. The inner-worldly mystic must *struggle* continuously to accept the world, whose challenge is ever renewed.

If we add to Weber's observations of "broken humility," the view from the object-relations theorists of widespread deficits in the modern West in sense of self and self-esteem, based on a uniquely early emphasis in child rearing on separation and exaggerated autonomy, then the tendency in our era to seek solutions to alienation through an inner-worldly mysticism must involve a heightened sensitivity of feeling to these conflicts as well. More specifically, an inner-worldly mystical openness to immediate experience entails an openness to the very narcissistic and schizoid dilemmas that Fairbairn, Winnicott, and Kohut were first locating and analyzing from the 1950s through the 1970s. These would include the widespread sense of not feeling alive or present, of not feeling real or having a true self, and lacking any intrinsic sense of self-esteem—all continually stimulated by a hyper-competitive society intent on establishing a basic sense of worth only in terms of outward accomplishments. Accordingly, any contemporary practice of felt presence, to paraphrase and extend Gurdjieffian "self-remembering," will mean cultivating a felt sense of "I am here now, in this situation, feeling awful about myself, withdrawn, unreal, abandoned, shamed, enraged, or desperately grandiose"—all the self-pathologies of modern times. So unless these dilemmas are going to be dealt with directly, as with Almaas and some Jungians, then New Age mysticisms, even though called forth to resolve this need for a greater felt presence or felt reality in the here and now, will at times stir up more pain than the individual can handle.

From this broader perspective we can return to the debate over whether the contemporary Western mysticisms, broadly inner-worldly, are inherently narcissistic and create a self-preoccupation that interferes with the demands of citizenship in a modern democratic state. Troeltsch had already wondered if that could be the price for these movements, however much they were also a positive response to the dilemmas of modernity. Meanwhile, Bellah and Hillman argue that the psychotherapeutic ethic itself, along with New Age spirituality, actually encourages a narcissism that further isolates us from the fabric of community and the commitments of citizenship needed to make modern society work.

However, there are other ways to look at these issues. The people that are most drawn to inner-worldly mystical groups are by definition, if Weber is right, already in the throes of a painful alienation. The practices themselves then usually require much time and discipline, so people will not commit to such practices unless they already feel a longing for the sense of meaning and presence absent from their everyday lives. They are already struggling with the narcissism and schizoid isolation of modern society, and its values of secular individualism and individual over community, for which New Age mysticism and psychotherapy cannot be held responsible. Both contemporary spirituality and psychotherapy are attempts, ultimately workable or not, to resolve dilemmas already produced. Bellah himself uses the writings of de Tocqueville, the French aristocrat who toured the United States in the 1830s, and who in his *Democracy in America* commented with amazement on the radical individualism of Americans at that time, suggesting that if it continued it would impede any viable family and community structure.

The radical individualism of modern society is required by its economic organization. The alienation thereby created will call forth a characteristically mystical solution because this alienation is already experienced as something inner, private, and personal. It seems meaningless to argue that the resultant tendencies to mysticism create a lack of community that was already beginning in the 1830s, or a narcissism that is the exaggeration of our resultant hyper-autonomy. Instead, an inner-worldly, directly experiential spirituality becomes the only possible direction for people in such a situation, from the perspective of Weber and Troeltsch, whether that attempt is ultimately successful or not in resolving the deep sense of alienation and confusion involved. Certainly the appearance of inner-worldly mysticisms among the more educated classes in a materialistic, sensate era, where normality is defined in terms of culturally unprecedented levels of self-preoccupation, would entail that these movements and creative individuals may appear narcissistic. Indeed, these practices could actually make certain forms of narcissism at least temporarily more extreme. But from a macro-sociological point of view, these are the problems already endemic to our society, with inner-worldly mysticism inevitably partly their expression, partly their attempted resolution.

What also seems historically unique to our situation, with its unprecedented expansion of an educated middle class, is that there has never before been such a large portion of a society ripe for the turn to the directly experiential resolution of mysticism. This will make the narcissistic issues, thereby also exacerbated, all the more culturally obtrusive. Yet, rather than "causing" increased narcissism, the deeper forms of inner-worldly mysticism—for instance, in the work of Nietzsche, Emerson, Jung, Gurdjieff, Heidegger, and Almaas—are the major attempts of our culture to face it directly and at least attempt its transformation. The unity experiences of essential states are perhaps the major source for the transmutation of narcissism and reconciling its sense of isolation and defensive grandiosity, through an encompassing sense of meaning and felt reality that also has the potential to connect and unite the people who come to share in it. For Durkheim (1912), after all, it is a shared spirituality that most directly expresses the unity of a society.

At the same time, inner-worldly mysticisms within our uniquely complex and hyper differentiated civilization will have vulnerabilities beyond the intrinsically "broken" humility and hypersensitivity located by Weber. The inherent compromise between inner-worldly mysticisms and their immediate social order means that they may offer a less full development of the all-inclusive formless dimensions than do the classical other-worldly mysticisms, even though they will also center on the cultivation of a needed personal essence. Similarly, in terms of Almaas on the multiple aspects of essence, it seems inevitable that many forms of inner-worldly mysticism will remain relatively one-sided. New Age mystical groups and our precursor visionary figures develop more within strength, joy, will, power, or brilliancy, but these are less often balanced and integrated with each other, let alone with compassion and love. A new mysticism of essential strength, will, and power will certainly compensate for an historical one-sidedness in Christianity, and also "sacralize" the more secular values of our competitive, individualized society, but it will risk a one-sidedness and extremity of its own. With figures like Nietzsche and Crowley, or Jung and Heidegger during their brief early fascination with the Nazis, there is an imbalanced concentration on essential strength, power, and will. The resulting one-sidedness can be associated with the development of what Almaas calls the false forms of essence—as in the stridency of the later Nietzsche in his false strength and will, the false power and schizoidness of Crowley, and the periods of narcissistic grandiosity in Jung.

Other-worldly mysticisms seek the formless One, a dissolving into an impersonal and transcendent unity, often referred to as experience "without seed" (Eliade 1958). By definition, inner-worldly mystical movements are working with more worldly forms and symbols of the numinous. These are the mysticisms "with seed," using evocative metaphors that certainly open out beyond the ordinary sense of self, and so expand a sense of meaning well beyond the categories of everyday experience. These include images of energy, sexuality, or nature, the latter of such primary importance in the "nature mysticisms" of Nietzsche, Emerson, Thoreau, Jung, and Heidegger. Later we will also consider the gender symbols central to modern feminist mysticism, again in reaction against the traditional and one-sided patriarchal imageries of Christianity. More dangerously there are the imageries of race and national origin which were so tempting for a while to Jung and Heidegger, and developed to visionary extremes by the actual proto-Nazi occultists. All these forms or structures can be used to evoke the numinous, since they are more "expanded" and "far out" than everyday ego, and so potentially mediate its opening. Yet they are also specific enough that they can have the opposite effect of falsely concretizing or fixating the numinous.

For instance, the categories of "transpersonal" experience mapped by Grof (1988) in his psychedelic drug research, such as extra-terrestrial scenarios, past lives, out-of-body travels, phylogenetic regressions, birth and pre-natal states, all show this simultaneously opening yet limiting impact. Emerson comments to similar effect on Swedenborg, a prototypical inner-worldly mystic, concerning his elaborately detailed visions of levels of hell and heaven: "It is dangerous to sculpture these evanessing images of thought. True in transition, they become false if fixed" (1850:65). Another way of saying this is that anything more specific than light or shining darkness as the metaphor that evokes the felt meaning of the numinous risks being falsely literalized at some point, or in Otto's terms preemptively "schematized." Numinous or essential states are so powerful in their impact and so dissolving of the ordinary sense of self that they will also be defended against and fixated when their effects prove too threatening. Metaphors less open than the all-inclusive felt sense of the "mysterium" and its "not knowing" thereby risk a defensive acting out in terms of sexuality, dominance, or group identity. Specific imageries that may initially be truly opening for the person will also lay a limiting structure over the experience that can curtail his/her later development.

Inner-worldly mysticism is the characteristic form assumed by historical mysticism in the West, aside from monastic Catholic mystics like Meister Eckhart and those individuals who today enter fully into Eastern other-worldliness. Despite some of the similarities that we will trace across time in these Western inner-worldly mysticisms, from Plotinus, the Gnostics, and the Greek-Roman mystery cults on, there is more generally a lack of historical continuity and direct influence among them. Troeltsch (1931) commented on their purely personal and local basis and lack of permanent form. Whereas the other-worldly mysticisms and prophetic movements create lines of relatively unbroken transmission, the inner-worldly mysticisms keep re-inventing themselves, as if continually reconstituting the photographic negative of our predominantly extraverted and individualistic civilization.[4]

The Hellenistic mystery cults, Christian and non-Christian Gnostics, and mystery schools like that of Plotinus disappear with the triumph of Christianity, but similar inner-worldly mysticisms reappear in the Middle Ages with the Kabbalah, Catharism, and the Free Brethren—the latter in sexually open and egalitarian communes soon annihilated by the armies of the Church. They reappear again in Renaissance magic, alchemy, and visionary figures like Giordano Bruno, who do appropriate to their own times earlier neo-Platonic and Hermetic traditions. Yet none of these have much direct influence on the later emergence of visionaries like Swedenborg or William Blake. The New England transcendentalists Emerson and Thoreau rediscover their own Gnosticism, and read in Sufism, but they in turn had no direct impact on the larger scale mass movements of spiritualism, occultism, and theosophy that appear in the late-nineteenth century. And it is generally similar with the independent appearance of Jung, Gurdjieff, and Heidegger in the 1920s, the psychedelic and Eastern meditation movements of the 1960s, and now the New Age spiritualities and cults.

One explanation for this relative lack of cross-referencing would be that Western civilization, according to both Weber and Jung, has been characteristically extraverted in its values, and based around the notion of the individual. Accordingly, the openness to inner-worldly mysticism in the West is going to be more specific to time and place and to the individuals involved, making the unbroken lineages of the East less likely. It is this very individualism of the West that would require an inner-worldly mysticism as both its expression and the reconciliation of its alienation. Whenever the conditions are ripe for mysticism these groups and individuals reappear, and then disappear as outer social conditions make their more restricted metaphoric "forms" seem idiosyncratic and dated. The result is a recognizable form of radical religiosity appearing and reappearing within the educated classes—its organizing metaphors a constantly varying mix of crisis and resolution.

PART **II**

The Historical Roots of Inner-Worldly
Mysticism: Prototypes of Crisis and Resolution
in Plotinus, Epictetus, and Gnosticism

CHAPTER 4

Plotinus and Hellenistic
Inner-Worldly Mysticism

The origins of a Western this-worldly mysticism can be traced to Plotinus and other Hellenistic and Roman mystery schools, emerging as fusions between the many earlier ecstatic mystery cults and the more abstract influences of Plato and Socrates. They will offer a historical template and primary illustration for our discussions of the phenomenology of essential states and for the typologies of Weber and Troeltsch, along with an early awareness of the potential metapathologies of spiritual practice.

Reflecting the typologies of Almaas and Laski, we find two poles within these first identifiable inner-worldly mysticisms. At the one extreme, there is the group of mystery schools of which Plotinus is the best representative, focusing on the formless dimensions, which for Plotinus culminate in the Absolute or all-unifying One. We will deal with the closely related but more overtly dualistic Gnosticisms in the next chapter. Plotinus, who died at the age of 66 in 270 A.D., is generally considered part of philosophical neo-Platonism, developing Plato's later, more speculative and visionary thought of the *Timaeus* and *Parmenides*. Plotinus's mystery school was as much a contemplative practice as it was a system of thought or philosophy. Educated within the esoteric traditions of Alexandria, Christian and non-Christian, Plotinus arrived at a postmythological abstract mysticism by combining the later metaphysics of Plato with the ecstatic mystery cults. It is "inner worldly" because students came to the school, located in Rome, to learn its understandings and attendant contemplative practices, and thence realize them in their own lives. It does not seem to have been an "other-worldly" ashram-type setting. In fact, what little is known of the life of Plotinus, apart from his being the upper-class intellectual Weber would predict, includes the fact that he adopted and raised numerous orphan children brought to him in trust by families who knew of him. It is also said that as a child he insisted on nursing until he was eight years old. There are fragments of passages from his teachers Ammonius and Numenius that are startlingly like the more extant writings of Plotinus, collected as *The Enneads*, so he seems to represent the greatest surviving development of a widespread mystical perspective.

The other pole of Hellenistic mystery schools, also treading the line between philosophy and contemplative practice (Hadot 1995), is centered on what Almaas would call the cultivation of personal presence. These are the schools of the Stoics, Skeptics, Cynics, and Epicureans. Their practitioners concentrated on the handling of daily life issues and events in the immediate present, to be understood and accepted with an inner detachment as expressions of Divine Will. The cultivation of a spiritual self in touch with divinity, widely understood as an inner daimon, was very much inspired by anecdotal tales of the life and daimon of Socrates that circulated throughout this era (*Diogenes Laertius*). These schools are most fully developed in the Stoics and their attempts to achieve a personal autonomy and detachment in the midst of a full participation in the situations of everyday life. The most complete surviving expression of the many Stoic schools from the late Greek and Roman periods is found in the *Discourses* of Epictetus. He died around 100 A.D. and was a freed slave, later exiled by Nero. So his ability under the circumstances to avoid being killed, while being outwardly indifferent to its possibility, says something both about his teachings and the perils of his times.

Epictetus and Personal Presence

Epictetus was explicitly elaborating the basic principles of conduct actually implied by the life and behavior of Socrates as these were then understood. This entailed cultivating a capacity for discriminating in here and now social situations what is within one's own personal control and what is not, with the latter to be accepted as God's will. Certainly, along with death and accident, what other people do, or think, or say, is not in our control. Therefore moral categories do not pertain to it, and it is neither good nor evil. Morality only pertains to what is within one's own choice, what is naturally given to us as within our power in a given situation. This is ultimately and primarily to discriminate that situation as fully as we can and to act justly, courageously, and honestly within it, regardless of what others do or do not. It was a demanding way of life. From the perspective of Almaas such a practice involves a capacity for the essential strength of personal autonomy and a capacity for discrimination in the heat of the moment. Epictetus's descriptions of his approach to problematic life situations also imply the essential will to steadfastly accept all that is happening outside of one's own control as a direct expression of God's will.

The situations to be thus lived and mastered, but not transcended, range from the ordinary to life-threatening extremes. So when a student tells him that he fears people might be thinking ill of him or pitying him, when that is not warranted, Epictetus tells him that if he is so upset about being pitied, when that is not actually within his own control, then he is deserving of pity after all—for so confusing what is in his control versus what is not. In more extreme situations, Epictetus seeks to persuade his hearers that a detached, careful discrimination and the essential will of acceptance are the only means of connection to one's inner spirit:

This is the law which God has ordained, and He says, "If you wish any good thing, get it from yourself." You say, "No, but from someone else." Do not so, but get it from yourself. For the rest, when the tyrant threatens and summons me, I answer, "Whom are you threatening?" If he says, "I will put you in chains," I reply, "He is threatening my hands and my feet." If he says, "I will behead you," I answer, "He is threatening my neck." If he says, "I will throw you into prison," I say, "He is threatening my whole paltry body." And if he threatens me with exile, I give the same answer. Does he, then, threaten *you* not at all?—but if I feel that all this is nothing to me,—not at all; but if I am afraid of any of these threats, it is I whom he threatens. Who is there left, then, for me to fear? The man who is master of what? The things that are under my control? But there is no such man. The man who is master of the things that are not under my control? And what do I care for them? (Epictetus, *Discourses*: 1.187–89).

Who can hinder me any longer against my own views, or put compulsion upon me? That is no more possible in my case than it would be with Zeus. (Epictetus, *Discourses*: 2.275)

Indeed, there are various stories of Stoic philosophers going to their death with just that attitude. This is only possible through the cultivation of a detached inner guidance, what Socrates called the daimon, the God within, later the Roman *Genius* (Onians 1951)— a notion also reminiscent of Almaas on "essential identity":

> But does anyone go so far as to tell you *this*, namely that you possess a faculty which is *equal* to that of Zeus? Yet none the less He has stationed by each man's side as guardian his particular genius,—and has committed the man to his care,— and that too a guardian who never sleeps and is not to be beguiled. For to what other guardian, better and more careful, could He have committed each of us? Wherefore when you close your doors and make darkness within, remember never to say that you are alone, for you are not alone. Nay, God is within, and your own genius is within. And what need have they of light in order to see what you are doing? (Epictetus, *Discourses*: 1.105)

This Stoic contemplativeness is presented as a neo-Socratic teaching, and from our perspective it becomes possible to understand Socrates himself as the first Western inner-worldly mystic— with his daimon and his acceptance of "not knowing" anything beyond its guidance. Certainly for mainstream Athenian piety, contact with an inner daimon was a radically new form of spirituality (McPherran 1996). From Almaas' perspective, Stoic and neo-Socratic practice involved a specific cultivation of the sense of a here and now presence, also related to personal essence, with the formless level of the Divine only implied. The Stoics show a radical autonomy, vital fullness, and a sensitive, discriminated contact with the here and now of everyday social life. They are not having visions of heavenly realms, as in the mystery cults and more abstractly in Plotinus. It is an in-the-world practice, with an impact very much like the early Christians, but by means of the development of essential strength and will rather than essential compassion and love. Indeed, descriptions of both groups in the face of danger, condemnation, and political strife are very similar. The difference between practicing Stoics and the early persecuted Christians lies in the more contemplative spirit of the Stoics. They are not behaving this way in the world in order to be "saved," but to better read God's intentions and understanding. Epictetus actually expresses puzzlement about the "Galileans," and says that if they can do what they do out of prophetical frenzy, his followers should be able to achieve as much by detachment, autonomy, and discrimination.

Plotinus and the Formless Dimensions

The Enneads of Plotinus is best understood as offering a contemplative practice, full of the abstract visual-spatial metaphors of Laski and Almaas, leading to an understanding and direct realization of the transcendent, formless dimensions of the numinous. At times reading Plotinus is like being coached along by a very abstract kind of guided imagery. As with the later Heidegger, what appears at first to be a conceptual system is meant to be directly sensed and felt, and Plotinus often slips into a more ecstatic mode of presentation (Hadot 1993). It is a neo-Platonic philosophical system meant to be experientially realized in a visionary mode, and as such it also had a tremendous influence on the early Christian mystics.

The system is a guide for the soul to return to and contemplate what Plotinus variously terms the Absolute, One, Good, Love, or God—as the source from which all things emanate. This is done by experientially ascending through the series of "hypostases" that are the different levels of created being. "Hypostasis" comes from "stasis," meaning "foundation," as in basic levels of reality, while "hypo" means less than or subordinated to. So the contemplative passes up through the hypostases, as emanations subordinate to the One, seeking formless union and dissolution within it—as in the classical all-unifying mysticisms. As we will see with Gnosticism, most in-the-world practices do not get quite that far. They tend to stay on a dualistic level because of the sheer tension of being fully open to living in the world. Accordingly, the full reconciliation of good and evil as ultimately one is absent in most of the figures we are considering. We have seen from a contemporary perspective how much depends on the degree of reconciliation of the splits within ordinary personality. Personal development is both more necessary and more problematic for inner-worldly spiritual practice.

The One, which Plotinus usually prefers to speak of as the Good or Love, is understood as the source of all-that-is. Conceptually it is derived from Aristotle's notion of an unmoved mover. The One, as all-embracing source, naturally wells forth in its plenitude and absolute generosity, aside from which nothing further can be said about it. Almaas (1995, 1996) similarly describes experiences of the Absolute as self-annihilating and only recognizable as such when the experience is

over, evoking Laski's imagery of dissolution into pure luminous blackness. The One overflows in its plenitude into the next lower level of
hypostasis, the *Nous*, which is open to the soul as a direct ecstatic
awareness. Such a direct awareness is only possible when the contemplating soul turns within (Laski's "inside" words) and follows the
descending radiance of Being back to its source ("up," "flow," and "luminosity" words). *Nous* is often translated as Intellect or Reason, but
we need to realize that our connotations for these modern usages are
misleading. *Nous* or Intellect for Plotinus is synonymous with God,
Being, Presence, and the Platonic forms in general—number, beauty,
justice, and all the archetypal forms of experience. So *Nous* is not reason in our sense. It is more like a structured intuition, or the intelligence of the arts, than it is like our logic or reason, which Plotinus,
very unlike Plato, explicitly subordinates to aesthetics.

The *Nous*, as an extension of its source, also irradiates and emanates forth, but the emanation of the *Nous*, as with all other subsequent levels, has two phases. The first phase naturally turns back in
upward contemplation of the One that has given birth to it, and it is in
ecstatic response to this source that, filled with this emanating flow
and luminosity, *Nous* generates the next layer down. We can already
see in Plotinus's metaphysic the abstract expression of a principle of
self-reflective, mirroring contemplation, developed in visionary practice for its own sake and independent of a lower, essentially practical
reason. It is his implicit cognitive psychology of essential states.

The next hypostasis is the layer variously discussed as the "All-
Soul" or "We," the source or principle of life. It is the equivalent of
the Logos in related Hellenistic traditions. It is here that sequential
time enters, as the vital world-soul's imitation of the sense of timelessness and eternity in the higher formless dimensions. It is this
soul/life principle that in its downward phase creates nature and
matter, while in its upward phase it contemplates the pure Being of
Nous. For Plotinus nature is primarily an expression of this creative
principle, so the contemplation of the beauty of nature, a pantheistic
nature mysticism, is the initial way to approach the emanating
Source—although nature will have a very different significance in
the dualisms of the Gnostics. The All-Soul is the locus for Plotinus of
the Stoic Creator God, or Plato's demiurge—again the place of a deep
splitting for the competing Gnostics. The All-Soul turns back, contemplates the Platonic forms in sheer ecstasy, and thus inspired, emanates the cosmos, in what we would see today as the Big Bang of
creation, but whose most direct and pure expression is the human
soul. The All-Soul within us is our highest essence, our intuitive

potential for the aesthetic contemplation of formlessness, while the discursive knowledge and memory of our reasoning capacity is the intermediate human soul, and the unreasoning or animal soul of sensation is our lower soul.

Matter itself is the end of this system of emanations. Formed matter is impressed by the higher divine and Platonic forms to varying degrees, but the very stuff of matter, what the Greeks understood as unformed chaos, reflects the point of final dissipation of the energies of emanation. Matter per se is for Plotinus the only hypostasis that does not look back toward the higher, but just finally spends itself. This failure to mirror back its own source is how Plotinus understands the privation that is evil. Unlike the Gnostics, evil is not seen as a separate principle in its own right. It is more that matter itself is unproductive, a necessary residue of creation, which in the form of the lower soul pulls us down and away from the pure contemplating potential of mind. We will explore below the resonances here to Winnicott on the failures of early mirroring and to Freud's purely dissipative Thanatos, for there is also a very modern psychodynamics embedded within this contemplative system.

Contemplative practice for Plotinus is the turning away from the dissipative tendencies of external world and personality, back toward the path of "ascent," which can eventually open into the intuitive unity experience of the One. This contemplative path is variously termed (and translated) "return," "conversion to the source," "introversion" and "interiorization"—very much implying its cognitive basis in a heightened self-awareness or reflexivity. The final intuition is clearly of Otto's "wholly other," which can only be rendered in terms of what it is not (via negativa). It is beyond even Being, aspatial and atemporal, yet present everywhere in creation. In his *Enneads*, Plotinus evokes this felt sense of absolute source in the partial metaphors of flow and emanation already familiar from Laski and Almaas:

> From this Principle which remains internally unmoved, particular things push forth as from a single root which never itself emerges. They are branching into part, into multiplicity, each single outgrowth bearing its trace of the common source. (Plotinus, *The Enneads*: 165)

and later:

> Imagine a spring that has no source outside itself; it gives itself to all the rivers, yet is never exhausted by what they

take, but remains always integrally as it was; the tides that proceed from it are at one within it before they run their several ways, yet all, in some sense, know beforehand down what channels they will pour their streams. (Plotinus, *The Enneads*: 245)

This sense of a source that gives forth all things in pure generosity or love, but does not show itself as such, has very strong parallels to the later Heidegger. In *On Time and Being* (1962) Heidegger plays with etymologies in a way evoking Plotinus. In German the phrase "it is" is written *es gibt*, which literally and originally means "it gives." Abstracting this phrase into a contemplative first principle, all-that-is has been "given" by an impersonal "it" that remains implied but impossible to further specify. Heidegger goes on to state that since we say "there is Being," "there is time," we can ask what it is that *gives* Being, what it is that *gives* time. Then in passages very reminiscent of Plotinus, he evokes a source ("it") that cannot be further specified other than as an inherent "welling forth"—the source that gives forth all Being and simultaneously conceals itself behind that very gift:

A giving which gives only its gift, but in the giving holds itself back and withdraws, such a giving we call sending. According to the meaning of giving which is to be thought in this way, Being—that which It gives—is what is sent. . . . This giving proved to be the sending of Being, as time in the sense of an opening up which extends. (Heidegger, *On Time and Being*: 8, 17)

For Almaas too, as also for William James, consciousness as such is revealed by a self-reflectiveness cultivated for its own sake and independent of its ordinary subordination to practical intelligence. It can be metaphorically evoked by imageries of "streaming" and liquid-like "flow." To fully realize this as an experiential or presentational state is literally to experience one's essence as a fluid medium, welling forth in a way directly metaphoric of the generosity of altruistic love. To fully sense and live these primal self-referential metaphors is to become the numinous—the more abstract and open the metaphor, the more formless the realization.

It is clear that the contemplative turning away from the everyday self as described by Plotinus leads to transient, state-specific transformations of consciousness. This is not intellectual knowledge in our sense. It is based on a radical simplification of the ordinary personality, leading to states of openness that encourage but cannot compel that experiential realization:

> Withdraw into yourself and look. And if you do not find your-
> self beautiful yet, act as does the creator of the statue that is
> to be made beautiful; he cuts away here, he smooths there, he
> makes this line lighter, this other purer, until a lovely face
> has grown upon his work. So do you also: cut away all that is
> excessive, straighten all that is crooked, bring light to all that
> is overcast, until there shall shine out on you from it the god-
> like splendor of virtue. . . . When you know you have become
> this perfect work, when you are self-gathered in the purity of
> your being, nothing now remaining that can shatter that
> inner unity, nothing from without clinging to the authentic
> man, when you find yourself wholly true to your essential na-
> ture, wholly that only veritable Light which is not measured
> by space, . . . —, when you perceive that you have grown to
> this, you are now become very vision: now call up all your
> confidence, strike forward yet a step—you need a guide no
> longer—strain and see. (Plotinus, *The Enneads*: 54–55)

The individual soul in this contemplation does not disappear for Plotinus, instead it becomes a pure form stripped of what we would call personality. This is strongly reminiscent of what Almaas calls essential identity, a sense of self still more fundamental than the fullness and contactfulness of personal essence. Here one's identity is felt as presence or beingness per se, with all more specific identifications and self-images dissolved.

Plotinus and Almaas seem to agree, within their respective languages, that any sense of self beyond this sense of bare presence is dangerous when experiencing the formless dimensions, since it can turn into narcissistic inflation or grandiosity. We will see later how Plotinus regarded the Gnostics as unwittingly under the sway of Narcissus, his version of a spiritual metapathology disturbing the authentic presence needed for communion with the One.

Cognition and Contemplation: The Plotinian Psychology of Silberer and Jung, and the Origins of Transpersonal Psychology

Plotinus views the process of contemplation as a self-reflection or introversion that reveals the higher forms of experience. This was first given a naturalistic psychological translation by Herbert Silberer and Carl Jung. In distancing themselves from Freud, they independently documented how the direct observation of ongoing spontaneous imagery could transform the usual contents of experience into more fundamental, and so abstract, forms.

Silberer (1909, 1912) initiated this work through his interest in his own visual imagery at sleep onset. It seemed to reflect a heightened self-referential or "autosymbolic" capacity, creating a step in such self-awareness that transformed the imagery and revealed its normally invisible inner structure. Silberer (1914) and Jung (1912) eventually came to understand this self-induced transformation of consciousness as the core of a psychology of spiritual development. Observing his own spontaneous hypnagogic imagery, Silberer noticed two different kinds of image, which he terms "material" and "functional." The material autosymbol is the more typical and lower form, in that it literally translates the content of verbal thought into a visual image— the image of what you have just been thinking about. For instance, on one occasion Silberer (1909) is thinking while he falls asleep, "I should dissuade someone from carrying out a dangerous decision or resolution. I want to tell him, if you do that grave misfortune will follow." Immediately as he falls asleep he sees an image that startles him awake: "I see three gruesome looking riders on black horses storming by over a dusty field under leaden skies." So the verbal thought, "don't do this or you'll get into trouble," is directly translated into an image that expresses the content or material of the thought.

Functional autosymbols are in a key sense more abstract. They show not what the mind is thinking about, but how the mind itself is functioning. They depict the form of one's experience more than the content. So this involves a deeper self-reference, in that consciousness is shifting toward depicting its own cognitive processes. For instance, just before falling asleep Silberer wants to review a philosophical idea, the explicit content of his ongoing thought, but exhausted, he repeatedly forgets key aspects and soon falls asleep, only to be suddenly awakened by the image of a morose secretary who refuses to give him a file he has requested. The image here does not render the content of his experience into metaphor, but instead its form—the failed attempt to recover the memory "file." As another example, with parallels to some accounts of near-death experiences (Moody 1975), Silberer (1914) was struck with how often immediately before he awakened from dreams and sleep onset imagery, he would come to a road or a stream or a fence, and awaken just as he stepped across it. He suggests that what is being functionally auto-symbolized here is the actual transition in state of consciousness—again, not its content but its form.

Silberer (1914) suggests that the typical cross-cultural motifs of mythology show a special development of functional autosymbolism, here revealing the basic forms or structures of human nature. These are what Jung would later term archetypes. Silberer and Jung both advance a view similar to some of the dialogues of Plato, that the imagery and metaphor of myth have a deep self-reflective property that directly evokes the basic forms of human knowledge in a way that discursive language can only approximate. It is also the principle of the contemplation of *Nous* for Plotinus, which will spontaneously abstract the basic forms out of a lower worldly content. Silberer was explicitly aware that he was building a naturalistic psychology of transpersonal development out of neo-Platonism and the related symbolisms of Renaissance alchemy. He posits a cognitive process which he terms "intro-determination," reminiscent of Plotinus on the heightened self-reflectiveness of spiritual introversion. Intro-determination turns material autosymbols into functional ones, and so forms the basis for the contemplative path. Jung's (1916) own term for intro-determination was the "transcendent function."

Silberer and Jung both distinguish between two kinds of dream imagery and dream interpretation, which Silberer (1914) called the "titanic" vs. "anagogic," and Jung (1912) characterized as regressive vs. progressive. Again, we have the lower and higher levels of soul for Plotinus. Titanic dream imagery expresses most directly the primary sexual and aggressive impulses of Freud. Anagogic imagery is based on forms of experience not yet developed in the person's life and so foreshadowing future growth—what Jung (1928) would later see as the guiding and compensating function of the archetypes. As an example of how the same dream can be given both a dynamic and "transcendent" interpretation, Jung (1916) describes the dream of a woman in therapy involving her possessing an ornamented ancient dagger. On the dynamic or regressive level this would be a phallic symbol expressive of aggression, but more "progressively" or "constructively" can be taken as the personal will absent in her life and which she was beginning to develop. For Silberer (1914) dreams of flying or descent into water can be interpreted anagogically as the process of contemplative introversion itself. Both the titanic and anagogic levels of meaning can be present in the same dream, or one or the other may predominate. This duality of meaning is also found in hunter-gatherer shamanism and Yogic dream interpretation (Hunt 1989).

Jung (1928) later developed a specific method of psychological inquiry to move from the dynamic content of waking imagery toward more abstract archetypal forms, which he calls "active imagination." By intensifying imagination and pursuing it for its own sake, the imagery undergoes a "sublimation" that gradually purifies it of its dynamic content and reveals the archetypal forms of human identity. Jung classifies these forms in terms of shadow, anima-animus, wisdom, and deity figures, which together constitute the total potential Self of the human being. Note that these inner forms or archetypes both mirror the total unrealized Self and compensate for the one-sidedness of the ordinary ego attitude. Where Plotinus would speak of ascending from lower to higher hypostases, Jung's language describes a spontaneous self-referential imagery that fills in what is lacking in one's present circumstances, thereby compensating, expanding, and guiding the way to deeper realization. Jung's Self mixes features of personal essence, with its fullness, and essential identity, with its openness to Being and the forms of *Nous*.

To begin to trace a transition toward the abstract synesthetic features of numinous states, and so complete our Plotinian cognitive psychology, it is important to realize that for Jung the imagery of heightened self-reference can become quite abstract. Jung (1950) became particularly interested in what he termed mandala imagery. These are abstract geometric patterns, often brilliantly colored and aesthetically complex, that can appear spontaneously in hypnagogic imagery, visionary states, psychedelic drugs, the imagery of alchemy, and cross-culturally in sacred art. For Jung, these mandala images, which he encouraged his clients to paint, are literally abstract forms of active imagination. Their geometric properties, colors, and overall centeredness or imbalance are interpreted as a purely formal Rorschach ink blot depicting the unfolding of the true self. Mandalas are abstract functional autosymbols, a terminology which can also be applied to Laski's quasi-physical sensations of ecstasy and the dynamic features of essential states for Almaas—in which complex synesthesias and felt physiognomies load and foreshadow essential realizations.

The following account from Almaas moves from these specific physiognomies of essence, and their attached dynamic personal issues, toward the more abstract access levels of the Plotinian Absolute. Almaas (1995) describes himself as awakening one day in an inexplicably sad mood, without knowing why. As he contemplates this, without rejecting it but just letting it be there, the sadness shifts and he realizes that it involves a loneliness. He then becomes specifically curious about the painful feeling of aloneness, while continuing to witness his total state:

> Memory reminds me of the experience of the last few days, that of the simplicity of presence and witnessing. Reflecting on it, I intuit that there is a connection between the experience of simple presence and the feeling of loneliness. My curiosity intensifies, a throbbing sensation at the forehead begins to luminate. The throbbing lumination at the forehead reveals itself to be a diamond-clear and colorful presence. The more passionate the naturally curious contemplation is about the loneliness, the more alive and brilliant becomes this presence, manifesting spacious and discerning clarity. I recognize the variegated, scintillating presence as the discriminating intelligence, the true *Nous*, which appears as a presencing of the intensification of consciousness. . . . (Almaas, *Luminous Night's Journey*: 3–4)

Curiosity itself appears here as a functional autosymbol, which for Almaas represents the *Nous* of Plotinus. He then realizes that the loss of ordinary identity implicit in his experiences of the simplicity of presence has been unconsciously linked to a sensed loss of others, who are connected to his ordinary sense of self. It was this loss that led to his loneliness. As he continues to observe, the transformations of consciousness evoked by abstract synesthesia continue, and in the terms of Plotinus, he ascends towards formlessness:

> Recognizing that the source of the feeling of loneliness is my association of the painful loneliness of the past [childhood] with the state of aloneness of presence in the present, liberates the sadness, allowing it to evaporate, leaving a sense of transparent depth to the dark abyss, a spacious depth. The feeling is centered in the chest. . . . The chest feels empty, but curiously quiet, peaceful and still. I recognize the state as a luminous black spaciousness, which is the unity of stillness and space. There is immaculate, glistening emptiness, but the emptiness has a sense of depth. The depth seems to be the felt aspect of the blackness of space. It is like looking into, and feeling into, starless deep space. . . . Intimacy discloses itself as an inherent quality of this black inner space. . . . No loneliness and no sense of aloneness. Simplicity of Being has ushered me, through the

door of aloneness, into its inherent intimacy. (Almaas,
Luminous Night's Journey: 6 7)

A spontaneous self-reflective capacity, witnessed and allowed for its
own sake, brings forth abstract spatial metaphors that are vehicles
evoking the formless levels of transpersonal states. It amounts to a
Plotinian cognitive psychology.

Object-Relational Patterns in Plotinian Contemplation: Mirroring and Splitting

The cosmology of Plotinus, with each level of emanation from the
Absolute turning back to its source in a self-reflective mirroring, ab-
stracts and exteriorizes the mother-infant mirroring pattern as understood by Winnicott and Kohut. For Winnicott, the infant's
experience of itself as real, alive, and present—its sense of Being—
depends on the recognition of its own spontaneity and expressiveness
as reflected back in the face and the manner of those who behold it.
The infant's experience thereby becomes self-aware, making its aliveness, joy, and sadness into experience in the human sense. The symbolic mind, for Winnicott and the object-relations theorists, is the
interiorization of this dialoguing pattern, which becomes the basic
form of human experience. We see this most obviously in the later
"inner speech" of verbal thought but it is equally true of imagery, both
image and verbal thinking involving a back and forth between interior observing and sending processes. For Kohut, mirroring also regulates and guides the infant's state and overall level of arousal. The
mothering one's vocalizations and gestures back to the baby not only
allow the infant to know its own state, but they equally calm the hy-
perexcited infant by lowering parental tone of voice, or raise the slug-
gish infant's interest by qualities of compensatory excitement. If the
baby is screaming, then if it is fortunate, the parenting one does not
scream back, but holds and calms the baby, which optimally both mirrors what is happening and regulates and balances it.
    It is this total pattern that becomes visible as the inner form of
our consciousness when it is witnessed and so exteriorized in sustained contemplation. The same mirroring and compensatorally
guiding structure is intrinsic to Silberer and Jung's transforming au-
tosymbolisms, Almaas on essential inquiry, and the ascending contemplation of Plotinus. The above example from Almaas illustrates
this inner structure of a dialoguing consciousness. Contemplating

his curiosity about his loneliness, the curiosity itself becomes experienced as a faceted diamond centered in the forehead, a functional autosymbol of the original curiosity. This abstract imagery then guides and leads toward an answer to what the loneliness is about, which in turn elicits the intimacy with all things characteristic of the more formless dimensions. For Plotinus successive cycles of mirroring and compensation go all the way within his experiential cosmology to final mergence with the One.

It is the purified or Platonic form of mirroring that reappears in mystical contemplation of the One. For Almaas and Jung, the sustained contemplation of ordinary experience will gradually release its inner mirroring structures as direct states. Our psychodynamics, witnessed in sustained self-reflection, become a transpersonal progression. Again, however, where there has been fundamental trauma and flaw in the laying down of that early mirroring, then narcissistic, paranoid, and schizoid dilemmas will be stirred up by these transpersonal practices. If so, the potential for transpersonal development will appear first as regressive pathology or metapathology, which must then be metabolized as part and parcel of any further realization.

Some reflection of such conflict can be found in Plotinus' account of evil as the unformed matter at the terminus of the emanation of the One. The failure of matter is that it does not reflect back—mirror—its source. Just as for Winnicott the infant can not develop a sense of Being and feeling real where mirroring is inadequate, so the unformed matter that cannot mirror, as the very nature of evil for Plotinus, has no real existence. His description of primal matter is also reminiscent of Freud's orally frustrated infant:

> Some conception of it would be reached by thinking of . . . the unshaped against a principle of shape, the ever-needy against the self-sufficing: think of the ever-undefined, the never at rest, the all accepting but never sated. . . . (Plotinus, *The Enneads*: 58)

We also see here a version of Freud's (1919) Thanatos, where the infant's energy, if not bound and contained by what Winnicott and Bion would later understand as maternal holding, follows a path of pure discharge—endangering the development of organized experience.

Despite the Plotinian emphasis on the One, his account of unformed matter as evil shows an incipient splitting and dualism. The physiognomy of a dense blackness is associated with both the originating Absolute and its final end in the unformed stuff of matter, yet while neither reflects "back," one is "the Good" and the other explains "evil." Later in mystical Sufism, where Plotinus was an explicit source, the first was the creative "luminous night," while the second was a dull, heavy darkness (Corbin 1978). Yet the split in both Plotinus and Sufism is tacit. Unlike the Gnosticisms, both assert a contemplative monism.

Of course, Freud would understand the entire process of contemplative self-referral in Plotinus as itself narcissistic—as in his discussion of mysticism as regression to the "oceanic feeling" of primary narcissism (Freud 1930). Such a reductionist view is complicated, first, by object-relations reformulations of classical psychoanalysis that would reject the concept of any primary undifferentiation or narcissism (Mahler's "autistic" phase of the first three months) in favor of a primacy of interpersonal relating, first manifested in neonatal mirroring behaviors. Second, and in his own anticipation of mind as interiorization of the mirroring process, Freud (1923) posited the energies of a secondary narcissism as the source of the dialogic structure of the early super-ego. Narcissism for Freud came to do a double, if unacknowledged, duty. It is both pathology and theory of mind (Hunt 1989)—also true for Plotinus.

Plotinus on the Metapathologies of the Gnostics

It seems significant, given the inevitable superimposition of the regressive and progressive in transpersonal development, that Plotinus himself is aware of the danger that a higher contemplation can *become* narcissistic. This is his own equivalent of the idea of spiritual metapathology. He sees narcissistic grandiosity as the specific vulnerability of his opponents, the Gnostics. For Plotinus, the Gnostics are under the sway of the figure of Narcissus in Greek mythology, who was fascinated by his own bodily reflection, or in our terms, by his ordinary self-image. The Gnostics do not specifically disengage from the lower soul, and thereby become inflated as they approach the formless dimensions.

The alternative model for the ascent of the soul in Plotinus is that of Odysseus, who at a certain point in his life adventures simply turns back and leaves everything behind him in his journey home—the return to source. This also seems to be an implication of Almaas on essential identity as the needed simplification of self, in contrast to the metapathology of narcissistic self-inflation. For the Gnostics, the divine nature of man means that all human beings are potential Angelic

Beings, higher than the traditional Creator God or Demiurge—and it is this that Plotinus finds inflated. He states:

> We must not exalt ourselves in a boorish way, but with moderation, and without raising ourselves higher up than our nature is able to make us rise; we must not rank ourselves alone after God, but recognize that there is room for other beings in his presence besides ourselves; otherwise, we are merely flying in a dream and depriving ourselves of the possibility of becoming like God, as far as this is possible for a human soul. . . . If a person who had been previously humble, mediocre, and ordinary were to hear: "You are the son of God; those others, whom you used to hold in awe, are not sons of God" . . . then do you really think other people are going to join in the chorus? (*Hadot, Plotinus, or the Simplicity of Vision*: 67)

Another related criticism of Plotinus against the Gnostics pertains to their explicit dualism, in which the material world and ordinary personality is evil, created by a lower, literally idiot god, also with delusions of his own omnipotence. Dualism becomes the perennial dilemma of all inner-worldly mysticisms, and we have seen how it is even implicit in Plotinus's account of a split-off, "evil" matter. The Gnostics, however, can only attain to their true nature by escaping (splitting off) the entire lower order of natural and worldly creation, thereby being elevated directly as beings of light or angels. For Plotinus it is the beauty of this world and the higher capacities of the human soul that best attest to the all-reconciling unity of the One and Intellect. So, reflecting Plotinus's criticisms, it is of interest that in object-relations theory, narcissism and false self-idealization become one major defense against the splitting between the all good and all bad mother images of Klein's paranoid-schizoid position.

Although we will deal with the major Gnostic systems in the next chapter, an illustration of this co-relation of narcissism and splitting as potential metapathology comes from the *Pseudepigrapha* of the *Bible*, specifically from the books of *Enoch I* and *II*, written from within the Essene and Judaic traditions between 100 B.C. and 70 A.D., and *III Enoch*, written around 600 A.D. as part of the Jewish Merkabah mysticism that was a precursor of the Kabbalah (Charlesworth 1983). The *Pseudepigrapha* anticipate the tendency of Renaissance alchemy to increase the authority of contemporaneous writings by attributing them to great visionaries or gods of the distant past, as also

in the numerous false dialogues of Plato. Here the narrative is attributed to Enoch, seventh descendant of Adam and Eve, and so pre-
dating the Mosaic tradition. In *Genesis* 5:24 he is briefly described as
walking with God and then vanishing, "for God took him." In their
elaborations on this story, the books of Enoch reflect the early
Jewish side of Gnosticism (Bloom 1996), as we will later trace its
Hellenistic Christian, Persian, and Egyptian versions. Suddenly
we find the prophetical dimension and ethical emphasis of Judaism replaced by a visionary and mystical attitude, as if the *Bible*
were being rewritten from a shamanic perspective.

In the core story, common to all three books, Enoch is relating
his visionary experiences of being suddenly raised through the seven
levels of heaven to behold God face to face, which would be certain
physical death in what is actually the older Mosaic prophetical tradition. In *I Enoch,* his face must first be frozen or else no human
could ever look at him again without being themselves annihilated.
A permanently fixated expression on his face, mirrored from seeing
God directly, would destroy all lesser mortals who then looked at
Enoch. God uses Enoch to rebuke the higher angels, fallen angels,
and Satan, showing them all that they are now lower than Enoch. In
II Enoch he is raised permanently to be with God as the "Son of
Man," and by *III Enoch* he has become Metatron (the second throne),
and the "lesser Yahweh." So it is interesting to find what for Plotinus
would be narcissistic grandiosity side by side with exaggerated expressions of a permanent dualistic split between good and evil,
rather than the visionary unifications of the fuller mysticisms.

In *II Enoch*, Enoch is told that the fiery red angels around God,
created on the first day, do not understand the scheme of God's creation as He is about to relate it to Enoch. Enoch is then shown the
separate layers of Heaven where the evil and fallen angels have
been segregated. The "angelic watchers," originally sent to instruct
human beings, lusted after women and procreated giants with them,
and so these fallen angels were imprisoned in darkness in the second
heaven, while the demons who are the spirits of the dead giants are
held beneath the earth—and certainly we note the absence of all
such beings in the monism of Plotinus. Finally, Enoch learns that
Satan and his allied angels of rebellion are imprisoned in the fifth
heaven, all awaiting the Day of Judgment. Enoch himself returns to
his children to tell them about these and numerous other visions of
the spiritual cosmos, before being brought back to stay permanently
on the level of Yahweh, above the angels. He is an ordinary human
being raised to the level of God.

This is very different from early Christianity, where God descends to become a full human being—an expression of Almaas's "personal essence"—or from Plotinus, where personality is first dissolved before visionary ascent, as in Almaas on "essential identity." The danger of this early version of the Gnostic path is that premature direct experience of the formless dimensions can both falsely narrow sensed transcendence and falsely inflate self-image. We are about to see how the deep stresses of daily life in the Roman Age become similarly reflected in the more conflicted inner-worldly mysticisms of the later Gnostics.

CHAPTER 5

Gnosticism: Mystical Dualism and
the Metaphysics of Hate

The term "Gnosticism" is derived from the neo-Platonic "Nous," referring to a direct knowledge of "experiential acquaintance." Gnosticism covers a diverse array of esoteric visionary groups extending through the Mediterranean regions controlled by Rome. It flowered between the first and seventh centuries, and was finally, and inevitably, suppressed by the dominant Christian Church. Versions of Gnosticism emerged from very different cultures, under the impress of common pressures on the educated classes under Roman rule, so that there are distinctly Jewish, Greek-Hellenistic, Egyptian, Iranian, and heterodox Christian versions. Until the discovery of the buried Nag Hammadi library in rural Egypt, containing many of these sources, we were largely dependent for our knowledge of these often extreme teachings on the detailed denunciations of the early Church Fathers, which have actually turned out to be remarkably accurate in their representation of the offending documents.

Given the diversity of these inner-worldly mysticisms of the Hellenistic-Roman era, the question has arisen whether Gnosticism should really be seen as a single coherent category (Williams 1996). Certainly if we use the generic meaning of gnosis, as an esoteric visionary knowledge contrasting with the more predominant prophetical roots of the early Church, then it comes to include Plotinus, who himself attacked the "so-called gnostics," as well as the later medieval Kabbalah. Thus expanded, the term does indeed lose its usefulness, becoming identical to Weber's inner-worldly mysticism, rather than the characteristically conflicted form of Weber's category that is our present focus.

Such definitional critiques, however, ignore Wittgenstein (1953) and William James (1902) on the actual "family resemblence" or "collective name" basis of our concepts. Our most serviceable concepts—as in "games" or "religion" itself—rest on no defining essence, but on a collection of features, any partial grouping of which constitute the working criterion for the loose categories that most usefully organize our thought. Here, and with most of the key authors on the topic, such as Jonas (1963), Layton (1987), Filoramo (1990), and Rudolph (1987), "Gnosticism" describes an eclectic range of visionaries whose mysticism remains dualist—with the creation of the world viewed as an act of ignorance or outright malevolence.

The task of the adept in these generally small groups was to gather the sparks of an original divine luminosity, shattered in the mistaken lower creation, and reassemble the original spirit of humanity. Thereby he/she becomes higher than the God of all material creation—the primal human Anthropos as mirror of the Absolute, or the condition of Adam and Eve before the Fall, or even before Creation itself. Instead of being unified in an all-inclusive One, the everyday life world and ego are to be escaped through "transcendence." This is similar to many contemporary New Age practices, except that then the escape was conscious and deliberate rather than tacit. The result of such a false or incomplete transcendence is that the dilemma of "evil" is not resolved, and one is left with a dualism in which, in Almaas's terms, there is no "metabolization" of hatred, of an inevitable rage against a frustrating world.

The Elements and Social Background of Gnosticism

Hans Jonas (1963), an early student of Heidegger, describes the Gnostic attitude in terms of a set of prototypical dimensions involving a characteristic theology, cosmology, anthropology, eschatology or doctrine of salvation, and morality. Philip K. Dick, whose later "science fiction" was largely inspired by his understanding of Gnosticism, weaves these dimensions together in a prototypical portrait:

> In Gnosticism, man belongs with God *against* the world and the creator of the world (both of which are crazy, whether they realize it or not). The answer to [the] question, "Is the universe irrational, and is it irrational because an irrational mind governs it?" receives this answer, . . . "Yes it is, the universe is irrational; the mind governing it is irrational; but

above them lies another God, the true God, and he is *not* ir-
rational; in addition that true God has outwitted the powers
of this world, ventured here to help us, and we know him as
the Logos. ∴ ." (Dick, *Valis*: 59)

With respect to theology, then, and following Jonas, we find in
these movements a radical dualism between the human and divine,
with the goal of the adept being nothing less than escape from the
world and the regaining of our original nature as a "being of light" at
or near the level of the Absolute. Experiences of direct illumination,
often combined with magic spells, allow the inner spirit to ascend
the levels of creation in a way often reminiscent of some contemporary accounts of the out-of-body experience (Whiteman 1961; Monroe 1985). The cosmology thereby traversed usually involves seven
lower levels of material creation, presided over by the Archons or
Rulers, as lower powers of evil under the sway of a Creator God derived from Plato's notion of the Demiurge. In contrast to Plato and
Plotinus however, this lower god creates the world and most of humanity out of ignorance, dementia, or evil—these views being co-
terminus with the Judeo-Christian derivation of Satan (Pagels
1995). The Judeo-Christian God of creation is understood as a monster. For the Gnostics, this world is a hell and our bodies the prison
of the divine sparks from the original formless dimensions of light.
The result for these visionary practitioners was inevitably a nihilist
and essentially paranoid attitude on a worldly level and an elitist,
potentially grandiose spirituality. The latter was reflected in their
elaborately satirical cosmological narratives, in which, for instance,
Eve was higher than Adam and the Serpent the secret messenger of
the higher God.

The prototypical Gnostic anthropology posits both a higher and
lower origin for humanity—the lower, of bodily animality, reflecting
the demented Demiurge, the higher, of pure spirit (Pneuma), reflecting the Absolute. Spirit, for those who possessed it, is hidden within
the outer person in a way reminiscent of Winnicott's "true self" of
being. Spiritual realization involved the experiencing of this spirit
within and its gradual release and raising to the level of the inherent peace and repose of the Absolute: "Within me was stillness of
silence . . . through which I understood myself as I really am" ("The
Foreigner," in Layton 1987:145). This intimation of the peace and
stillness of what Almaas terms "essential power" also implies a more
ordinary sense of helplessness and powerlessness in everyday life, in
which we are lost in a benumbed, intoxicated "sleep." Salvation was

an "awakening" brought about by a messenger from the light, either as the purely spiritual Christ or as one's personal angel or genius. The messenger or savior came not to pardon sin or reconcile us to the world, but to reunite the lost sparks of an originary and divine true self: "The Gnostic Savior comes to save himself" (Filoramo 1990:106). Ascension restored the original divinity of the individual, reconstituting the fallen Anthropos or Adam before the Fall. This higher spiritual self, superior to the Demiurge and the lower angelic powers of creation, was often understood as female and/or androgynous.

The resulting ethics was the typical, and controversial, "elitism" of mysticism, although in practice many of the Gnostic groups were radically egalitarian within themselves, with women often playing key roles (Pagels 1979). All these "pneumatics," however, were well above the mass of average humanity. Their inner liberation freed them from traditional morality and placed them, in the varying senses of the classical mysticisms "beyond good and evil." While most groups practiced an extreme asceticism, like the early Christian mystics, some showed the antinomianism and libertinism sometimes characteristic of inner-worldly mysticism. In the years immediately after the death of Jesus, Simon Magus travelled in the same regions of Palestine with Helena, an ex-prostitute, who he said was the incarnation of Sophia or Higher Wisdom. They advocated a sort of Western Tantricism of free love as spiritual practice, since sex was the only earthly reflection of the principle of unity in the Higher Divinity (Jonas 1963). Wilhelm Reich's (1949) therapeutic release of the "orgasm reflex," as a reflection of a higher Orgone or life energy of the cosmos, offers a contemporary parallel.

Meanwhile, a few Gnostics apparently went further in the direction of Fairbairn's "evil be my good" of the modern schizoid dilemma, and advocated, at least according to their Christian critics, the systematic breaking of all the ten commandments of the Judeo-Christian monster god as the only means for direct liberation from his lower realm. How far the Carpocratians and Messalians actually went in these directions we will probably never know (see LaCarriere 1989, for some convincing speculations), but on the more obviously destructive side, it does make Charles Manson, and his advocacy of murder as spiritual liberation for his victims, a modern representative (Sanders 1971).

The setting for these quite various Gnosticisms was the Hellensitic world under Roman rule, arising not in Rome but in the more distant melting pots of Alexandria and Antioch. Weber (1922b) had suggested that these movements were the creation of the "marginalized intellegentsia" of the outer provinces of the empire. In modern terms, Rome was, after all, a kind of fascist state—the roads into its major cities periodically lined with crucified dissidents. Among the few freedoms permitted the conquered were the new religious movements, as long as they had no obvious nationalistic implications. It does not need much speculation to see the Archons and demented Creator God as emblems of the crushing power of Roman rule, and the deep worldly pessimism of the Gnostics as the echo of largely disenfranchised educated classes. The visionary direction of their alienation emerged as what Raschke (1980) has called the "aristocratic shamanism" of the Gnostics. Indeed, in addition to attacking their affinity for the myth of Narcissus, Plotinus attacked the Gnostics of his era for their unending complaints about the disparities and injustices of society, which he saw as inevitable and to be accepted, but they saw as evidence for the evil, demonic nature of creation itself.

We can see how a systematic dualism would be the price for an inner-worldly mysticism under these conditions, while leaving us all the more respectful of Plotinus's own unitive achievement. The reconciliation of a directly experienced divine principle with a material cosmos of such crushing power would be difficult. The heightened sensitivity and openness of an inner-worldly mystical path, will, in such a world, occasion deep suffering. We could say that the metaphysics of such strife, and its attendant hatreds, was Gnosticism. In contemporary object-relational terms, the result would be a "paranoid-schizoid" dilemma—manifested simultaneously in a defensive narcissism, in which the individual prematurely rushes to be the direct mirror of the Absolute, and in a paranoid terror of the world and its blind, demented, and, most particularly, malevolent creator. The temptation towards a premature and incomplete transcendence becomes inevitable. What would be most difficult in such circumstances would be the development of the essential strength needed for a genuine individual autonomy within the world and the development of personal essence. Jesus was not the only religious teacher of those times to end up on a cross.

Contemporary parallels seem clear, even as the power of the modern multinational economy over the individual is more "abstract." Globalization produces a similar powerlessness and frustration on local levels and an analogous alienation and inward turn among much of the educated middle classes. One could even argue that the independence from national control by multinational corporations is analogous to the growing independence of the vast provincial agrarian estates from Rome, which was Weber's explanation for the actual decline of the Empire (Kasler 1988). Our own attendant New Age spirituality has its foreshadowings and anticipations in some of the key cultural figures we will later consider. In contemporary psychological terms, the Gnostic "pneumatics" would be those high on traits of "openness to experience" (McCrae 1994) and imaginative creativity (Murray 1938), and so most sensitive to the crises of "meaning" and "purpose" personally described by Nietzsche, Heidegger, Jung, and Gurdjieff.

Nietzsche's creative visionary "overman" becomes the new individual of the future who replaces God as the true source of the numinous, while Emerson's and Thoreau's earlier divinity of immediate experience, in the new "self-reliant" individual, is directly Gnostic. Heidegger articulates an everydayness inherently alienated in its helpless "thrown-ness" and dread, yet still with the inner potential of the individual to attune to Being as such—the original source of Nietzsche's dying Judeo-Christian God. Jung develops what he at first termed a "gnostic psychology" (Noll 1997), in which the experience of the numinous becomes a natural human potential whose fruition is the Self—the perfected Anthropos of the alchemists he later found so fascinating. Meanwhile, Crowley developed his own visionary magic rituals to ascend past the threatening demonic powers of the lower cosmos, and Gurdjieff's brilliant adaptation of Sufi self-remembering partly foundered on its own dualism and false will. Finally, contemporary feminist mysticism can be seen as its own re-constitution of the Gnostic Sophia, whose fall and redemption was so central to the Jewish and Christian Gnosticisms to be considered below.

Some Specific Gnosticisms: Metapathologies and
Implied Dynamics

EGYPTIAN HERMETICISM

Hermeticism, a tradition independent of the Judeo-Christian Gnosticisms, was developed in Egypt out of the earlier so-called Chaldean Chronicles (actually Egyptian) and the Orphic mystery cults of neo-shamanic soul travel. It appears in written form between the second and fourth centuries, later collected as the *Corpus Hermeticum* (Copenhaver 1992). Like the incipient shamanic mysticism of the Jewish books of Enoch, this work is another example of pseudepigrapha, the claim being that it was dictated to an ancient Egyptian priest by Hermes Trismegistus—"thrice great" Hermes, or Thoth, the god of knowledge. So convincing was this attribution of an ancient priestly authorship that until the Renaissance many Western thinkers saw these works as the source of the later Plato, rather than more obviously the other way around. Hermeticism did, however, appear to have had some influence on Plotinus, and the closely related cosmology of the Chaldean Chronicles appears to have been cited by his teacher Numenius (McKenna 1991). Consistent with such links, Hermeticism is the least dualistic of all the Gnosticisms.

The highest divinity in this teaching is Pure Intellect or Poimandres, meaning "knower of Ra" in Coptic. From it descends a second level, usually translated as "Forethought," a feminine (or androgynous) principle common to most Gnosticisms and an apparent equivalent to "pure awareness" in Buddhism.[1] There is no inherent split between these higher levels and the Creator God or Craftsman, probably adapted from Plato's Demiurge, whatever its possible earlier origins in Pythagoras or elsewhere. Creation was an attempt to organize the chaos at the outer reaches of divine emanation by instituting the seven spheres and their governors. The original spiritual man, Anthropos, was created as the mirror image of the highest God so He could enjoy his own perfection—since "even God had a burning desire for its own form" (Layton 1987:454). The descent of the Anthropos into the lower orders of the cosmos, however, was a mistake. We saw our own primordial reflection in the chaos below, and fascinated by our beauty, reached out for it and fell into creation, accumulating the fates of each level and our human form as we descended. The visionary reascent of the spirit is based on secret names and spells (gnosis) that allow the adept to slip the knots of the seven spheres to return to our origin in the eighth sphere, or Ogdoad. At death, the souls of those not so prepared are eaten by the Archons as their food—an image later revived to powerful effect by Gurdjieff.

The distance here from Plotinus lies not so much in dualism but in the inherent narcissism and implied grandiosity of this imagery—which indeed seems to be an abstract rendering of the earlier myth of Narcissus. Narcissus, scorning true Eros, falls in love with his own watery image and drowns. We see this narcissistic imagery, which Plotinus already saw as a dangerous inflation, twice over, both in the fall of primordial humanity and in the need of Pure Intellect for a mirrored self-image of light. On the one hand, there is the equivalent notion of an inner core of humanity as the essential self of pure being in Almaas or Winnicott, and on the other, an almost Nietzschean sense of God as a kind of projection of our highest nature, and so as paradoxically a lesser being. An implied narcissistic inflation seems clear in this passage from the *Corpus Hermeticum*:

> For the human is a godlike living thing, not comparable to
> other living things of the earth but to those in heaven above,
> who are called gods. Or better—if one dare tell the truth—the
> one who is really human is above these gods as well. . . . For
> none of the heavenly gods will go down to earth, leaving be-
> hind the bounds of heaven, yet the human rises up to heaven
> and takes its measure. . . . Therefore, we must dare to say that
> the human on earth is a mortal god but that god in heaven is
> an immortal human. (Copenhaver, *Hermetica*: 36)

Almaas (1988) and Epstein (1998) have suggested that the meditative cultivation of the experience of a transcendent, all-perfect
One must inevitably stir up deep feelings of deficiency by contrast
with the necessarily egoic nature of the practitioner. A resultant defense would be a premature and so inevitably narcissistic identification with that higher principle, as a denial of one's sensed personal
inadequacy. So it is interesting to find some reflection of the potential painfulness of this contrast in the *Corpus Hermeticum*:

> God lacks for nothing, to become evil in longing to possess it.
> Nothing that exists can be lost to him, to cause him grief in
> losing it (for grief is a part of vice). Nothing is stronger than
> god, to make an adversary of him (nor does he have a com-
> panion to give him injury); nothing is more beautiful, to
> cause desire in him; nothing is unheeding of him, to make
> him angry; and nothing is wiser, to make him jealous.
> (Copenhaver, *Hermetica*: 21)

In leaping to identity with their Primal Source, hermeticist visionaries would be similarly spared any such more direct personal
comparisons.

BARBELITES, CAINITES, OPHITES, AND SETHIANS:
MYSTICAL SATIRISTS OF THE OLD TESTAMENT

Who these groups were and whence their origins is unknown. We
have only their texts and the bitter denunciations of the church
fathers for their systematic inversion and intricate mockery of the
stories of biblical Genesis, picturing the Creator God, here called Ialdabaoth, as a demented monster. These are some of the earliest Gnostic texts, dating to the first century, and perhaps systematically
developing the similar teachings of Simon Magus, but we have no idea

whether they were written by heterodox-Hellenized Jewish visionaries, the Essenes, or dissident and possibly anti-Jewish Christians—or,
variously, by all of the above.[2] One could, in the abstract perhaps, de-
rive something like these astounding versions of a dualist divinity by
combining the visionary, quasi-shamanic ascent described in the first
book of Enoch (first century B.C.) with the more abstract cosmology of
Plato. Then Yahwah becomes the Demiurge, re-christened Ialdabaoth,
and now more easily assimilated to the rebellious angels and Satan,
while the ascending human spirit belongs with the One or Absolute.
Certainly all these groups had in common the placing of a mystical visionary layer, endlessly elaborated from Plato, over a Judeo-Christian
prophetical layer—with the result an unbridgeable split between a
higher divinity and lower god, good and evil.

To generalize across these groups, they posit a First or Parent
Principle that is ineffable and, like Plotinus and the early church
mystics, only knowable in terms of what it is not—the mystical *via
negativa* of something wholly other and beyond. In *The Secret Book
According to John* we find:

> It is not fitting to think of it as divine . . . for it is superior to
> deity; nothing presides over it, for nothing has mastery over
> it. . . . It is unlimited because nothing exists prior to it . . . ;
> unfathomable, because nothing exists prior to it so as to
> fathom it; immeasurable, because nothing else has mea-
> sured it; . . . ineffable, since nothing has been able to reach it
> so as to speak of it. . . . It is not corporeal, it is not incorpo-
> real, it is not large, it is not small. . . . It is not something
> among the existents; rather it is something far superior to
> these; yet it is not as though it were "superior." (Layton, *The
> Gnostic Scriptures*: 29)

As with Plotinus, this One as source is only known by what it
emanates from out of its uncharacterizable fullness, except that instead of Love, the emphasis in this group of writings is on a second
and feminine principle of pure awareness, often translated as "Forethought" and sometimes named Barbēlo—that probably derived
from "emission" or "projectile."[3] She is the first expression of the pure
repose and stillness that is the major positive attribute of the Parent
Principle—thus the "Barbelites." It is she who creates the aeons,
corresponding to the formless dimensions of mysticism, that come to
include Christos, the Primal Adam or Anthropos, Seth, and finally at
the outer perimeter of this pure emanation of the realms of light,

Sophia—the feminine principle of wisdom. Wisdom or not, it is Sophia who commits the fatal error that leads to material creation, again essentially a disorder of narcissism. She longs to continue and further the divine emanation, and so creates out of herself, alone and without any higher consort, a separate being, who is also thereby an abortive monster, Ialdabaoth. He has the head of a lion and a body of serpents, and it is he who will become the Creator God. Note that these Gnostics are here simultaneously lampooning not only Yahwah but also Mithra, sacred deity of the Roman legions, with his lion's head and human body entwined in two serpents.

Sophia is horrified at the monstrosity she has brought forth, and flings him into the outer regions of chaos. There, he comes to himself and, believing he is unique, omnipotent, and alone in the universe, decides to create his own cosmos, his assistant Archons, and finally human beings as his own "perfect" reflection. The result is a wormlike Adam whom Sophia, or in some accounts Christos, then secretly imbues with a redeeming pneuma. In some versions it is Eve who is created first. Dimly sensing that their creations are actually their spiritual superiors, the Archons attempt to gain this power, in some accounts pursuing Eve through Eden in order to rape her—making them the father of Cain and Abel and perhaps opening the way to the former's higher awakening for the group calling themselves "Cainites."[4] At any rate, Eve's spirit escapes the Archons by hiding in the serpent—thus the "Ophites" or snake worshipers. This divine serpent later provides instructions concerning the tree of gnosis, which restores to Eve and Adam their true spiritual nature—leading to their expulsion by the jealous Ialdabaoth and his subsequent enraged destructions of humanity by flood and fire. For the "Sethians," only they, as the descendants of Seth, and so born exclusively of Adam and Eve, are free of these early taints and constitute the hidden, elite race of "pneumatics." The pneumatics only await "awakening" by the divine messenger sent from the realms of light, in order to realize their true origin. This is the task of the Gnostic Jesus, who provides the secret understandings and magic spells to allow the ascent of the adept past Ialdabaoth and the Archons to become the true Anthropos.

These spiritualities, which from a contemporary perspective seem so strangely paranoid and over-elaborated, enshrine many of the object-relational dilemmas of dualist inner-worldly mysticisms. Most of their accounts of the First Principle emphasize its "repose," "stillness," and "quiet," implying a one-sided development of essential power, the black, and a lesser articulation of both strength (vital autonomy) and compassion, and with obviously no valuation of anything like a this-worldly personal essence. The magically controlled ascension of the contemplating soul past the Archons may also indicate a form of false will, very distinct from any "surrender." What we would today see as narcissistic dilemma is also multiply reflected in their mythologies, both in Sophia's original creation out of herself, and Ialdabaoth's similar narcissistic, purely self-gratifying generation of the lower Adam as his personal mirror. Ialdabaoth himself has all the grandiosity and false omnipotence of Freud's own vision of the withdrawn narcissism of the infant, and he creates and responds largely out of what Kohut might regard as narcissistic rage at his own denied inferiority. The visionary path of the adept functions purely as an escape from this world. We could also guess, from the complaints of both Plotinus and the early Christians, that the discovery that one was actually a Sethian risked an elitist self-inflation that could lead far away from the "broken humility" of the more complete inner-worldly mysticisms.

VALENTINUS AND PTOLEMY: HETERODOX CHRISTIAN GNOSTICS AND THE REDEMPTION OF SOPHIA

Valentinus and his student Ptolemy wrote between 140–180 A.D., and are associated with what amount to alternative Christian gospels, the "Gospel of Truth," and "Gospel of Philip," respectively. These offer versions of a more mystical Jesus, and are more or less as old as the canonical gospels of the *New Testament*. This Jesus emerges as a purely spiritual emanation who could not thereby undergo a crucifixion of the body. His purported sayings primarily invite a contemplation of the individual's own inner divinity. Begun more as a Christian mystery school, these teachings were declared heretical only after the final triumph of the Church of Rome, but continued through at least the eighth century as monastic groups within the more mystical Eastern Church.

The Valentinians saw the origin of evil as resulting from a failure of communication within the higher divine realms, as an interior tragedy, and so partly avoiding the more radical dualism of the Sethians. Here again, the first principle, variously termed Forefather or Abyss, is described predominantly in terms of a pure repose or stillness. The second principle, named Ennoia, sometimes referred to as the Higher Sophia, is female and described as "first thought" and "silence." Together they generate the *Nous*, or Father, the beginning of all things, as well as a conjoined female principle, Aletheia or Truth, completing the first Tetrad within the Divine Pleroma of abyss and silence, mind and truth. The next level of emanation produces word (Logos) and life, humanity (Anthropos) and church, all as elements of formless dimensions that constitute the original Ogdoad. From here there are many further purely spiritual emanations, so that the whole is actually reminiscent of the later Sephiroth of the Kabbalah, and culminates in the last nonmaterial level, the Lower Sophia—also called Achamōth.

Suffering and redemption within the Valentinian vision belong entirely with the Lower Sophia, rather than being centered on Jesus. It seems that each of the higher emanations, which end in the Lower Sophia, has less and less contact with the originating Abyss, and she finally comes to feel this separation acutely. Her passionate longing to continue the divine light results in the first appearance of the emotions of grief, fear, and confusion, which become a fog that congeals into matter. In an attempt to bring order to this primal chaos, she generates out of herself, again alone, the Demiurge who then creates the physical cosmos and human form, not out of evil, but out of ignorance. The higher Christos, seeing her suffering and confusion, comes to illuminate and save her. This is the central "redemption of Sophia." Then and secondarily, in repentance, she sends Jesus as her purely spiritual agent to redeem the sparks of pneuma present in some, but not all, of humanity. Here Jesus is not the primary focus, since he is a secondary stratagem to deceive the Archons and begin the ascent of the pneumatics toward the higher realms—and the "mystical marriage" to which they are destined.

The controversy surrounding the Valentinians within what was to become orthodox Christianity centered around this "mystery of the bridal chamber." It remains unclear whether the union of the female pneuma within the adept and one's corresponding higher male angel was purely visionary, a specific ritual, or at times physically acted out. At any rate, the original separation of Adam and Eve was thereby undone and the primal Anthropos re-constituted within what was most probably a predominantly symbolic expression of the libertinism often associated with inner-worldly mysticism. Jung's (1928) own notion of the inner reconciliation of the opposite-sex identity within, as anima or animus, seems to have been a direct influence. An antinomian and elitist aspect is also present in Valentinianism. Of the three layers of humanity, "material" or fallen, "psychic" or possessing a soul to be educated by orthodox Christianity, and "pneumatics" or "spirituals," only the last could not be sullied by any conduct whatsoever. "Beyond good and evil," the true Valentinian pneumatic was immune from any consequences of unethical conduct. Thus in Ptolemy:

For just as the element that consists in "dust" cannot have a share in salvation—for . . . it is not capable of receiving it— so also the spiritual element . . . cannot receive corruption, no matter what sorts of behavior it has come to pass its time in company with. For a piece of gold does not lose its beauty when it is put into filth but rather keeps its own nature, since the filth cannot harm the gold. (Layton *The Gnostic Scriptures*: 294)

For the Valentinians, evil ceases as soon as it is fully understood. In the *Gospel of Philip* we find: "Lack of acquaintance is a slave; acquaintance is freedom" (Layton 1987:352). There is the implication here, similar to Jung on owning and metabolizing the shadow archetype, that only some degree of conscious living out of our lower nature can truly expose and release it as such. Jung, in a letter discussing Gnosticism, says:

It is certain that no one is redeemed from a sin he has not committed, and that a man who stands on a peak cannot climb it. The humiliation allotted to each of us is implicit in his character. If he seeks his wholeness seriously, he will stray unawares into the hole destined for him, and out of this darkness the light will arise. (Jung, *Letters*: 2.74–75)

The temptation in such practices would be toward a narcissistic grandiosity, splitting, and self-idealization. The more orthodox Christians were bitter over the Valentinians' contempt for the social order and their readiness to lie about being Christians to avoid the Colosseum, when the Pauline Christians were duty bound to assert their faith and die a sacrificial death. The Valentinians saw this as pointless. Some of their versions of the crucifixion itself echo a similar disdain, with a purely spiritual "laughing Jesus" (later of such fascination to James Joyce in *Ulysses*), who could of course not be physically killed, observing from an adjacent hill as the confused Romans crucified the wrong man. The rejection of the inferior Creator God of *Genesis* would, from a traditional perspective, convey a similar perceived arrogance: "In the world human beings make gods and bow down to their products. It would be more fitting for the gods to worship human beings!" (*The Gospel According to Philip*, in Layton 1987:344). In actuality, there may have been a range of Valentinian inspired groups, with some acting out a false inflation and power, and others more like modern Jungians, inwardly metabolizing the schizoid and depressive dilemmas implied in their cosmology. Absent further documentary discoveries, we will never know.

MANICHAEANISM: A RADICAL PROPHETICAL DUALISM

The most widespread form of dualist gnosticism, actually predominant over Christianity at the time of St. Augustine's own shift of allegiance, were the Manichees, followers of Mani, who was himself martyred in 275 A.D. Although Manichaeanism, initially centered in Syria and Persia, was a remarkable syncretic mix of Christianity, Zorastrianism, and Buddhist compassion, it may not properly belong with the more mystical forms that are our focus. Accordingly, it may help us to better understand and apply Weber's typology of radical salvation movements.

Based ultimately on the much earlier teachings of Zoraster, one of the first true ethical prophets, Manichaeanism posits an elaborate cosmology based on an eternal war between the co-equal realms of good and evil—ruled over by Ormuzd and Ahriman. The Manichee "elect"were to avoid marriage, property, and work, and subsist on charity. Their task was to wander, like Jesus and the Apostles, and teach the workaday "hearers" about the ethical conduct that would aid in extracting and liberating divine light from the evil and darkness that has invaded the world. Sexuality, within or outside marriage, only perpetuates the dark power of matter. The consciousness of the sin involved in ordinary life is overwhelming, and extends to compulsory vegetarianism so as not to consume the fragments of divine light in animals.

Jesus is a messenger from the realms of light to awaken the elect and distill light from the suitable virtuous souls of the dead, which takes place on the moon—imagery later taken up by Gurdjieff. This emphasis on a spiritual liberation based on ethical conduct and occurring only after death, with the apocalyptic notion of an end of time, places Manichaeanism more within radical propheticism than inner-worldly mysticism. There is the same elaborate visionary cosmology, highly simplified in the present account, but the emphasis is on an extreme asceticism, at least for the elect, which itself is the most direct means to prepare for the all-important afterlife—a release into light delayed until after death in the manner of the inner-worldly propheticisms of ethical salvation and in obvious competition with the similar thrust of a Judeo-Christian Day of Judgment. The experientialism of true mysticism is always here and now. Mystics are individual afficionados of a felt eternity, and are usually strangers to any final, communal End of Days.

One element, however, that Mani's intricate cosmology has in common with the immensely elaborated mystical visions of Valentinus and the Sethians, is the sheer detail of the spiritual realms to be envisioned and the absence of the ultimate ineffability and "not knowing" that defines the more complete mysticisms. Although this sense of absolute mystery is part of the "repose" and "stillness" of the Parent Principle or Abyss of the Sethians, their remaining "formless dimensions" are rather amazingly filled in with the false specificity that can creep into less-developed inner-worldly mysticisms and make them sound more like infinitely detailed paranoiac delusions than evocations of the numinous. This was the criticism of the various gnosticisms by the classicist Arthur Darby Nock (1972), who found them lacking in what Keats had called the "negative capability" of remaining open to and allowing mystery—which is, after all, the core of the numinous. The hyper-detail of the Gnostic visionaries is finally all too effable. Paradoxically or not, it is precisely essential intelligence or brilliancy, the mysticism of knowledge in someone like Eckhart, that appears in a false and impossibly over-specified form in these mysterious figures. Here, again, the separation from Plotinus could not be more obvious.

"Please Allow Me to Introduce Myself": The Problem of *Splitting in Mystical Gnosticism*

Satan appears even in the relatively late *Book of Job* as part of the Divine realms, an angelic being seated on the left hand of Yahweh. Pagels (1995) traces the original meaning of this "stn" root in Hebrew as "one who opposes" or "acts as an adversary." Yet in *Job* this opposition is still in service to Yahweh, as a means of testing human beings. Later, in the years of bitter sectarian division among Jewish spiritual groups under the impact of Roman rule and the fall of Jerusalem, one's theological opponents were seen as influenced by a Satan now taken as an increasingly separate and lower principle of evil. This separation becomes reflected in the tales of Satan's fall, understood as a matter of his pure malevolence, based variously on hatred, arrogance, envy, and lust—as seen, for instance, in the early books of Enoch. Some of the epithets and alternate names for Satan, such as Samael or "blind," Mastema or "hatred," are identical to the characteristics being simultaneously attributed to the Gnostic Ialdabaoth.

Adding to this push towards cosmological dualism, with separate realms for good and evil, was the Iranian and Zoroastrian influence from the East (Cohn 1993). Increasingly, the material and social world seemed ruled by a principle of malevolence and evil, whether as a lower or as a co-equal entity, but radically separate from the realms of divinity, at any rate. It became an obvious step for the alienated Hellenistic visionaries, whether Jewish, Christian, Egyptian, or Syrian, to assimilate the Platonic Demiurge to Satan, or to the evil Zoroastrian Ahriman, and thereby envision the entirety of natural creation and the corresponding lower soul of humanity as "evil."

Of course there is a difference in the inner "psychology" of the Ialdabaoth and Satan figures, whatever their overlap in underlying malevolence. Ialdebaoth is a demented and utterly inflated narcissist, unconscious of his evil and driven by envy and rage. Satan, on the other hand, is conscious of his evil and his prideful separation from an opposing realm of the Good. Yet they draw together, as more and more groups under Hellenized Roman rule came to see the everyday social order as under the sway of a principle of evil, whether taken as a source of ambivalent temptation or an occasion for flight.

Part of the difference between the more prophetical and more mystical responses to escaping this horror of ordinary living was that the contemplative path involved an openness to direct experience, the necessity of a "direct acquaintance" as reflected in "The Gospel According to Philip." As with Almaas today, it is only the direct experience of hatred, feeling it as fully as it insists on being felt, that can dissolve and release these impacted energies. These same pressures could instead lead to an antinomian acting out and indulgence, which psychologically could only reinforce, perpetuate, and intensify psychic splitting. Most of Gnosticism sought a direct transcendent experience of escape from the lower order. The psychology here is ultimately schizoid.

Whatever the complex cultural and doctrinal sources of the appearance of the Satan/Ialdabaoth figure in the Hellenized Mediterranean world of the first century, they do not explain its spread and widespread appeal to the residents of the great provincial cities of the Roman Empire. For that, with Weber, we might appeal to the demanding quality of life under the urban conditions of empire, and the very different impact of those alienating pressures on the lower vs. the educated classes. The latter groups, increasingly disenfranchised from real power in their own cities, turned within to the individualized visionary path of the mysticisms, while the former were more open to the widespread popular appeal of a renewed ethical being-in-the-world of the early Christians. For both, the intensified cruelties and necessary compromises of daily life under Roman rule pushed them towards a radical spiritual dualism as the most accurate representation of their actual life experience—enshrining as more or less normative what in modern terms would have to be seen as a paranoid-schizoid splitting.

It is interesting in this context to recall Philip K. Dick's interesting statement in *Valis*, his portrayal of a contemporary gnosticism: "The Empire never ended." In the sense of Weber's socio-economic analysis of the pressures of a progressive rationalization and disenchantment in complex capitalist societies, Dick was right. And how are we today to deal with the resulting fear, hatred, and rage in the context of reinventing our own spiritualities within the now pervasive educated classes? The mandate is for direct experience, but what if the very core of the soul that then opens up seems to be based on hatred?

Freud's Gnostic Metapsychology of the Newborn

For Almaas (1986a), as more recently for Diamond (1996), hatred and anger have very different bases and potential resolutions. Anger is more a frustrated autonomy that lashes out against restrictions to our independence, expansion, and self-assertion. It can appear as a more extreme narcissistic rage where our self-esteem has been the most crushed. The positive potential of what anger and rage seek is related to Almaas on essential strength. Anger moves toward the spontaneous heat and expansiveness of the red. It seeks an essential autonomy and aliveness. Accordingly, its primary developmental era within the psychoanalytic template falls into Mahler's (1975) analysis of the separation-individuation phase of the second and third years of life—into the incipient narcissistic grandiosity of the "practicing" stage of the recklessly exploring toddler, and the more balanced autonomy and personalness of the "rapproachment" period. For Almaas (1988, 1996) these stages are the developmental templates for a later spiritual individuality—a sense of one's "essential identity" as pure being and of "personal essence" as a more personal sense of fullness and potential contactfulness with others.

Hatred, on the other hand, has a somewhat different psychology, and one that can have its first origins earlier in both Freud's and object-relational developmental frameworks. Hatred is more the outcome of a denied, even humiliated, love. We cannot truly hate, as so many now see, what we have not originally loved. Hate itself is "cold" and "silent," and once chronic it becomes calculating and willing to wait. It comes out of a perceived separateness, which painful as it may be on a deeper level, must be preserved. It seeks the quiet and ultimate safety of knowing that one's enemies are gone, ideally dead, so that one can finally relax. Accordingly, its positive spiritual aspect is what Almaas terms the peace and black stillness of essential power.

In the unitive mysticisms, the black repose of the Absolute and its emanation of light as love are inseparable—two faces of the same all-encompassing source. But where hatred predominates, the person is cut off from love and in a place of utter helplessness—thus the false but temporarily gratifying power of intensely felt hatred. For Almaas, as for Fairbairn (1954) earlier, the early failure of the infant to have its love mirrored back and/or to experience an unconditional love from the parents, separates and splits love and hate. Love is then felt as weak and endangered, and hatred as all powerful. Cold, withdrawn hatred is an inevitable feature of Fairbairn's schizoid dilemma, in which our deepest and most fundamental capacity for love is rejected or shamed. Fairbairn extends its first point of potential developmental fixation back into the first months of life, in the stunned withdrawal and "quiet" of traumatized or chronically neglected neonates. For Freud (1919) the first response of the frustrated infant to its surrounding environment was held to be hatred, which for Klein leads to the split between all-good vs. all-bad experience that she found characteristic of early infancy (Klein et al. 1952). More generally, hatred becomes a dynamic issue in any developmental era where power and love become separated, so that love seems weak or absent, and anything powerful becomes by definition malevolent and terrifying (Almaas 1988).

Accordingly, we could say that the major Gnostic systems—then and now—are hate based. The Absolute is characterized one-sidedly in terms only of its repose, stillness, and quiet, that is, the "black" of essential power. Compassion enters in with the messenger of awakening for a fallen humanity, but the result is never the red of a vital essential strength or the this-worldly expansiveness of the autonomy and contactfulness of personal essence. Instead, the goal is a transcendent escape entirely past the cosmos of creation and personality into a pure and radically separated stillness and repose. Good and evil are not experientially reconciled in an all-one, as psychologically demanding as that of course must be, but instead remain split within an essentially paranoid cosmology. The inevitable result of such visionary practices would be the narcissistic grandiosity and elitism of which Plotinus and the Church Fathers complained. The Gnosticisms become the very definitions and illustrations of spirituality as false power and premature escape, rather than the more arduous integrations of the psychological inner-worldly mysticisms of Emerson, Jung, Gurdjieff, and Almaas—in which we must actually feel our innermost negativities as the dissociated life energies and expressions of love which we need to re-empower.

It seems of special interest then that the metapsychologies of infancy common to the first great developmental psychologists of the modern era, Freud (1923) and Piaget (1962), actually enshrine as normative a portrayal of the baby as essentially "narcissistic," "schizoid," and "autistic"—as an encapsulated Ialdabaoth, demented and screaming. For Freud, the energy metabolism of newborn experience is organized in terms of a primary narcissism, turned back entirely within itself on the metaphor of an egg, and essentially a continuation of the fetal state. For Piaget the first organization is one of "autism." There is nothing here of Winnicott and Fairbairn on the primary relatedness of the neonate to the mothering one, supported by Meltzoff and Moore's (1992) more recent studies of simple mirroring behaviors from birth.

Instead, for Freud, these internally bound up energies, shielded from external impingement by an autistic "stimulus barrier," must be gradually and secondarily directed into interpersonal relating by the instinctual satisfaction of nursing. In a related notion, the actual instability of the neonate's capacity for organization (Freud's Eros) means that the infant is especially vulnerable to the primary discharge of energy that is the underlying principle of Thanatos—his death/entropy drive. This proneness to discharge of all impinging energies manifests first in what Freud calls the primary or automatic anxiety of infancy—the baby screams and kicks helplessly—and then in a more organized way in the hate and rage directed at any impingement from the environment. This means that for classical Freudian thought the first response to the awareness of an external world that does not fit with the infant's primary narcissism is hatred. The infant becomes aware of reality in the first instance by hating it. Tension discharge is the primary instinctual response, rather than infant object seeking, curiosity, and relating—which in a sense also offers an unwitting "metapsychology" of the inevitability of heroin.

Freud was himself fascinated with the what we can now see as spontaneous Gnosticism in the paranoid delusions of Judge Daniel Paul Schreber, as described in the latter's *Memoirs of My Nervous Illness* (1903), the basis for Freud's (1911) own case-study analysis. Judge Schreber, having partially survived a childhood of bizarre intrusion from his famous pedagogue father (Niederland 1974), suddenly found himself persecuted by what he came to regard as the lower God, whom he called Ahriman. The only way to prevent his own death and that of humanity was if, at the behest of the higher God, Ormuzd, Schreber could be transformed into a woman—so as to procreate a redeemed human race. The somatic hallucinations from which Schreber suffered, similar in form to those explored by Angyal (1936 and discussed in chapter 2), entailed a demonic suffering and torture from which only his version of himself as a reconstituted Sophia could save him. Otherwise all he could do was "bellow" to discharge energy, and so prevent the more complete release of death. In Freud's interpretation, the destructive side of deity in Schreber's delusions reflected the primal father and his threat of castration, while Schreber's original cosmology of energies bound up in a narcissistically organized higher God constituted an autosymbolic and projected depiction of Freud's own psychology of a primary narcissism:

> It remains for the future to decide whether there is more delusion in my theory than I would like to admit, or whether there is more truth in Schreber's delusion than other people are yet prepared to believe. (Freud, "Psycho-analytic Notes Upon An Autobiographical Account of a Case of Paranoia": 466)

We might today conclude that both are true, provided we see Freud's psychology of infancy as itself depicting not a normative but a deeply traumatized pattern of development.

In fact, Freud's psychology of the infant offers a perfect fit for the characteristics of Ialdabaoth—narcissistic, terrified, and full of rage and hatred—as also for his precursor in the Egyptian god of primal chaos, Apophis, blind, and screaming for all eternity (Cohn 1993). Even the "blindness" of these gods of the lower material cosmos fits widespread earlier beliefs that newborn infants lack any organized perception, now so throughly refuted in terms of both perceptual discrimination studies (Bower 1977) and early mirroring behaviors (Meltzoff). The dementia of these gods similarly reflects both Klein's and Freud's now strange assumptions of a normative schizophrenia in the newborn.

More mainstream psychoanalytic attempts by Jacobson (1964) and Kernberg (1984) to save Freud's model by rephrasing his primary narcissism as a "primary undifferentiation" ignore this empirical evidence of a differentiated relatedness to the mothering one from birth. They unwittingly preserve a view of the infant that ignores or minimizes its actual sensitivity and complexity. And so they leave in place a tacit picture of the infant as schizoid, narcissistic, and paranoid, and which thereby implies the inevitability and unresolvability of such conflicts—in contrast to the primary wholeness and relatedness postulated by Fairbairn, Balint, and Winnicott. These latter theorists see the defensive splitting of these pathologies as something secondary and contingent. Played back through the Gnostic mythologies, the British object-relations theorists could be said to picture the newborn as the Higher Adam/Eve or Anthropos, the immediate dyadic reflection of an Absolute in which stillness, power, and love are inseparable. Meanwhile Freud, Piaget, and by implication Mahler, unwittingly picture the newborn infant in terms of Ialdabaoth, Apophis, and Satan—a cut-off demented being, manifesting itself mainly through energetic discharge.

Given the socio-economic tensions of modern Western civilization, perhaps it was inevitable that our first naturalistic psychologies of infancy would reflect the same dualism and splitting as the visionary Gnostic reactions to Empire. Our first psychologies were unwittingly Gnostic in terms of the very weaknesses first discussed by Plotinus. It is not surprising then that the renewed inner-worldly mysticisms called forth in modernity would so often founder on this same tension between the longing for unitive oneness and a more obvious but chronically conflicted dualism. The invitation to here and now experiencing as the path for a renewal of charismatic enchantment, in a complex society such as ours, leads sooner or later to the dilemma of what to do with the ensuing terrors and hatreds that must also arise with the presence-openness of here and now beingness.

All of our key precursor figures of a contemporary transpersonal spirituality struggled with this Gnostic dualism, and most foundered on it. It remains an open question whether any of these figures, except perhaps Emerson, reconciled the deep inner splitting of the paranoid-schizoid and narcissistic dilemmas of modern character. The struggles and incompleteness in these audacious pioneers will attest to the very real difficulties in the way of a contemporary spiritual renewal truly congruent with our era—as well as to the integrity and sincerity of their quest.

PART III

Transpersonal Anticipations and Conflicts
in Nineteenth-Century Precursors to
a Naturalistic Inner-Worldly Mysticism

CHAPTER 6

Nietzsche

Friedrich Nietzsche (1844–1900) is central to the experiential shift of modernity, of which the tendency towards a this-worldly spirituality is perhaps an underlying force. That Nietzsche's thought includes a naturalistic mysticism is most apparent in his fascination with ecstasy, both personally and as a specifically human capacity (see also Roberts 1998). Nietzsche does not speak of "mystical experience," but he repeatedly uses terms like ecstasy, intoxication, and creative frenzy, which he interprets in this-worldly terms. He is radically opposed to what he sees as the rejection of life and humanity implied in all supernatural dogma, but he wants to reconceptualize the ecstatic states that are traditionally at the core of religious experience in human terms as reflecting our highest creative potential. In the notes that constitute *The Will to Power* he even calls for a "physiology" of ecstasy. Especially given his own quasi-medicinal experiments with opium and hashish, he would presumably have been especially intrigued by the LSD research of the 1960s.

We will look at Nietzsche in terms of his work and especially in regard to his tortured personal life—to see how dynamics related to hatred, withdrawal, and narcissism distorted or narrowed his own spiritual development prior to his final breakdown in 1889. His decline, although doubtless complicated by the considerable dynamic issues in his life, was ultimately due to an organic dementia related to the effects of tertiary syphilis.

Aspects of Essence in Nietzsche's Thought and Experience

There is much debate in approaching Nietzsche over whether to consider his work primarily as a system of thought and so open to criticism and refutation on logical grounds, or whether he is better understood in terms of a radical pragmatism of direct experience, loosely based around certain key insights that are not really intended as a philosophical system.

Nietzsche is perhaps the first modern figure to present a radical perspectivism and relativism in which there are no conceptual, metaphysical, or religious absolutes, but all knowledge is always relative to the living of human life—to be evaluated only in terms of whether it is life affirming or life denying (Jaspers 1936; Kaufmann 1956). Nietzsche sums up the full consequences of this relativism in his famous phrase "God is dead," and thereby predicts a crisis of nihilism and futility of meaning in the modern era to come. While Nietzsche understands God as a projection of human nature, to which Freud's later view of religion would be limited, he also opens up the possibility of a naturalistic understanding and appropriation of the energies at the core of ecstatic visionary states:

> Where is God gone? . . . We have killed him,—you and I. . . .
> Has it not become colder? Does not night come on continu-
> ally darker and darker? How shall we console ourselves? . . .
> Is not the magnitude of this deed too great for us? Shall we
> not ourselves have to become Gods, merely to seem worthy of
> it? (Nietzsche, *The Joyful Wisdom*: 167–68)

Nietzsche's answer to this dilemma is his own version of the Gnostic Anthropos: the *Übermensch*, or overman. The overman is the higher, creative human being of the future understood as becoming in certain key respects god-like. The stance usually associated with Nietzsche is his foreshadowing of modern nihilism, in that he is calling attention to a fundamental crisis in terms of loss of meaning in the traditions of Western civilization. Here he had a direct impact on Weber's understanding of rationalization and disenchantment. Yet for Nietzsche it is the capacity of the fully realized, creative person of the future for a direct contact with the lived sources of ecstatic experience at the core of traditional spirituality which could ultimately allow a higher acceptance or "yea saying" in the face of this nihilism and its pervasive sense of futility. This ecstasy is no longer to be projected onto some supernatural realm, but experienced as the highest life potential of the human being. So there is a sense in which Nietzsche can be taken as advocating a kind of naturalistic mysticism, or what today would be regarded as a transpersonal psychology, dramatized in terms of the higher person or essential self of his poetic masterwork, *Thus Spake Zarathustra*:

> Behold I teach you the overman. The overman is the meaning of the earth. Let your will say: the overman *shall be* the meaning of the earth. I beseech you, my brothers, *remain faithful to the earth*, and do not believe those who speak to you of other-worldly hopes. (Nietzsche, *Thus Spake Zarathustra*: 125)

It is clear from his letters (Middleton 1969) and from his autobiographical *Ecce Homo*, which he wrote just before his breakdown and which Jaspers (1936) believed shows the beginnings of his dissolution, that Nietzsche based his portrayal of Zarathustra on his own ecstatic states:

> Can anyone at the end of this nineteenth century possibly have any distinct notion of what poets of a more vigorous period meant by inspiration? If not I should like to describe it. Provided one has the slightest remnant of superstition left, one can hardly reject completely the idea that one is the mere incarnation, or mouthpiece, or medium of some almighty power. The notion of revelation describes the condition quite simply; by which I mean that something profoundly convulsive and disturbing suddenly becomes visible and audible with indescribable definiteness and exactness. . . . There is an ecstasy whose terrific tension is sometimes released by a flood of tears, during which one's progress varies from involuntary impetuosity to involuntary slowness. There is the feeling that one is utterly out of hand, with the most distinct consciousness of an infinitude of shuddering thrills that pass through one from head to foot;—there is a profound happiness in which the most painful and gloomy feelings are not discordant in effect, but are required as necessary colors in this overflow of light. (Nietzsche, *Ecce Homo*: 896–97)

This is an example of Rudolph Otto's account of the energy and fascination side of numinous experience. For Almaas, it shows essential joy, rather than the frenzy of a more secular kind of happiness, because it is clear from Nietzsche's accounts that the joy is paradoxical, leaving him simultaneously deeply saddened, and bringing with it a broader detachment. The joy comes out of an affirmation and acceptance of everything that is also most painful about his own life, which was considerable. Most of his descriptions of essential states come from his breakthrough period between 1880 and 1883, when he generated the key concepts of his naturalistic inner-worldly mysticism, to be published as the *Joyful Wisdom* and *Thus Spake Zarathustra*.

Essential will is also a key aspect of Nietzsche's understanding, initially as *Amor Fati* or love of fate. The stance of the overman, to which Nietzsche aspires, is to accept and so will whatever happens in life. For Almaas, the difference between ordinary personal will and essential or spiritual will comes with this paradoxical quality of surrender. One's personal will is aligned with the sense of a universal will as something sacred and beyond oneself. For Nietzsche this became the capacity to will one's fate, and his had indeed come to involve a huge suffering.

Nietzsche soon develops *Amor Fati* into his notion of the "eternal recurrence of the same," his fullest nihilist vision of a meaningless mechanistic universe, in which each moment will lawfully recur in some further universe through eternity, and whose acceptance or yea-saying is the ultimate challenge to the creative overman of the future. In affirming one's present moment, one is also affirming its joy or suffering forever. This becomes a naturalistic paraphrase of the each moment-as-eternity experience so characteristic of the fully developed mysticisms.

Yet this most controversial of all Nietzsche's notions can be understood in two very different ways, both present in Nietzsche's writings. On the one hand, eternal recurrence is part of a very questionable quasi-scientific metaphysics. Nietzsche really thought that the fullest development of modern science would show this kind of endless, essentially pointless, deterministic recurrence, such that over billions of years everything recurs again and again and in all possible variations. Nietzsche personally found this a deeply upsetting idea, but the logical conclusion of a mechanistic science, and the ultimate challenge to a Dionysian affirmation of life as it is. However, as Karl Lowith (1997), one of Heidegger's major students, points out, the doctrine of eternal recurrence taken as conceptual system is deeply flawed logically, not to mention scientifically. Nietzsche is portraying a universe of absolute determinism, although human beings, at least in their higher form, are to have the freedom of will to choose its affirmation. Yet the yea-saying of the overman itself can only be a further reflection of this determinism, and thus cannot triumph over it.

The other view of the eternal recurrence, and the one most relevant to our reading of Nietzsche here, is that he is not really prescribing a conceptual metaphysics at all, but an attempted experiential realization guided by ideas whose value is pragmatic rather than systematic—a view most associated with Walter Kaufmann (1956, 1980). The experience sought is one of joyous acceptance or yea-saying in the face of a modern loss of meaning. Eternal recurrence is the notion intended to sharpen this potential nihilism to the maximum, in order to transcend it by the life-affirming yea-saying of the overman. Nietzsche's approach to classical metaphysics is always to find the life that is repressed within and release it, so why would this first thorough-going pragmatist substitute his own conceptual absolute?

In favor of this experiential view, the notion of eternal recurrence was both terrifying and exhilarating for Nietzsche personally, and seen by him as a vehicle of potential transformation. Lou Andreas-Salome, possibly the one woman Nietzsche loved, only to have any relationship thwarted by his outraged mother and sister, gives the experiential flavor of his first formulation of the eternal recurrence during the time of their brief contact:

> To me the hours are unforgettable in which he first confided it to me, as a secret, as something he unspeakably dreaded to see verified. . . . Only with a soft voice and with all the signs of deepest horror did he speak of it. And in fact he suffered so deeply from life that the certainty of the eternal recurrence of life had to entail something ghastly for him. (In Lowith, *Nietzsche's Philosophy of the Eternal Recurrence of the Same*: 197–98)

By this time Nietzsche was suffering from unbearably painful migraines and vomiting, and could only read and write for a few hours a day, so the eternal affirmation of such experiences, juxtaposed though they be with periods of creative ecstasy, was clearly asking a lot.

In *Joyful Wisdom*, written in 1881, where Nietzsche first introduces the eternal recurrence, its intended impact on personal realization is clear:

> If that thought acquired power over thee as thou art, it would transform thee, and perhaps crush thee; the question with regard to all and everything: "Dost thou want this once more,

and also for innumerable times?" would be as the heaviest burden upon thy activity! Or wouldst thou have to become favorably inclined to thyself and to life, so as *to long for nothing more ardently* than for this last eternal sanctioning and sealing? (Nietzsche, *Joyful Wisdom*: 271)

Nietzsche is describing a naturalistic version of the exultation of the moment in mysticism generally. The challenge is to live each moment so fully that you could will it as eternal presence, and the pragmatic effect of this attitude becomes an in-the-world version of an attunement to and acceptance of the unfolding here and now that is basic to all meditative techniques. In the language of Almaas, Nietzsche's "eternal recurrence" would be his approximation to the surrender to universal will.[1]

The final and especially controversial orienting concept in Nietzsche's later writing is the "will to power"—also open to understanding in terms of essential or numinous experience, and so further demonstrating Nietzsche's creation of a naturalistic mysticism. For Nietzsche, the will to power is the fundamental dynamism or energy that humanity and the universe share. It is a principle of the vital expansion of life and accumulation of force, whose highest development is in the creative artist and the religious ascetic, not in the simple dominance of one person over another—despite his occasional use of metaphors of warfare and political power. In some of the unpublished fragments collected as *The Will to Power*, Nietzsche says that ecstasy is the conscious feeling that goes with the maximum expression of the will to power, making its meaning as direct experience also related to the alive expansiveness and "red" of essential strength.

His sometime metaphors of violence and ruthlessness were seized on by Nazi ideologues in the 1930s, who tried to make Nietzsche a major apologist and precursor for Hitler's Nazism, and its advocacy of a false will, strength, and power—false in the sense of lacking the paradoxicality and balance central to Otto, Laski, and Almaas. Context usually makes clear that Nietzsche on "power" and "force" is discussing an inner creative struggle. He broke off relations with his sister owing to her public advocacy of anti-Semitism, which he found disgusting.

If Nietzsche anticipates a naturalistic inner-worldly mysticism, we would also expect to see some of the instabilities and contradictions located by Weber and Almaas in such attempts. We have seen the close relation between the overman and the Gnostic Anthropos, the primal human being who, fully realized, is higher than God. For

Nietzsche, however, this also involves a this-worldly naturalism. The highest potential of the human being is to experience the world in the way of the traditional spiritual visionary, but not to project that onto a supernatural realm beyond the human. The aim is to understand as inherently human the direct experience of fullness of meaning, acceptance and yea-saying, joy, and essential will and strength—all the immense energies of ecstatic states. The overman is higher than God because as a human projection God does not exist, and so was really expressing the highest creative potential of the individual all along.

The question inevitably emerges, also pertaining to much of the current enterprise of transpersonal psychology, whether the phenomenology of the numinous as an encounter with something sensed as "wholly other" and intrinsically ineffable—as an experience that has you, rather than you having it—is something that can be meaningfully and safely understood as human, however logical the basis of that insight. Plotinus and the Gnostics agree on the sheer beyondness of the One, its pure empty stillness and all-encompassing otherness—in short its *non* humanness. So is it possible, given this phenomenology of the full numinous experience, for it to be experienced as "ourselves"—that is, without the risk of major inflation and narcissism? Indeed a narcissistic stance is already a metapathological risk of any direct spirituality, and it would seem potentially exacerbated in any naturalistic and/or humanistic conceptualization of the essential dimensions, since that violates their actual phenomenology. Certainly Nietzsche himself came to show such an inflation, both in his idealized Zarathustra/Dionysius figure and in his later personal life, as he writes his greatest works under the increasing pressure of an approaching organic dementia.

As we will see in more detail, Nietzsche remains a necessarily incomplete inner-worldly mystic. His work and life show clear signs of essential strength, will, and joy, but a complete absence of essential love and compassion, which he could only see through the lens of a Christianity he found hypocritical—and no evidence of any direct experience of the formless dimensions. As he becomes more withdrawn, lonely, and inflated by the mid 1880s, very much overdetermined by the course of his disease, his writings show more and more strident expressions of what becomes a false strength, with its endless discussions of "becoming hard," as well as a false form of will, in terms of willing the eternal recurrence. An agitated frenzy comes to replace an earlier numinous joy, and there is none of the paradoxical stillness and inner quiet of an essential power. With respect to the latter, and all the false power implicit in his metaphors of domination and conquest, we would look for specific blockages around unassimilated hatred as a major barrier to development. Quite apart from his appalling final fate and its growing physiological pressures on him throughout his most creative working years, Nietzsche's early life was the occasion for an almost insurmountable withdrawal and emotional ambivalence that both led to and distorted his mature search for a new form of self-realization.

Nietzsche's Life: Dynamics and Tragedy

We do not have to follow the overly detailed speculations of Alice Miller (1990) on Nietzsche's childhood. Jaspers's (1936) more conservative account is more than sufficient to locate long-term themes originating in childhood suffering, which will have impacted strongly on a sensitive and imaginative child. First, at age four, there is the death of his father, thence running through his life as a thread of longing and search. His father was a pastor, also his grandfather in this very religious family. His recollections of his father were positive, if idealized, and certainly in comparison to his later hatred for his mother. The father's improvisations on piano also became the favorite recreation for the adult Nietzsche, although their manneredness could be off-putting to listeners. His father was thirty-five at the time of his death from what was described by his mother as a head injury, a trauma that took about a year to kill him. So there was some sort of deterioration ("brain softening"), probably from the time Nietzsche was three and a half, whether directly due to an injury or brain disease is ultimately not clear. His younger brother died the next year, after Nietzsche had a terrifying dream, on the night before the brother's unexpected illness, of his father returning from the grave and taking the boy. Throughout his childhood and youth he would on occasion hear the "warning voice" of his father, which he later linked to the daimon of Socrates (Köhler 2002). He also suffered nightmares throughout his life.

Not surprisingly, by the time he is five and six, the young Nietzsche is described as having an unusually quiet and serious demeanor, spending long periods alone in nature. Children in the neighborhood nicknamed him "the little pastor," and did not treat him all that kindly, one gathers. The longing for the absent father and the deep wound at his loss extends through his life in ways both idealizing and quite disastrous. It fueled his early brilliancy, which filled the hole left from a missing sense of masculine energy, and later led him to Wagner as mentor. Pletsch (1991) has suggested that Nietzsche learned from his close association with the world-famous Wagner what it meant to be a genius and take one's own stance, daringly and with a self-sustaining steadfastness and even grandiosity. The initial support and recognition he received from Wagner was incredibly important to Nietzsche in finding his own original authorial voice. The final break, so common in mentor relationships of that intensity (Levinson 1978), cost Nietzsche tremendously. He was sad and bitter about it for years afterwards, and wrote a final denunciation of Wagner in 1888, the year before his breakdown.

The negative side of this intense identification with the missing father appears in Nietzsche's unshakable belief, by the time he is an adolescent, and in contradistinction to his mother and sister, that his father had died of a hereditary insanity and that he, the young Nietzsche, had the same symptoms—namely, the severe migraines that he had begun to suffer as a child. We will see that these headaches probably had more to do with his mother than his father, but a young child under the impact of such a loss will not know that. The headaches become more crippling as he got older, further solidifying this sense of tragic identification with the father. In the late 1870s they are aggravated, along with chronic nausea, vomiting, and myopia approaching blindness, as the early effects of the syphilis, which he probably contracted in the mid 1860s when he was briefly in the army. By the late 1870s the symptoms are bad enough that he is having difficulty fulfilling his philology professorship at the University of Basel, where he is already highly controversial for his heterodox views in *The Birth of Tragedy,* alienated from Wagner, and teaching, however brilliantly, at times to empty classrooms (Gillman 1987).

In 1879 he finally gives up the professorship and with his small pension sets off with one trunk, filled with books and medicines, to wander mostly alone, across southern Europe, seeking the seasonal climates in Turin, Nice, and Sils-Maria that lessened his almost overwhelming symptoms, and growing gradually alienated from all but a few of his previously wide circle of friends. People who encountered him during the 1880s during his long hikes in the mountains, often not knowing until later who they were meeting, describe him as touchingly kind and gentle, very much in contrast to his increasingly grand and sarcastic literary persona (Gilman 1987).

He is thirty-five years old, in 1879, when he begins this period of lonely wandering, at exactly the age that his father died. He himself believes he is about to die, writing to several people that his brain

symptoms are obviously getting worse and that the hereditary insanity is closing in. So there is the confluence here of both his tragic
identification with his father and the beginnings of an actual organic
brain disease. He believes, and is of course correct, that he does not
have much time. What follows is his extraordinary creative period,
to end in 1889 in Turin when an alarmed boarding house owner
sends for help to his friend Overbeck, after he collapses in the street
trying to stop a horse from being beaten by its enraged owner. Up
until 1881 his writings were extremely original and powerful, but
not as radically original as they would become. Starting in 1881 with
Joyful Wisdom and extending in a period of astonishing incandescence to *Thus Spake Zarathustra,* the first three books of which are
written in ten days each in 1883 and 1884, he proceeds with growing
stridency to *Beyond Good and Evil, On the Geneology of Morals, Twilight of the Idols, The Antichrist*, and *Ecce Homo*, the last three all
written in 1888. He writes throughout amidst daily and weekly
bouts of incapacitating migraines, stomach pains, and vomiting.

Then there is the mother. After the father's death, Nietzsche's
mother went to live with her sisters, and the resulting home atmosphere seems to have been rigid and cold in the extreme, with all the
false piety and sanctimony that would later fuel his attacks on Christianity. His mannered and precocious formality as a child seems to
have been a reaction formation, perhaps triggered by the deaths of
his father and brother, to the toddler temper tantrums that apparently made such an impression on the family. The mother later spoke
with pride of the following incident, when Nietzsche at about age
seven was late returning home from school during a torrential downpour. Only after all the other children had rushed by, did they see
Nietzsche in the distance, walking slowly and deliberately through
the downpour, head down in his usual formal and serious demeanor.
He explained that the headmaster had told them at the beginning of
the year that on leaving the school they should always preserve a
decorum and not run or jump, so of course he had followed the rules
on this occasion as well.

It was during these years that Nietzsche largely withdrew from
other children and sought solace in nature. This early use of nature
as a kind of alternative maternal holding environment will be characteristic of several of the figures we are considering, including
Thoreau, Jung, Heidegger, and Crowley. In Kohut's (1984) terms, instead of allowing the young Nietzsche the maternal support and mirroring he would need in the wake of his father's death, the mother
used the boy as her own "narcissistic self-object," pushing him

toward the "perfection" that would best support her own image. The same usage of the child to mirror maternal identity will also appear in Thoreau and Heidegger, where it led to a similarly painful "negative merging." The fatefulness of Nietzsche's own relation with his mother, and later his sister, is attested by the depth of his later hatred for them. He broke with his sister in the mid 1880s and came close to severing relations with his mother, only to end up during the final eleven years of his organic dementia first in the care of his mother, then of his detested sister. By then he seems not to have cared, but during his creative period both his attacks on what he saw as the hypocrisy of Christian love and his periodic misogynist outbursts seem to have been responses to the household of his youth.

The pattern is reminiscent of Fairbairn's (1954) discussion of the schizoid dilemma as a sense of inner isolation, outward aloofness, extreme formality, and unassimilated hatred—in response to the early failure to genuinely mirror the young child's spontaneous love, with a resulting shame, hatred, and distrust of love.

> At the absurdly tender age of seven, I already knew that no human speech would ever reach me: did anyone ever see me disconsolate therefore? Today I still possess the same affability towards everybody, I am even full of consideration for the humblest: in all this there is not an ounce of arrogance or contempt. He whom I despise divines the fact. . . . My mere existence angers those who have bad blood in their veins. (Nietzsche, *Ecce Homo*: 853)

In the Reichean bioenergetic tradition, hatred is often held in the eyes or the ocular muscular segment. So it is of interest that by the age of seventeen Nietzsche had semi-constant headaches, centered in his eyes, and that a physician who examined him then described "his wild threatening stare" (Miller 1990).

Also consistent with Fairbairn's discussion is a lifelong loneliness and longing for intimacy. Nietzsche describes a devastating sense of loneliness present from childhood on. For Almaas and Laski it is the full acceptance of the hole of aloneness that opens into the higher intimacy of essential states, but by the late 1880s Nietzsche's sense of a painful isolation had become intolerable, closing in with growing intensity after his expansive period of essential realizations was replaced with agitation and inner frenzy. In an 1886 letter to Overbeck, one of his few remaining friends, he expresses his growing despair:

> If only I could give you an idea of my feeling of *loneliness*! I
> have no one to whom I feel related, as little among the liv-
> ing as among the dead. This is unimaginably terrifying.
> Only . . . a step by step development from childhood on in
> my capacity for bearing it—this alone enables me to com-
> prehend how I have not yet perished on account of it.—For
> the rest, the task for the sake of which I live confronts me
> clearly: it is a *factum* of unimaginable sadness, albeit
> transfigured by the consciousness that there is *greatness* in
> it. . . . (In Krell, *Nietzsche*: 274–75)

and a year later:

> I yearned for human beings, and I searched for them. I al-
> ways found only myself,—and I am no longer yearning for
> *myself*! . . . Nobody comes to me any more. And as for myself,
> I went to all, but I *reached* nobody! (In Jaspers, *Nietzsche*: 87)

And that same year:

> I have forty-three years behind me, and am just as alone as
> when I was a child. (Middleton, *Selected Letters*: 276)

The opposite side of such isolation is the deep need for intimacy
and symbiotic relatedness. This is expressed in his capacity for ex-
quisite gentleness and grace with others, often described as deeply
touching, and only sometimes as mannered. Several people talked
about an almost feminine tenderness, and, not yet knowing who he
was, that they were changed in his presence—"becoming more themselves" (Gilman 1987). However, by the late 1880s his hypersensitivity to others, also a prominent feature of Fairbairn's portrait, led to a
deeper sense of futility and withdrawal. In a letter from early 1888 he
writes:

> The perpetual lack of a really refreshing and *healing human
> love*, the absurd isolation which it entails, making almost
> any residue of a connection with people merely something
> that wounds one. . . . (Middleton, *Selected Letters*: 282)

And later that year:

> There is indeed a great *emptiness* around me. Literally, there
> is no one who could understand my situation. The worst thing

is . . . not to have heard for ten years a single word that actually *got through* to me. . . . (Middleton, *Selected Letters*: 300)

By the end, the predominant impression he made on both those who knew him and those who did not was one of "strangeness."

Much of Nietzsche's earlier capacity for intimacy was bound up with the series of close male friendships now exhaustively documented by Köhler (2002), along with his circle's fascination with a Byronesque romanticism of "twin-soul" friendship based on Plato's *Symposium*. Köhler assumes at least a periodic homosexuality, but it seems more difficult to determine how much of this was a sublimated Greek classicism or whether Nietzsche's definite homoeroticism was more or less suppressed than the heterosexuality that led him to such a painful infatuation with Lou Andreas-Salome—who was also aware of the bisexuality of Nietzsche's inner identity. The sense of "mystery" and "secrecy" of which Köhler makes so much should not merely be reduced to a hidden sexuality, since it is a major part of the more general structure of the schizoid dilemma for Fairbairn and Khan—with its impacted frustration and ambivalence over all forms of mirroring intimacy. We can certainly conclude that Nietzsche longed for a deep "something" from others that he never found, and that his sexuality and its confusions played their own painful part therein.[2]

His abrupt collapse in January 1889 has always engendered controversy. Popular opinion at the time had it that his ideas had finally "driven him mad," and Carl Jung (1961) was typical of later nineteenth century youth, in the face of such warnings, reading the forbidden Nietzsche in secret. And like R.D. Laing and Carlos Castaneda more recently, it was also true that the unstable and hypersensitive were thereby unerringly drawn to such "dangerous" books. Yet all the neurologists and psychiatrists directly consulted at the time, including Binswanger, head of the widely known Burgholzi asylum, agreed that Nietzsche's dementia was not schizophrenic but the general paresis of tertiary syphilis—and this in an era that, lacking knowledge of the causation of psychosis, concentrated on a refined diagnosis of differentiated syndromes (Podach 1931; Jaspers 1936).

In addition, there is the unconfirmed report that Nietzsche had already consulted a physician in 1865 over syphilitic symptoms. By the time of his resignation and lonely wandering in 1879, his migraines had become incapacitating, and he suffered from vomiting, dizziness, and hypersensitive vision and reduced eyesight, in addition to complaints of the first episodic feelings of paralysis. The latter is an early sign of the general paresis syndrome, and by 1887

others were noticing the stiffness in his gait and his posture (Podach 1931). Also from 1887 there is a new pomposity and manneredness with people he meets on the streets and store owners,
another sign of the neurological syndrome of tertiary syphilis, and
which intensifies to delusional proportions after 1889. In his letters, he describes periods of involuntary grimacing in the streets,
also symptomatic.

The picture is of course complicated by the mid-1880s by the
powerful drugs he is using in order to self-medicate his pain and insomnia and to continue writing. These include the highly addictive
sleeping medication chlorolhydrate, along with opium and hashish—
all widely prescribed in this era. However, a final convincing sign of
an organic dementia is the complete absence of any reference to his
earlier ideas after 1889 and his eventual loss of the ability to read.
In the final years, before his merciful death in 1900, his sister would
grant important visitors some time with her brother and on occasion
prop a book in his hands, but he was sometimes observed to be holding it upside down. By that time Nietzsche was passive and quietly
dependent on his sister, with oral symptoms of placing brightly colored objects in his mouth, and the utterly blank facial expression,
seen in final photographs, that also goes with general paresis.[3]

Relations between Pathology, Creativity, and Essential States
in Nietzsche

Karl Jaspers, who, along with Heidegger and Lowith, wrote
major reinterpretations of Nietzsche in the 1930s, was a well-known
psychiatrist of his day, before developing a philosophy of Existenz
somewhat parallel to Heidegger. In 1922, in *Strindberg and Van
Gogh*, Jaspers identified two different ways in which psychosis,
whether functional or organic, can impact on major creativity.
Strindberg would show the pattern in which psychotic anxieties and
pressures actually begin to enter the creative work, giving an impression of bizarreness and paranoidal strangeness in certain of his
later plays and autobiographical writings. In Van Gogh, on the other
hand, and he would later add Nietzsche, a pathological process first
energizes the creative work, as a steady pressure from outside that
appears initially as an intensified drivenness behind the work, and
then eventually shuts it down altogether. Van Gogh went through
this cycle several times, and Nietzsche permanently in 1889, after
which this incredibly prolific author does not set pen to paper. For

someone who wrote in short aphorisms, one would think there would still be a few brief expressions, but not even in his speech, which was grandiosively delusive and mostly about entertaining royalty—all further reinforcing the impression of syphilitic dementia. For Jaspers, Van Gogh's art, and Nietzsche's books up until *Ecce Homo*, do not actually show psychosis. Instead, a striking drivenness, from the pressure of incipient pathology, pushed each in a very short time period far beyond what they might otherwise have attained—until it abruptly stopped them altogether.

In viewing Nietzsche as a naturalistic inner-worldly mystic and as anticipating twentieth-century developments of an experiential spirituality, it will help to combine Jaspers's analysis with Almaas on true and false forms of essence. It appears that true forms of essential strength, will, and joy in Nietzsche do grow out of an acceptance of the specific suffering and felt deficits blocking each aspect. We can see this "doctrine of holes" and later defensive shifts from true to false forms in the several phases Jaspers locates within Nietzsche's work. From 1871 to 1879, when Nietzsche wrote his earliest works, his physical symptoms develop slowly but progressively, with incapacitating headaches, stomach pain, resulting exhaustion and limitation of his daily working hours, and a growing isolation to protect himself. In a formal sense this period would bring about what Almaas and Laski regard as the deficiency or desolation states that have the potential to open into direct experiences of the numinous. Indeed, this period is followed by his major creative breakthrough, from 1880 to 1884, during which the manifestation of an essential brilliancy is attested by *Joyful Wisdom* and *Zarathustra*, and his texts and letters describe specific states of essential realization based on joy, will, and strength.

From the perspective of inner spiritual development, it probably does not matter whether the hole of suffering is based on psychological pain, physical pain, or both. After all, physical self-punishment and adversity have been associated with ecstatic states from shamanism through Christian flagellation, not to mention the considerable pain of prolonged meditative sitting. Not only does Nietzsche suffer emotionally, as we have seen, believing that he has his father's hereditary brain disease, but the physical toll is staggering. So there are the headaches and their periods of intellectual incapacity as the hole of brilliancy, misery and despair as the hole of joy, exhaustion and weakness as the hole of strength. Of course there is the continuing struggle to accept his fate. What we then see in the early 1880s is a qualitative breakthrough in the power of his intellect, ecstatic states of joy, and, in his account of the overman, descriptions of expansive alive strength, along with an astonishing demonstration of his own personal autonomy and courage. His acceptance of his suffering as *Amor Fati* attests to the presence of essential will.

Nietzsche himself arrives at a theory of his own development reminiscent of Almaas on the holes of desolation both preceding and sometimes following essential states:

> In the midst of torments which accompany an uninterrupted three-day cranial pain . . . I possessed a dialecticians clarity *par excellence* and very deliberately thought things through for which I am not enough of an acrobat, not cunning and not cool enough under healthier conditions. . . . Concerning torture and denial, my life during my last years may be matched with that of the ascetic of any time, . . . only my complete loneliness made me discover *my own resources.* (In Jaspers, *Nietzsche*: 113)

And in 1887 he writes:

> With every increase of greatness and height in man there is also an increase in depth and terribleness. . . . The more radically one desires the one, the more radically one achieves precisely the other. (Nietzsche, *The Will to Power*: 531)

Interestingly, given his own illness and chronic exhaustion, Nietzsche sees a "great healthiness" as a key attribute of the higher overman. The Dionysian individual is preeminently "healthy," but for himself he saw this "higher health," reminiscent here of Maslow on self-actualization, as the product of deep physical suffering:

> And as for my long sickness, do I not owe it indescribably more than I owe to my health? I owe it a *higher* health . . . *I also owe my philosophy to it.* Only great pain is the ultimate liberator of the spirit. (Nietzsche, *Nietzsche Contra Wagner*: 680)

From 1884 his periods of expansive ecstasy are replaced by more abrupt euphorias and "black despair," and there is a quality of frenzy and stridency in his letters about his own experience. He complains that his feelings are now out of control.

My feelings undergo such violent explosions that one single moment literally suffices to produce a change . . . that makes me thoroughly ill (this happens about twelve hours afterwards and lasts two to three days). . . . Of what avail is the most sensible way of living if at any moment the vehemence of feeling may strike into it like lightning and upset the order of all bodily functions? (In Jaspers, *Nietzsche*: 96)

He is now increasingly isolated, unbearably lonely, and impressing others with his "strangeness."

From Almaas's perspective one would expect anyone experiencing such openings of essential joy, strength, and will to encounter the dynamics and conflicts thereby stirred up, and to struggle with the appearance of the false forms of these same essential states—and especially so with someone of Nietzsche's painful upbringing. But with these pressures themselves pushed forward by the organicity of his syphilis, combined with his drug use, he had no chance whatsoever to fully comprehend what had happened to him experientially or intellectually—no chance to stabilize and consolidate by facing his more personal issues.

It seems inevitable then that false forms of essence, as distortions of the numinous, would predominate in his final years of inner urgency and desperation. The aliveness of an earlier essential strength becomes a praising of "hardness" and "cruelty," channeled into his increasingly strident attacks on Christianity. Dionysian joy becomes manic and frenzied, by 1888 with bizarre paroxysms of laughter in which he falls helpless to the floor. He becomes increasingly isolated and withdrawn, losing an earlier detachment. In a letter from 1887:

The vehemence of my inner pulsations has been terrifying, all through these past years; now that I must make the transition to a new and more intense form, I need, above all, a new estrangement. . . . So it is of the greatest importance what and who still remain to me. (Middleton, *Selected Letters*: 280)

His understanding of his actual historical importance becomes the posing, merely provocative narcissism and false grandeur found in *Ecce Homo*. By January 1889, he describes himself in his final letter as slapping people's shoulders in the street, saying "Are we happy? I am God, I made this caricature" (Middleton, *Selected Letters*: 348).

Meanwhile, the "eternal recurrence," fully spelled out, does not develop towards the "letting be" of the formless dimensions, but ends as its more artificial conceptual approximation, with a forced yea-saying to an eternity that is understood as something horrible and persecutory—essentially a malevolent paraphrase of Ialdabaoth in its meaninglessness and indifferent mechanism. As we have seen, there is nothing of the peace and repose of essential power, but an increasing resort to imagery of a life force as pure dominance.

Yet Nietzsche's own psychological understanding of the issues that frustrate his further development includes the view that the hatred linked to "will to power" contains a life energy that needs to be reassimilated, or as Almaas would say, metabolized.

> This yea-saying book sends out its light, its love, its tenderness, over all things evil, it gives them back their "soul," their serene conscience, their high right and privilege of existence. . . . My danger is the loathing of mankind. (Nietzsche, *Ecce Homo*: 887, 929)

His own hatred does remain unassimilated, of course, and his closest approach to the deeper repose of Plotinus and the higher Gnostics became the final passivity and apathy of advanced general paresis.

The pressure and increasing deficit of the paresis first energized his creative period and its approximations of essential will, strength, and joy, and then shut them down. Like Van Gogh, when his symptoms are at their worst he simply cannot work, and when they alleviate he writes with a passion and directness that otherwise he might never have attained. The organic progression, intensifying in the late 1880s, meant that the dynamic emotional conflicts inevitably stirred up by such openings could have no chance of resolution. There would be no possibility of integrating his early trauma and rage, on the one hand, and the split-off persona and narcissistic ideal of his Zarathustra, on the other. Like the Gnostics, Nietzsche is ultimately held to a dualism and the similar inflation of a higher God-man. It is a tragic and powerful story.

The Nietzschean Psychologists and Abraham Maslow

Nietzsche often called himself a "psychologist," so it is of interest that in addition to his most obvious philosophical inheritors, Heidegger, Jaspers, and Lowith in the 1930s, and Foucault and Bataille more recently, there is a corresponding group of what could be termed "Nietzschean psychologists."

Strictly speaking we would not include Freud here, despite his praise for Nietzsche's psychological acumen. Not only did Freud deny reading extensively in Nietzsche, but the side of the latter's thought reflected in Freud is primarily the more reductionist analysis of unconscious motivation underlying cultural sublimations. Nor would one necessarily include, in the present context, Adler. Although his view of the primacy of dominance and self-assertion, referenced to will to power, is obviously an explicit development of Nietzsche, it is without the central linkage to ecstasy and essential realization. Rather it is Carl Jung, Otto Rank, Wilhelm Reich, and later the transpersonal psychology of Abraham Maslow wherein we find explicit psychologies of the Dionysian life affirmation of the overman— Nietzsche's own answer to critical nihilism.

Jung, of course, developed his own naturalistic understanding of the numinous, while also connecting the spiritual individuation of Self to Nietzsche's concept of overman. Reflecting the complex battle during the 1930s for the essential soul of Nietzsche's thought, Jung taught an ongoing seminar on *Thus Spake Zarathustra* between 1935 and 1939 to his closest followers (Jung 1988), treating it as an example of his own self-realization method of active imagination. Zarathustra is understood as an idealized archetypal wisdom personification of the kind sometimes emerging in multiple personality. Jung was especially inclined to draw attention to the grandiosity of Zarathustra as reflecting the imbalance of Nietzsche's own development. Ironically, he does not share Freud's high opinion of Nietzsche as psychologist. One suspects that Nietzsche's inflation was too close to Jung's own anxieties (Parkes 1999).

Otto Rank's existential "will psychology," also of the 1930s, was even more explicit in its debt to Nietzsche. This is most obvious in *Art and Artist*, with its detailed contrast of creativity and neurosis, and his view that the self-actualized life of the creative person of the future would be based on treating one's own life as a work of art—one to be based on a full acceptance of the non rational sources of life:

> For . . . a re-discovery of the natural self of man, it is not sufficient to *see* the importance of the irrational element in human life and point it out in rational terms! On the contrary, it is necessary actually to live it and of this only a few

individuals in every epoch seem to be capable. . . . Man is
born beyond psychology and he dies beyond it but he can *live*
beyond it only through vital experience of his own—in religious terms, through revelation, conversion or re-birth.
(Rank, *Beyond Psychology*: 14, 16)

Wilhelm Reich (1897–1957), our era's version of Simon Magus,
only cites Nietzsche in passing. Yet he is surely our most Dionysian
psychologist, with the development of his early psychology of orgasm
into a theory of universal life energy (orgone), whose direct experience within is understood as the genuine core of a falsely projected
classical mysticism. Reich, having been indirectly responsible for the
horrible suicidal death of his mother, who had been having an affair
with his tutor and about which he told his father, later succumbed to
his own grandiosity and paranoia. Convicted of medical quackery
largely through his own stubborn identification with Socrates,
Jesus, and Giordano Bruno, he insisted on being so treated and died
in jail (Sharaf 1983). This is an ending that in its sheer unwarranted
tragedy does rival that of Nietzsche.

The most directly Nietzschean psychology, however, is Abraham
Maslow's (1908–1970) account of self-actualization, with his naturalistically interpreted "peak experiences" as its inner marker. At his
most controversial, where Maslow describes self-actualizers as the
"superior biological specimens" of humanity, who should thereby
guide and determine values for the rest, he explicitly cites his closeness to Nietzsche on the overman (Maslow 1971). In his earlier work,
also influenced by Adler, Maslow (1936, 1939, 1942) extended his first
observational research on healthy vs. unhealthy dominance in primates into highly original interview studies of what he called "dominance feeling" in young women. Its features of strong self-esteem,
capacity for constructive and nurturant leadership, a strong healthy
sexuality, and an experiential openness are an obvious developmental precursor to his later description of midlife self-actualizers.
Indeed, his discussion of the experiential sensitivity and high hyp-
notizability of his female interviewees sound very much like contemporary research by McCrae (1994) and Tellegen and Atkinson
(1974) on "openness to experience" or "absorption" as a basic dimension of personality—and one similarly correlated with altered and
transpersonal states of consciousness.

Most remarkable, however, are the personal parallels between
Nietzsche and Maslow. There is the same unassimilated hatred for the
mother, battles with exhaustion and depression, over-idealization of
their self-actualizer/overman figure, and hypersensitive narcissism.

Although Maslow somewhat resented his father's emotional distance, he truly hated his mother, denouncing her in print during her life and refusing to attend her funeral (Hoffman 1988). He variously described her as "cruel," "ignorant," and "schizophrenogenic." He describes her as killing before his eyes the forbidden kittens he had nonetheless brought home, by smashing their heads against the kitchen wall.

> I was a terribly unhappy boy . . . my family was a miserable family and my mother was a horrible creature . . . I grew up in libraries and among books, without friends. With my childhood, it's a wonder I'm not psychotic. (In Hoffman, *The Right to be Human: A Biography of Abraham Maslow*: 1)

Personally quiet and gentle, it was not surprising that Maslow complained in his journals (Lowry 1982) of a lifelong isolation and loneliness and found graduate students a perpetual threat to his precarious self-esteem, while publicly and privately insisting that his high I.Q. (196) meant that others should simply defer to his insights. His late-life depressions, and struggles with his "unexpressed anger," attest to an unmetabolized hatred, juxtaposed against his outwardly predominant enthusiasm and genial optimism. Near the end of his life he came to see his portrait of the self-actualizer, which he initially based on perhaps somewhat idealized versions of his most influential teachers, as a specific reaction against his mother's traits:

> I've always wondered where my utopianism, . . . stress on kindness, love, friendship . . . came from. I knew certainly of the direct consequences of having no mother-love. But the whole thrust of my life philosophy and all my research and theorizing has its roots in a hatred for and revulsion against everything she stood for. (Lowry, *The Journals of Abraham Maslow*: 245)

In a final parallel with Nietzsche, Maslow's first detailed formulations of self-actualization and peak experience in the 1950s emerge during a period of unaccustomed vitality, directly following several years of physical and emotional exhaustion and initial coronary symptoms—showing again how the expansiveness of essential strength and joy can emerge out of their deeply felt deficiency, within which the physical and psychological can be indiscriminable. In his final years heart attacks and depression closed in again, and his journals document a professional bitterness and disengagement from empirical research during the time of his greatest public recognition.

Unlike the secularization of the Protestant Ethic found in Freud's extolling of "love and work" (Homans 1989), the "Nietzschean psychologists" primarily value "meaning" and "sense of Being," sought through direct ecstatic experiences of essential joy, strength, will, and power. Since as secular values these latter have become the predominant concerns of a materialist society extolling individuality and autonomy, it makes sense that they would be the aspects of the numinous most emphasized in any mystical re-enchantment that would mirror the life issues of the modern alienated individual—so similarly understood by Nietzsche, Heidegger, Jung, Rank, Reich, and Maslow. The exception, as we will see further below, would be Kierkegaard, who, in a burst of utterly original writings between 1842 and 1855, attempted to revitalize a Christian love, compassion, and faith. Yet he also begins with his own powerful evocations of a very modern dread, despair, and loneliness, only later moving back towards his own restatement of an ethical prophecy in his final Christian sermons.

The worst-case dangers for a new this-worldly mysticism are clear enough, on the level of mass society, in the "holes" of strength, will and power whose denial was also central to Hitler's National Socialism—with its false hardness, willful control, cruel dominance, and the frightening mass appeal of its projected hatred (chapter 8). Meanwhile, our increasingly globalized contemporary society extols the media image of a triumphant individuality, interchangeable autonomy, and control of just about everything, while real people suffer increasing powerlessness and doubtful self-esteem. The broader cultural shift toward a more radically experiential attitude offers the progressively isolated individual his/her own secularized versions of transcendence in the form of drugs, thrill seeking behaviors, extreme sports, an obsession with bodily perfection and fitness, and endless sexual entertainment and experimentation. These, in Almaas' terms, are expressions of false strength, will, power, and joy. On the level of explicitly spiritual movements, the issue becomes how the true forms of these aspects of the numinous are to be developed and balanced with each other, *and* with the forms of love and compassion at the center of the Christian spirituality whose secularization Nietzsche was one of the first to understand. What Nietzsche lacked above all was a genuine compassion for himself and his extraordinary suffering. Instead, what we get are various versions of "what does not kill me, makes me stronger"—which in his own case, while true in passing, could not have been more finally incorrect.

CHAPTER 7

Emerson, Thoreau, and Hiram Marble:
New England Transcendentalism and
a Brief Look at Spiritualism

The New England transcendentalists, Ralph Waldo Emerson and
Henry David Thoreau constitute a nineteenth-century inner-worldly
mysticism with striking resonances to Plotinus, as well as to certain
elements and dilemmas of Gnosticism—of which Emerson, as a Harvard educated Unitarian minister, was certainly aware. Emerson
and Thoreau fell out of favor in contrast with the more revolutionary Nietzsche, Jung, Gurdjieff, and Heidegger, in part because their
exquisitely beautiful writing became widely familiar as a style of
rhetoric. However, Emerson had a direct influence on Nietzsche,
being one of the few nineteenth-century authors who Nietzsche took
seriously, and was a precursor to Heidegger on primordial Being experience. There are also striking parallels between Emerson and
Jung's archetypal imagination (Bickman 1988). Contrawise, we will
later locate an unexpectedly Kierkegaardian resonance within
spiritualism, that more plebeian mediumistic movement scorned
by both Emerson and Thoreau, yet also a part of the inner-worldly
spirituality of their times.

Emerson's Eternal Moment of Being

For Ralph Waldo Emerson, who was born in 1803 and died in
1882, it is the cultivation of the soul, defined as the ongoing attunement to one's own immediate experience, that *is* divine and the closest

147

we can come to God. This is a notion of the supremacy of the human individual as the fullest and most complete expression of divinity. Emerson began as a minister, but by his late twenties he was resisting, then refusing, the practice of communion, since he had concluded that there could have been no original Fall of man and therefore no need for any redemption by crucifixion. Each of us in our heart is already the perfect Adam—the Adam before the fall so central to the Gnostic Anthropos. For Emerson there is something already god-like in any individual who fully trusts their own immediate experience, and this is, at its core, what Weber meant by innerworldly mysticism—that God is in the here and now moment. From Emerson's point of view, revelation is literally the continued attention to one's immediate situation:

> Let us be poised, and wise, and our own, today. Let us treat the men and women well; treat them as if they were real; perhaps they are. Men live in their fancy, like drunkards whose hands are too soft and tremulous for successful labor. It is a tempest of fancies, and the only ballast I know is a respect to the present hour. Without any shadow of doubt, amidst this vertigo of shows and politics, I settle myself ever the firmer in the creed that we should not postpone and refer and wish, but do broad justice where we are, by whomsoever we deal with, accepting our actual companions and circumstances, however humble or odious, as the mystic officials to whom the universe has delegated its whole pleasure for us. (Emerson, Experience: 262)

Again, what Emerson is teaching is not so much an ethics of the moment as its revelatory aesthetics.

Emerson's understanding of this moment by moment "vast flowing vigor" of "first cause," which, like Almaas, he also terms Essence, anticipates the key insight of Heidegger:

> In our more correct writing we give to this generalization the name of Being, and thereby confess that we have arrived as far as we can go. Suffice it for the joy of the universe that we have not arrived at a wall, but at interminable oceans. Our life seems not present so much as prospective; not for the affairs on which it is wasted, but as a hint of this vast-flowing vigor. (Emerson, Experience: 268)

The dogma of religion, the creeds of theology, all cloak an immediate experience of ongoing beingness available in the here and now and nowhere else.

Openness to the experience of Being is helped by a process of "compensation," remarkably akin to Almaas on the doctrine of "holes," Laski on the experience of existential deficit, and Jung's own concept of archetypal compensation for the narrow one-sidedness of ordinary consciousness:

> Our strength grows out of our weakness. The indignation which arms itself with secret forces does not awaken until we are pricked and stung and sorely assailed. A great man is always willing to be little. . . . When he is pushed, tormented, defeated, he has a chance to learn something; he has been put on his wits, and on his manhood; he has gained facts; learns his ignorance; is cured of the insanity of conceit; has got moderation and real skill. The wise man throws himself on the side of his assailants. It is more his interest than it is theirs to find his weak point. . . . Every evil to which we do not succumb is a benefactor. (Emerson, Compensation: 184)

That which appears in these openings to Being is ultimately the "Oversoul," which he takes from Plotinus. It is the Great Nature which in moments of inspiration we sense as our source:

> Man is a stream whose source is hidden. Our being is descending into us from we know not whence. . . . We live in succession, in division, in parts, in particles. Meantime within man is the soul of the whole; the wise silence, the universal beauty, to which every part and particle is equally related; the eternal One. And this deep power in which we exist and whose beatitude is all accessible to us, is not only self-sufficing and perfect in every hour, but the act of seeing and the thing seen, the seer and the spectacle, the subject and the object, are one. (Emerson, The Over-soul: 262)

This is one of many allusions to Plotinus in the mature Emerson, in this pantheistic nature mysticism somehow revised out of New England Protestantism.

Nature provides for Emerson the primary language of the soul, and it is this insight that Thoreau actively practiced as a method of consciousness transformation. Inspired by his own readings in German idealism and romanticism, Emerson anticipates Heidegger and especially Jung, in the idea that all of our deepest self-awareness rests and relies on physical metaphor. The properties of nature are the primary mirror within which we see ourselves. Emerson's insight includes but goes beyond the observation first made by Vico (1744) that all words for experience in all languages rest on natural phenomena originally used metaphorically—as in wind (pneuma) for spirit and the "ang" root of anger, anguish, and anxiety, which originally in European languages meant being caught in physical straits or narrows. Rather, he approximates Jung, and more recently Lakoff (1987) and Johnson (1987), for whom the forms of our more developed self-awareness are actually created out of our experience of the dynamics of physical nature as primary mirror, and could not exist without them.

In his 1836 essay "Nature," the first of his major post ministry works, Emerson sees that this identity of consciousness and physical nature goes deeper than a proto-cognitive theory of "metaphor":

> It is not words only that are emblematic; it is things that are emblematic. Every natural fact is a symbol of some spiritual fact. Every appearance in nature corresponds to some state of mind, and that state of mind can only be described by presenting that natural appearance as its picture. . . . Light and darkness are our familiar expression for knowledge and ignorance; and heat for love. . . . Who looks upon a river in a meditative hour, and is not reminded of the flux of all things? (Emerson, *Nature*: 12)

In this essay he goes on to anticipate recent discussions of chaos modeling and non linear dynamics in calling attention to the way in which the same form constants in nature occur on level after level of reality, including consciousness itself. The same patterns of flow found immobilized in rock and lava, he says, move faster in water, and still faster in air. All forms are modifications of each other, and the highest form of nature is human consciousness, which in turn expresses the divine.

In this strikingly Gnostic passage, human beings, as the most complex embodiment of the principles of nature, are the closest we can come to the creative source of all things:

> A man is a god in ruins. . . . Man is the dwarf of himself. Once he was permeated and dissolved by spirit. He filled nature

with his overflowing currents. Out from him sprang the sun and the moon: from man, the sun; from woman, the moon. The laws of his mind, the periods of his actions, externised themselves into day and night, into the year and the seasons. But having made for himself this huge shell, his waters retired; he no longer fills the veins and veinlets; he is shrunk to a drop. He sees, that the structure still fits him, but fits him colossolly. Say, rather, once it fitted him. . . . Yet sometimes he starts in his slumber, and wonders at himself and his house, and muses strangely at the resemblance betwixt him and it. (Emerson, *Nature*: 35)

This really sounds like the primordial Anthropos, the realization of the pre-fall Adam as God-like. Nature is pure emanation, and as such it is an "ecstasy" that terminates in the human individual as its fullest realization. At the same time we are the only true mirror of that source, which in its elevation of the individual is reminiscent of Nietzsche's overman.

Dynamics and Openings to Essence in Emerson's Life

Emerson's upbringing is strikingly similar to Nietzsche. His father was minister of the First Congregational Church of Boston. He died when Emerson was eight, a brother having died four years before. So again, it is a childhood of powerful early grief. Like Nietzsche he was then raised by his mother and an extended family of aunts, but unlike Nietzsche one of these aunts played the crucial inspirational role in his intellectual education. He was raised to be a minister, with strong values of self-abnegation and suppression of personal will. However, the death of his young wife had a shattering impact on him. Every day for a year he walked into Boston from Concord to visit her tomb and then one day he opened the coffin and looked at her body, and was never the same person again (Richardson 1995).

His journal now emphasizes a surrender to the experience of the present moment reminiscent of Almaas on essential will, and using a suddenly rich descriptive imagery for his new experience that also reflects an expansiveness of essential strength in its recurrent references to fire, light, volcanoes, and molten lava. Suddenly, everything he experiences is enhanced and significant, with a special aliveness full of possibility. There is an extraordinary expansion of an intellectual, inspired brilliancy and a new power of expression. Eight months later he resigned his ministry, finally refusing to give communion as inconsistent with the potential God-likeness of each individual, although his congregation offered numerous compromises to keep him.

His essays and journal entries from this point show a Dionysian, expansive joy. He experiences each day as simultaneously the dawn of all creation and the day of judgment. He speaks of having reached a "habit of enthusiasm," and there is much mention of delight, wildness, and exhilaration.[1] He anticipates Nietzsche on ecstasy and Maslow on peak experience as naturalistic states. Each person can have moments of extraordinary experience, the highest experiences of the soul, and he understands these in a way reminiscent of current chaos models of brain dynamics, as a natural process that can be understood as a higher version of the flow dynamics of rivers (Richardson 1995).

Emerson is also presenting a doctrine of personal essence—of the inherent autonomy and self-sufficiency of the individual as the highest spiritual principle. He writes expansively of America as the new Eden, thereby evoking the Gnostic pre-fall Adam, and states that his era is "the age of the first-person singular." Personally, in these years of essential opening, Emerson is clearly a charismatic figure. Those who knew him described a sense of presence, and a personal aliveness, autonomy, sweetness, and capacity for a truly intimate contact with others (Richardson 1995).

What is absent in Emerson, but present in Thoreau, and probably one of the reasons why they could not ultimately be of help to each other, is what Almaas would call the power of the essential black, manifested most fully as a sense of peace and inner stillness. In fact, Emerson only shows an approach to this peace in the later stages of what seems to have been an organic loss of cerebral capacity. By his mid 50s Emerson begins to suffer a loss of energy and a dimming of his earlier brilliancy. Indeed, his writing had already lost much of its qualities of incandescence after the death of his son by his second marriage at the age of six (Bickman 1988). A quiet loneliness begins to manifest, certainly exacerbated by the multiple deaths of loved ones, and his closest friends find him increasingly inaccessible. His daughter said that whenever he attempts to talk about anything deeply emotional he now becomes inarticulate and upset and says that he cannot continue.

Emerson's last truly original writing was his unsparingly honest eulogy for Thoreau in 1862, but his late essays mostly have a tone of negative resignation rather than anything like his earlier acceptance and surrender. Then there is the increasing loss of memory, so that eventually he cannot anymore deliver his frequent public lectures, let alone write new ones. Lecturing had been his post ministry livelihood, so not surprisingly, there is a period of intense shame and anguish over not even being able to read from his lecture notes. Yet later, in the final years of his life, everyone who knew him described his unusual happiness and contentment. In the classical mysticisms of the Eastern traditions, "losing one's mind" is sometimes described as a necessary step for the higher enlightenment of the formless dimensions. So in a much happier way than Nietzsche, such a loss of mind seems to have been physiologically mediated for Emerson, and the outcome was the peace and quieter joyousness described by his wife during his years of senility: "He is the happiest person she ever knew" (Richardson 1995: 571).

Emerson, Thoreau, and later William James, Walt Whitman, Richard Bucke, of course Nietzsche—and earlier Blake and Carlyle, and the British and German romantic tradition generally—were all engaged in the celebration of individual character as a scared enterprise. The inner development of character is the highest form of spirituality. Almaas understands this in terms of personal essence, as the integration of spiritual and worldly orientations, and there is a deep consistency here with Troeltsch on inner-worldly mysticism as the new spirituality of modernity. Yet by the turn of the century, New England transcendentalism had disappeared, assimilated into a narrower secular American functionalism. The practices of an inner-worldly mysticism would instead have to return to North America in the 1920s and 30s through Jung, Gurdjieff, Steiner, and Eastern teachers of Vedantic and Buddhist meditation (Taylor 1999). In retrospect we could say that without the techniques of imagistic elaboration, self-remembering, and meditation from these more specifically articulated systems, the earlier spiritualization of character was too difficult to teach and pass on.

Emerson and Thoreau developed a deep understanding of personal essence but without a specific path and technique of practice. Their spiritual way remained characteristically intangible, as with the Greek imitation of Socrates. Of course we have seen that inner-worldly mysticisms will come and go more rapidly than more independent and self-sustaining spiritual traditions. The Civil War and its aftermath of rapid industrialization left Thoreau's use of the woods around Concord, as the means to operationalize Emerson's insights, a cultural anachronism. Still, it is ironic that the immediate roots of what are now called transpersonal psychology, had, apart from William James, to return from Europe, since its essentials had already been laid out by Emerson and Thoreau.

Thoreau: The Woods of Concord as Mirror of the Soul

Henry David Thoreau died early of tuberculosis at the age of forty-four in 1862. In 1846 and 1847 he had retreated to a hut on Walden Pond, keeping a journal that he developed into *Walden* and published in 1854. We will see how Thoreau directly practiced Emerson's method of "compensation" by using nature as a continuously unfolding mirror of the otherwise implicit life of immediate consciousness. Personally Thoreau is very much the opposite of Emerson, his mentor. There is none of Emerson's joy, expansive strength, and personalness, but instead a fascination with the blackness and silence of essential power, along with the issues of a schizoid aloneness and hatred that run through Thoreau's life—and both feed his experiences and eventually block them in crucial ways. Thoreau is a complex and in some ways tragic figure, aptly called by one of his major biographers "Dark Thoreau" (Bridgman 1981). In place of Emerson's celebratory imagery of fire and volcanoes, we find the silence of the night, the quiet of the woods, and the deep inner stillness of winter ice.

As with Emerson, it is the immediacy of the moment that most fully reveals the sacred, and Thoreau understands this not primarily in ethical terms, but in terms of its felt aesthetics. For Thoreau this attitude opens into a direct sense of presence or beingness, especially in the stillness and power of nature. It is this orientation to experience of the moment, supported by his explicit interest in Sufism, that reflects an inner-worldly meditative attitude:

> Men esteem truth remote, . . . behind the farthest star, before Adam and after the last man. In eternity there is indeed something true and sublime. But all these times and places and occasions are now and here. God himself culminates in the present moment, and will never be more divine in the lapse of all the ages. (Thoreau, *Walden*: 349)

There is also a Gnostic flavor here, in that the average person, who is not in the revelation of the unfolding moment, is seen as "asleep." The key is to become fully alive by "waking up," and we can only keep ourselves awake "by an infinite expectation of the dawn" (Thoreau, *Walden*: 343).

Emerson's notion of compensation is directly applied to the immediate experience of nature, as the ongoing mirror of Thoreau's momentary subjective state, in a way reminiscent of Almaas on the "holes" of felt deficiency expanding into aspects of essence. Thoreau finds this entire sequence of deficiency and opening mirrored back to him as he walks and observes the same woods day after day. What he observes each time depends on his immediate state, especially his emotional pain, which is then transformed and redeemed as he continues to observe. In psychological terms he has located a way to exteriorize Silberer's autosymbolism by following his own spontaneous shifts in attending to his surroundings:

> A few weeks after I came to the woods . . . I doubted if the near neighbourhood of man was not essential to a serene and healthy life. To be alone was something unpleasant. But I was at the same time conscious of a slight insanity in my mood, and seemed to foresee my recovery. In the midst of a gentle rain while these thoughts prevailed, I was suddenly sensible of such sweet and beneficient society in Nature, in the very patterning of the drops, and in every sound and sight around my house, an infinite and unaccountable friendliness all at once like an atmosphere sustaining me, as made the fancied advantages of human neighbourhood insufficient. . . . Every little pine needle expanded and swelled with sympathy and befriended me. I was so distinctly made aware of the presence of something kindred to me, even in scenes which we are accustomed to call wild and dreary, . . . that I thought no place could ever be strange to me again. (Thoreau, *Walden*: 382–83).

This pattern is repeated over and over through *Walden* and the journals. Different forms of suffering are first reflected in his surroundings and then answered by the aspect of essence felt to be missing, as in this journal passage from 1858:

> I was feeling very cheap, reduced to make the most of dry dogwood berries. Very little evidence of God or man did I see then, and life not as rich and inviting an enterprise as it should be, when my attention was caught by a snowflake on my coat sleeve. It was one of those perfect crystalline star-shaped ones. . . . This little object, which, with many of its fellows, rested unmelting on my coat, so perfect and beautiful, reminded me that Nature had not lost her pristine vigour yet, and why should man lose heart? . . . We are rained and snowed on with gems. . . . I was beginning to

> believe that Nature was poor and mean, and I was now con-
> vinced that she turned off as good work as ever. . . . I may say
> that the maker of the world exhausts his skill with each
> snowflake and dewdrop that he sends down. . . . In truth
> they are the product of *enthusiasm*, the children of an ec-
> stasy, finished with the artist's utmost skill. (Bode, *The
> Portable Thoreau*: 578–79)

As with Emerson, and later Jung, Nature fully contemplated offers a mirror for our inner experience that goes deeper than we could
articulate with ordinary language alone. It does seem that the essential aspects of the numinous, the access levels of mysticism, are
based on the felt embodiment of the luminosity of open space, the
gentleness and beneficence of wind, and the silence and dark stillness of night. These physiognomies are constituent of the experience
itself. This is very much what Thoreau is practicing, giving himself
contemplatively to nature and so inviting it to reflect the immediate
state of his soul.

Thoreau's Life and Dynamics

Thoreau is explicit that the mirroring and support he gets from
nature is maternal:

> This vast, savage, howling mother of ours, Nature, lying all
> around, with such beauty, and such affection for her chil-
> dren. (Thoreau, Walking: 621)

> I make it my business to extract from Nature whatever nu-
> triment she can furnish me. . . . I milk the sky and the earth.
> (Bode, *The Portable Thoreau*: 686)

Yet Thoreau feared the true wilderness. He returned to Concord
woods shaken and agitated from his trip to the mountains of Maine,
where he was repeatedly lost and panicked. He needed a safe, do-
mestic woods as an alternative, maternal holding environment.

Thoreau offers a good illustration of Weber on the "broken" quality of inner-worldly mysticism. Certainly we see themes of shame,
dilemmas around hatred, schizoid withdrawal, and a painful hypersensitivity to others, often with a defensive grandiosity and haugh-
tiness. His relation to his mother is not so different from Nietzsche

and Maslow, and his life-long attempts at independence continually fail in one way or another. An exception to many of the people we are studying, his father does not die in childhood, but was, while well liked in the village, looked down upon by the mother as lacking in ambition. Although earlier accounts of Thoreau's psychology have emphasized the Oedipal pattern of his relative distance from his father and closeness to his domineering mother (LeBeaux 1977, 1984), as reflected also in his curious surrogate mother relationship with Emerson's wife Lydia, the pre-Oedipal psychologies of the mother-child dyad of Winnicott and Kohut will seem the more appropriate.

Thoreau's mother was, by most accounts, dominating, gossipy, malicious, and cruel. Although he was her favorite child, some flavor of his deep ambivalence about her comes from this extraordinary outburst from one of his travel essays, *Cape Cod*. The circumstances he attributes to a local woman, briefly glimpsed in passing, reflect his own resentment over what he saw as his mother's lack of grief over the deaths of both his brother and father, in contrast to his own deep grieving over his brother:

> We saw one singularly masculine woman, however, in a house on this very plain, who did not look as if she was ever troubled with hysterics, or sympathized with those who were; or, perchance, life itself was to her a hysteric fit,—a Nauset woman, of a hardness and coarseness such as no man ever possesses or suggests. It was enough to see the vertebrae and sinews of her neck, and her set jaws of iron, which would have bitten a board nail in two in their ordinary action,—braced against the world, talking like a man-of-war's man in petticoats, or as if shouting at you through a breaker; who looked as if it made her head ache to live; hard enough for any enormity. I looked upon her as one who had committed infanticide; who never had a brother, unless it were some wee thing that died in infancy,—for what need of him?—and whose father must have died before she was born. (Thoreau, *Cape Cod*: 55–56)

His mother also grew up without a father and lost a brother in infancy.

His mother doted on Thoreau, simultaneously dominating and favoring him over his older brother, who was more like the father and very popular in the town. On the one hand, she sends Thoreau to Harvard on her limited funds, and not the older brother, which would have been the normal course of things on the basis of his age

and superior academic performance. Yet there are later accounts of
dinner at the Thoreau household that describe Thoreau, by then
very well known, talking to a guest, his mother interrupting him,
and Thoreau simply ceasing all interaction until the maternal ha-
rangue had ceased, then to resume his sentence at the exact point
where he had stopped. It is not surprising then that Thoreau grew
up as a grave, withdrawn, and rather cold child. Where other children called the mother-dominated Nietzsche "the little pastor,"
Thoreau was called "the judge." He and his mother were about
equally unpopular in Concord.[2]

Thoreau's relation to his older brother John is especially interesting, because it involves a mirroring or symbiotic twinship pattern
consistent with the dyadic identifications studied by Kohut, Winnicott, and Khan. It is the brother, genuinely beloved by the town and
by Thoreau himself, who teaches him about the woods and passes on
Indian lore and how to find arrowheads. Thoreau steps aside when
the two fall in love with the same young woman, and never forgives
her for rejecting his brother's proposal. It seems to have been the
only romantic love of his life. In 1842 the brother dies of lockjaw,
brought on by a minor infection. Thoreau nursed his brother all during the illness, not allowing anyone else near him. Deeply distraught
after his brother's death, he developed sympathy symptoms, entirely
psychosomatic but convincing at the time. It is only after his
brother's death that Thoreau takes to the woods on his own. His two
years at Walden Pond are deeply linked to the dead brother. It was
then that he wrote his first book, *Ten Days on the Concord and Mer-
rimac Rivers*, as a eulogy to his brother based on his journal of their
earlier canoe trip together (Harding 1965).

Walden Pond also had much to do with his need to escape the
town's judgment upon him. It was made clear to him that the wrong
brother had died, a point on which he might have secretly agreed.
He was already known as cold and supercilious, walking past people in the village without greeting. There is also the implied, if explicitly denied, shame over an incident in which he and a friend
accidentally set fire to the woods he would later make so famous.
Were it not that the other man was the son of a favored family, they
would have been charged legally. The friend goes to arouse the town
and when the local men arrive back to fight the large fire, including
his volunteer fireman father, Thoreau continues to sit alone on a
large promontory rock above the burning area, watching their efforts, and according to his journals, waxing philosophical that he is

no more to blame than the lightening that could as well have done the same thing. The incident was never forgotten in the town.

Doubly out of favor, he begins his famous night walks in the woods, literally feeling his way down the trails by his feet. These are experiences of profound silence and stillness, where, consistent with Almaas on essential power, he is at peace. *Ten Days* comes out in 1849, a total commercial failure, and he is full of bitterness at Emerson, who had initially been so supportive, owing to some critical personal comments on the book. By 1855, a year after the instantaneous success of *Walden*,[3] Thoreau began to suffer from a lingering illness never diagnosed, but leaving him too physically weak to walk or even use his writing hand. The mysterious lassitude and weakness lasted several years, and would constitute the hole of that essential strength and joy so available to Emerson. The two are later reconciled, but Thoreau writes little after *Walden*, although he recovered enough to resume his walks and journals. By 1860 he has the tuberculosis that will kill him two years later. In the proximity of death he pulls together some of his earlier unpublished essays, writes some new work, and experiences a touching reconciliation with some of the townspeople he had believed still hated him. Others still did.

The dynamics of Thoreau's personal life reflect what Fairbairn (1954) has termed the schizoid dilemma, which fits well with what we know of his relation to his mother and his use of nature as an alternative symbiotic support. There is his long struggle with themes of withdrawal and isolation, shame, and feelings of hatred, which on the positive side could periodically open into the states of essential power and stillness described in his journals, but would at the same time prevent the integration of the expansiveness and vitality of essential strength, as well as essential joy, and compassion. The blue of awareness and the black of peace and silence are highly developed in Thoreau, but their associated conflicts block any genuine autonomy and personalness. Thoreau remains astonishingly impersonal and cold, in a way very different from the expansiveness of either Emerson or Nietzsche. Instead, we find the pseudo autonomy of isolation. Emerson had all the expansion and vitality that Thoreau lacked, and Thoreau had all of the stillness and detachment absent in the personally contactful Emerson, but somehow they could not put that together fruitfully between them. As much as Concord woods allowed Thoreau to open to essential realization, they were also a refuge—as also for the use of nature by Nietzsche, Jung, and Heidegger.

Thoreau himself was at times acutely aware of his defensive aloofness from others, and the difficulties he had managing his own hatred and bitterness. From his journals:

> I have seemingly preferred hate to love . . . concealed my love, and sooner or later expressed all and more than all my hate. . . . I am under an awful necessity to be what I am. (Bridgman, *Dark Thoreau*: 265)

Here we see Fairbairn's "hate be my good" of the schizoid reversal of values. At another point he says he got so little from his friendships, "because I gave so little" (Bridgman 1981: 267). Emerson's eulogy for Thoreau calls him a New England Socrates, and at the same time captures the extremity of Thoreau's relations with others:

> There was somewhat military in his nature not to be subdued, always manly and able, but rarely tender, as if he did not feel himself except in opposition. He wanted a fallacy to expose, a blunder to pillory. . . . It cost him nothing to say No; indeed, he found it much easier than to say Yes. . . . No equal companion stood in affectionate relations with one so pure and guileless. "I love Henry," said one of his friends, "but I cannot like him; and as for taking his arm, I would as soon think of taking the arm of an elm tree." . . . Such dangerous frankness was in his dealings that his admirers called him "that terrible Thoreau," as if he spoke when silent, and was still present when he had departed. I think the severity of his ideal interfered to deprive him of a healthy sufficiency of human society. (Emerson, *Thoreau*: 137, 148)

To complete this picture of austere coldness and perfectionism, only truly absent in his affectionate dealings with the Emerson children, there is the hypersensitivity that is also part of Fairbairn's picture—Emerson pointing out that Thoreau could not stand the sound of his own feet walking on gravel. Acceptance of this imposed sensitivity could and did open Thoreau to silence and stillness. There could be the repose of the Gnostic One evoked by the silence of the woods at night and the purity of the ice in the winter. Yet the failure to develop the strength of autonomy and merging love for real others would block any manifestation of personal essence in Thoreau's writings.

The sense of futility that Fairbairn finds to be the central affect of the schizoid dilemma predominates through most of Thoreau's post

Walden years. During his period of apathy and lassitude, the journals change in their tone and become more an obsessive cataloguing of what he encounters on his walks, often a list of the dead animals he had seen. At the same time, in order to gain some financial independence from his family, since he is now living at home again and managing his late father's pencil factory, he does surveying work in the very woods whose doom he had earlier foretold as he saw his neighbors surveying and fencing their property lines. Now he himself does what he had once described as the work of the Devil, helping in the first destruction of the American wilderness. But not without mixed feelings. He says that he feels like he has committed suicide (Bridgman 1981). The only recovery of strong emotion comes in 1858 when he is so moved by the inspirational terrorism of the abolitionist John Brown, that he listens to him speak with fists clenched in rage and writes an impassioned defense after Brown's death. The man who had been the first to articulate the principle of non violent protest (Civil Disobedience 1849), now favors murder in a just cause.

The other affective pole of the schizoid dilemma is the intense feeling of shame, linked to a fragility of self-esteem, with or without defensive grandiosity, and some attempt at affective suppression and withdrawal. Despite the idealization of his literary persona, as characteristic of *Walden* as it is of Nietzsche's *Zarathustra*, and his distancing use of irony, Thoreau's vulnerability to shame and his avoidance of the eyes of his neighbors is all too clear. Here he describes his relation to the town during his time at Walden Pond:

> The houses were so arranged as to make the most of mankind, and lanes fronting one another, so that every traveler had to run the gauntlet, and every man, woman, and child might get a lick at him . . . For the most part I escaped wonderfully from these dangers, either by proceeding at once boldly and without deliberation to the goal, as is recommended to those who run the gauntlet, or by keeping my thoughts on high things, like Orpheus, who "loudly singing the praises of the gods to his lyre, drowned the voices of the Sirens and kept out of danger." Sometimes I bolted suddenly, and nobody could tell my whereabouts, for I did not stand much about gracefulness, and never hesitated at a gap in a fence. . . . and so escaped to the woods again. (Thoreau, *Walden*: 417–18)

It would be unmetabolized hatred and shame that block Thoreau from the aspect of essential strength and vitality, with essential joy (as "exaltation") only appearing on his deathbed. The expansive life energy and Dionysian spirit so central to Nietzsche and Emerson must be morally condemned in Thoreau. It is an "animalistic" something he cannot deal with:

> We are conscious of an animal in us, which awakens in proportion as our higher nature slumbers. It is reptile and sensual, and perhaps cannot be fully expelled; like the worms which, even in life and health, occupy our bodies. Possibly we may withdraw from it, but never change its nature; I fear that it may enjoy a certain health of its own; and we may be well, yet not pure. . . . I fear that we are such gods or demigods only as fawns and satyrs, the divine allied to beasts, the creatures of appetite, and that, to some extent, our very life is our disgrace. (Thoreau, *Walden*: 465–66)

Instead of anything Dionysian, any hint of sexuality, in this isolated life, whatever its literary gain and partial openings to essential power, there is a growing physical exhaustion, jaundiced bitterness, and lack of heart. In Jungian terms neither shadow nor the feminine anima within are assimilated, and the resulting spiritual development is as austerely impressive as it is imbalanced. Certainly in touch with his hatred, it drives his essential unfoldment while distorting it. The contracted sense of self at the core of the schizoid dilemma (Guntrip 1968) would block any opening into formlessness, and he would have to rely on darkness of night and winter ice for its partial intuition.

Hiram Marble and Spiritualism: Kierkegaard's Knight of Faith at Dungeon Rock

What is missing in Thoreau is present in abundance in Hiram Marble, and vice versa. Marble, born in the same year as Emerson, 1803, was a mason in western Massachusetts. He lost his second son, George Henry, to illness at the age of thirteen in 1850, and was devastated. He was soon impacted by the rapid spread of mediumistic spiritualism, after its origins in the house of the Fox sisters in Acadia, New York in 1848 (see chapter 12). Within a few years there were a million self-declared adherents in the United States, and channeling mediums in essentially every medium sized town in the Western world (Isaacs 1983). In itself the remarkable spread of this modern form of communion with the spirits of the dead attests to the real decline in Christianity so variously diagnosed by Nietzsche and Kierkegaard. As Webb (1974) points out, spiritualism is the deepest of heresies from the perspective of an earlier Christianity. Literally it is the practice of "necromancy," and in the Renaissance would have required magic pentangles to protect from the satanic powers being invoked. Its popularity shows the actual secularization of Christian belief despite a still high level of church attendance.

Up to the point of his son's death Hiram Marble describes himself as an "unmitigated infidel" with "frigid principles" and "no sort of belief in man's immortality" (Lewis and Newhall, 1865:218–19). There are also hints of Fairbairn on the schizoid dilemma, in the writings of the sixteen-year-old medium Marble later used for channeling, when she speaks of "the painful absence of mother love," "the battle of living without love," and "the terrible sternness of a disappointed man" in the book based on her trances (Enesee 1856:1). In grief, Marble had turned to spiritualism for contact with his dead son. Hearing of Dungeon Rock, a huge outcropping of granite in Lynn Woods, with its legend of buried pirate gold, he began digging, using local mediums to guide his excavations, most especially Nanette Snow Emerson (no relation!)—hence Enesee. She trance channels the long dead pirates and they tell him which direction to dig. He digs not primarily for the reputed gold, but as a test of the spiritualistic truth of a life after death: "I will either prove the truth of spiritualism or dig its grave" (Provenzano 1987: 43).

A local legend inspired it all (Snow 1944). In 1658, the pirate Thomas Veal had in fact fled inland from the pursuing British Navy, perhaps with a chest of treasure, perhaps living for a time in a cave in the huge granite rocks of Lynn Woods and trading with local townspeople. There was a large earthquake in 1727, supposedly eliminating the cave and burying the pirate and his treasure inside—thus the name of the rock—although Veal would have by then been quite old and rather introverted for a pirate. Yet there may also have been an earthquake in 1659 (Lewis and Newhall 1865). At any rate, legends well established, even linking Captain Kidd to the Rock, treasure seekers began digging in the 1830s, ostensibly with no luck. This was part of an earlier east coast "pirate gold" version of the western gold rush that Thoreau so scorned. Marble purchased the area around Dungeon Rock in 1852 and moved his family to the house he built on the site. There he spent the rest of his life, until his death in 1868, digging and blasting through the thick New England granite in search of a treasure that would prove his son's eternal life. When he ran out of money, he sold shares to be redeemed on recovery of the treasure. The tunnel he dug was continued by his first son Edwin, until he struck water near the end of his own life in 1880 and finally desisted.

The result is a tunnel two hundred feet long through solid granite, at least seven feet high and wide, and, amazingly enough, extending gradually down to seventy five feet beneath ground level. Its seemingly arbitrary twists and turns were dictated by Enesee, who also channeled a stickily romantic tale of the pirates and their women—an unchained anima/animus fantasy first published in 1856. To this day a pile of granite fragments lies outside the entrance to the tunnel, still deep within miles of pristine woods. Dungeon Rock has been the delight of generations of local children, who soon realize that Marble was not digging in the direction of any conceivably possible earlier cave or buried gold.

As a means of discovering treasure the tunnel is impossible and absurd. It goes down into solid granite and angles increasingly away from the likely locations of any cave. To actually discover treasure by this meandering descent through solid rock would clearly *be* a miracle —and that was exactly where Marble put his extraordinary faith. The turns of the tunnel literally follow the changing advice of Enesee's pirate voices. Transcriptions of the guiding spirit voices convey "their" sense of amazement, and one would hope some embarrassment, over the demonstration of faith and will that had actually unfolded:

> My dear Marble . . . I am aware you feel not discouraged; but you feel that after ten years' hard labor, you should have had more encouragement than you have seemingly had. But, dear one, we have done the most we could for you, and though we may be slow to advise you in reference to that which your highest ambition seems to be—the establishment of a truth which but few comparatively now credit, or cannot believe, from the grossness of their minds. But Marble, you have done a work that will tell when you shall be as I am. The names of Hiram and Edwin Marble will live when millions of years shall from this time have passed, when even kings and statesmen have been forgotten. . . . What shall you do? seems to be the question. Follow your own calculations or impressions, for they are right.

And in another message:

> Don't be discouraged. . . . Moses was by the Lord kept forty years in his circuitous route. . . . Cheer up, Marble; we are

with you, and doing all we can. (Lewis and Newhall, *History of Lynn*: 247–48)

It is important to note, in the face of all this visionary strangeness, that Marble's character was a source of deep affection and respect to those who knew him, whether believing spiritualists or skeptics. He had a personal presence and charismatic quality that impressed, even moved, others:

> He welcomed all to his humble abode, whether believer or skeptic, with the same good natured, honest expressions of interest and assurance in the work, that he fully believed was given to him to do by disembodied spirits, receiving as he sometimes said all things as compliments, whether donations of money, provisions, or a profusion of wordy advice or ridicule. (Enesee, *The History of Dungeon Rock*: 81)

> He is communicative, and in his conversation there runs a pleasant vein of jocularity. He is now verging upon old age . . . He is ready to converse on his plans, fears, and hopes; and with great good nature, and sometimes with an apparently keen relish, alludes to the jeers and taunts of those who seem disposed to rank him with lunatics. It is refreshing to observe his faith and perseverance, and impossible not to conclude that he derives real satisfaction and an enjoyment from his undertaking. (Lewis and Newhall, *History of Lynn*: 246)

Robust until nearly the end of his life, Hiram Marble thrived on the huge effort, and delighted in the visits and advice of fellow spiritualists from all over New England. Unfortunately his son Edwin did not thrive in the same way, the cold damp air of the tunnel apparently affecting his health, and he sickened and died prematurely—suffering the tragedy, perhaps, of having a charismatic father.

We begin to see here why we might need Kierkegaard, writing contemporaneously with Marble's digging, to fully appreciate this New England version of Don Quixote. Hiram Marble represents, better than any historical figure I know, Kierkegaard's "knight of faith," who in the face of an impossible love makes a "leap of faith," gaining this faith precisely by virtue of its very impossibility, even absurdity. In *Fear and Trembling,* Kierkegaard, having broken with his beloved fiancée ostensibly because he felt she would not ultimately be happy with him, displaces his grief and passion into the *Old Testament* story of Abraham and Isaac. This he retells with modern variations and paradox. In contrast to the traditional account, his Abraham, as the knight of faith, goes forward in a paradoxical joy, with the faith that what should happen finally will happen as the actual expression of divine will, and that somehow this must include his love for the son he is also prepared to kill:

> The knight of faith . . . renounces claim to the love which is the content of his life, . . . but then occurs the prodigy, he makes still another movement more wonderful than all, for he says, "I believe nevertheless that I shall get her, in virtue, that is of the absurd, in virtue of the fact that with God all things are possible. . . . " So he recognizes the impossibility, and that very instant he believes. . . . To him who follows the narrow way of faith no one can give counsel, him no one can understand. Faith is a miracle, and yet no man is excluded from it; for that in which all human life is unified is passion, and faith is a passion. (Kierkegaard, *Fear and Trembling*: 57–58, 77)

Marble, in the face of all rationality, truly seems to believe he will find gold in this manner, and if he had, it could *only* have been proof that the spirit messages were objective—and if so that the same would have to be true of his contact with his dead son. Unlike Thoreau, who is more the tragic hero, Marble seems to have triumphed over his pain and hatred by virtue of the immense physical work of digging his absurd yet oddly inspiring hole, to prove, out of love, that there is no such thing as death and that his son was not truly gone. In joy and certitude, Marble was digging to prove the existence of God. Thoreau loved the truth, and approached it with a clarity and brilliancy conspicuously absent in Marble, but Hiram Marble loved his lost son, and like Orpheus descending, goes after him. The digging itself is a gesture of faith, else why not dig rationally? Instead, the activity becomes an end in itself, a vital embodiment of the red of essential strength and the "gold" of essential love.

Of course, what Marble does could be dismissed as an "acting out" or "literalizing" of essential states. It may also have been the fullest expression of passion and heart possible in that life. The sheer effort and energy of digging into solid granite would be a means—certainly exteriorized—of expending his hatred in a way that Thoreau could not. The positive side of an essential power as peace and repose, renewed each day in the physical expenditure of the work, emerged in place of his earlier cynicism and "frigid principles." Marble is thereby left with an essential joy of fully living in the moment. It is true that this idiosyncratic synthesis of love, strength, joy, and power comes at the cost of what James Hillman (1980) terms the "lunacy" or "inflation" of the white—the concretization of his faith as a false, over-determined will that could not surrender to the pain of his son's death. Where Thoreau succumbs to apathy and despair, while also realizing a clarity of essential awareness, Marble bypasses this clarity of the alchemical blue for a mysticism of love, not of knowledge. Where Thoreau has his austere purity, Marble has his charming lunacy.

Thoreau's "black" is the black of "illuminated night" in classical mystical accounts (Corbin 1978). It is the felt embodiment of the clear dark space of his night walks. Marble's "black," on the other hand, has the dense, velvet texture of the pitch black of his tunnel after one has extinguished one's light—a local rite—or the denseness of the granite through which he dug. Almaas (1986b) makes a distinction relevant here between experiences of clear or open black space, which he finds associated with the resolution of issues related to one's private or inner sense of identity, and experiences of a dense black space, related more to an inner bodily sense of self and anxieties around death and annihilation. It makes sense then that Thoreau's encounter with essential power and its attendant dynamics around hatred centers more on his personal loneliness, narcissistic issues, and shame, whereas Marble is wrestling with the meaning of death and the core of aliveness. Marble, in one sense, goes further toward the realization of the this-worldly "philosopher's stone," as personal essence, but at the price of intellect and clarity. Meanwhile, Thoreau manifests a brilliancy and power but sacrifices heart. His luminous cold eyes in several photographs reflect his widely attested lack of personal contactfulness and engagement.

It might seem tempting to regard Thoreau's life as showing at least the approach to the reorganization of self that comes with true spirituality, and Hiram Marble as showing more of a delusional disorder. Yet Anton Boisen (1936), a protestant pastor who underwent his own psychotic breakdown, reframed this distinction between mysticism and psychosis in a way that highlights their common crisis in meaning and value. Their distinction would ultimately rest not in the original labels, but in the precarious balance between the spiritual victory vs. spiritual or moral defeat that can emerge out of either pattern:

> Certain types of mental disorder and certain types of religious experience are alike attempts at reorganization. The difference lies in the outcome. Where the attempt is successful and

some degree of victory is won, it is commonly recognized as religious experience. Where it is unsuccessful or indeterminate,
it is commonly spoken of as "insanity." In those constructive
transformations . . . the individual is relieved of his sense of
isolation and is brought into harmony with that which is
supreme in his hierarchy of loyalties. . . . effecting a synthesis
between the crisis experience and his subsequent life. . . . In
. . . "mental illness," no such synthesis is achieved. The patient
may get well but he may not solve his problem. (Boisen, *The
Exploration of the Inner World*: viii)

In these terms both Thoreau and Marble are spiritual figures, but
Marble may come closer to "relieving his sense of isolation" and
"coming into harmony with what is supreme in his hierarchy of values." If so, Marble's life is also a reminder of the depth of courage,
faith, and the real risks involved in the modern inner-worldly spiritual path. Meanwhile, Thoreau did not "solve his problem." Acknowledging the high personal price paid by both figures, my own
deeper admiration goes to the spiritualist and not the transcenden-
talist. Marble seems the more alive and fully present within his own
life, the more attuned perhaps to the expansive joy of the early
Emerson, and certainly to the passion of Kierkegaard.[4]

Emerson and Thoreau looked down on spiritualism as credulous
and plebeian. While that may be true, both William James and Jung
were at least open to the inquiry. Emerson and Thoreau missed any
opportunity to dialogue in some form with the most widespread post-
Christian spiritual movement of modern times. It was destined, as
we shall see, to segue into Blavatsky's Theosophical movement and
so introduce Eastern thought on a popular level to the West. Emerson speaks of the "many men renowned and reckoned of excellent
sense [who] tumble helplessly into mesmeric spiritualism and prove
its most credulous dupes" (Emerson *Journals*, 15: 424) and of the
"squalor" of these "cat and mouse revelations" (Emerson *Journals*, 6:
209). Thoreau visited and lectured in Lynn several times, and although Marble was by then a local legend, Thoreau's copious *Journals* make no mention of any visit. It would have been beneath him.

The possibility for any American bridging of transcendentalism
and spiritualism ended with William James, who courted serious
controversy in the new scientific psychology by finding spiritualism
worthy of empirical investigation. The rich conceptual understanding of Emerson and Thoreau, and later James, was certainly lacking
in the popular triumph of mesmeric revelations and spiritualism.

Yet, the inner-worldly spirituality of the transcendentalists, as fore-runner of transpersonal psychology, would have to be returned to the shores that invented it by visiting Eastern gurus, on the one hand (Taylor 1999), and, on the other, by the active imagination techniques of the Jungians—adapted by Jung from his own early studies of mediumistic trance (Jung 1902).

PART **IV**

Some Political Ambiguities in the Development
of Presence: Inner-Worldly Mysticism,
Metapathology, and National Socialism

CHAPTER 8

Jung, Visionary Racial Occultism, and Hitler

Carl Jung's brief flirtation in the early 1930s with National Socialist racial ideology, so similar to that of Heidegger at the same time, provides an important cautionary tale of the ways in which otherwise viable versions of a naturalistic inner-worldly mysticism can go at least temporarily wrong—based on what Almaas would call false will and power and narcissistic inflation, and what Jung himself came to see as an acting out of the shadow archetype. Spirituality fused and confused with collective political ideology is an inherent risk for all forms of *inner-worldly* religiosity, and one with generally destructive results. At the same time, one way of seeing how far Jung and Heidegger were from serious Nazi ideology, even during a time of apparent political temptation, is to examine some of the visionary occultist movements on which the Nazis based their most extreme racist doctrines. While this "mystical" or visionary wing was central to the development of Nazi thought, Hitler, who certainly was a charismatic personality, was himself in Weber's sense an example of the primitive prophet.

Self, Archetypes, and Collective Unconscious

Carl Jung (1875–1961) both offers a psychology of individual transpersonal development and was himself an important exemplar of the inner-worldly mystic, having several periods of intense visionary experience in his life, beginning in childhood, and on which he based his psychology. Jung understood what he was doing as a kind of post-Christian Nietzschean psychology, and specifically linked his early insights to Hellenistic and Gnostic imagery (Ellenberger 1970; Noll 1997). For Jung, as important as Taoism (1929) and Tibetan Buddhism (1939) were for comparison, there is a this-worldly mysticism specific to the West. Rooted in our culture and values, its renewal as a psycho-spirituality could be guided, but not replaced, by the Eastern mysticisms.

The empirical core of Jung's psychology of numinous experience was based on his technique of active imagination, which involves a deliberate absorption in ongoing imagery, balanced with an attitude of non controlling detachment—partly inspired by his early studies of the spiritualist trances undergone by his cousin (Jung 1902; Goodheart 1984). Guided by his readings in pagan and Gnostic mythology, Jung found that these images tended to cluster around successive archetypal identities, reflecting compensating forms of potential human experience not yet lived out in the person's life and very close to what Almaas terms aspects of essence. Imaginal dialogues between the ordinary self and these autonomous expressions of numinous imagery gradually expand and recenter the ego, until it approximates the totality of what Jung terms the Self. It is the Self that balances and integrates the different archetypal identities with the ego.

Depending on the context of his discussion, Jung's Self has features relevant to both essential identity and personal essence, but predominantly centered on the former. Indeed, Jung (1959) considers Buddha and Jesus as the most complete exemplars of what he means by Self, so it is identity as Being that he seems to intend. The core archetypes include the shadow, or the potentially evil and destructive side of the person, the anima/animus, or the latently opposite gender identity within men and women, and various wisdom or guidance figures. These are the inner Platonic forms of being human, which, along with their potential integration as higher Self, define the "collective unconscious." This is Jung's early notion of an unconscious deeper or higher than Freud's "personal unconscious," and his way of describing/ explaining cross cultural similarities in religious experience and mythology. Jung's process of individuation or self-actualization reflects an inner-worldly, form-based understanding of spirituality, and does not offer his Western subjects specific guidance within the formless dimensions of Plotinus and other-worldly Eastern mysticisms. The aim is more the expansion and recentering of personal identity rather than its dissolution.

Jung (1928, 1938) is more clear than some contemporary transpersonalists that archetypal experiences, whether induced or spontaneous, are immensely impactful and can develop in a positive, integrated way or in a more disintegrative, psychotic fashion. When not successfully balanced and integrated with ordinary ego identity, these states can either release a latent psychosis or appear in more contained versions as the inflations and/or withdrawals that we have discussed as "metapathologies." Jung's ambivalent response to Hitler in the mid 1930s, and his willingness at the time to link his "collective unconscious" to Nazi ideology, which he later saw as a serious mistake, reflect the inflation or grandiosity side of spiritual metapathology. We will consider this below in terms of his own unanalyzed and unassimilated narcissism.

Jung here shows the dangers for any inner-worldly movement of using symbolic forms that are related to the categories of nation or race as vehicles for the imaginal expansion of ego identity. We saw how inner-worldly mysticisms approach formlessness by means of powerfully evocative this-worldly forms that do expand consciousness beyond its usual range. For instance in contemporary UFO cults, there are specific entities beyond the terrestrial that are encountered in visionary states, and which have been interpreted by Jung (1958) and others (Ring 1989) in terms of archetypal imagination. Or, in accounts of so-called phylogenetic regression or animal identification experiences in LSD (Grof 1980) and shamanism (Winkelman 2000), as well as in psychedelic experiences of birth and fetal states, we find natural forms or categories experientially embodied so as to powerfully expand ordinary identity.

Certainly such categories are broader than how we normally experience ourselves. However, imaginal forms based on sexuality and aggression, on a personal level, and national and racial identity, on a collective level, are also potentially dangerous ways of self-expansion. They are expanded, but not expanded enough, and so lend themselves to a concrete acting out in the world. We will see this in relation to Crowley's use of sexuality, and in Jung's use of the categories of nation and especially race as layers in his collective unconscious.

From the time Jung first put forward his notion of a collective unconscious, in his 1912 *Symbols of Transformation*, wherein he declares his independence from Freud, it receives two potentially inconsistent formulations: one in terms of imagination and its creative development, and the other in terms of memory and its supposed ancestral bases. On the one hand, Jung puts forward a notion of different forms of thinking, reminiscent of more recent formulations by Gardner (1983), in which verbal, sequentially ordered thought is contrasted with a more immediate imagistic thinking. Operationally defined, active imagination fits best with this first concept, in which self-actualization is based on a self-referential inner dialoguing with imagistic states, bringing forward Platonic or archetypal patterns. It is this side of Jung that was further unfolded in his studies of alchemy (1944), and later developed by Michael Fordham (1958) and James Hillman (1975) into a cognitive theory of archetypal imagination as a metaphor-based embodiment of the basic forms of physical nature. On the other hand, Jung, under the influence of the subsequently refuted Lamarckian view of evolution, also understood these archetypes as the traces of an ancestral or evolutionary layer of a collective, in some sense inherited, psyche. Here we have a "memory," or "evolutionary memory" model in contrast to an "imagination" one.[1] It is this view that has been developed by the contemporary Jungian Anthony Stevens (1982) and explicitly based on MacLean's questionable triune model of the human brain as containing mammalian and reptilian layers (see Hunt 1995a). Jung first derived his ancestral memory account from Nietzsche's early *Human, All Too Human*, and by the early 1900s it had become part of popular imagination and a staple in the novels of Jack London.

Logically, however, if ancestral levels of mind are to include cross-culturally common forms from human evolution, and earlier phylogenesis, they could also include more superficial layers specific to racial and even national ancestry. Accordingly, psychologies of human development will need to be specific to these groups:

> Thus it is a quite unpardonable mistake to accept the conclusion of a Jewish psychology [i.e. Freud's psychoanalysis] as generally valid. Nobody would dream of taking Chinese or Indian psychology as binding on ourselves. The cheap accusation of anti-Semitism that has been leveled at me on the ground of this criticism is about as intelligent as accusing me of anti-Chinese prejudice. No doubt, on an earlier and deeper level of psychic development, where it is still impossible to distinguish between an Aryan, Semitic, Hamitic, or Mongolian mentality, all human races have a common collective psyche. But with the beginning of racial differentiation essential differences are developed in the collective psyche as well. (Jung, *Two Essays on Analytical Psychology*: 152)

It becomes obvious how such passages could be used by a Nazi ideology of racial inferiorities and superiorities. Unfortunately, for several years Jung proved willing to play that hand himself, or at least acquiesce in his theory being so used.

Carl Jung's Dance with the Devil

Jung claimed at the time (1934), and later (1946), that what he was principally trying to do in the 1930s was to protect his Jewish therapist colleagues in Germany, after Hitler had banned all forms of psychoanalysis and specifically banned Jews from any memberships in German professional organizations, starting in 1933. Kretschmer, the well-known psychologist of body types, had resigned the presidency of the General Medical Society for Psychotherapy, protesting Hitler's decrees banning Jewish memberships—the same thing also happening to university professors at the time. The Swiss Jung agreed to take on a new international presidency and the editorship of the journal, the *Zentralblatt für Psychotherapie*, on the condition that the Jewish therapists in Germany could be members in the new international section. Of course, the organization and the journal were still largely controlled by the Nazis. The new president of the German society and later coeditor of the journal through the 1930s was Matthias Göering, psychiatrist cousin of Herman.

Although Jung did what he said he would in including the disenfranchised Jewish members, and in fact privately assisting several therapists in emigration (Maidenbaum and Martin 1991), the Freudian psychoanalysts, predominantly Jewish, soon came to feel that Jung was actually exercising vengeance against Freud in a move for power that was explicitly and blatantly anti-Semitic. Nor, in terms of the increasingly virulent racist politics of the day, can they be blamed, especially given Jung's first editorial as journal editor, which he remained until 1939:

> The differences which actually do exist between Germanic and Jewish psychology and which have long been known to every intelligent person are no longer to be glossed over, and this can only be beneficial to science. (Jung, Editorial: 533)

While he explicitly states that such differences imply nothing about superiority or inferiority, the timing, along with his next response, after being publicly attacked by the analysts, was hardly reassuring:

> The Jewish problem is a regular complex, a festering wound, and no responsible doctor could bring himself to apply methods of medical hush-hush in this matter. (Jung, A rejoinder to Dr. Bally: 539)

The best-case scenario here would be that Jung was remarkably obtuse politically, which was certainly true (Stern 1976). The obtuseness is also surprising because he had a number of close Jewish colleagues and followers in Germany who were writing him out of personal concern and giving him the frightening details of their daily lives—although admittedly prior to the publically sanctioned physical violence of the later 1930s. Yet in the face of this knowledge we have the following remarkable passage, from a 1934 article in the *Zentralblatt*. After the war, Jung did acknowledge this to be "embarrassing nonsense":

> The Jews have this peculiarity in common with women; being physically weaker, they have to aim at the chinks and the armor of their adversary, and thanks to this technique which has been forced on them through the centuries, the Jews themselves are best protected where others are most vulnerable. Because, again, of their civilization more than twice as ancient as ours, they are vastly more conscious than we of human weaknesses, of the shadow-side of things, and hence in this respect much less vulnerable than we are. . . . The "Aryan" unconscious, on the other hand, contains explosive forces and seeds of a future yet to be born. . . . The still youthful Germanic peoples are fully capable of creating new cultural forms that still lie dormant in the darkness of the unconscious of every individual—seeds bursting with energy and capable of mighty expansion. The Jew, who is something of a nomad, has never yet created a cultural form of his own and as far as we can see never will, since all his instincts and talents require a more or less civilized nation to act as host for their development. (Jung, The state of psychotherapy today: 165–66)

Of course many Germans at this time, who later thought better of it, still believed that Hitler's cultural renewal had just such a potential, but the language of "nomads" and "host," with its parasitical implications, was the precise language of the Nazi ideologues—surely kerosene on the fire, even accepting Jung's continuing protestations that he was not in the least personally anti-Semitic.

Jung, however, as one would expect from someone of his training who found himself in the grip of what he would term a "power complex" or "inflation," was showing a growing ambivalence—privately and in print. He was becoming aware of a Faustian element in his own fascination with Hitler. In May, 1933 Jung attended the Berlin Congress on Psychology and, while praising the contributions of Freud in his talk, also praised Hitler in a Radio Berlin interview, where he described Jewish psychology as "hostile to life," and extolled "the blood and exclusiveness of the race."

Afterwards he received an invitation to visit Goebbels, the infamous propaganda minister, and they have the following conversation, as reported an hour later by Jung to his Jewish follower James Kirsch over lunch:

> GOEBBELS: "You wanted to see me, Dr. Jung."
> JUNG: "No, you wanted to see me."
> GOEBBELS: No, you wanted to see me."
>
> (Kirsch, Carl Gustav Jung and the Jews: 77)

At which point Jung turns, walks out of the room, and vomits. Now Goethe's *Faust* was almost a cultural bible for German speaking peoples, so both Jung *and* Goebbels would be well aware that their situation was the familiar meeting of the learned professor and Mephistopheles. Jung certainly knew this or else he would not have left abruptly and thrown up. The role of Goebbels is similarly clear. It is as if he were saying: "You've been saying some interesting things on the radio, Dr. Jung, that we very much like. What would *you* like. What can we do for *you*? Perhaps a much larger format and audience??" Jung sees the temptation and rejects it, telling it as a humorous story to his Jewish friend. And it *is* a powerful little story.

By 1936, and his first published essay explicitly on National Socialism, although not appearing in the *Zentrablatt*, he has become more obviously critical. He now states that National Socialism is a revival of the archetype of Wotan, the Dionysian Germanic god of storm and frenzy, and also of magic and art. Which side will predominate is not clear to him, but he is now clear for the first time that the German people are more its victims than its agents:

> The impressive thing about the German phenomenon is that one man, who is obviously "possessed," has infected a whole nation to such an extent that everything is set in motion and has started rolling on its course towards perdition. (Jung, Wotan: 185)

Jung then cites the dangers of inflation and disintegration on a societal level when collective archetypal energies cannot be assimilated in a balanced way. Yet he remained co-editor of the *Zentralblatt*, a journal also publishing all of the crackpot skull measurement and pseudo biology of racial features of Nazi Aryan theory. Jung's name stays on the masthead of what is becoming in large part a Nazi rag until 1939. Then, in his post-war writings, he continues the critical social analysis of the Wotan essay. National Socialism is now a "mass psychosis," but he avoids any discussion of his more ambiguous personal flirtations from 1933 and 1934. In private, when challenged by a former Jewish friend, he says " I slipped up" (literally "I lost my footing") (Jaffe 1971).

What to conclude? From the careful assessments of the Jungian Andrew Samuels (1992) and the collection of papers by Jungian analysts in Maidenbaum and Martin (1991), certain points do stand out. In fact, it does not seem that Jung was personally anti-Semitic. Freud's published hint to this effect in 1914 was unfair, since most creative students break, often painfully, with their mentors, and Jung was personally stung by the accusation. After all, for a Protestant pastor's son, from rural Switzerland, to apprentice himself in 1907 to Sigmund Freud, the urban Viennese Jew, is not the act of somebody who is racist or bigoted. What Jung did was rare for the time and place, and Freud knew it, as surely as Husserl knew it of Heidegger. Later, Jung had many Jewish followers and friends whom he did not lose as a result of the events of the 1930s. Jung did try to protect the Jewish therapists in Germany although with very limited success, since being a member of an international society, when forbidden to practice in your own country, is at best symbolic. He also helped many Jewish refugees in Switzerland, and there is the curious story of Jung offering, through an intermediary, a large sum of money to Freud in 1938 as a bribe to secure the latter's emigration from Nazi-controlled Austria. Freud angrily declined it (Ellenberger 1970).

Certainly Jung was politically obtuse and naive. Even the more sympathetic among contemporary Jungians speak here of his undeveloped feeling function, by which they mean his extreme egocentricity and lack of empathy in a time of calamity, and which extended to some with whom he had been in intimate contact (Maidenbaum and Martin 1991). This is only fully intelligible if we add in Jung's own failure to understand and assimilate his own shadow— his own split-off hatred. Blind to the underlying dynamics of his relations with Freud, and provided with the opportunity, Jung became a political opportunist. He saw the opportunity for exercising a predominant cultural influence and took it. Freud had once said, in an exchange of letters with Jung, that whoever controlled German psychotherapy controlled the future of psychotherapy generally. Samuels (1992) concludes that the opportunity of controlling European medical psychotherapy was just too big an advantage over the Freudians to throw away, especially if it could be rationalized as a rescuing on a more personal level. Jung himself would have to characterize this as a grandiosity and inflation, towards which he had a certain leaning anyway. Almaas might understand it in terms of a false power of dominance and a false will of control—based ultimately on a deep lack of inner support and trust extending back into early childhood.

Narcissistic Vulnerability in Jung's Development

Characterological narcissism can appear not only as a meta-pathological byproduct of the impact of essential states, but also as a major blockage to the realization of essential identity and personal essence. Narcissistic issues run all through Jung's life, and it is striking how much Jung's preoccupation with the archetypal significance of his childhood and adult visions kept him from also considering the personal dynamic conflicts they also enshrined (Hunt 1992)—and this despite his formal statements that psychodynamic issues from childhood must be clarified and assimilated for self-realization to proceed in a balanced way. Kohut (1977, 1984) found that narcissistic clients are especially unable to tolerate interpretations in terms of oedipal and interpersonal dynamics. Their sense of self is so vulnerable and easily disrupted that all talk of their jealousies, guilts, and griefs are experienced so much as an insult or a wound that they often cannot stand to remain in traditional psychotherapy. For Kohut, before including such more standard interpretations, a great deal of empathic work must be done to strengthen and expand the core sense of self—allowing, in Winnicott's sense, a growing capacity for feeling real and present in one's immediate situation. It seems relevant then that the core of classical Jungian therapy concentrated on the expansion of ordinary ego into Self.

D.W. Winnicott (1964) understood the childhood reminiscence chapters of Jung's autobiography *Memories, Dreams, Reflections* as showing the dilemmas of the split self—with its struggles between the sense of a hidden true self and an outer protective false self. The marks of this central vulnerability in sense of self are the absence of a sense of Being, or feeling real, often manifested in a search for a sense of meaning in life, and a painful loneliness and inner isolation.

Kohut also adds a lack of empathy, often coexisting with an intuitive hypersensitivity to the inner states of others. From the perspective of contemporary personality research, we could say that Winnicott is describing the traumatized, dissociative side of the more general personality dimension of absorption/openness to experience (Hunt 2000). Jung's own portrayal of himself touches on many of these themes, positive and negative:

> As a child I felt myself to be alone, and I am still, because I know things and must hint at things which others apparently know nothing of, and for the most part do not want to know. Loneliness does not come from having no people about one, but from being unable to communicate the things that seem important to oneself. . . . The loneliness began with the experiences of my early dreams, and reached its climax at the time I was working on the unconscious. . . . It is important to have a secret, a premonition of things unknown. It fills life with something impersonal, a numinosum. . . . For me the world has from the beginning been infinite and ungraspable. . . . I had to learn painfully that people continued to exist even when they had nothing more to say to me. . . . I was able to become intensely interested in many people; but as soon as I had seen through them, the magic was gone. In this way I made many enemies. . . . The world into which we are born is brutal and cruel, and at the same time of divine beauty. Which element we think outweighs the other, whether meaninglessness or meaning, is a matter of temperament. . . . Life is—or has—meaning and meaninglessness. I cherish the anxious hope that meaning will preponderate and win the battle. (Jung, *Memories, Dreams, Reflections*: 356–59)

So much has been written on Jung's life and its relation to the development of his theory, from inside and outside Jungian circles (Hayman 2001; Hannah 1976; Stern 1976; Ellenberger 1970), that we will concentrate here more on overall patterns than specific detail. The sections of *Memories, Dreams, Reflections* that Jung, as an old man, wrote entirely by himself, describe the really quite extraordinary visionary experiences he experienced during his troubled childhood, marked by marital strife between his parents. These experiences, along with his cultivation of intense archetypal imagery after his split from Freud, and during which he feared psychosis, formed the basis of his later psychology of spiritual individuation. It is fascinating that in his accounts of his childhood dreams and visions, he does not connect them to the familial and interpersonal dynamics occurring at the same time, even when the circumstances are fairly blatant. He does tell us that his mother was severely depressed and absent from the home, and probably hospitalized, several times during his early childhood. For Winnicott, the stony visage of a depressed mother leads to a situation of insufficient mirroring, and a tendency in the child towards withdrawal to protect a sense of an inner, but hidden, alive self. So we find Jung as a child spending much time alone in nature, and developing within the same isolated personal enclave as Nietzsche. Again, there is the feckless but kindly Protestant pastor father, and the intensely devoted but periodically cold and detached mother, whom he often found uncaring and frightening.

Of course, we would not expect Jung to engage in psychodynamic reductionism with the beginnings of his own essential states, out of which he later created the first naturalistic psychology of spiritual development—as for instance Erich Fromm (1963) would do in an early mean-spirited review of *Memories, Dreams, Reflections* or as Winnicott (1964) himself at times approaches. Yet Jung, who discusses both regressive and constructive interpretations of client dreams, will have none of it with his own experiences, which had after all offered him his only support for his secretly unfolding inner self. Thus, his early dream vision at age three, of a huge phallus on a throne in an underground chamber, is never connected to the possibility of any reactive or precocious sexualization in the wake of the tension within his parents' tortured marriage—but treated exclusively as the unifying intuition of a god-image. Then there is the episode from his later childhood where he secretly places a mannikin in a box, along with certain "special" stones and hieroglyphic signs, and hides it. For Jung, this is a harbinger of the archetypal Self of later individuation. We have to read between the lines to realize that it might *also* have something to do with the concomitant birth of an unwelcome sister for this hitherto only child, who had not consciously noticed any change in his mother's body and so felt betrayed and distrustful of her after the birth.

In adulthood there is much indication that this gifted therapist and spiritual guide, who could in brief one-time consultations offer uncannily intuitive interpretations to clients that would occupy them for years, was nonetheless curiously insensitive to his impact on others and lacking in genuine empathy in more ordinary social contexts. His astonishing obtuseness to the actual effects of his pronouncements about an Aryan and Jewish unconscious in the 1930s is actually part of a long series of analogous situations. There is his embarrassingly self-serving letter to the mother of Sabrina Spielrein, after she had become upset, reasonably enough, about the acted-out eroticism of her daughter's involvement with Jung, in what may be the first recorded symbiotic transference-countertransference. It was all new territory for deep therapy, of course, but Jung's letter is widely seen as a self-righteous special pleading (Kerr 1993). Then there is his insistence that his later paramour-anima Antonia Wolff attend Sunday lunches with his wife and children, to the embarrassment of everyone except Jung himself (Stern 1976).

My personal favorite, however, is Jung's puzzled complaint in *Memories, Dreams, Reflections* that he was apparently not trusted by his new psychiatrist colleagues after he arrived at Burgholzi to work with the famed Bleuler, while he later tells us he had at the same time begun a secret study of the family genealogies of these same colleagues for evidence of schizophrenia. It seems not to have occurred to Jung that they might not even need an uncanny intuition of the kind that he did possess, and use to good effect, in order to feel legitimately uncomfortable around Jung.

Although Jungian individuation emphasizes the assimilation of the shadow, and this is far more developed and explicit in Jung's own life than for Nietzsche or Thoreau, there is still much evidence, certainly including his destructive grandiosity over National Socialism, of an unmetabolized and dissociated hatred. For Almaas this becomes a blockage to the peace and inner silence of the black aspect of essential power, and it is part of Fairbairn's view of the schizoid dilemma. The driven and passionate Jung only came to such a contentment partially and later in his life—beginning after a major heart attack in 1944, wherein he speaks of the importance of life finally "busting" one and the release that brings. Yet as an old man there are still huge rages, for Kohut a major sign of remaining narcissistic vulnerability, often over pencils left in the wrong spot on his desk (Jaffe 1971).

Most telling here is his life long fascination with stone and its progressive alchemical animation as true self, and which he does *not* link to his frequently cold and stonily withdrawn mother. In childhood there is his favorite stone. He would go out into the woods and sit on this large stone and enter into an absorbed state in which he no longer knew whether he was the child Jung sitting on the stone or he was the stone being sat on. Later there are powerful archetypal dreams of knights in armour. Then in 1923, beginning in the months after his mother's death, he begins construction of a stone tower to which he retreats for periods of contemplation and to be with his various mirroring anima women over the next years. Here he also does his own intriguing carvings in stone, representing specific visionary experiences. For Winnicott, the child with the stony, cold mother will not easily own its own responsive hatred. Instead it becomes a detached part of one's soul.

Outwardly Jung was energetic and expansive, but many became aware of an inner, more withdrawn self, and we can see over the course of Jung's realization a progressive coming to life—an animation of the unyielding stone. Thus, in his tower, he literally lives inside the maternal stone, and comes to a secret aliveness inside it. He expanded the tower periodically in response to inner developments and finished it in the months after his wife's death. Meanwhile, over the last twenty years of his life he had shifted his major interest to Renaissance alchemy, with its own animation of leaden stone into the red and gold of the Gnostic Anthropos (Jung 1944, 1955). Alchemy, with its physical processes of firing, dissolving, and sublimation as the outer metaphors of an inner self-realization, was the most precise historical parallel and precursor to Jung's active imagination. Of course, Jung links this spiritualization of matter, his proto-cognitive theory of metaphor, to the archetypal feminine Mater as the ultimate support or ground of self awareness—but never to his own mother.

From the perspective of Almaas we find in Jung's own life a huge expansiveness of essential strength (the alchemical red) and a capacity for a Dionysian joy (the alchemical yellow and gold of the this-worldly Self of the philosopher's stone). His late-life detachment and acceptance, along with his fascination with synchronicity as the meaningful coincidence of inner archetypal experience with external "extrasensory" events, suggest a growing manifestation of essential will. Unassimilated issues of shadow, as a largely dissociated hatred, keep him from the repose and peace of essential power. Jung remains largely impersonal, and without the genuine empathy and contactfulness of personal essence. Not surprisingly, his life and system reflect issues both leading to and distorting the development of essential identity—Jung's Self. Jung's practice is one of the mutual balancing and modification of ego and Self, and in this it is also the first naturalistic psychology of inner-worldly spirituality. The major barrier to the realization of Self in Jung's own life remained his struggles with a metapathology of

grandiosity, shown in his brief fascination with Hitler and National Socialism and in the narcissistic inflations appearing in the
wake of his major periods of archetypal visions (Noll 1997). After
all, if these developments were easy, we would have more evidence
than we do of their increase and widespread attainment. In this regard, however, Jung does finally show a fuller essential realization
in his personal life than Nietzsche, Thoreau, or Maslow, and even
more obviously, Crowley.

From "Collective Unconscious" to "Objective Psyche": Jung's Shift from Pseudo-Biology to a Cognition of Metaphor

Some of Jung's lack of insight into the political implications of
his concept of collective unconscious, as a racial or ancestral psyche,
came from its similarity to a widely popular Germanic *Volkische* romanticism, which was equally prominent in liberal and conservative
political ideologies (Sluga 1993). It was the conservative form that
came to have the racist implications of Fascism. The earlier German
romanticisms of Schelling, Goethe, and Hölderlin, for instance, were
themselves approaches to an inner-worldly mysticism, broadly understood. There was a rebellion against industrialization, the notion
of a return to origins, and a longing for lost roots in the land—in
short the same re-enchantment sought by Blake in England. A major
divide enters, however, in how these roots and origins are understood. The land of a lost rural life can be understood, with Emerson,
Thoreau, and the later Jung, in terms of a physical nature—of woods
and fields and their animal inhabitants—or in terms of a return to
the settings and values of village life, the German *Heimat*, much as
in Quebec separatism today.

Understanding "origins" as felt resonance to the patterns of
physical nature or as village ways of the ancestors could run together, but their implications were potentially quite distinct. After
all, most of the Concord villagers found Thoreau's self-reflective use
of the woods and night quite strange. The *Volkische* utopian movements that were especially prominent in Germany, owing to the dis-
locations of its later and rapid industrialization, were centered more
on a longing for the revival of a rural "Volk," as a lost Golden Age of
national and racial identity. People so drawn dress up in traditional
garb and dance at festivals, they do not go alone to experience nature. The widespread popularity of Wagner's operas, which Nietzsche came so to abhor, were a significant part of this political pan

Germanism—so different from the pantheistic nature mysticism of Schelling or the later Heidegger.

Volkische pan Germanism did also become associated with a romanticization of the old Teutons of pagan Europe, of the shamanic roots of the Aryan peoples, supposedly best preserved in the Eddas, the Icelandic sagas of the ancient Norse (Goodrick-Clarke 1985). The result was a neopaganism, with different cults and movements developing from the late 1800s, integrating in various measures, sun and nature worship, vegetarianism, sexual liberation, hiking, and drugs—all practices of the "wild men" with beards to their knees camping in the mountains around Ascona, Switzerland. Noll (1994) refers to these as Nietzschean cults, and places Jung and his closest followers in the 1920s as their culmination.[2] However, there were already obvious differences between those whose paganism was classical and Hellenistic and those, to be discussed below, who sought a specifically racial and national purity, and a spiritual renewal, by "channeling" ancient Aryan spirits.

Jung's *Symbols of Transformation*, in the cultural context of 1912, would have been widely understood as a visionary solar mythology, recast in the language of a naturalistic psychology of symbolism (Noll 1997). At this stage he was presenting a pagan psychology consistent with these sun-worshiping cults, the divine hero doing battle with the negative monstrous mother. So it is interesting that Jung's first conceptual framework was not primarily or exclusively "racial." Rather, he invokes what was called at the time "landscape mysticism," after C.G. Carus, who put forward the view that the basic psychological differences between peoples are the result of their identifications with their surrounding geography. After his 1930s debacle, Jung would return to a more cognitively sophisticated version of this model, with basic dynamics from the natural environment—as reflected also in alchemy—providing metaphors and mirrors for normally unconscious levels and potentials of the Self.

Jung's initial way of viewing how the land creates the collective psychologies of peoples, from essays in 1927 and 1918, was more mysterious, with some now strange pseudo-biological overtones. The wilds of the primeval forests of North America would create not only an Indian-like identity in us, but even a corresponding physique—the collective psyche speaking through us in the language of the land:

> Certain Australian primitives assert that one cannot conquer foreign soil, because in it there dwell strange ancestor-spirits who reincarnate themselves in the newborn. There is

a great psychological truth in this. The foreign land assimilates its conqueror. (Jung, Mind and earth: 49)

The mystery of the earth is no joke and no paradox. One only
needs to see how, in America, the skull and pelvis measure-
ments of all the European races begin to Indianize themselves
in the second generation of immigrants. That is the mystery of
the American earth. (Jung, The role of the unconscious: 13)

In the 1930s Jung was tempted by the more prophetical and political
language of a racial and ancestral layer of his collective unconscious,
rather than the more mystical and cognitive language of nature and
land to describe the same layers of the psyche. The point being that
the *volkische* mentality so significant to the early Jung was far
broader, however still falsely biologized, than the racial occultism
that would directly feed into Nazism.

Jung's later solution, similar to that of Heidegger at the same
time, was to understand the source of an archetypal collective psyche,
to be recontacted as spiritual realization, as an evocation of physical
metaphors from nature, very much like Emerson and Giambattista
Vico before him. In part because of what had become the "racial" connotations of his "collective unconscious," Jung often replaces the term
with "objective psyche," by which he means to describe subjective
states so phenomenologically powerful that they are felt as "objective."
It is the level of psyche central to creative imagination and is reflected
from the patterns of nature as metaphor. Since these patterns have a
level that is universal, they explain the cross-cultural parallels of
myth and mysticism on quite different grounds than Jung's "collective
unconscious" of the 1920s and 30s. Now we have a purely cognitive
psychological understanding of those similarities, widely missed in
textbook treatments of Jung, not in terms of ancestral memories, but
by means of a creative imagination that engages nature as mirror and
therefore produces highly similar states. This is the form of Jung's
thought developed by Hillman (1975) and Fordham (1958). It also fits
well with the nature metaphors that structure what Laski terms the
quasi-physical aspects of ecstasy—light, darkness, flow, and fire.

Anthony Stevens (1982), on the other hand, has continued to
look for an ancestral unconscious in terms of phylogenesis, bypass-
ing race and going down to specifically mammalian and reptilian
levels of the brain to explain certain visionary states involving animal identification experiences. The virtue of Hillman's more cognitive "imaginal psychology" here is that it can also interpret these

experiences as themselves felt or embodied metaphors. If a subject under LSD or a shaman in trance becomes hallucinatorily a crocodile, that is not necessarily because of any activation of a reptilian level of the brain stem. A more psychological and parsimonious way of interpreting such states is to say that the crocodile/reptilian pattern is being used by creative metaphoric imagination as the best mirror for the mixture of egoic and essential aspects being developed (Hunt 1989, 1995a).

What initiated this change away from biologized "memory" and towards creative imagination is Jung's insight that the elaborate operations and transforming substances of the alchemists offered the most precise metaphorical system for the process of spiritual individuation he had been trying to describe all along. In Hillman's (1978, 1980, 1989, 1993) hands this becomes a physiognomy of archetypal dimensions in terms of the qualities of the metaphoric black, white, blue, yellow, and red, which parallel Almaas's dimensions of essence (see chapter 2, note 2).

This shift to a cognitive psychology of archetypal experience as embodied natural metaphor is foreshadowed in the impact of nature on Jung as a child. Jung's (1961) own earliest life memory was of a nature-based ecstatic experience, while he was in his pram—a feeling of "indescribable well being" while watching the sun glittering through leaves. There are of course two sides to this unusual first memory, which might more commonly have had an interpersonal content. His other early memory is of the sensory qualities of the taste and smell of milk and bread, similarly consistent, as Feldman (1992) points out, with the tendency of infants who are not succinctly mirrored and held to use sensory qualities of the physical environment as an alternative maternal support. At the same time, what we also see in Jung's first memories of the beauties of nature is his perhaps compensatory, but nonetheless obvious, cognitive precocity within a developmental line of metaphoric-aesthetic sensitivity which would become the core of his later theory of spirituality.

Aryan Racial Occultism: Why Jung is not a Nazi

One of the best ways to see how far Jung and Heidegger were from Nazi ideology—even at their most grandiose and opportunistic— is to consider the utterly bizarre visionary movements of racial occultism from which Hitler, Himmler, and Rosenberg drew their key ideas on race and ancestry (Levenda 2002; Goodrick-Clarke 1985).

These cults of Ariosophy—the philosophy of the Aryans—have the surreal, paranoid, and hyperliteralized qualities of some of the more extreme Gnostics. Indeed both movements were inner-worldly mystical
responses, in alienated visionaries, to the social and cultural disloca-
tions of their respective eras. So there *was* actually a Nazi mysticism,
but it bears no relation to Jung. It was instead a virulent, ultra right-
wing, distorted funhouse-mirror version of the more liberal New Age
spirituality of our own times.

Guido von List (1848–1919) and Lanz von Liebenfels (born in
1874 and through some perversity of history, not dying until 1954)
were the key inventors of these syncretic visionary cults, fusing
Volkische pan Germanic nationalism, Aryan racism and virulent anti-
Semitism, and the occult belief, popularized by Madame Blavatsky's
Theosophy (chapter 12), in Atlantis—here understood as the original
homeland of the racially pure Aryans. Since all races prior to the At-
lantan Aryans were partly animal, who destroyed the *übermenschen*
Atlantans by interbreeding, the future task of mankind would be to
reassert the purity of Aryan (German) rule, in order to reconstruct
the ancestral Golden Age through eugenic reform and genocide
(Goodrick-Clarke 1985; Webb 1976).

Von List's many books were hugely influential in the revival of
Wotanism and sun worship as the original Germanic religion—an
Ur-shamanism disrupted first by Rome then by Christianity. List
produced utterly idiosyncratic translations of the runic writings of
the Eddas, a pseudoscience of runic letters and ancient Teutonic
emblems that he claimed to be the original language of the Aryans.
He introduced the swastika as the emblem of the many List societies spread over Germany and Austria by 1908, with tens of thousands of members—essentially a Germanic Ku Klux Klan. These,
and related groups, proliferated even further in right-wing circles
with the economic and social disasters after World War I. In fact,
the Thule Society, which stockpiled weapons and trained political
assassins and, in 1919, put all its resources and funds at Hitler's
disposal, was the political wing of the *Germanenorden*, a later
descendent of List societies.

All these societies were modeled on the earlier esoteric traditions
of the Freemasons and Rosicrucians, with secret rituals and grades of
development moving up the hierarchy of ancient priest kings toward
the status of Aryan god-man. Von List called for a pan German empire of a master race dominating inferior slave races. There would be
laws for racial purity, with each family responsible for establishing
the purity of its own blood line. This later became direct Nazi policy.

List's other speciality, having added the "von" to make himself more aristocratic, was what he called archeological occultism. He would go to pagan sites and ruined German castles and trance-channel their Aryan prehistories, with fellow clairvoyants then confirming his findings—creating a metaphysics of hatred and revenge to contrast with the romantic pirate mysticism of Hiram Marble. Astonishingly enough, before his death List predicted 1932, the year of Hitler's election, as the time when the divine forces of the ancient Aryan gods would descend and re-possess German consciousness.

Lanz von Liebenfels, who similarly added the "von Liebenfels" to his original name of Lanz to render himself more aristocratic, built upon the visions of List. Although he also wrote numerous books, it was his magazine *Ostara* that was read by Hitler, who thereby got essentially the comic-book version of these intricate groups. The story goes that during his impoverished period in Vienna, when he turned to anti-Semitism after his second rejection for architectural studies, Hitler visited Lanz's apartment in search of the two issues missing from his collection, which he received for free (Waite 1993). It was, however, Himmler, Rosenberg, and Hess, the true Nazi occultists, who read deeply in List, Lanz, and others, and incorporated their racist pseudo-biologies and prescriptions for slavery and genocide.

In his more extensive writings, Lanz was attempting the visionary reconstruction of the prehistory of the Aryan race. His trances taught him of the primeval struggle between the god-like Aryans and the submen, or *untermenschen*, also termed "apelings," sent to subvert Aryan racial purity by a lower evil force—once again a Gnostic dualism of sorts. Before this fatal interbreeding the Aryan god-men had natural capacities of telepathy, clairvoyance, and omniscience—in short, an approximation to the Gnostic Anthropos. They were seduced by "love pygmies"—beings of immense sexual perversion, gifted in the arts of sensuality and seduction. The only way to reverse the resulting creation of the inferior human races would be enforced sterilization, castration, and "brood mothers" served by pure-blooded Aryan stud males, with inferior races to be enslaved, or else incinerated as sacrifices to the Aryan gods—the direct source of Himmler's later advocacy of polygamy for S.S. officers and racial genocide.

Lanz felt he had located archeological depictions in Assyrian base-reliefs of these "love pygmies" being led as tribute to Ashurnasirpal II. It is perhaps a failure of contemporary imagination that to present eyes these look very much like roughly rendered representations of ordinary monkeys by artists to whom they would be relatively unfamiliar. Were it not for the horrific effects of these bizarre visions, Lanz would deserve our grudging respect for the title alone of his 1905 masterwork: *Theozoology: The Lure of the Sodom-Apelings and the Electron of the Gods*. X-rays had only recently been discovered, and Lanz's trance-channeled imagery showed him how the pineal glands of the ancient Aryans had emitted N-rays which gave them their praeternatural cognitive powers. Thousands of members in multiple cults, including Lanz's Ordo Novi Templi (the new crusade), believed and shared in this sort of thing in the years leading up to Hitler. (We will see later, Aleister Crowley's connection to these groups.)

Other German spiritualists and occultists added in the facial and bodily racial diagnostics of Houston Chamberlain (1855–1927), along with astrology, the Templars, the Grail, and even the Kabbalah— very much as captured in the Spielberg movies. Friedrich Marby (1882–1966) transformed runic designs into Aryan yoga postures and even invented a rune yodeling as the Aryan mantras needed to channel ancient energies. We can laugh now—but tragically not enough people did then. Ironically, most of these prominent occultists were exiled, jailed, or otherwise silenced after Hitler came to power, since he feared these associations would hurt him with the lower-middle and working classes, who were the key to the popular appeal of National Socialism. As we will see, Hitler's version of National Socialism was very much an inner-worldly prophetical movement, and he himself had little real interest in its occult, inner-worldly mystical wing, with its experiential appeal to marginalized intellectuals like Himmler, Hess, and Rosenberg.

The major exception to this relative suppression of the racial occultists was Karl Maria Wiligut (1866–1946), a German hero of World War I, S.S. officer, and genuine aristocrat, who was protected for a time as Himmler's personal mentor and friend (Goodrick-Clarke 1985). Wiligut's visions had shown him to be the last descendant of ancient German sages and he was able to reactivate within himself clairvoyant ancestral memories dating back to 228,000 B.C.—when there were three suns in the sky and the earth was populated by giants, dwarfs, and Aryan god-men. In other words, this is Jungian active imagination done by really disturbed people, the very definition of narcissistic grandiosity leading to the false strength, will, and power of a Nazi spirituality. Wiligut, with his office next to Himmler's, was head of the S.S. "Prehistorical Research Division," which sent out teams to trance-channel ancient Teutonic and Norse ruins. Aside from designing the death's head ring for the S.S., his chief duties were talking to Himmler and committing his ancestral memories to paper. He developed elaborate S.S. rituals, which Himmler envisioned as the core of a new occult religion after the war, and drew up plans for a monumental pagan S.S. vatican. Wiligut fell victim to his bureaucratic enemies, who unearthed documents showing that he had been hospitalized for schizophrenia in the mid-1920s, forcing his resignation. Himmler protected him for the duration of the war and in a rare gesture of sentimentality, kept Wiligut's S.S. ring and dagger in a box in his office.

Hitler as Charismatic Prophet

Despite the role of these visionary inner-worldly mysticisms in Nazi ideology, Hitler himself is more clearly an auditory, "ethical" prophet in Weber's sense, a point also made by Redlich (1998). Hitler's charismatic speeches portrayed a future utopia for a morally purified race, and induced falsely literalized and concretized states of strength, will, and power. Hitler inspired primarily with a message pertaining to values and conduct. His Nazism was, after all, about social action. His well-attested public raptures, and those of his followers, were always through "the word." Apart from the states of rapture, false expansion, and domination that he entered during the frenzied later parts of his speeches, and the leftovers of an earlier aesthetic-architectural fascination he shared with Albert Speer, his inner states were predominantly blank, bored, and empty (Sereny 1995; Waite 1993). Hitler well understood that National Socialism was itself a religious movement—in Weber's terms, of "radical salvation"—and he repeatedly compared himself to Jesus Christ. As early as 1923, one of his close followers complains, "Something has gone completely wrong with Adolph, with that damned whip of his, shouting "I must enter Berlin like Christ in the temple!" (Bromberg and Small 1983:167).

Hitler's earliest adolescent enthusiasms were of course aesthetic, but even in the descriptions of Kubizek, his close and only friend in Vienna when they were studying art, his preoccupations are prophetical not mystical, and his ecstasies come always while speaking—Hitler holding forth to trees if Kubizek was not available. After one Wagner opera, Kubizek observes:

> It was as if another being spoke out of his body, and moved him as much as it did me. . . . I felt as though he himself listened with astonishment and emotion to what burst forth from him with elementary force . . . it was a state of complete

ecstasy and rapture. . . . He saw himself . . . as the Messiah of his people. He spoke of a mandate, which, one day, he would receive from the people to lead them out of servitude to the heights of freedom. . . . He spoke of a special mission which one day would be entrusted to him. (Waite, *The Psychopathic God*: 178).

And this at seventeen.

At thirteen Hitler had been relieved at the death of his hated and genuinely brutal father. At least he no longer had to run away from home to escape. His mother's Jewish doctor later said he had never seen such a close relation between mother and son, their intense mirror connection perhaps further intensified by the incestuous quality already present in the father marrying his own niece. Klara supported Hitler in his aesthetic and architectural studies, emotionally and financially, until her death of debilitating cancer when he was eighteen. It was at this point that Kubizck saw the earlier ecstasies transformed by rage and hatred. His newly virulent anti-Semitism has been variously ascribed in the literature to the ethnicity of the mother's doctor, the possibility that the father had secretly converted from Judaism, or his rejection for advanced artistic studies ("For this the Jews will pay"), combined with his readings in *Ostara*.

His practice speeches to Kubizck were now infused with a new hardness and hatred, the earlier expansive joy largely gone:

> I had the impression that Adolf had become unbalanced. He would fly into a temper at the slightest thing. . . . He was at odds with the world. Wherever he looked he saw injustice, hate, and enmity. . . . Choking with his catalogue of hates he would pour his fury over everything. . . . (Waite, *The Psychopathic God*: 190)

Driven by an intolerable sense of shame, he gave up his unrequited secret love for a romantically idealized young woman, ceased all contact with his only friend, and disappeared into the slums of Vienna, living a hate-filled and embittered poverty until World War I. By 1919, when he first discovered that his messianic rants could have a powerful social impact, he is already described as having a voice that inspired enthusiasm—strident versions of a narrowed strength, will, and power—while his eyes remained "cold," "staring," "blank," "cruel," and/or "extraordinary." His mother had the same blank uncanny stare. It is the very portrait of a cold schizoid hatred, underneath a narcissistic grandiosity, and now energizing a new prophetical movement of radical social transformation.

His mother's death, his total isolation, and the years of poverty unleashed an intensified narcissistic pattern based on inflation, humourlessness, shame, diffuse rages, and deep distrust and secrecy. There were also features of a borderline syndrome that included a "hypnotic" and manipulative role playing, perverse sexual proclivities of the kind that Khan (1979) found to be an inferior sensual mysticism, and an extreme splitting between idealization and a projected hatred (Bromberg and Small 1983). Fortunately there was also the dissociated self-destructiveness that would actually subvert his most grandiose plans precisely at the points they seemed finally attainable (Loewenberg 1988).

In short, this is the picture of a secularized inner-worldly propheticism, its false essential states twisted by a degree of pathology only approached among the major figures we are considering by Aleister Crowley. Hitler functions, in Weber's terms, as a primitive auditory prophet whose charisma inspired essential states in others in a way that provided the felt meaning for a program of "ethical" transformation of an entire society. Again in Weber's terms, it was Himmler and other anti-Semitic occultists who illustrate the more aesthetic, mystical side of National Socialism. Here we find doctrines reminiscent of the Gnostic metaphysics of hatred and radical dualism, with the call to experience a higher humanity, a new Anthropos, similarly based on narcissistic pathology. The combination of this false propheticism and false mysticism produced a this-worldly disaster. No wonder Jung and Heidegger, whatever their own grandiosities and opportunism, indignantly rejected suggestions that their thinking was fascistic and racist. They are both distant indeed, from List, Lanz, and Wiligut.

Max Weber on Spirituality and Politics

The racial occultists, Jung and Heidegger, *and* the latter's recent critics do have something in common. They all make the same mistake, from Max Weber's perspective, in thinking that transpersonal states and spiritual realizations had concrete implications for politics. Weber in his 1918 essay "Politics as a Vocation" points out that all spirituality has an ethic of ultimate ends—and so, we can add, is necessarily elitist, with its gurus, visionaries, and prophets guiding their followers to specific felt realizations. Politics in a modern society, on

the other hand, is based on a relative ethic of competition and compromise, *and* a responsibility for social consequences in the real world.

> He who seeks the salvation of the soul . . . should not seek it
> along the avenue of politics. . . . Everything that is striven for
> through political action . . . following an ethics of responsibil-
> ity endangers the "salvation of the soul." If, however, one
> chases after the ultimate good in a war of beliefs, following a
> pure ethic of absolute ends, then the goals may be damaged
> and discredited for generations, because the responsibility for
> *consequences* is lacking. (Weber, Politics as a vocation: 126)

To say that the naturalistic and inevitably "elitist" spiritualities
of Jung and Heidegger are fascist or Nazi in their political implications is to make a category mistake and confuse two separate frames
of human intelligence—politics and spirituality. The confusion is the
same whether it is Jung and Heidegger themselves who briefly
thought this or their contemporary critics. It is like saying that the
aesthetic rigors of master wood carving has fascist political implications because of its elitist master-apprentice structure. The wood-
carver ethos is only fascistic if someone seeks to impose it in the
sphere of politics, as in Plato's image of the philosopher-king, briefly
so appealing to Heidegger.

Jung and Heidegger did indeed risk "discrediting for generations" their essential realizations by making the same category mistake made by all those who confuse the spheres of spirituality and
politics. The list certainly includes Himmler, as well as Christian
and Muslim fundamentalists everywhere who seek the political im-
plementation of religious ethical doctrine. It also includes those who
reject the very form of a naturalistic inner-worldly mysticism because of its supposedly inherent political implications—which it
cannot possibly have, because it is *not* politics (N. Hunt 1994).

Of course history, ancient and modern, is replete with eras and
societies who have not made this distinction. Accordingly, it is helpful to note how the romantic mysticism reflected in modern revivals
of shamanism can appear to have either conservative or liberal consequences if taken politically, depending on the overall cultural context. The kind of Ur-shamanism advocated by the sun and Wotan
worshiping occultists of Europe, and especially as developed by List
and Lanz, clearly fits into the right-wing political ideology of the
times. On the other hand, current North American interests in
shamanism as an inner-worldly mysticism, with very cosmopolitan

people going on ritual peyote hunts and learning shamanic healing techniques, seems to fit with a clearly liberal, ecological, feminist, and multi-cultural politics.

That the same movement of Ur-shamanic revival can be part of extreme right or left wing politics, depending on the social context, further underlines Weber's caution on confusing spiritual realization with specific political ideology. Wilhelm Reich (1976) provides a further illustration of how a post-Nietzschean psychology of vitality and presence, also in Germany of the 1930s, could be linked to, and temporarily confused with, radical Marxism. The danger here is not that an in-the-world spirituality will lead to political commitment per se, spirituality hopefully not precluding citizenship, but that *specific* essential realizations will be felt to have *specific* political implications. Then the necessary relativities of political life become inflated with the felt "absolutes" of either mystical or prophetical numinous experiences. Current spiritually sanctioned political extremisms, of both right and left, show that we are hardly past such vulnerabilities.

CHAPTER **9**

"Triumph of the Will": Heidegger's Nazism
as Spiritual Pathology

Martin Heidegger (1889–1976), with Wittgenstein, is widely regarded as either the first or second major philosopher of the twentieth century. He can also be seen as central to the post-Nietzschean attempt to understand and cultivate the experiential core of spirituality as an inherent human capacity. Yet any consideration of Heidegger as a seminal spiritual thinker will require a careful consideration of his enthusiastic assumption of the Nazi rectorship at the University of Freiburg in 1933, in order to extend the National Socialist revolution within the universities, along with his sometimes duplicitous behavior while rector, until he abruptly resigns in 1934. Recent cultural debates have made this episode increasingly notorious. Opinions range from the view that his National Socialism was a temporary aberration with no inherent relation to his philosophy, to the conclusion that his entire work is thereby revealed as implicitly Nazi or fascist—rendering Heidegger essentially unreadable for many. The present approach eschews both these extremes.

Rather, if Heidegger's work *is* a major development of modern spirituality then the moral failing of his Nazism would show a metapathological or spiritual crisis *within* that development. The three forms of metapathological reactions, for Almaas, are grandiosity, or what Jung similarly termed "inflation;" "negative merging," or the defensive symbiosis with destructive relationships and groups; and withdrawal or isolation. We will see that they are all present in Heidegger. The first two predominate during his rectorship. The third, a more schizoid isolation and sensed futility, arises periodically but is especially marked after 1946 as his reaction to the de-Nazification

199

hearings in which he was banned from teaching until 1950, experienced a deep sense of despair and humiliation, and suffered a brief psychiatric breakdown.

Heidegger as Spiritual Thinker

For Heidegger the human sense of the transcendent rests on our capacity for wonder and awe at the sheer "facticity" of things, that anything is at all—the "primordial experience" of Being. The early Heidegger crossed his initial studies in medieval scholasticism with the phenomenology of Husserl (Kisiel 1993) to arrive at a structure of human existence or *Dasein* in which the openness of time ahead into the unknown offers the "horizon" for the sense of Being as such. Since our temporality entails the intrinsic anxiety of a "being-to-wards-death," our openness to Being is also readily occluded. For Heidegger that has become a specific characteristic of the modern West. This is the burden of the *Daseins-analysis* of *Being and Time* (1927), including Heidegger's discussion of the potential for an individual authenticity that allows a re-attunement to Being.

After 1935 Heidegger's writing becomes more evocative and poetic in its treatment of Being as the hidden "disposition" (Heidegger 1938), or latent felt meaning within the concepts of Western metaphysics. Heidegger's evocations of "the holy" through the poetry of Hölderlin and the abstract animism of the pre-Socratics show more clearly what has been termed the "mystical element" in his philosophy.[1] In addition to the specific physiognomies of essence to be traced below, his words to describe the direct sense of Being-as-such echo Otto on the numinous. With Otto, he describes qualities of "awe," "wonder," "mystery," "strangeness," "uncanniness," "stillness," and "wholly other" (Heidegger 1938: 1936–38). That Heidegger's thought is itself a form of mysticism is clearest after 1950, when his writings become more directly reminiscent of Meister Eckhart on the paradoxical nothingness of the Godhead (Caputo 1986) and Buddhist views of the void as compassion (Guenther 1984).[2] He writes Being as B̶e̶i̶n̶g to convey his sense of a pure facticity of isness that gives forth specific beings while withdrawing behind them as an ostensible nothing (Heidegger 1956). In *Time and Being* (1962) Heidegger also echoes Plotinus on the Absolute as an infinitely generous welling forth.

As with Jung, Heidegger is calling attention to the necessity of physical metaphor for any encompassing reflection on human existence, which similarly replaced his earlier preoccupation with the cultural renewal of the German *Volk*. For Jung *psyche* could only be adequately reflected by cross-cultural metaphors abstracted from nature, best illustrated in his re-use of alchemy as a psychological language. For Heidegger, the "welling forth," "shining," "radiance," "clearing," and "opening" of Being should not be considered as a mere animism or anthropomorphism, since that presupposes that we actually know what humanity is (Heidegger 1936b). Rather our being is concealed and mysterious, much as Jung sees alchemical imagination as a knowing the unknown (mind) by means of the unknown (matter-based metaphors). For the later Heidegger our being is a "dwelling" and "giving," not as an explicit and so limited metaphor, but because Being actually does *shelter* and *hold* us. There are no other words to convey this sense of the Being that somehow "allows" and "lets" our existence. If, with Nietzsche, the holy is a projection of our own nature, it becomes equally clear that such "projection" is only possible for us as self-aware beings because we are also the expressions of that same Being.

As to whether Heidegger himself had essential experiences, his is not the ecstatic mysticism of the heart, but clearly belongs with Plotinus as a mysticism of knowledge. The directly charismatic impact of his lectures was widely attested, and the mantra-like repetition of his highly abstract written evocations of the multiple facets of Being can unquestionably induce essential realizations in the reader. Accordingly, more than with any of our other precursor figures, it will be textual analysis, coupled with simultaneous events in Heidegger's life, that will allow us to trace an interplay of essential openings, painful inner deficiency, and false essence.

The Rectorship

Our discussion of Heidegger's one-year assumption of the first Nazi rectorship of a major university, widely publicized within Hitler's Germany, must remain on the level of an overview that will begin to highlight its more conflicted and confused aspects. Heidegger, after the sensational impact of *Being and Time* (1927), and the end in 1928 of his passionate four-year affair with Hannah Arendt, his student and Jewish muse, was personally adrift, full of self-doubt, and in search of some sort of "new beginning."

He was drawn towards National Socialism by the same neo-romantic concern with roots and renewal that also drew Jung.

Despite some recent accusations, Heidegger's behavior seems neither racist nor merely opportunistic. Even in his rectorate speeches praising Hitler's revolution, he avoids the crude racism and pseudobiological doctrines that defined Nazi orthodoxy, and he was accordingly criticized by the Nazi ministry of education (Farias 1989). Heidegger was especially drawn to the Röhm faction of the S.A., not for its notorious thuggery, since by all accounts he was quite timid, but for its call for a second and permanent cultural revolution, to follow Hitler's political one, and which Heidegger naively thought he could lead within the universities. Idealistically, he had long advocated the elimination of departmental divisions, curtailing of the role of occupational training, and a grounding of all disciplines in ancient Greek thought. He was also fascinated with the nationalist and romantic ideology of the *Freikorp* veterans and the S.A.'s youth camps, whose student campfires and Black Forest retreats Heidegger attended enthusiastically and later made compulsory as Rector. He actually thought the Nazis represented a rejection of technology, which surely shows the danger of truly non political people getting caught up in mass movements. He resigned just before the brutal 1934 assassination of Röhm and his major followers, which he later said opened his eyes to the violence of the regime.

In 1934 he was quoted as saying that the rectorship was "the greatest stupidity of my life" (Petzet 1993). After the war he made several very private confessions of shame—for the rectorship, for not attending the 1938 funeral of Husserl, for the loss of his friendship with fellow philosopher Karl Jaspers and the latter's Jewish wife, and for his temporary estrangement from Hannah Arendt, whom he later came to see as the love of his life. It is important to note that, although he did not resign from the party, he began speaking out in his lectures against National Socialist doctrines from 1935 on, which seems relatively courageous for the inwardly frightened person described by Arendt (Ettinger 1995). This sufficiently annoyed the ministry of education that he was actually under surveillance by the S.S. from 1936 on, and was briefly mobilized in 1944, at age fifty-five, as part of Germany's desperate final defense, while younger colleagues at Freiburg were spared. None of this mattered in the de-Nazification hearings of 1946, partly because of the prominence of his early support, partly because of the self-serving nature of his written "apology," and partly because Heidegger's stridently Nazi and racist wife was so unpopular in Freiburg (Ott 1993).

Evidence of metapathology or spiritual crisis in all this is striking. Certainly there are signs of inflation and narcissistic grandiosity. Jaspers concluded at the time that Heidegger hoped to be "spiritual

Führer" of Germany—that he would somehow influence Hitler directly as a sort of Platonic philosopher-king of culture and education (Oliver 1994). Despite his later attempts to minimize these early fantasies, those close to him saw his intoxication and excitement and his personal identification with Hitler (Safranski 1999). His grandiosity is also reflected in the bombast of his speeches as Rector (below) and in the way he shaved his moustache to look like Hitler's.

Most shocking, however, is the mendacity and cunning of his actions as Rector. This is actually a complex story. Some of the rhetoric around Heidegger's rectorship is unfortunate. The truth is generally bad enough, without the exaggeration to which many in our current "culture wars" are prone (Ettinger 1995; Farias 1989; Wolin 1990). Thus Heidegger was not responsible for banning Husserl from the university library (Ott 1993) and seems not to have been anti-Semitic in his personal dealings at all (Neske and Kettering 1990; Young-Bruehl 1982). He had already had a typical mentor-student falling out with Husserl from 1927, and actually tried, with only the most minimal success, to delay the anti-Semitic decrees of the education ministry, as well as various book burnings. He did, sadly, make anti-Semitic comments where he thought it would further his administrative goals. Heidegger was already under suspicion by the Nazis as an opportunist, regarded as soft on race. There are ministry documents criticizing him for close ties to Jewish students, and for his "Talmudic" and "schizophrenic-degenerate" writing style (Farias 1989). It seems likely that, in part, some of his rather two-faced behaviors were fruitless attempts to compensate for rumors of such accusations.

Not surprisingly, by 1934, Heidegger was distrusted by all sides. He finally resigned when he realized that all his would-be university reforms would be blocked at the ministry level and truly had nothing to do with National Socialist plans. As Hans Gadamer (in Neske and Kettering 1990), his early student, observes, if he were merely an opportunist he would have been more of a racist in 1934 and more of a democrat after 1946, but instead he was utterly naive politically and personally "deluded." In 1933 he was forty-four years old and at the height of vulnerability to the male midlife crisis as portrayed by Levinson (1978).

Heidegger's Spiritual Crisis and its Partial Resolution

We will now see how Heidegger's spiritual crisis and its later resolution can be traced through his writings beginning from 1928 and through 1944, culminating in his "dark night" crisis after

1946. These crises, exacerbated by his own characterological narcissism, offer a powerful illustration of the vulnerabilities and
"broken" quality of inner-worldly mysticism. Yet whatever Heidegger's personal failings and grandiose ambitions, he does deserve
some credit, in the fuller context of the deeply compromised elite of
German academia under Hitler, for his continued scorn of the
pseudo-biology of Aryan purity and the false "gigantism" of the rallies. Heidegger paid heavily in the later de-Nazification hearings,
while many of the archeologists, anthropologists, and historians
who had been opportunistically drawn into the crazed research
sponsored by Himmler's S.S., moved seamlessly into prestigious
post-war academic careers.

    As we will see, his essays from 1928 through 1931 show Hei-
degger immersed in what Almaas would term the holes or felt
deficits of the lack of Being. He is in the painful throes of Winnicott's dilemma of being or feeling real. This period is abruptly replaced by the false, strident versions of essential will, power, and
strength seen in Heidegger's rectorship speeches and lectures in
1933 and 1934. If his Nazism is rightly to be taken as a spiritual
crisis or metapathology, then these speeches should differ as much
from his 1928–1931 essays as from the more evocative, genuinely
essential imagery that appears in his writings after 1935—and
this seems to be the case.

    In terms of Evelyn Underhill's (1955) stages of mystical real-
ization, the work culminating in *Being and Time* in 1927 can be
taken as Heidegger's initial "awakening," which is centered on the
personal presence or self-actualization side of essential development. He would fail to realize that in his own life, and completely
side-step it in his final more "transcendent" writings. The suffering
and painful sense of deficiency that appears from 1928 through
1931 reflects Underhill's notion of a second stage of "purgation."
Her next stage, "false illumination," then corresponds with Heidegger's Nazi period and its manifestations of false essence. Underhill's
"true illumination" follows in the striking manifestation of separate
essential aspects in his powerfully evocative essays of the later
1930s and 1940s. Heidegger's collapse and despair following the de-
Nazification humiliation approach Underhill's "dark night of the
soul," from which he never entirely emerges. Accordingly, his more
"formless" later writings constitute only a partial version of Underhill's final stage of "unitive life." They are being more an "escape to
transcendence," which, while conceptually revolutionary, still left
him subject to frequent despair and loneliness.

1924–1927: Spiritual Awakening

With *Being and Time* Heidegger had completed his analytic of *Dasein*, or human existence. It began, in the early 1920s, as a very abstract version of the traditional theology of the "heart" of Augustine, Luther, and Kierkegaard, reinscribed as an authentic care implicit in the openness of time. His notion of "authenticity," based on presence, care, and solicitude for the same presence in others, is close to Almaas on "personal essence" as a sense of autonomy and contact—also implying a goal akin to the vitality of the this-worldly alchemical red of Jung's Self. There is a still more obvious relation to Almaas on "essential identity," since the core of authenticity is the realization of our Beingness. *Being and Time* culminates in an intricate analysis of the way in which the "ecstasies" of temporality, the flowing of past, present, and future into one, allow *Dasein*—"cleared by light"—to break into a sensed spaciousness. This happens in the fullness of the "moment of vision." Heidegger's stated task at the end of the uncompleted *Being and Time* is to move from the analysis of temporality, as the horizon of Being, to the felt sense of Being as such. Henceforth, he will seek to directly (poetically) "say" and evoke the spaciousness of the moment.

1928–1932: Purgation

An early stage of the alchemical work, following Jung, is the *nigredo* or blackening, the encounter with suffering. This is well reflected within Heidegger's writings from 1928 and 1929 in their evocation of the dread, despair, and the nothingness of a sensed loss of support. In these essays we find the "holes" of essential will, strength, and power.

By 1928 Heidegger is left with the fame and notoriety of *Being and Time*, the recent deaths of both his parents, and the ending of his tortured, hidden affair with Hannah Arendt. All this is reflected in his preoccupation with the existential analysis of apathy and futility in "What is Metaphysics?" (1928) and *The Fundamental Concepts of Metaphysics* (1929/30). He speaks of "profound boredom drifting hither and thither in the abysses of existence like a mute fog," "a queer kind of indifference," "empty silence," the solitude of "abandoning" oneself to "emptiness," and above all of "nothingness." We have seen how Fairbairn locates futility as the fundamental emotion of the schizoid dilemma, which Almaas discusses, with coldness and hatred, as indicating the hole or sensed deficit of essential power. A defensive withdrawal must lack inner stillness and peace.

A felt deficit of essential strength and autonomy seems also reflected in "What is Metaphysics?" in references to the way *Dasein* "quivers" with the "pulsation" of dread—a pulsation greatest in the "courageous," who "let themselves go into Nothing." Given that Almaas sees the dimension of essential strength as the core of a vitality that opens into the freeing spaciousness of spiritual experience, it is interesting that in *The Fundamental Concepts of Metaphysics*, Heidegger explicitly rejects any connection between his understanding of *Dasein* and aliveness or bodily vitality. Consistent with the possibility that his work finally fails to develop the red of strength/vitality, it is interesting that later, when his friend Medard Boss asked Heidegger why he ignored the phenomenology of the body, the latter responded, "Because this is the most difficult thing" (Craig 1988). In these years, Heidegger is trapped.

A felt deficit of essential will, based, for Almaas, on anxieties over lack of support, appears in Heidegger's discussion of the "abyss" of nonsupport or "groundlessness." Thus, in *The Essence of Ground* (1929) "freedom" is merely the "groundlessness of existence" and our nature is one of "abandonment." In this regard, Heidegger ends these 1929 reflections on groundlessness and nonsupport with, "For only in its *Dasein* with others can *Dasein* surrender its individuality in order to win itself as an authentic self" (1929:31). To paraphrase Heidegger's famous 1966 interview (in Neske and Kettering 1990), where an older and more despairing Heidegger said "Only a god can save us now," it is as if, in 1929, he is saying "Only a group can save us now." His wife, an overly dominating influence as we shall see, joins the National Socialist Party in 1929. By 1932, in his still untranslated lectures on Plato's *Republic*, he actually says that collective liberation from forgetfulness of Being can only come through "violent action," because people have become too "comfortable." Speech is no longer relevant, "we merely have to act" (Safranski 1998).

1933–1934: FALSE ILLUMINATION

One danger of the alchemical work of spiritual development is a premature or false development to escape suffering, rather than accepting it so as to allow its potential for transmutation (Jung 1944; Kugler 1993). Thus, from the Jungian perspective, overlapping here with Almaas, we can speak of a false red coming too soon, or the false marriage of red and the manic yellow of enthusiasm, or the more malevolent fusion of red and black. Heidegger manifests all of these in 1933–34, along with what the Jungian James Hillman

(1980) calls the "lunacy of white"—an inflation that has about it the "snowblindness of purity." Indeed it is interesting that Jaspers later described Heidegger as entering National Socialism "like a dreaming child" (Ott 1993).

We have already seen the grandiosity of Heidegger's behavior as Rector. It remains to trace the rhetoric of a false will, power, and strength through his speeches and articles at the time—so entirely lacking in both the paradoxical coincidence of opposites of his post-1935 writings and the felt deficiencies or "holes" of personal presence so striking from 1928 through 1931.

It begins in 1933 with his infamous Rector's Inaugural Address "The Self Assertion of the German University," whose appeal to a re-grounding in classical thought earned the initial praise of his friend Karl Jaspers, who was soon to conclude quite differently. We hear that "German destiny must now come to power in the will to essence," which is inseparable from "the will to science." Prometheus—with his seizure of the powers of the gods—is accordingly presented as the first philosopher. "The spiritual world of a people" is "the power that most deeply preserves [their] earth-and blood-bound strengths." Most astonishingly, given essential will as an allowing and surrender, we find him saying "This people . . . ready for battle . . . wills to be a spiritual people." One wonders how such a thing could be *willed* in the sense Heidegger apparently meant. He closes with Plato's phrase, again intriguing in terms of the latter's near lethal role as advisor to the Tyrant of Syracuse, "All that is great stands in the storm" (in Neske and Kettering 1990: 6–13).

In later addresses and articles from 1933–34, Heidegger speaks of the necessity of a "new courage" for this "hard race," which must "remain tough." To an audience of students, complete with Nazi salute, he says "Ideas shall no longer govern your existence," but instead the Führer and his "glorious will." They must have the "courage to cut loose from what exists, and either to grow or break" in a new spirituality "motivated by the toughness and danger of human existence" (in Runes 1965: 25–35). This is a near perfect description of the false will soon to be celebrated in the Nuremberg rallies of 1936 and preserved in Leni Riefenstahl's infamous documentary "Triumph of the Will."

Heidegger's prose here is consistent with a metapathology of inflation based on false forms of will, power, and strength, and the defensive "negative merging" with a mass movement. We can see these speeches, so different from anything he wrote before or afterwards, as premature attempts to fill the "holes" of the 1928–1931 essays. If so, then beginning with his return to original writing and lecturing in 1935, following the personal impact of his resignation, we might expect to find genuine or essential forms of the alchemical white, black, and red, and the appearance of new dimensions previously blocked. That is precisely what occurs.

After his resignation from the rectorship, Heidegger entered a new but briefer period of futility and despair. In a letter to Jaspers he describes himself after 1934 as in a state of *Ratlosigkeit*—loosely translatable as "at sea," with connotations of perplexity, helplessness, and embarrassment. This is part of the hole of lack of support, the sensed deficiency of essential will. Heidegger's earlier grandiosity has been replaced by shame over his alienations from Jaspers, the Husserl family, and Hannah Arendt. He responds at first with withdrawal and silence. He has had the strength to resign, and even, in the face of the Röhm assassination, to begin to criticize mainstream National Socialism in his lectures. He has had no choice but to accept his isolation and aloneness.

1935–1944: True Illumination—Direct Manifestations of Essence

Beginning with his more evocative essays/lectures of 1935 and 1936, we find the first appearance of the paradoxical phraseology of essential will, power, and strength, now often explicitly contrasted by Heidegger with their false forms.[3] The genuine or true black of essential power, the alchemical "illuminated night," is discussed in terms of a peace and stillness taming an inner agitation. The true white of an essential will (the alchemical *albedo*) also appears, based now on a "letting be." The earlier abyss of groundlessness is replaced by a "serene dwelling." Yet there is also an impersonality in the imagery of these writings. It increases as he moves toward his major preoccupation with *logos* or essential intelligence in the 1940s and into the 1950s—a permanent move away from the more "personal" aspects of resolve and solicitude in *Being and Time*. Vulnerabilities of character to be discussed below seem to have predisposed Heidegger to a "coldness of soul" in which feelings of relatedness disappear. This will become more striking after 1946.

Gone, in the 1935 lectures later published as *Introduction to Metaphysics*, is the nothingness, groundlessness, and futility of 1928–1931. Now the sense of Being is to be approached by amplifying the pre-Socratic sense of *physis*—"nature" as a self-opening or spontaneous emergence from "the hidden" into the "clearing" and "lighting" of space. The text is full of the imagery of light and fire as an illuminating or shining forth, usages similar to the early Emerson. A sense of the essential strength of this opening into spaciousness is implied by the way it flares up and shows itself, in contrast to what Heidegger now terms the "false appearing" of fame and glory. There is still an imagery of strife and struggle, but it is more internalized. Heidegger still uses the loaded German word, *Kampf*, but the strife is now within *logos* or knowing itself—as the attempt at "gathering" and "holding" the contending opposites of beings.

In "The Origin of the Work of Art," from later in 1935, this inward strife of *logos* moves towards resolution. Now art—as the essence of thought—gathers across the rift between *physis* and human world. In a favorite image, the dark, cold material of the stone of a temple, overlooking the sea, stands in this rift and "draws up out of the rock the mystery of [its] spontaneous support." The lustre of the stone "first brings to light the light of the day, the breadth of the sky, the darkness of the night. [Its] towering makes visible the invisible space of air." There is still a "battle" but it is now between the concealment and unconcealment of truth, and so contained within *logos*. The "concentrated agitation" of this "primal conflict" has now become a "repose" (Heidegger 1935b: 42, 57–58). Here an essential power emerges in Heidegger's imagery as both the dynamic radiance of the "illuminating" or true black and as its inner peace and stillness, both reflected in an imagery of the natural and crafted stone that also fascinated Jung.

The expression of an essential will or support comes to the fore in "Holderlin and the Essence of Poetry" (1936a) as a "letting be" and "abiding." The poet is said to evoke the openness of a ground that "shines." To "dwell poetically" is a gift of Being that Heidegger uses to characterize human existence as such. The notion of a ground-less abyss henceforth largely disappears from his writings and lectures.

There is also the appearance of essential joy, an aspect new for Heidegger, in "Remembrance of the Poet" (1943a). For Hillman (1989) the alchemical yellow is an expansiveness and enlivening of the white. Consistent with the "coincidence of opposites" that is key to numinous qualities, we find Heidegger saying, following Hölderlin, "the Most Joyous . . . declares itself to me now, in this grief "—in the sadness of "homecoming" and in "waiting" in the "proximity" of god's absence. In accepting this sadness the poet arrives at "the Serene," which "allots each thing . . . [its] place of existence." "The Serene . . . holds everything in tranquility and wholeness. The Serene is fundamentally healing." "Homecoming is the return into the proximity of the source," which is an inherent "mystery" and "the holy" (Heidegger 1943a: 247–62). Here for the first time we see in Heidegger the sense of basic trust implicit in an allowing of joy.

In addition, there are Heidegger's writings from 1937 through 1945 on "thinking" as an opening to Being in its own right. There is a distinct quality in these writings that fits well with Almaas (1988) on essential intelligence and brilliancy as an aspect of spirituality. Essential intelligence, as reflected for instance in the "mysticism of knowledge" in Eckhart or Plotinus, offers its own access to all other aspects of essence—strength, will, joy, compassion, etc. After all, Heidegger is above all a thinker, and it is at this point that he comes to see that thought itself—what he will later (1959) term "presentational thinking"—*is* Being. For Hillman (1993), this is related to the alchemical blue, and associated with the "wisdom of Sophia."

In his lectures on Parmenides (1942/43) and Heraclitus (1943b, 1944), essential thought emerges as a paradoxical acceptance of "mystery" and openness to "not knowing." Thought is the unconcealing of the concealment of Being. The basis of all thinking is an openness to mystery that shelters the gift of Being itself. The *logos* is a "gathering" that is no longer a strife but instead lets things "lie together" as they come to "shine" in presence. In "Conversation on a Country Path," not published until later but based on conversations that Heidegger said took place in 1944–5, this "letting" of thought reflects a "highest willing." Here thought looks into the "openness as such" of the sky's horizon—of the blue—which is "an enchanted region where everything belonging there returns to that in which it rests" (64–65). Thought-as-such entails a generosity of attitude and a *thanking* that seems reminiscent of compassion in Mahayana Buddhism. His discussion of a felt "releasement" (*Gelassenheit*) into the open spaciousness of "that which regions" directly evokes Meister Eckhart, for whom it was a key term.

Heidegger's writings between 1935 and 1945 represent the furthest Heidegger was to go in bringing together the aspects of essential power, strength, joy, compassion, and especially will in their more impersonal aspect. They show a triumph of essential will as a "letting be" that offers an appropriate counterpoint to the triumph of false will in the Nuremberg rallies. However, the pain and further withdrawal consequent on the events of 1946 prevented Heidegger from integrating this work with the more personal sense of Being in his work from the 1920s, and pushed him further towards the more formless levels of mysticism in his final writings. Quite simply, he was never able to address the personal implications of his Nazi temptation. Instead there was only his much criticized "silence" about the war, and especially about the death camps.

Vulnerabilities of Character

We have seen how spiritual metapathology can be especially exacerbated where earlier development has left a predisposition to narcissistic and schizoid conditions. It is widely acknowledged, however, that psychobiography of the famous—and especially so with someone as secretive as Heidegger—often miscarries through purely speculative attempts to reconstruct early-childhood etiologies for adult problems (Runyon 1982). Unlike Nietzsche, Emerson, Thoreau, Jung, and Crowley, we know almost nothing personal about Heidegger's childhood. Accordingly, the majority of our discussion must concentrate on establishing the presence and depth of narcissistic and schizoid *themes* in Heidegger's adult character, and so minimize speculation about his early childhood.

Certainly Heidegger's adult life shows the thematics of Winnicott on the split between an inner "true self" and an outer, falsely accommodating self, as well as Kohut on the vulnerability to shame in narcissism, and Fairbairn on the schizoid dilemma of futility, emptiness, and loneliness. It seems fitting that Winnicott (1971) sees early deficits in sense of support and mirroring as associated with the inability to feel real and alive—the same failure in sense of Being wherein Heidegger locates the dis-ease of the twentieth century. Many accounts of Heidegger emphasize his timidity, shyness, and childlike vulnerability, also reflected in his inability to meet the gaze of others, and a watchful distrust that under pressure appeared as a more active cunning (Ott 1993; Ettinger 1995; Petzet 1993). We learn with surprise that when directly contradicted on points of philosophy, Heidegger retreats into inaccessible silence (Picht, in Neske and Kettering 1990). Yet many also emphasize the sense of charismatic excitement and mystery he could evoke in the classroom, heightened, or perhaps not, by his idiosyncratic version of rural "Black Forest" clothing. Something of a self-confession may be present in this passage from *Being and Time*:

When . . . one's knowing-oneself gets lost in such ways as aloofness, hiding oneself away, or putting on a disguise, Being-with-one-another must follow special routes of its own in order to come close to Others or even to 'see through them.' (Heidegger, *Being and Time*: 161)

There is a strong sense of aloneness and solitude in Heidegger, also reflected in his months of long isolation in his mountain cabin while he wrote. In the older Heidegger this aloneness became particularly painful, something else he shares with the older Jung (1961). In a late interview (in Neske and Kettering 1990: 106) he states "Yes, . . . I am lonely, how lonely you don't know." It is interesting that after his brief psychiatric breakdown in 1946, he said of von Gebsattel, intriguingly enough the "existential" therapist assigned to him, that all he did was to take him on hikes in the nearby forest snow. "That was all. But he showed me human warmth and friendship . . . I came back a healthy man again" (Ott 1993: 319). In short, he is recognized not as a great (or evil) philosopher but in his personal being.

We see something of the contrast between the sense of deficient emptiness and the openness that can emerge from its acceptance in the contrast between his postwar "depressions," the crises of futility and inability to work from which Hannah Arendt's visits could rescue him, and a more reparative and quiet kind of sadness from which his creativity emerged. On visits his friend Medard Boss was struck by the way Heidegger would fall into an apparent aloof depression during their morning walks—"as if wounded in some undiscoverable way." (Boss 1988: 8). In explanation Heidegger said that this was the time when he became spontaneously immersed in thought. "Always at this time of day 'the thinking' comes over me. Then, if I don't want to do myself painful violence, I have to surrender myself to it." This pattern emerges after his breakthrough in the late 1930s into a "more serene and composed" attitude and replaced what Heidegger termed an earlier "constant pressure to think."

Herein we also see at least a hint of the reparative sadness that Winnicott (1963b) makes central to the creative capacity and which Balint (1968) sees as a mourning for the sense of "basic fault." Thus we find Heidegger in "The Thinker as Poet" linking his "thought of Being" with the spontaneous lifting of an implied mourning. "When . . . a ray of the sun suddenly glides over the gloom of the meadows: We never come to thoughts. They come to us" (Heidegger 1947a: 6). Many who met the older Heidegger sensed a quiet sadness (Neske and Kettering 1990).

Winnicott (1971) and Kohut (1977, 1984) cite the deep need for recognition and mirroring in those with a fragile sense of self, as also illustrated in the centrality of exclusive "muse relationships" in the highly creative (Khan 1974). We can see several times over in Heidegger's life the importance of a total support from those around him. Indeed, the people he most seriously betrayed during the rectorship were former students who had deviated from his thought in some way. Similarly, Hannah Arendt's importance to Heidegger during their secretive affair in the 1920s very much included her role as privileged confidant and witness to his work. Even after the renewal of a close friendship in 1950, he later ignored her for almost two years after she had sent him some of her own already widely known writings. Arendt saw this as testimony to his deep need for her to play the exclusive role of supportive muse to his own thought (Ettinger 1995).

Heinz Kohut (1977) and the Jungian analyst Jacoby (1994) both stress the vulnerability to shame in the narcissistic character, rather than guilt, as the basic response to a felt inadequacy in sense of self. Almaas (1988) understands shame as part of the hole of essential will—the felt sense of non support, non recognition, and not being valued in one's own right. In contrast to the guilt that seeks to assuage itself by making amends and confession, shame is silent and seeks to hide. This is perhaps the best explanation for Heidegger's supposedly notorious "silence" on the holocaust and rectorship in his postwar writings. Privately he told several of his "shame," but he visibly froze and withdrew at any suggestion of a public statement (Neske and Kettering 1990). Karl Jaspers, who had written an influential essay on German guilt, finally broke with Heidegger in the late 1940s over Heidegger's failure to admit his "guilt"—this despite Heidegger's statements of deep shame in several letters (Ott 1993). Karl Jaspers seems to have missed what for Kohut would be the gulf between the separate psychologies of guilt and shame. From Heidegger's point of view, whatever he had *done*—which, after all, *included* resigning, criticizing the regime, and helping several Jewish students—would have paled beside what he had *shown*—his inner grandiosity and his capacity for vengeful cunning. Guilt may seek some sort of public reparation, but shame seeks only to hide.

In their letters (Kohler and Saner 1992), Jaspers and Arendt agreed that Heidegger had "no character," and she repeatedly refers to him therein as "the fox," in the years immediately before their reapproachment in 1950. Such ascriptions fit well with Winnicott (1960) on the opportunism and secrecy of the false-self dilemma. It is interesting that Jung also (1961) was puzzled that so many people found him similarly "cunning." The list of those in Heidegger's life who came to see an expediency thinly covering his own agenda is too long to be indicative of anything but the truth. It includes the de-Nazification committee, the National Socialists themselves, Husserl and his phenomenological circle, and his Ph.D. supervisor, Heinrich Finke. The latter withdrew all support from Heidegger in 1916 when he realized that Heidegger's commitment to "Catholic philosophy" was, by that point, only because the funds allowing his studies came from the church.

The origins of this false outward accommodation are instructive. Heidegger's parents were rural, very religious, and comparatively poor. Heidegger's early intellectual precocity came to the attention and sponsorship of the parish priest. The only educational path forward under such circumstances was a church-sponsored boarding school in the city of Constance, starting from age fourteen, with the aim of training for the priesthood—specifically for the Jesuits, given his intellectual brilliance. Until his early twenties this seems to have been Heidegger's deep aspiration as well. The only financial resources for such an education, one so significant for his family, were local scholarships through the church. With constant reapplications and uncertainty, these supported Heidegger's studies beginning with boarding school, his abortive pastoral training, and finally through graduate studies in Catholic philosophy.

By the time Heidegger was seventeen, however, his teachers were already commenting that his theological studies were suffering from his passion for German literature. Five years later, in the midst of university training, he hoped to study with Husserl, but money problems kept him where he was. There was even a period of economic crisis around this time when the man destined to be one of the central philosophers of the century seriously contemplated becoming a high school mathematics teacher, so as to be finished with his studies and finally self-supporting (Ott 1993). By the time of National Socialism and its takeover of the universities, Heidegger had been well schooled in the necessary opportunism of the impoverished student with a true gift. He had learned how to "pass" with his own agenda. Of course, it was naive of him, if not obtuse, to think he could do the same with Hitler. Similarly, it was perhaps inevitable that he would continue the attempt with his self-serving "apology" to the de-Nazification hearings in which, like Jung after the war, he claimed that his rectorship was only intended to protect academia.

The depth of the conflict between an unsupported, unrecognized true self and an outward false self in Heidegger's life is attested by his periodic "psychosomatic" crises. These begin during the first weeks of his long-awaited and consciously desired Jesuit training. His sudden heart palpitations and difficulties in breathing, then termed a "nervous heart disorder," made him unsuitable for the rigors of the Jesuits. The same mysterious symptoms end his next attempt at pastoral training in 1911, again within a few weeks. A similar "heart disease" and "neurasthenia" after his Ph.D., and which he attributed to exhaustion and lack of adequate food, keep him in the university and out of World War I until 1918 (Ott 1993). It is not known if this pattern recurred in 1928 when he was described by many who knew him as "in crisis" (Farias 1989), or in 1934, but it seems likely to have been part of his 1946 withdrawal and hospitalization—which is also described as "psychosomatic" (Ott 1993). All this occurs in a man who lived to an age of 87 and was especially known for his robust hiking and physically daring skiing. Whatever else was involved, these episodes sound like "panic attacks," the bases of which appear to have been unconscious for Heidegger. They can also be seen as a series of quasi-Socratic "No's"—protecting his latent sense of inner mission from the socially enforced engulfments that threatened it.

We can only speculate on the familial origins of Heidegger's vulnerabilities in sense of self, especially since his only published reminiscences are so extremely sketchy and idealized. In a short autobiographical essay, "The Pathway" (1947b), he describes his father, the church sexton and local cooper, as "laboring thoughtfully" in his workshop. His mother "watched over everything" and sent him off "well provided with words of warning." His student Max Mueller (in Neske and Kettering 1990) later described Heidegger's mother as "too pious" and suggested that Heidegger never managed a separation and independence from her—as illustrated perhaps by the fact that her picture on his desk was the only decoration in his otherwise spartan study. We might speculate that Heidegger's early and lifelong recourse to surrounding mountain forests constitutes an alternative maternal holding environment, as we have also seen in Nietzsche, Thoreau, and Jung. If part of the schizoid dilemma for Fairbairn (1954) is not being valued in one's own right, it may be that her ambition for him to become a priest, resulting in his leaving home for boarding school, would be unconsciously felt as a deep rejection. The impact of this leave-taking must have been considerable, since Boss (1988) reports that the only dream the older Heidegger could recall was a repeating anxiety dream, ending only in the late 1930s, of his school entrance exam, with his new teachers grilling him mercilessly.

The "inherited social awkwardness" that Arendt reports Heidegger attributing to himself (Ettinger 1995) probably also describes his taciturn father, who like Heidegger had married "up" in

socio-economic terms. Along these lines it is interesting to note that
Heidegger's younger brother, Fritz is described as conveying a
"deep-seated sadness" and suffering much pain over "a small speech
impediment" (Petzet 1993). It seems also relevant that Heidegger's father had suffered the death of his own mother at age four,
which might be expected to be part of a tendency to depression in
both brothers.

The closest, at present, that we can approach Heidegger's early
relations with his mother is by inference from the pattern of his relationships with his wife, Elfride, and his lover, Hannah Arendt.
With Elfride, we do find reflections of the coldness and dilemmas
over closeness that Winnicott (1971) and Fairbairn (1954) make central to a schizoid dimension. Were the mother to resemble Elfride
she would indeed have been dominating and cold, and this on multiple accounts (Ott 1993; Ettinger 1995). Elfride was widely resented
in Freiburg for her behavior while in charge of civilian mobilization
for defense in 1944, during which she insisted on including new
mothers and patients in hospital in the sandbag brigades. She was
also well remembered for her direct and personal anti-Semitism
(Neske and Kettering 1990).

Heidegger's behavior with Arendt during their passionate affair
illustrates his need for intimacy and the deep anxieties it stirred. Heidegger insisted on a complete physical and emotional passivity from
Arendt, with her forbidden even to write unless he wrote her first and
gave permission. Early on he insisted she transfer universities to keep
her at a still accessible distance that was safer for him. She describes
her painful experience of "endless waiting" for his periodic calls to ren-
devous, while at the same time aware of his childlike vulnerability
and his deep need of her (Ettinger 1995). Heidegger's need for elaborate control, extending well beyond the caution actually required,
evokes Fairbairn on the schizoid dilemma of regulating distance and
closeness—an intimacy desperately needed at one moment suddenly
turning into a threatening engulfment to be escaped. Arguably we
may find in this tortured affair the echo of a distancing endured by a
much younger Heidegger.

George Steiner (1999), in his review of the German edition of
the letters of Heidegger and Arendt, compares the life-altering impact of their relationship to Abelard and Eloise, or Kierkegaard and
Regina. It may well be that Heidegger lost what chance he had for a
personalness and intimate "solicitude" in his break from her. It probably says much about his despair and emptiness after 1928. Certainly his Nazism would have been impossible if he had had the

courage to follow his heart. Arendt and Heidegger remained the mutually declared loves of each others lives.

Heidegger emerged from childhood with a deep fearfulness and shyness, a lack of felt support, and a degree of cunning to get it— none of which he ever lost. "I'm always so frightened," the elderly Heidegger says to Arendt before a lecture (Ettinger 1995). Always for him there is the personal issue of how to be and feel real and alive. Heidegger remains caught within the deficits of personal essence and the inability to trust merging love. The themes of "separation" and "homecoming" run all through his writings. He continually speaks of the source, one's true home, always ahead of us, and of "homecoming" as "the arrival of a distant origin" (Heidegger 1947b). Almaas (1988) states that the ultimate barrier to spiritual enlightenment is the inability to separate from one's mother, meaning the mother image within. Heidegger's bitterness, confusion, and loneliness after 1946 block any chance of genuine surrender to the sources of his suffering.

After the de-Nazification hearings and his brief psychiatric hospitalization, Heidegger feels shamed and dishonored. He complains of being "solitary and alone," a "comic figure to the world," and his despair and depressions often slow his writing. His earlier playful humor becomes markedly bitter and caustic (Petzet 1993). The shift in his writings is abrupt. There is a marked contrast from the joyfully unfolding essential aspects of the 1930s and 1940s. In 1946, in "What are Poets For," he writes that our era is "defined by the god's failure to arrive. . . . Divine radiance has become extinguished in the world's history." In the "Letter on Humanism" (1947c) we find: "The unique disgrace" of this age is that "the dimension of grace has been closed," while in "The Thinker as Poet," "We are too late for the gods and too early for Being" (Heidegger 1947a). This failure of Being to turn its face toward us reflects Heidegger's own withdrawal and isolation.

The years after 1946 constitute a penultimate "dark night of the soul" in which, Heidegger, as a person, seems to have largely remained. Heidegger's vulnerabilities in sense of self prevent him from the full acceptance of suffering that would be necessary for its opening into an essential strength and compassion. It was hardly the height of personal integration and insight for Heidegger to say, "I'll aplogize when Hitler comes back and apologizes to me" (Petzet 1993). His bitterness and defensiveness keep his writings on a more impersonal level. Yet by the mid 1950s this also allows the intellectual power and beauty of his final writings on the more formless or transcendent dimensions of Being. There is the sense of an emptiness that "wells forth" (Heidegger 1962) like the Buddhist void, and a *logos*, or essential intelligence, attuned, as "thanking" (Heidegger 1954) to the mysterious "it gives" beneath time and Being. Herein we do find a spontaneous contemporary intuition of Plotinus's Absolute.

Conceptually, the totality of Heidegger's work constitutes a complete noetics of the sense of Being as the experiential core of spirituality, with personal, essential, and formless aspects. However, it is a framework that Heidegger as person does not integrate. The intellectual triumph and centrality of Heidegger's noetics of the transpersonal conceals a more personal tragedy. What is missing is the "heart" basic to inner-worldly mysticism.

Dilemmas of Inner-Worldly Mysticism

JUNG AND HEIDEGGER

The similarities between Heidegger and Jung, both of whom pursued "naturalistic" versions of inner-worldly mysticism in this secular century, are striking. Both exemplify in their own lives Winnicott's split between true and false self, with a concomitant painful loneliness, especially in old age, and indications that they were exposed to a relatively cold mothering (Winnicott 1964; Hunt 1992). Both came from relatively poor, rural, and deeply religious backgrounds. They rejected these religious upbringings for their own explicitly post-Nietzschean articulation of a more mystical and "natural" spirituality. Both apprenticed themselves to Jewish mentors, unusual for that time and place, and turned the secular systems of Freud and Husserl into versions of an inner-worldly mysticism, understood phenomenologically rather than supernaturally, but nonetheless to the horror of their teachers. The inevitable break from their mentors was followed by accusations of anti-Semitism, which seems unlikely, as such, given the continued association of both Heidegger and Jung with Jewish pupils. Both engaged in significant liaisons with much younger Jewish anima figures, Jung with Sabrina Spielrein (Kerr 1993) and Heidegger with Arendt. These constituted crucial mirroring relationships during their initial years of original creative breakthrough.

With respect to the background of their brief involvements with National Socialism, both Heidegger and Jung were already oriented to a neo-romantic revival of mythological and metaphoric modes of thought, which they saw not as "primitive" but as a needed return to origins. They were initially drawn by the National Socialist rhetoric of radical cultural renewal. Both justified their involvements in the early 1930s in ways that later seemed opportunistic and self-serving. While there was a partial truth in their explanations, each also ignored the more grandiose and self-serving aspects of their behavior.

Why in retrospect has Jung fared better than Heidegger in the eyes of history, even considering the intense postwar criticism from psychoanalysis (Glover 1956) and the more recent sober reassessments by Jungians (Maidenbaum and Martin 1991)? In part, it is due to character and personal development. Jung's theoretical work was inseparable from his personal realization, and inseparable from specific techniques of active imagination to aid the process. Jung went further in healing his own true-false self-division and had more fully assimilated the anima and shadow sides of his own life. Jung was more able to see the Faustian element in his fascination—as in finding humor in his vomiting after meeting with Goebbels. Heidegger would have explicitly rejected any view that his version of National Socialism had to do with his own shadow side.

In part, however, the differing public fates of Heidegger and Jung are due to luck. Jung lived outside Germany and so could not assume a formal role of the sort available to Heidegger. Also Jung was well past the mid-life crisis he suffered in the years after he split from Freud, and so could not be engaged with the totality and intensity of the mid-life Heidegger. By the 1930s, whatever his initial fascination with the mythology of National Socialism, it was peripheral to the already integrated fundamentals of Jung's own spiritual development. One might expect, however, that were Jung to become as prominent in North American academic circles as Heidegger has been in recent years, then the "politically correct" culture wars now current against all that is perceived as "elitist" and "non rational" would have no difficulty including Jung within what is after all a very traditional condemnation of the only avenue of spiritual renewal that Weber, Troeltsch, and Durkheim (1912) saw as open to modern culture.

Socrates and Heidegger

An instructive, if discouraging, series of parallels can also be drawn between Heidegger and Socrates—that originary Western inner-worldly mystic and prototype for its "not knowing" and "openness to mystery." In these comparisons Heidegger often emerges as the distorted reflection of Socrates, attesting perhaps to the vulnerabilities in sense of self in the modern West and their disturbing impact on essential realization.

Both Heidegger and Socrates experienced an internal daemonic "No" that visibly guided their lives, although for Heidegger it took the form of a psychosomatic collapse that sustained the direction of his actual inner genius. Both apparently had infamously cold and dominating wives. Elfride, with her more virulent version of National Socialism, appears here as the contemporary reflection of Xantippe, wrathfully pursuing Socrates through the market place. Heidegger very much needed some of the cheerful "Much good may it do her" spirit of Socrates in response to such incidents (Epictetus). Hannah Arendt regarded her as the "disaster" of Heidegger's life (Ettinger 1995).

Both Heidegger and Socrates were publicly lampooned and ridiculed—Socrates in Aristophanes' "The Clouds" and Heidegger for his essay "What is a Thing?" Both lived in tenuously democratic countries taken over by fascist movements. Both were initially friendly to these seizures of power, while later withdrawing when asked to participate in ways that went beyond their own beliefs and standards. Of course, it was Socrates who abruptly declined to participate in the arrest of fellow citizens ordered by the Tyrants, some of the latter being his former students. Heidegger equivocated and manipulated for a year before he resigned. Both then quietly but distinctly criticized their respective tyrannical regimes, at some ostensible risk, but were more or less ignored.

The usual comparison is between Plato's near-fatal tutelage of the Tyrant of Syracuse and Heidegger's fantasy of being Spiritual Führer, with one of Heidegger's colleagues actually saying "Back from Syracuse, Herr Heidegger?" on first seeing him after his resignation (Ott 1993). Nonetheless, it was both Socrates and Heidegger who were put on trial after the return of their more egalitarian democracies, both under suspicion, if we follow I. F. Stone (1988) on Socrates, for cooperating with the very tyrants they had repudiated. Both are then accused of "corrupting the youth" of their respective nations with the intent of banning them from teaching. Heidegger's trial has been the more prolonged, with various critics still in search of family and university documents. However, neither figure ever endorsed democratic values nor apologized for their brief involvements, each insisting that political values were not relevant to their more spiritual-philosophical concerns—Heidegger coming to this conclusion in the 1966 *Der Spiegel* interview and considerably later than Socrates.

Both defended themselves against their accusers with "Apologies" of sorts. Here the contrast is perhaps the greatest, between

Socrates' stoic repudiation and gentle taunting and Heidegger's temporizing and incompleteness. Yet it is fascinating, in passing, that I. F. Stone's attempt to make the Athenian position against Socrates more plausible and sympathetic uses arguments about the "elitist" and "anti-democratic" nature of spiritual thought *identical* to the recent critics of Heidegger (Farias 1989; Wolin 1990; Rockmore 1992). And just as both Socrates and Heidegger had little understanding of the necessity and value of democracy, it is equally clear that Stone and Heidegger's recent critics, perhaps also confusing an essentially political frame of reference with an inner-worldly spirituality, can find no value in the latter.

Heidegger and Weber

Neither Heidegger nor Jung could fully comprehend Max Weber's insight on the necessary separation of church and state in complex modern societies, as inherently distinct spheres of human life and intelligence whose fusion seems inevitably to end in the alchemical *monstrum*.

Heidegger and Weber represent complementary understandings within a twentieth-century inquiry into the nature of human spirituality that also includes William James, Jung, the transpersonal psychologies of meditative states, and Almaas's recent synthesis of spiritual realization and object-relations psychoanalysis. Although both Heidegger and Weber were deeply preoccupied with what they saw as the historically unique development of spirituality within the Western tradition, it is Weber who best illuminates the socio-cultural forms of charisma within complex historical societies. In particular, Weber shows how the inner-worldly mystical orientations, which Weber and Troeltsch foresaw for the modern West, will have a necessarily "broken" quality, since they cultivate a vulnerability and openness to experience in the midst of complex social constraints that will not be supportive of such sensitivities. This "broken" quality is, indeed, well illustrated in the metapathology of Heidegger's rectorship and in the "dark night" of his post war struggle.

Heidegger's noetics of Being provides the fullest conceptual context for the "naturalistic" understanding of the transpersonal as also developed by Weber, Jung, and Almaas. They in turn make far more sense of Heidegger's own spiritual path, suffering, and metapathology than he could for himself.

PART V

Roots of a Contemporary
This-Worldly Spirituality

CHAPTER 10

George Ivanovitch Gurdjieff: A Near Eastern
Inner-Worldly Mysticism in the Modern West

The Gurdjieff-Ouspensky movement directly anticipates our current crossing of psychodynamic object relations and the transpersonal perspective. In fact, Almaas's Diamond-Heart perspective is in part a refinement of the Gurdjieff perspective with respect to its more psychological side. We will see later how the life and character of Gurdjieff shows his attempts to master some of the anxieties outlined by Klein, Fairbairn, and Balint, while his system provides his own anticipations of these later developments of psychoanalysis.

Gurdjieff's Life and Teachings

Gurdjieff is a controversial and sometimes enigmatic figure. He made up different stories about his early life, many of these as a deliberate provoking and testing of his students, so that we are not even certain of his exact date of birth—estimates ranging between 1866 and 1877. What is known is that he was born in the Georgian and Armenian section of Southern Russia, as a young man travelled throughout the Near East and possibly Mongolia and Tibet, and then emerged in St. Petersburg and Moscow in 1912 with a fully complete system of inner-worldly mystical practice based on meditative techniques of self-remembering—the self-observation of one's immediate presence. He referred to his this-worldly teaching as a "fourth way" tradition, separate from the traditional paths of the yogi, magician, and saint. The system aims at the cultivation of a sense of presence or Being in the midst of everyday social involvements. After guiding

225

his core followers through the perils of post-revolutionary civil war in Russia, he established his Institute for the Harmonious Development of Man in a large chateau at Fontainebleau, outside Paris, in 1922. There he attracted some of the major intellectuals of the day, including the literary figures Katherine Mansfield and Alfred Orage, the architect Frank Lloyd Wright and his group at Taliesin, and several Jungian psychologists. He abruptly dismissed most of his followers between 1927 and 1934 in order to concentrate on writing, sold the chateau due to lack of funds, and finally returned to the teaching of small groups from his flat in Paris. By the time Gurdjieff died in 1949, he had established teaching centers in England, Germany, France, and the United States, which have continued to develop and proliferate to this day (Webb 1987; Moore 1991).

In addition to his methods of challenging and provoking students, there is also much controversy over the origins of the system, which appeared full-blown in 1912 and 1913, and was described in detail by P.D. Ouspensky (1949), his major follower from those years. There are several sides to this complexly syncretic system. Its more psychological side is based on methods of self-remembering and self-observation that would be largely Sufi in origin—and he does describe travels to Sufi monasteries in Afghanistan (Gurdjieff 1963). His attendant portrayal of ordinary personality, anticipating object-relations theory, may be based on his own studies of hypnotism and the contemporary psychiatric literature on multiple personality. Both Tart (1994) and Almaas (1988) offer current developments of these practices.

A second side of the system, most intensively taught in the early 1920s and late 1940s, and sometimes absent from contemporary Gurdjieff groups, consisted in Gurdjieff's music, dances, and complex rhythmic movements. He staged various ballets and public exhibitions of these dances, including Carnegie Hall in the 1920s. The dances themselves are certainly derived from Sufi temple dances, but it is also clear that Gurdjieff added his own music and complex movements that represented concepts from his original cosmological system. Many of the dances helped to heighten self-awareness by means of contrary movements that might involve doing one rhythmic movement with the left hand, a completely different rhythmic movement with the right, with legs directed separately and one's face making the characteristic grimace of a different emotion, from envy to rage or love. On a more prosaic level, but central to his teachings throughout, there were also the numerous "work projects." Here self-remembering was to be cultivated during gardening, housekeeping, and outdoor construction work—all under varying degrees of social and personal stress. It is meditation sustained through movement that makes the practice fully "this-worldly."

The third aspect was a theoretical cosmology, which involves an almost surreal neo-gnostic myth of creation, based on a view of the average human life as a pointless feeding of required psychic energies to the cosmos—the result of a vast mistake in creation which only those who "self-remember" can escape. The whole system is based on the musical octaves as vibration patterns that underlie different layers of reality from matter to spirit, with an elaborate pseudo-biochemistry or alchemy of "hydrogens" that purports to explain how the different energies that enter the body—food, air, and psychological impressions—are modified and specifically developed into higher "octaves" by those practicing self-remembering techniques. He divides his cosmology and inner alchemy into a "law of three" reminiscent of Hegelian dialectic, and a neo-Pythagorean "law of seven." The latter assimilates all patterns of organic development to a musical template, with "discontinuities" in the octave requiring special energies or "shocks." It is difficult to know whether Gurdjieff in the end intended this system side of his practice literally or more as an engaging metaphor for those of his followers who were more intellectual and needed an elaborate conceptual system to go along with their practices of presence.

It is the sources of this cosmology that are the most debated. On the one hand it is very reminiscent of some of the Gnostic heretical traditions, whose often satiric creation myths also influenced Jung. This has led J. G. Bennett (1973) to suggest a further Sufi influence, in that some of the desert Sufi monasteries that Gurdjieff probably visited may be survivals of much earlier Gnostic traditions that assimilated to a later conquering Islam and so formed the historical nidus of its mystical Sufism. On the other hand, much of the system may be derived either from Blavatsky's contemporaneous theosophical movement (see chapter 12), with its own synthesis of a science of subtle material "vibrations" with Hellenistic hermeticism, or from Gurdjieff's own studies of Renaissance hermetic writings. The latter contain at least anticipations of Gurdjieff's teaching diagrams of the nine-fold "Enneagram" of personal and spiritual transformation (Webb 1987). What is clear is that Gurdjieff's final system contains a set of practices largely derived from Sufism, with a more western psychology of the multiplicity of ordinary personality, all synthesized within an original version of Gnosticism and an attendant highly technical alchemy of inner experience. Finally, Gurdjieff mentions sources from Greek Orthodox monasteries around Mount Athos, which themselves preserved a more Gnostic version of Christianity, and he sometimes referred to his practice as "esoteric Christianity." Beyond that no one really knows.

One of the more controversial aspects of his teaching was his use of specific emotional challenges to instill, in his students and at times himself, the energy needed for cultivating a sense of presence. For Gurdjieff, self-remembering was worthless unless it could be done in everyday life, for which the energy from negative emotions would be necessary in order to strengthen the practice. What this meant was that Gurdjieff deliberately provoked and at times insulted his pupils. For instance, the aristocratic ex-army officer DeHartmann (1964) was told to sell carpets near a club frequented by his old associates. Once Gurdjieff thought they had mastered self-observation sufficiently, he gave his students what he himself termed "shocks," which usually hit the emotional area in which the individual was most vulnerable. At times this was done with considerable humor—at least to others—as when he persuaded an embarrassed student of the desirability of putting mustard on her ice cream (Peters 1964).

The doctrine that "shocks" can intensify a sense of presence is consistent with reports of "being experience" triggered by spontaneous situations of high arousal (Hunt 2000). It also makes sense of otherwise inexplicable, even self-destructive features of Gurdjieff's own behavior, as well as some of the rather abrupt "discontinuities" in the course of his teachings. In other words, if Gurdjieff was to provide periodic "shocks" to his followers to maintain the direction of their growth, who was there to provide these abrupt energizations to Gurdjieff other than Gurdjieff himself? Accordingly, there is his abrupt sacrifice of any use of his unusually developed hypnotic abilities at a point of early crisis and near suicidal despair, the sudden decision to leave Russia, his initial extreme push for the public presentation of the dances, and the curious episode of his 1924 automobile crash. He enjoyed taking considerable risks while driving, but on this particular occasion he had the car checked before he left, gave power of attorney to one of his major followers, refused to take his secretary along as was his usual custom, and then ran into a tree, quite possibly deliberately. He was found lying on a cushion beside the wrecked car and later very nearly died (Peters 1964; Webb 1987).

Whether the accident was consciously deliberate or more of a premonition, after a slow recovery Gurdjieff did use it to re-direct his life. This ostensibly very non literary man, disappointed in the defection of Ouspensky, on whom he had counted to write an overview of the system, suddenly decided on a writing career. He dismissed many of his pupils, ostensibly for their own good, but also telling them that he decided on this sacrifice to stimulate his own creative efforts. After three years of frustration, he repeated this again in 1927, sending away his very closest pupils as the deliberate sacrifice of those who made him the most comfortable.

Then in 1935, during the writing of his third book, none being published during his lifetime, he broke off in mid-sentence, following a major financial setback, and then mysteriously disappeared for three months. He reappeared in Paris where he began the teaching of small groups that he continued for the rest of his life. Finally, in 1948, the year before he died, there was another near-lethal car crash, this one clearly not his fault, but followed by an equally remarkable energization of his declining powers—again illustrating the role of "shocks" in his understanding. It was Gurdjieff's use of shocks, often brutally embarrassing to new pupils and appropriately penetrating to his more advanced followers, that made him so controversial and meant that many of his major followers, including Ouspensky, eventually left. Although many returned during his final, calmer years and resumed the practice. Gurdieff's approach here is actually an extension of a heterodox Sufi tradition called the Way of Blame, or Malamat, in which Sufi masters would insult, provoke, and otherwise upset their pupils in order to test their degree of attainment and meditative abilities (Bennett 1973).

Gurdjieff's books, perplexing to some but widely appreciated, continue his sometimes frustrating practices in literary form. His first and most ambitious book was titled *All and Everything: Beelzebub's Tales to His Grandson* (1950). It is 1200 pages long, surreal, and deliberately written to be extremely difficult to read—with stories that he re-wrote chapters when his students found them too understandable. Most of its sentences are a page or so long, and full of clauses, parentheses, and addendums of all kinds, telling long impossible stories inside impossible stories, within which the reader becomes lost—a bit like the *Arabian Nights*. The book consists of the stories told by Beelzebub, misunderstood as the devil, to his endlessly inquisitive grandson, Hassein, about the misguided history of the earth—while both travel back to earth on the spaceship Karnak so that Beelzebub can make one last attempt to wake up human beings, in the tradition of Jesus and Buddha, so that we can finally remember ourselves and cultivate a sense of presence. His explanations of why this is necessary provides an elaborate and often absurd history of the earth, starting with the civilization of Atlantis and proceeding with a fractured and

satiric history of the world through World War I. It will indeed frustrate the average reader in much the way that Gurdjieff would challenge one in person. The preface states that its aim "is to destroy,
mercilessly, without any compromises whatsoever, in the mentation
and feelings of the reader, the beliefs and views by centuries rooted in
him, about everything existing in the world" (1950: v). Depending on
one's point of view, the book is either delightful or maddening.

Gurdjieff's second effort was the strange but more accessible
Meetings with Remarkable Men (1963), which purports to be the
story of his childhood and his wanderings in Afghanistan and Persia,
his encounters with various holy men, and the people who accompanied him on this journey to the East in search of ancient mystical
wisdom. Again, the book is an indeterminable mix of probable truth
and obviously wild stories. The portraits of his father and of his first
tutor, a local priest, are very persuasive, powerful and personal, but
once he gets out onto the steppes of Asia we find stories of crossing
the Gobi Desert during sandstorms by walking on stilts, in order to
be above the storm, or selling sparrows as rare canaries by painting
them yellow.

His final book, *Life is Real Only Then, When "I Am,"* is the most
practical and accessible. It was not published until 1975; up until
then it was privately circulated among Gurdjieff groups. It tells a
much more believable story of his early wanderings and spiritual
crises, something of what he learned in Sufi monasteries, and specific instructions on various techniques of self-observation and self-
remembering. He wrote and rewrote essentially nonstop between
1924 and 1935, again with this last work ending in mid-sentence
and to which he never returned, even though he lived until 1949.[1]

As to how Gurdjieff himself has been represented in print by
those who knew him, we find diametrically different views, depending on who wrote them and when they were written. Not surprisingly, given his use of emotional shocks and his deliberate tendency
to present himself as a charlatan or huckster as a test and challenge
to prospective new students, and also given that his sense of humor
was a bit reminiscent of the Marx Brothers, many of the accounts
that were written about him during his life were quite negative
(Pauwels 1964). Early accounts were often based on the outrage and
injury felt by somebody he had insulted and who had left the teaching. It is also the case that between 1917 and 1924 he drove himself
and his followers very hard (DeHartmann 1964). There was a widely
remarked sense of emergency and even desperation in his approach,
and there were some breakdowns and suicide attempts in disaf-

fected followers during those years. All of this combined during his lifetime to give the public impression of an almost malevolent figure, reminiscent of Aleister Crowley (see chapter 11), even though he was also drawing the serious attention of many intellectuals of his day. After 1935 he softened his methods and became considerably gentler, while still administering his own brand of emotional shocks. He is often described in these final years as conveying a sense of detachment, a quiet sadness, and more obvious compassion, with a kinder acceptance of the limitations of his students (Bennett 1962; Hulme 1966; Peters 1965; Popoff 1973).

Common to the earlier controversial accounts and these later accounts from the followers who stayed with him throughout, are descriptions of his powerful presence, and extraordinary humor. The following relatively benign example comes from his early Russian period:

> On one occasion a small group of us came to the apartment . . . at the appointed time . . . When we . . . were admitted in the, by then, familiar state between fear and almost aching anticipation, we found the door to the room where we were to foregather locked. What to do? We stood in the little hall, silent, looking at each other without looking, each hoping someone else would take the initiative. While we were standing there awkward and uneasy, Mr. Gurdjieff appeared from the kitchen and looked us over. . . . Stroking his moustache, he said in a tone of distress, "Oh, is scandal! Such important people to be kept waiting! Where is Lise? Where is key?"

> This did nothing to allay our awkwardness and unease. Somehow we were more aware than ever before of our total *lack* of importance. But to disclaim importance was as out of the question as was pulling ourselves together to pretend it. We were totally exposed, frozen in our inability to find a formula for behavior. . . .

> Still murmuring about "scandal" and "important people" Mr. Gurdjieff disappeared into the kitchen and returned bearing in his hand an absolutely gigantic screwdriver and a miniature tack hammer, apparently with the intention of taking the hinges off the door so we could be admitted and not kept standing any longer. Unbelievably, he looked precisely like any clown you might see in a circus, embarrassed and apologetic, engaged in a hopelessly impossible task

with totally unsuitable tools. How could anyone offer to help him? No one can help a clown! We were more paralyzed than before, if such a thing is possible. Surely this was an hallucination. . . .

After a few minutes more of his struggle with the giant screwdriver and the minute hammer, attended with no effect whatever on the door hinges, by the way, Lise returned with her shopping basket. . . . She listened quietly, put down her basket, reached up to the lintel over the door and got the key from its resting place there. She unlocked the door in silence, and in silence we sheepishly filed into the room. . . . (Stavely, *Memories of Gurdjieff*: 11–13)

Gurdjieff's Anticipations of Object-Relations Theory

Gurdjieff is reminiscent of both Heidegger and Winnicott in his view that people in the modern West have lost their capacity to Be— to have a sense of presence and of their own existence as such. The best way to see how Gurdjieff anticipates the interface between psychoanalytic approaches to narcissism and current transpersonal psychology is through his portrayal of what he takes to be the inner condition of the average civilized Westerner. Here he is holding up a challenging mirror to his pupils, and it shows the same dilemmas of narcissism and schizoid sense of self described by Winnicott, Fairbairn, Kohut, and Balint—and this beginning in 1912. Reminiscent of Winnicott on dilemma in sense of true self, Gurdjieff describes his prospective followers as lacking any sense of inner essence, without a central "I" or "center of gravity." Essence typically stops developing in early childhood, so that our capacity to feel spontaneously real and present in the world stays at best on a four- or five-year-old level. Self-remembering, and later on, self-remembering with negative emotions, begins to build bridges from a current false self organization back to this stunted essence, so that essential development can continue into adulthood—a notion also central to Almaas. This is a process now made more difficult in a secular, alienated society where childhood presence is not mirrored by a corresponding adult sense of presence.

For Winnicott, too, our sense of a lost or inaccessible true self is covered by a false self based on a reactive outer accommodation. For Gurdjieff, the outer face of personality becomes a false mask covering, not essence, or a central self, but what he calls the many I's or egos resulting from its fragmentation, and among which we unconsciously shift based on inner and external dynamics—a view later developed more specifically by Fairbairn and Klein. This false personality, which Gurdjieff finds endemic in modern life, is based on a series of largely unconscious "identifications." Gurdjieff, and now Almaas, use the term "identifying" to mean getting lost or "hypnotized" in everyday life. In identifying, we are so over-involved in unconscious role playing with others that we lose or don't even notice our more fundamental sense of presence. Here Gurdjieff is reminiscent of Melanie Klein on introjective and projective identifications as a defense against a primal sense of anxiety emerging from the helplessness of the young infant—although Gurdjieff understands this more in terms of a fear of death.

Gurdjieff can also remind us of Fairbairn's view of a fundamental schizoid position based on a sense of inner emptiness and futility. For Gurdjieff, as for Jung, modern individuals are fundamentally running away from a sense of meaninglessness. Whereas for Fairbairn and Winnicott this creates an underlying withdrawal from fully embodied aliveness, Gurdjieff's version portrays the average person as "asleep," as if "sleepwalking" through life. This false detachment and its underlying schizoidness is conveyed by Walker in his over-view of Gurdjieff's system:

> I soon realized that Ouspensky was not speaking in a poetic or figurative manner about man's being asleep. He meant us to take his words literally, that we were all living in a sleepwalking world, a world inhabited by people who moved about in a twilight of consciousness and yet imagined themselves to be awake. (Walker, *A Study of Gurdjieff's Teaching*: 36)

A related way of describing this unconscious automaticity, lacking any sense of grounded presence or true self, is Gurdjieff's characterization of ordinary behavior as machine-like. Again, this is very reminiscent of Fairbairn and Winnicott on the artificiality and mechanicalness of schizoid clients.

Finally, there is a similarity between Klein on a fundamental paranoid position, ultimately based on early infant anxieties, Heidegger on the dread implicit in our human "being-towards-death," and Gurdjieff on the motivating power of becoming fully conscious of what he calls the "terror of the situation." He often illustrated this implicit terror underlying ordinary living with his parable of the magician and his many sheep. Not wanting to bother with a shepherd or a fence, the magician hypnotized them into believing they were immortal, that no harm was done to them when they were skinned, that it would even be pleasant and done out of love, and that whatever would happen to them would at any rate not happen just now:

> After this all his cares and worries about the sheep came to an end. They never ran away again but quietly awaited the time when the magician would require their flesh and skins. This tale is a very good illustration of man's position. (Ouspensky, *In Search of the Miraculous*: 219)

> In short, to look his own death, as is said, "in the face" the average man cannot and must not—he would then, so to say, "get out of his depth" and before him, in clear-cut form, the question would arise: "Why then should I live and toil and suffer? . . . Do not we, people, ourselves also feed, watch over, look after, and make the lives of our sheep and pigs as comfortable as possible . . . in order to slaughter them one fine day and to obtain the meat we require, with as much fat as possible. In the same way Nature takes all measures to ensure that we shall live without seeing the terror, and that we should not hang ourselves, but live long; and then, when we are required, She slaughters us. (Gurdjieff, *All and Everything*: 1225–26)

While we will see later some of the projective personal dynamics within Gurdjieff's Gnostic dualism, it is also true that most spiritual traditions, as also with Heidegger, use the inevitability of death as a wake-up call. Certainly, any individual in whom the dilemmas of self and sense of being described by object-relations theory were prominent and painful would have felt well recognized and mirrored in Gurdjieff's stark portrayal of false personality, multiple selves, and the need to awaken to essence.

"Self-remembering" creates the "first conscious shock" in Gurdjieff's inner alchemy. Along with attendant exercises in self-observation, it begins the building of the sense of a permanent I. Self-remembering is the attempt, in the midst of one's ordinary activities, to become aware of one's here and now beingness. Although it is a fundamentally nonverbal sense, were one to put it into words, it becomes, "I am here, now, in this situation, reading this book." A preliminary version of this state involves attempting to sense one's arms and legs while staying involved in one's activities and feelings, so that there is a simultaneity of doing and Being. This attitude goes very much against the grain of the involvements of ordinary life, within which we tend to lose ourselves. It is a combination of orientations that are ordinarily separate and in competition—a simultaneous outward participation and a witnessing self-awareness.

> To remember one's self means the same thing as to be aware of oneself, I am. Sometimes it comes by itself. It is a very strange feeling. It is not a function, not thinking, not feeling, it is a different state of consciousness. By itself it only comes for very short moments, generally in quite new surroundings and one says to oneself "how strange I am actually here." This is self-remembering. At those moments you remember yourself. (Ouspensky, *The Fourth Way*: 8)

There can also arise a sense of exhilaration and clarity in the midst of this here and now presence, reminiscent of Maslow on "peak experience" and some accounts of lucid dreaming. Lucid dreams can also involve a similar delicate balance between self-awareness and dream participation, with a correspondingly vivid sense of kinesthetic embodiment and energized presence, and even bliss (Hunt 1989). Here is a similar account of the effects of self-remembering practice from a later Gurdjieff student:

> To have the sensation, for the first time in my life, that my head and my body were working together and that this vibrating team possesses a tenfold energy. . . . A fleeting sensation of no longer being alone, separate, but reconnected to an immense presence. . . . One day, like a rain of gold showering down over my head, shoulders, and back, I was completely aglow, inundated by a grace both luminous and solid, which I received with surprise and wonder. . . . Is this what it is to be "touched by grace"? (De Vilaine-Cambessedes, No conscious effort is ever lost: 395)

Gurdjieff's "second conscious shock" involved the attempt to self-remember during "negative emotions," whether spontaneous or induced by "shocks." Certainly intense, unexpected stress can induce the closely related states of double awarenesses of being in a situation and sensing oneself as within it, also found in lucid dreams, out-of-body states, and near-death experiences (Green 1968a, 1968b).

Coming to recognize and use one's characteristic negative emotions as spontaneous "shocks" entailed a coming face to face with what Gurdjieff called one's "chief feature"—his last major parallel with contemporary object-relations theory.

One's chief feature is the fundamental character flaw or deficiency specific to each of us but which, in our narcissism and unconscious wish for perfection, we do not want to see. Gurdjieff here is very reminiscent of Balint's (1968) discussion of "basic fault." For Balint, near the end of deep therapy and preceding its potential for a "new beginning," the client must deal with narcissistic levels of dilemma in which he/she gradually comes to accept a sense of a basic flaw or fault in their lives that cannot be altered. Instead, it must be mourned with an acceptance and quiet sadness. This is also the mark of a new maturity for Melanie Klein (Klein et al. 1952) in her discussion of the "depressive position."

Gurdjieff seems to be calling attention to a very similar phenomenon, although the language he uses for identifying "basic fault" is typically colorful. Sometimes he calls it the confrontation with one's "inner animal," in the sense of our most ingrained emotional habits which we automatically indulge as the core of ordinary ego identity. At other times, he refers to it as "making the moon inside," alluding to his Gnostic cosmology of creation and its occasionally sci-fi version of metaphysics. Specifically, the "ray of creation" extends from the Absolute through the level of all suns and all planets to the moon as the densest level of matter in the universe. Energy vibrations are cycled all through this system, aided by humanoid "three-brained beings," of which we on earth are but one example. But in the creation of our particular "ray" something went terribly wrong, so that our moon split in two, and the entirety of our energies and lives had to go "to feed the moon." By the time this total drainage, rendering our lives pointless and without meaning, was no longer necessary, we were stuck in the habit of energy dissipation. Only the discipline of self-remembering can bring about the conscious acceptance of the inner moon in ourselves, paying it the energies needed for reciprocal maintenance of the universe via our *intentional* conscious suffering, and so liberating extra energies for the sense of presence that can then send energy upward again toward the Absolute. "Making the moon in ourselves" is the conscious acceptance of our inner version of this cosmic flaw, which alone can liberate the higher energies of presence.

In Gurdjieff's most pointedly entertaining version of chief feature, it is referred to as "crystallizing one's idiot." Later in life he developed a classification of twenty-one different kinds of idiot, or character structure, and he would preside over lengthy banquets with toasts to the different kinds of idiot, with each person required not to drink when their particular brand of idiocy was being toasted. By "crystallizing the idiot," Gurdjieff means that understanding one's chief feature does not lead to its elimination or "transcendence," but rather to its conscious acceptance as the specific form taken by one's inevitable human suffering—perhaps centered on jealousy, or pride, resentment, fear, etc. In *Secret Talks with Mr. G.*, purporting to be the written record of one of Gurdjieff's New York small groups, he says:

> I should mention, by the way, that your chief weakness will not only not be eliminated, but will be crystallized as an idiot permanently, thereby dashing all your hopes for purification. You would not wish this for yourself with vanity and self-love, because you do not wish to be objective idiot in any respect. [An objective idiot is somebody who knows they are an idiot.] But I assure you that a chief weakness is necessary as channel for higher influences in order to direct you in the Work. This is a wish contrary to your nature, perhaps even to your present whole being. As you are now, you would not like it. (Gurdjieff, *Secret Talks*: 84)

One's chief feature needs to be identified so it can become a "reminding factor" to assist self-remembering, rather than functioning as an automatic stimulus to deeper unconsciousness.

As with Balint on "basic fault," this work on chief feature is the final giving up of one's narcissistic fantasies of self-perfection. Gurdjieff is clear that sacrificing one's largely unconscious wish to be perfect will be painful. For Almaas (1988), Engler (1984), and Epstein (1998) a danger of long-term meditative practice for many Westerners will be a fueling of an underlying narcissistic fantasy of self-idealization. Narcissistic persons are often perfectionistic, and may be especially drawn to meditative practice as a way of becoming still more perfect. Yet sooner or later, if meditation is the actual observation of what is really present in consciousness, that will include the sense of personal deficiency, inadequacy, and emptiness basic to the ordinary defensively structured ego, pervasive in modern society. To persevere on the meditative path past that point it is necessary to consciously sacrifice "perfection" and accept inherent suffering, and on this point Gurdjieff was more precise than many contemporary spiritual teachers. Inevitably, many would-be students were disappointed.

Gurdjieff's understanding of "self-remembering" as a means to personal presence, and the attendant acceptance of ones chief feature, places Gurdjieff very much within the frame of Weber's inner-worldly mysticism. His system is an inner-worldly mysticism, first, because "self-remembering" is a practice to be done in the world—an "extraverted" meditation, so to speak. Second, the transcendence to more impersonal, formless states of consciousness, what Gurdjieff called "objective consciousness," was not part of his formal practice, since, with Almaas, he held that a permanent "I" was necessary first. As with what we can infer from many of the earlier Gnostics, objective consciousness for Gurdjieff would come principally after death, if a permanent soul (presence) had first been created by self-remembering. Reminiscent of the Tibetan Buddhist Bardo state, the energies of those who have a permanent "center of gravity" or soul expand at death up the ray of creation into higher levels of being.[2] Those who do not self-remember will "feed the moon." They "die like dogs." This "postponing" of classical mystical experience until death or near death is characteristic of the more inner-worldly spiritualities, both mystical and prophetical— the latter concretizing the formless states as "heaven."

Finally, Weber's "broken humility," as specifically characteristic of the inner-worldly mystic, is reflected not only in Gurdjieff's views on "intentional suffering" and "crystallizing the idiot," but more personally in his own shift from the demanding drivenness with his students, and himself, toward a deepening compassion, stillness, and quiet sadness after 1935—his own final acceptance of the inescapable limitations of his life and circumstances.

Object-Relational Dilemmas in Gurdjieff's Life and System

The object-relational vulnerabilities that Gurdjieff's teachings sought to address in his students, also appear in his own life. In both Gurdjieff's life and in the way in which his life issues appear at times projected within his system, we find some of the tensions of Kohut's narcissistic self-pathology and Klein and Fairbairn on the paranoid-schizoid position. Gurdjieff was obviously an extremely complex and controversial figure, and there is no consensus on his impact or on his system. Certainly in periods of his life, particularly between about 1917 and 1935, when he finished his writing, there is a quality of drivenness and desperation. Gurdjieff does appear at these times as a mystic on the edge of pathology and disintegration. We have seen how his system used felt deficits in sense of self as opportunities for self-remembering. Although he was capable of great subtlety and empathy, at times the "shocks" he administered were dislocating and disruptive in their effects, fixating the very dilemmas they were intended to transform. Yet the overall direction of his later impact on pupils moves more obviously towards an integration and coherence.

Gurdjieff's accounts of his childhood, found in *Meetings with Remarkable Men* and *Beelzebub's Tales* and in certain stories he told, are useful in indicating some of the object-relational dynamics that both drove his spiritual quest and at times blocked it as well. Although many of these stories may be exaggerated or even created out of whole cloth, they also illustrate the themes since explicated by the object-relations analysts and are consistent with his outward struggles as spiritual seeker.

THE SCHIZOID POSITION

We can locate aspects of Fairbairn and Winnicott on the schizoid dilemma in Gurdjieff's more autobiographical writings. Winnicott's notion of the sense of despair over a false self that blocks a higher true self, and Fairbairn on futility as the emotional indicator of the schizoid dilemma, are reflected in *Life is Real Only Then, When I Am*. There Gurdjieff discusses the overpowering disillusionment and doubt he faced near the end of his wanderings and search for teachers, over whether there was any true spiritual teaching. His deeply felt terror of "inner emptiness" is also reminiscent of Jung's autobiography, a dread of meaninglessness and its attendant despair that pushed the spiritual search of both men. Gurdjieff's attempts to move past this state were characteristically extreme, involving struggles over suicide and the enlivening shocks which he semi-deliberately administered to himself by seeking out situations of extreme physical danger—claiming to have been shot twice during his wanderings, and financing his travels by working for the Czarist secret police.

Another theme central to Fairbairn (1954) is the schizoid rejection of love as dangerous. Many have noted the absence of merging love in Gurdjieff's teaching, and of compassion during his more driven period. The dualism of good and evil in his system is consistent with early splits in a primal maternal image, and it is striking that the negative metaphysical forces blocking self-remembering are always understood as feminine—evocative of Klein and Jung on the imago of the "terrible mother." Thus the average person is lost in a withdrawn "sleep," until a feminine "Great Nature" eats us, consuming everything within at death. At times his cosmology almost seems a response to a lack of basic trust in Erikson's (1963) sense.

In one of his major teaching stories, the fourth way of the sly man involves tricking the devil into teaching us the means to develop a true soul and so outwit "Great Nature" and finally achieve immortality. Similarly his monstrous quasi-gnostic account of our ordinary energies merely going to "feed the moon" involves both orality and imagery of the destructive feminine. It is as though in Jungian terms Gurdjieff runs together the shadow and anima. Gurdjieff's comments about women also show a sharp ambivalence. At times he would say that women could only become spiritually developed through association with a man, or on occasion through sex with him—of which there are several stories. Yet it is also true that his major women followers were treated with respect and as independent seekers in their own right.

Fairbairn considers role playing and exhibitionism as a defense against a primary schizoid anxiety over any act of giving—love being sensed as a losing of oneself or being consumed by the other. That this would be part of Gurdjieff's own personal struggle is implied by his constant role playing. He referred to this extravagantly provocative behavior toward his pupils as "divine acting," which he himself links to a kind of withdrawal:

> In my youth, I too . . . worked on myself very much for the purpose of attaining such a blessing as I thought predetermined by Heaven; and after enormous efforts and continuous rejection of nearly everything deserved in ordinary life, I finally reached a state when nothing from the outside could really touch me internally; and, so far as acting was concerned, I brought myself to such perfection as was never dreamed of by the learned people of ancient Babylon for the actors on the stage. (In Nott, *Teachings of Gurdjieff*: 112)

Fairbairn also mentions the substitution of the compulsion to be hated as the deepest defense against anxieties over the wish to be loved. Gurdjieff developed an extraordinary refinement of the Sufi "way of blame," where the teacher deliberately and repeatedly puts himself in a bad or negative light in order to provoke and test the confidence of the pupil. On dynamic grounds this may have been especially congenial to Gurdjieff, and it can be seen as a systemization and sublimation of the conflict that Fairbairn is describing. For Gurdjieff, of course, intense love or hate from his students was a mark of identifying and a failure to self remember, but he often seemed most comfortable when provoking them.

He could accomplish [transformation] only through playing
roles. . . . Then one had to hold back from reacting badly and
not be resentful. Mr. Gurdjieff told me once that when I was
resentful it caused him pain. . . . However, the art with
which Mr. Gurdjieff brought us this pain was so great . . .
that . . . we were quite sure that there stood before us a cold
and even cruel man. . . . Protests exploded like gunshots. Mr.
Gurdjieff's face would begin at once to change. He resumed
his usual expression, but looked very sad and would walk
away without a single word. (De Hartmann, *Our Life with
Mr. Gurdjieff*: 43 and 103)

Some of the uniquely Gurdjieffian features of his cosmological
system also show a version of Freud's model of primary narcissism.
Gurdjieff portrays a time before the creation of the universe when the
Holy Sun Absolute was completely bound up within and sufficient
onto itself, which he refers to as Autoegocrat. The present universe of
reciprocally "feeding" vibrations is only created because the Absolute
notices a gradual shrinking that would eventually have entailed its
disappearance.[3] The resulting cosmos and its "three brained beings"
primarily serve to avoid this shrinkage. At best this leaves our universe as a kind of secondary narcissism. Absent here is any hint of the
pure generosity and nurturant gift of creation in Plotinus, Christian
mysticism, and Sufism (Izutsu 1984), all potential sources we might
expect Gurdieff to echo, and which are, in turn, more consistent with
Winnicott and Fairbairn's substitution of a primary relatedness for
Freud's primary narcissism.

Positing a primary narcissism actually implies a defensive contraction in the face of early trauma and neglect, and it seems relevant
that Winnicott makes dissolution and disappearance a "primal agony"
of a traumatized early relatedness. For Winnicott, both Freud's model
of infancy and Gurdjieff's account of cosmological "infancy" would unwittingly enshrine defensive reactivities in place of what the classical
mysticisms and object-relations theory both see as a primary fundamental relatedness. In this regard, even the heterodox Gnosticisms
relegated reflections of object-relational dilemmas to a later and secondary level of creation—involving the "mistake" of Sophia as consequence of her distance from a more primal and purely generous One.
On Gurdjieff's model, God ultimately needs *our* help, a theme in Jung
(1961) as well, and which itself echoes the tendency in young children
to take on the unacknowledged terrors of borderline or psychotic parents in an attempt to relieve the latters' pain (Searles 1979).

The Paranoid Position

It is not surprising then that we find reflections in this system of the splitting between all-good versus all-bad that Melanie Klein makes central to her "paranoid position" of dynamically conflicted infancy. We have seen that this kind of dualism between good and evil, higher and lower, tends to be the dilemma that inner-worldly mysticisms do not often resolve, rarely reaching into an all-reconciling One—"beyond good and evil." For Klein this splitting originates predominantly on a maternal level, it is pre-oedipal, and she understands the shift to the beginning of the oedipal position as a projection of one or the other of these ideal or persecutory personifications onto the father. Thus, the earlier split continues as the child's perception of an exaggerated division between the mother and father.

We do find some evidence for major splitting in Gurdjieff. A first example comes from comments that Ouspensky makes about Gurdjieff in the 1920s, which certainly need to be taken with a grain of salt, since in Gurdjieff's view Ouspensky had failed to respond as intended to a major shock/challenge, and much to Gurdjieff's regret had broken off all further contact.[4] Yet it is also true that many had similar views of Gurdjieff during his more conflicted period:

> His possibilities are much greater than those of people like ourselves. But he can also go in the wrong way. I believe that he is now passing through a crisis, the outcome of which no one can foresee. Most people have many "I's." . . . But with Mr. Gurdjieff there are only two "I's"; one very good and one very bad. I believe that in the end the good "I" will conquer. But meanwhile it is very dangerous to be near him. . . . He could go mad. Or else he could attract to himself some disaster in which all those around him would be involved. (In Bennett, *Witness: The Story of a Search*: 134)

It is interesting to note that Gurdjieff's mother is almost never mentioned in the autobiographical or pseudo autobiographical accounts of his childhood in *Beelzebub's Tales* or *Meetings*, while the father is absolutely idealized. Entirely true or intended more symbolically, we do get a hint of the thematics of Kleinian splitting and persecutory anxiety. Gurdjieff dates his awareness of what he later called "the terror of the situation," the inevitability of one's own death, to the death of his grandmother at the age of seven. He mentions the great influence his grandmother's death had on him, with the trauma probably magnified by the failure of his father's business soon afterwards and the necessity of the family moving several times. His description from *Beelzebub's Tales* does convey a strong persecutory anxiety and a resulting shift in the child's behavior between withdrawal and a driven acting out.

Gurdjieff is called to his grandmother's deathbed and she gives him the "strict injunction . . . somewhat angrily and imposingly. . . . In life never do as others do," after which she immediately died:

> All this made so powerful an impression on me at that time that I suddenly became unable to endure anyone around me, and therefore . . . stole away . . . and lay there, without food or drink, in a tempest of whirling and confused thoughts . . . right until the return from the cemetery of my mother. . . . I then immediately emerged . . . ran to her and clinging fast to her skirts, involuntarily began to stamp my feet, and why, I don't know, to imitate the braying of the donkey belonging to our neighbour, a bailiff. (Gurdjieff, *All and Everything*: 27–28)

He then continues to follow his grandmother's injunction at the subsequent requiem service:

> Suddenly without any rhyme or reason . . . instead of standing quietly as if overwhelmed with an expression of grief on one's face . . . I started skipping round the grave as if dancing and sang: "Let her with the saints repose, Now that she's turned up her toes." And just from this it began, that in my entirety a "something" arose which . . . always and in everything engendered what I should now call an "irresistible urge" to do things not as others do them. (*All and Everything*: 29–30)

We get the picture then of a powerful anxiety sweeping into his childhood with the grandmother's death and profoundly changing his sense of self. It is also interesting that the drivenness in his teaching methods accelerates after his mother and wife arrive at his Institute at Fontainebleau early in 1923, and that his crisis of 1927, when he sends away his closest pupils as a self-administered shock to energize his writing, comes in the year after the death of his wife, and in the midst of renewed thoughts of suicide. His mother died in 1925, and it seems relevant that he links her death to his decision to begin his writing, albeit in a deliberately provocative interview with a journalist. The latter was told, at least, that after his mother's death Gurdjieff had erected a tombstone with the inscription: "Here lies the mother of one who sees himself forced by her death to write the book *Les Opiumistes*" (Landau 1964: 151). No such book exists, and it seems very unlikely that this inscription would be on his mother's grave—although with Gurdjieff one never knows. Yet the linkage of women, mothers, death, loss, terror, and Gurdjieff's trickster role playing seems clear. We are told that Gurdjieff mourned both women deeply, but he never discusses them in his writings. The contrast with the strongly idealized father is all the more striking.

In this system the Holy Sun Absolute is thoroughly male, while the all-devouring moon and "Great Nature" are always referred to as female. Given Gurdjieff's Greek Orthodox background that is not surprising, but it does separate Gurdjieff from many of the Gnosticisms that may have been his indirect source. Sophia as higher wisdom is not part of this approach. How personal this split may have been to Gurdjieff comes through when he speaks of his own father. Ouspensky, who saw them together, said that Gurdjieff was especially respectful and attentive to his father when they visited. Gurdjieff describes his father's goal in life as being an inner freedom based on the development of will, which of course is later very much the focus of Gurdjieff's system. He also describes his father's teaching as "never to put much trust in anyone or anything" (Gurdjieff 1963: 39). While his accounts of his father's huge influence on him in this regard may be somewhat fictionalized as teaching stories, Gurdjieff's reminiscences of his childhood give the picture of somebody who is also quite overwhelming, especially if we think of these practices as applied to a small boy:

> My father took measures on every suitable occasion so that there should be formed in me, instead of data engendering impulses such as fastidiousness, repulsion, squeamishness, fear, timidity and so on, the data for an attitude of indifference to everything that usually evokes these impulses. I very well remember how, with this aim in view, he would sometimes slip a frog, a worm, a mouse, or some other animal likely to evoke these impulses, into my bed. . . . He always forced me to get up early in the morning . . . and splash myself all over with cold spring water . . . and if I tried to resist he would never yield, and although he was very kind and loved, me, he would punish me without mercy. (Gurdjieff, *Meetings with Remarkable Men*: 44–45)

Even making allowance for time and place, it is perhaps surprising how hard Gurdjieff sometimes drove his students, in the service of an ideal of self-sacrifice, to develop the values his father had instilled. Its overdetermination seems clear from how counterproductive it could be at certain times and with certain students. The system aims at a decidedly masculine "will" and "power," with the values of love and compassion implied in his overall cosmology but not developed as such. The schizoid and paranoid dilemmas implicit in his system, and at times explicit in his behavior, do show the kinds of tensions Gurdjieff was attempting to resolve for himself and for others. He himself lived his own system by using "shocks" to come to essence, and so surmount the "discontinuities of vibrations" that were not only part of his cosmology, but dominated his life.

THE DEPRESSIVE POSITION: MAKING REPARATION AND THE CAPACITY FOR CONCERN

While there are these indications that Gurdjieff was coping with specific paranoid-schizoid and narcissistic vulnerabilities, there are also signs both in the system and especially in his later teachings of some resolution of these difficulties. In Klein's terms the surmounting of paranoid-schizoid anxieties is based on a shift into the depressive position, manifested in a capacity for grief and guilt. This shift from relating to others in terms of all good vs. all bad personifications to a more ambivalent relation with a whole, complex, other—perceived as separate from, and not symbiotically fused with, onself—is also marked by a wish to make reparation for felt destructiveness. Winnicott (1963b) generalized Klein's depressive position into a capacity for concern for others as real separate beings, for whom one can feel responsible, in contrast to the more persecutory, self-punishing quality of guilt in the primitive super-ego. We have already discussed Balint's more inward version, as a mourning over and final acceptance of the realistic sense of inevitable deficit in oneself.

The goals of Gurdjieff's self-remembering practice are repeatedly described as the development of a central "I" capable of "genuine remorse" and "objective conscience." His system pictures the purpose of such a spiritual maturity as serving to help God in maintaining the ray of creation by means of an "intentional suffering," based on assuming a responsibility for a higher level of suffering than would ordinarily be one's lot. By fully opening to and accepting one's actual life situation, and its attendant potential for spiritual development, one was helping to "alleviate God's suffering." Correspondingly, Gurdjieff's personal behavior after 1935 increasingly manifested a quiet sadness and compassion, as if acknowledging that he had done the best he could to have a transformative impact on contemporary society and had finally accepted his own limitations and the realities of his times. So he settled more calmly into the teaching of smaller groups, without the drivenness and extremity that had characterized his earlier work. We have already seen the close parallels between acknowledging and using one's chief feature and Balint on the acceptance of basic fault as an ultimate letting go of the narcissistic need for perfection.

There are also reflections of Gurdjieff in Kohut's (1977, 1984) discussion of the therapeutic resolution of narcissism and the development of a higher sense of self. For Kohut the end of therapy with narcissistic clients is marked by the ability of the person to give up a sense of grandiosity and to move away from a false idealization of others towards a more realistic de-idealization and acceptance of the actual conditions of one's life. Certainly whatever else was involved in Gurdjieff's use of "emotional shocks" to lay bare "chief feature," it was designed to puncture people's grandiosity. Given the implied wish for a kind of perfection in the spiritual quest, such that many modern persons so attracted will inevitably have strong narcissistic issues, Gurdjieff's methods would quickly, if at times ruthlessly, determine how close an individual might be to the vulnerability and openness needed to let go of any inflated self-importance.

A process of radical de-idealization at the more advanced levels of the teaching is also implied by Gurdjieff's discussions of his own earlier disillusionments, and his repeated statements that the ultimate goal of a fourth way teaching is that the student reaches a point where they can let go of the teacher and let go of the system and become their own person—based on a direct openness to presence. Webb's discussion in *The Harmonious Circle* of the relation between Gurdjieff's early period of spiritual search and his later system fits well with Kohut on the role of de-idealization in the later stages of psychotherapy:

> At the beginning, [Gurdjieff] informed his pupils, he was "psychopathic." I believe that he meant this seriously. The journey of Hassein on the Karnak is a reflection of the progressive disillusionment of Gurdjieff himself. We can now date the point at which he recognized the extent of his disillusion. This is . . . in 1905, after he returned to Central Asia. . . . At the age of thirty-one, at last realizing that no one and nothing could help him to understand the meaning

of existence, Gurdjieff carried out a revision of the premises on which he based his life. He then set about perfecting a method which might allow his pupils to undergo the disillusioning process at "an accelerated tempo." (Webb, *The Harmonious Circle*: 556–57)

A further indication for Kohut of the resolution of narcissistic issues is the emergence of a full and genuine sense of humor. This is strikingly absent in narcissistic clients. Of course Gurdjieff's humor was extraordinary if often controversial. Jung also had a large and at times excessive sense of humor, whereas Nietzsche, Thoreau, and Crowley remain within a humor of irony, cynicism, and sarcasm— this more indicative of issues of unmetabolized hatred. Now Gurdjieff was no stranger to sarcasm, and his humor could be pointed and ostensibly cruel when "administered" as "shocks." Yet the range of his humor is amazing, extending from a sense of subtle irony to the social anarchy of the Marx Brothers. The stories of his behavior in the books of Fritz Peters (1964, 1965) and others are hilarious, and *Beelzebub's Tales* is genuinely funny, if exasperating. It is probably the only sacred book of a spiritual movement largely based on humor. A further part of the humor in all this is that so many of his followers were without any—including Ouspensky and his followers, and perhaps attesting to the very narcissistic issues they would initially bring to such a spiritual search.

Gurdjieff and Almaas

In many ways Almaas can be regarded as completing Gurdjieff's system, adding the object-relations analysis already anticipated in Gurdjieff's psychology and filling in Gurdjieff's briefly glossed "objective consciousness" with formless dimensions similar to the understandings of Plotinus, Sufism, Vedanta, and Buddhism. Gurdjieff's "essence," the sense of individual presence sought through self-remembering, becomes more fully differentiated by Almaas into essential self, or identity as being, on the one hand, and personal essence, with its more personal sense of fullness, autonomy, and contactfulness, on the other. Almaas (1984) sees a one-sidedness in Gurdjieff's approach to presence, since it centers almost exclusively on the development of essential will—"the capacity to do" via the "super-efforts" of self-observation. We can also see an expansiveness of essential strength, which would be the essential transformation resulting from the fear, shame, and anger created by Gurdjieff's "shocks." Compassion is *implied* in the idea of God needing our help and in Gurdjieff's later behavior, but it is not central to the practices of his students. Joy, merging love, and the spaciousness that opens to the more formless dimensions seem undeveloped and at most implicit as part of an afterlife.

Of course, we have to keep in mind that the more advanced teachings of Gurdjieff were given to single individuals or to very small groups, so our discussion pertains to the formal system and the access levels engaged by most students. On this level, the over-emphasis on personal will is striking, along with the danger of "false will." It is primarily the absence of "true will" in the ordinary person that self-remembering is supposed to address—which during the 1920s gives the impression of a false attempt to "storm heaven," prior to the deeper acceptance of essential will in the older Gurdjieff. The earlier pattern is very much like Heidegger in the early 1930s, Nietzsche on the "will to power" as the basis of "eternal return,"[5] and the view of William James (1897) that the "will to believe" could be the basis of a renewed spirituality. Yet however one-sided Gurdjieff's own system, we have seen how contemporary inner-worldly mysticism would need to shift the Christian emphasis on compassion and love to a sacralization of the values of the new materialism—especially will and strength. Gurdjieff was hardly alone during these initial years of a renewed inner-worldly spirituality in the attempt to "will" eternity. It continues to be the dilemma, explicit and more often implicit, in any "naturalistic" approach to the full potentialities of human consciousness.

A Final Note on Gurdjieff in Nazi-Occupied Paris

In contrast with the initial pull of a mystical political fascism for Jung and Heidegger, Gurdjieff, the perennial survivor, simply continued in the teaching of his groups in the occupied Paris of World War II, much as he had during the Russian Revolution. In contradiction to the bizarre and unsubstantiated speculations of Pauwels (1964) seeking to link Gurdjieff and Nazi occultism in a manner more applicable to Aleister Crowley, the recently published protocols of Gurdjieff's Paris meetings contain no political or war references—apart from a caustic reference that he did not care who won: "All have ideals, all kill" (Patterson 2000: 295). There was no interest in Nazi or any other kind of occultism. History and politics were, for

Gurdjieff, the inevitable backdrop of a deluded humanity against which the work of individual self-realization proceeded as best it could. It would be almost as difficult in peacetime as it was in war. Of course our contemporary democratic sentiments might prefer to hear that Gurdjieff actively supported the resistance and entertained Sartre and Camus at his continuing "toasts to the idiots," but no such luck—and no such inconsistency. Both Gurdjieff's work and his capacity to negotiate his way through the two major wars of his century were always about inner personal liberation.

CHAPTER **11**

Aleister Crowley, Sexual Magick, and
Drugs: Some Ambiguities of Sex, Will,
and Power in Inner-Worldly Mysticism

Aleister Crowley (1875–1947) was very consciously influenced by
Nietzsche. By the early 1900s, he was proclaiming a new mystical
religion based on a doctrine of free will and the use of magical practices to induce higher states of consciousness. In the spirit of Nietzsche he advocated a radical individualism as the conceptual frame
for a new spirituality—destined to last for the next 2000 years and
with himself as its messiah. So immediately we see in Crowley a
grandiosity that better locates Jung's and Heidegger's periodic
struggles with their narcissistic metapathologies within the wider
context of "wild gurus" and "holy madness."

Crowley's System of Mystical Will

The principles of his system, based on the Law of Thelema (or
Will, in Greek), were dictated to Crowley in visionary trance by his
holy guardian angel Aiwaas in 1904 (Crowley 1969; Symonds 1973;
Wilson 1987). He and his then wife were traveling in Cairo when she
went into a trance and told him that the Egyptian god Horus was
angry with him, and that he should be at a certain place on a certain
day to receive the god's message. On the three successive nights of
April 8, 9, and 10 he then heard a voice and wrote down what it said,
which emerged as the book *Liber Legis* or *Book of the Law*, announc-
ing the New Age of man. At first Crowley doubted the importance of
these revelations, other than as a further extension of his already

well-developed visionary occultism, but by 1907 *Liber Legis* was the basis of his own esoteric groups.

The Law of Thelema can be summarized in three core statements, with which he would abruptly open conversations when he sought to have a maximum charismatic effect on potential new followers: 1) "Do what thou wilt," understood as specifically contrasted with the Judeo-Christian "Thy will be done." 2) "Love, but love under will," again with very different implications than Augustine's "Love and do what thou will." We will see later how Crowley's notion of individual will in the end blocks any Plotinian sense of surrender to universal will. 3) "Every man and woman a star," this being a specific appeal to the notion of the Nietzschean overman who "wills" ecstasy as a natural phenomenon. Crowley's is a mystical religion of radical individualism, and in that regard on the same line as Emerson, Thoreau, Nietzsche, Jung, and Gurdjieff. He understood what he termed "ritual magick" as a fusion of the methods of science and the aims of religion. Rightly understood, "magick" was the *science* of the numinous, seen as subject to its own material laws, albeit far more subtle than those of ordinary physical reality. In this regard, with Nietzsche, Blavatsky, Gurdjieff, and the early Jung, but not Emerson or Heidegger, his is a kind of subtle reductionism. Emerson, Heidegger, and the later Jung certainly intend a naturalistic understanding of the numinous, but for them nature itself, as the inherent metaphoric language of the soul, is a true expression of the irreducible mystery of Being.

The Book of the Law describes several ages of mankind's spirituality. First, there was the age of Isis, the Egyptian mother goddess, as an age of matriarchy, and to which we will return in the next chapter on feminist mysticism. Then comes the Age of Osiris, the god of fertility and renewal, the Egyptian version of Dionysius, who ushers in the age of spiritual patriarchy whose bankruptcy had been finally diagnosed by Nietzsche. Crowley's own contribution is to announce the Age of Horus, the "aroused and conquering child," who as the son of Isis and Osiris, is to avenge Osiris's death—significant, as we will see, in relation to the early death of Crowley's own father. So *The Book of the Law* announces that the new 2000-year age of humanity is to be the "age of the child." The age of the child is explicitly opposed to the family, and especially to the tie with the mother—again highly resonant with Crowley's own horrific childhood. Crowley is saying that the nuclear family is dead, finished as the institution at the center of modern society. The same economic factors once holding it together are now pushing it apart (Crowley 1973). It is interesting that

this piece of contemporary sociology on the cultural implications of
our Western principle of radical autonomy and individuality is being
spoken into Crowley's ear by guiding spirits in 1904.

Crowley's vision of the new, post-Nietzschean age is most
clearly set forth in his later book *Magick Without Tears*, his more
central works being written in a grandiosely oracular and pompous
style. This makes them somewhat off-putting in the manner of
Jung's similarly grandio-eloquent *Sermons of the Dead*, his own
spirit dictated neo-gnostic work in the crisis period after he broke
from Freud. Here is Crowley's more directly stated version of his
denunciation of the family:

> If there is any truth at all in anything, or even any meaning
> in life, in Nature herself; then there is one thing, and one
> thing only paramount; to find out who one is, what is one's
> necessary way. . . . To the performance of this Work the near-
> est obstacle and the most obvious is the Family. Its pre-
> sumption is manifest, in that it expects everybody to yield it
> first priority. . . . It began when you gave your first yell; your
> personality is deliberately wrenched and distorted to the
> family code; and their zoology is so inadequate that they al-
> ways feel sure that their Ugly Duckling is a Black Sheep.
> Even for their Fool they find a use: he can be invaluable in
> the Church or the Army, where docile incompetence is the
> sure key to advancement. Curse them! They are always in
> the way. (Crowley, *Magick Without Tears*: 336, 335)

As with Emerson, the development of the individual and spiritual development are not separate for Crowley, but one and the same:

> Nothing can save the world but the universal acceptance of
> the Law of Thelema as the sole and sufficient basis of con-
> duct. Its truth is self evident. . . . It admits that each mem-
> ber of the human race is unique, sovereign and responsible
> only to himself. In this way it is the logical climax of the
> idea of democracy. Yet at the same time it is the climax of
> aristocracy by asserting each individual equally to be the
> center of the universe. (Crowley, *The Confessions of Aleister
> Crowley*: 849)

He often said that he was training his followers "to act as a Brain for
the human race . . . and assume Kingship to rule the disorganized

and bewildered mob" (Symonds 1973: 375). This is a disquieting thought, given some of the methods involved.

Crowley, a youthful minor poet in the tradition of Swinburne, but who already regarded himself as a literary giant, joined the Hermetic Order of the Golden Dawn in 1898. This visionary occult society, to which the Irish poet W. B. Yeats also belonged, had been founded by MacGregor Mathers and initially organized around his translation of a fourteenth-century manuscript, *The Book of the Sacred Magic of Abramelin the Mage*. It describes the form of ritual evocation of spiritual powers later practiced by John Dee and Edward Kelly in Renaissance England and generally referred to as Enochian magic—the Gnostics viewing Enoch as a bridge between the human and divine, as we have seen. Mathers organized the society in terms of grades, like the Rosicrucians and Free Masons. Following Abramelin, they distinguished good spirits, evil spirits, and elemental spirits of earth, air, fire, and water. The ritual techniques involved, really akin to a guided Jungian active imagination, were understood as a modified white magic, separate from the strictly Satanic cults also part of the European scene in these years. They contacted and used evil spirits and elementals, but in the name of higher or divine spiritual powers. The key step was to contact one's guardian angel, thus Crowley's preoccupation with Aiwaas, and then, under its guidance to evoke various demonic and elemental forces to do one's bidding. In Enochian magic, practitioners might seek to know the past or the future, conjure dead spirits (Helen of Troy being a favorite, as in Goethe's *Faust*), and contact spirit familiars in order variously to cause storms, turn men into animals, search for treasure, levitate, or alchemically transform lower matter into gold and silver.

Several occult societies in England and Europe were involved in this reinventing of earlier visionary rituals for the twentieth century, very much an inner-worldly mysticism in that the aim is certain transpersonal states, well short of the formless dimensions, whose impact is primarily aesthetic and experiential rather than ethical. What Crowley added to the Golden Dawn was his own highly idiosyncratic studies of the Kabbalah, which he synthesized with the version of the Tarot being developed by Yeats. In later years Crowley would also incorporate the Chinese I Ching and his understanding of yoga practices into an overall system, which, with *Liber Legis* as its framework, became what he taught to his own students after his inevitable split with the Golden Dawn. Inspired by his own version of Jung's archetypal imagination, he kept promoting himself to higher grades of initiation on his own, and he finally resigned in indignation when these were not recognized. The core of Crowley's innovations, and a major indication of his extreme grandiosity, comes with his re-interpretation of the Kabbalah in a way making its higher formless stages ostensibly available by means of ritualized sexual activity.

The Kabbalah is often understood as a Jewish Gnosticism and indeed shows a striking similarity in its depictions of higher spiritual realms to the Christian Gnosticism of Valentinus and Basilides, although its own origins were independent and not fully formed until the thirteenth century (Scholem 1946). Renaissance Christian magicians and occultists, and even the German racial occultists, relied heavily on the Kabbalah as a major living link to an earlier Gnostic and Hermetic form of mystical consciousness, since these latter had been suppressed by the Church as heretical.

The Kabbalah had its own semicontinuous development. It stretched from Merkabah (throne) mysticism, based on the *Third Book of Enoch* (600 A.D.), to a culmination in the thirteenth-century *Zohar*, to its later sixteenth-century development by Luria, and finally to Sabbatai Zevi's and Jacob Frank's antinomian and libertinian radicalisms of the seventeenth and eighteenth centuries—completing the parallels to an earlier heretical Gnosticism. Here also, evil is an independent reality, part of an overall divinity "beyond good and evil" but separate within it, its origins in the "breaking of the vessels" not able to contain the infinite light of the ineffable Absolute. Before this Fall, Adam Kadman, the primal Anthropos, was a cosmic Being higher than Metatron (chapter 4). The task of the visionary is the gradual return *(tikkun)* of the fragments of divine light scattered through material and lower spiritual forms back into the Absolute *(Ain)*, thereby completing and redeeming creation. The later more radical Kabbalists, with whom Crowley had the most in common, held that the sins of Adam were already redeemed, so that no true sin was possible for the adept, who was to fight true evil by enacting the ostensible evils prohibited in the Torah.

The central image of the Kabbalah is the tree of life, the symbolic diagram of spiritual forms that link the unknowable Absolute (Ain) with ordinary worldly experience through a series of powers or essences, the ten spheres or Sephiroth. These are to be contacted through ritual and visions, as the practice of spiritual ascent towards the One (see figure). The ten Sephiroth are connected by twenty-two different paths, and Crowley's contribution was his particular and heretical linkage of these paths with the major arcana

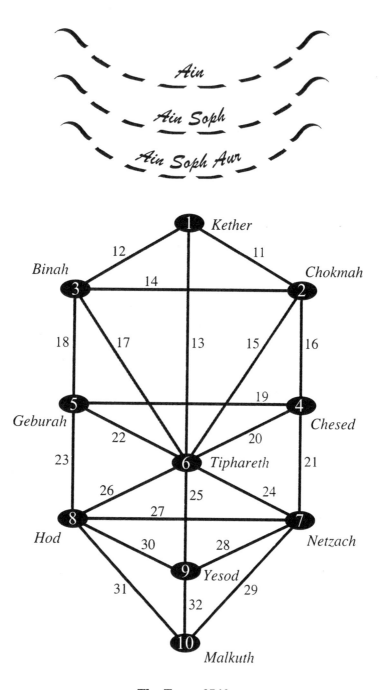

The Tree of Life

of the Tarot deck—which in Jung's terms depict basic archetypal identities. The Kabbalistic conception of the Absolute, its formless dimensions, and the Sephiroth can be roughly coordinated with Plotinus and with Almaas on essential aspects.

At the highest level is Ain, the Absolute or void, or as Crowley preferred to term it, the Abyss, with Ain Soph and Ain Soph Aur as graduations of its emanating light. Still within the formless dimensions, *Kether* is Primal Cause or Being, the equivalent of Nous for Plotinus, with *Chokmah* and *Binah* as its male and female and energy principles. The remaining Sephiroth are more equivalent to Platonic forms or essential aspects, from compassion *(Chesed)*, to strength *(Geburah)*, merging love *(Netzach)*, and brilliancy *(Hod)*. *Tipareth* (beauty, harmony, and surrender) corresponds to the letting be of essential will, and classically it was the highest level of ascent possible for human beings, such as Moses or Enoch—at least until Crowley's reformulations. It is the place of a direct consciousness of the formless realms, and the equivalent of the Valentinian Christos. Below it is Yesod, the giver of lower imagistic forms and the Kabbalistic equivalent of the lower creator God, or Gnostic Demiurge, and thereby linked to the material world *(Malkuth)*.

So what does Crowley do with this? If everyone is a star, a potential overman, then Crowley's ritual magick can, after suitable preparations, *start* from *Tipareth* and then *will* an ascent to the Absolute from there. *Tipareth*, as traditionally the highest point of human ascent, was often associated with the light and energy of the sun. But with everyone *already* a star, which Crowley also linked to the astrological procession from Pisces to Aquarius, he connected the right hand path of visionary ascent to the Star card of the major arcana of the Tarot (path fifteen) and thence to the Fool (path eleven), thus reaching to Nous *(Kether)* and the formless dimensions. These linkages of Tarot and Kabbalah very much reflect Crowley's own behavior. He is always the arrogant and narcissistic star, following paths fifteen and eleven as far as they will go—to the point of deliberate absurdity, self-parody, and moral outrage.

His is very much akin to the Sufi way of blame, also exemplified by Gurdjieff's own provocative behaviors to challenge his followers, but in Crowley's case it seems to be more literal disaster that he was courting—and this supposedly as a means of higher transformation. He was very pleased with his newspaper tagline "the wickedest man alive," until to his puzzlement it actually began to entail prejudice and ill treatment from powerful others. Thus, he thought it merely a private joke when his newspaper interview claim that he had "sacrificed

120 babies" actually referred to his use of birth control. He apparently felt that the negative energies he drew to himself as public anti-Christ would be transforming. In reality, he eventually drove away most of his direct followers by the extremity of his abusive and demanding behavior. A more benign illustration of this "right-hand" path of star and holy fool comes from a later letter to one of his correspondence students on how to live one's life from the "act of truth":

> You must invent your act to suit your case, every time; sup-
> pose you expect a cable next Friday week transferring cash to
> your account. You need $500 to make up an important pay-
> ment, and you don't know whether they will send even $200.
> What are you going to do about it? Skimp, and save your ex-
> penses, and make yourself miserable and incapable of vigor-
> ous thought or action? You *may* succeed in saving enough to
> swing the deal; but you won't get a penny beyond the amount
> actually needed—and look at the cost in moral grandeur. No,
> go and stand yourself a champagne luncheon, and then stroll
> up Bond Street . . . and squander $30 on some utterly useless
> bauble. Then the $500 will swell to $1,000, and arrive two
> days early at that! There are one or two points to consider
> very carefully indeed before you start: 1. The proposed Act
> must be *absurd*; it won't do at all if by some fluke, however
> unlikely, it might accomplish your aim. . . . 2. The Act must be
> one which makes the situation definitely worse. (Crowley,
> *Magick Without Tears*: 153–54)

Crowley practiced what he preached, usually to his seeming detriment.

The left-hand path from Tipareth is equally descriptive of an-
other side of Crowley's practices—and here even more destructively. Crowley links path seventeen to the Lovers and then path twelve to the Magician. Herein lies his way of "sexual magick" to engender the energies of spiritual transformation. Certainly by 1907 he was using increasingly perverse sexual practices to energize his rituals. His understanding of Kabbalah paths thirteen and fourteen as the High Priestess and Empress, respectively, fits with his later doctrine of "the scarlet woman." Women who were intimate with Crowley were required to take an oath of deliberately "shameless" sexual behavior, involving being sexually provocative with every man they encountered and especially with the potential male followers Crowley sought to influence—much as Charles Manson would similarly use

his women followers. Crowley was overtly sadistic and abusive to all his scarlet women over the years, with insulting names for them such as "dog," "camel," etc. and with several of them suffering psychotic breaks or committing suicide—the latter also true of several women close to Hitler. It is also of interest then, that path twenty-six, leading to *Tipareth*, was the Devil or Beast, which was the name given to Crowley as a child by his rigidly pious mother. Clearly, from a traditional Kabbalist perspective, Crowley's ritual mystical religion of the pure individual is a spiritual arrogance and inflation in the extreme.

The Practices: Astral Travel and the Invention of the Speedball

By the time he was done Crowley had combined, in truth with a breathtaking creativity, the rituals and Tarot of the Golden Dawn and his understanding of both the Kabbalah and the Chinese I-Ching on the one hand, with Yoga, as his path of introversion, and with his own version of out-of-body experience, understood as an astral travel to spiritual realms. This was to be explored by active imagination practices similar to those of Jung—as his path of extraversion. The imaginal out-of-body patterns were to be directed and guided in terms of the specific magical powers, demons, and spirits to be engaged. Crowley regarded himself as an experienced traveler on these planes, knowing how to interrogate the entities that appeared to find out if they were friendly or hostile, to banish or use them as needed. In one such visionary encounter:

> I began by asking for a vision containing a message. I first heard gurgling water and saw a dark farmhouse amid trees and green fields. The house and other things disappeared. . . . I then asked "Where will a message come from?" Immediately soldiers with guns appeared lounging around the place, and a [wizard] on a throne where the house had stood. I asked again for a message and saw an egg in which there were tiny convulsions of some flesh-like substance. . . . For him to say anything to me, I should have to build a fire of sticks, which he showed me how to do. There was a baby connected in some way with my act of building the fire; it was like a ritual. Then a most beautiful lion was standing by the fire. The wizard was still holding one or

two sticks. He smiled and said "Child." I then saw a most beautiful and naked boy of five or six years, dancing and playing in the woods in front of us. . . . The wizard was very happy and satisfied. . . . As we watched the boy, he put his left arm around me tenderly and he placed my head on the left side of his chest. He said, "It's all in the egg." (Symonds, *The Great Beast*: 242–43)

Jung would interpret these as fragments of an archetypal identity to be integrated—here, the divine child. For Crowley they are more literal manifestations of different spiritual realms.

Often these experiences were engaged in interactive tandem with a follower, usually with ritual sexuality to call forth the requisite energies. Here Crowley describes a mutually influenced and enacted imaginal state, generated in exchanges with his assistant Neuberg, following a bird sacrifice and probably Crowley's usual passive or, as he puts it, "sacrificial" role in ritual sodomy. They are outside at night in the Moroccan desert, and he has contacted the entity he terms the Dweller in the Abyss:

Choronzon appeared in many physical forms to us. . . . He took the form of myself, of a woman who Neuberg loved, of a serpent with a human head, etc. . . . His main object was to induce [Neuberg] to leave the [protective] circle or break into it; so as to obsess him, to live in his life. Neuberg had many narrow escapes. . . . There was now a gap in the Circle; and Choronzon, in the form of a naked savage, dashed through and attacked [Neuberg]. He flung him to the earth and tried to tear out his throat with froth-covered fangs. Neuberg invoked the name of God and struck at Choronzon with the Magical Dagger. The demon was cowed by this courageous conduct and writhed back into the Triangle. . . . During all this time I had astrally identified myself with Choronzon, so that I experienced each anguish, each rage, each despair, each insane outburst. My ordeal ended as the last form faded. . . . The work had lasted over two hours and we were both utterly exhausted. (Crowley, *The Confessions of Aleister Crowley*: 623–24)

So that would be an evening in the Moroccan Desert, if you were of that persuasion.

There were two levels to Crowley's rituals (Duquette 1993). The pentagram level involved the lower five Sephiroth, generally used to evoke or banish elemental powers. Experiences of the higher Sephiroth were based on hexagram rituals. Crowley developed ritual geometric patterns, elaborate gestures, and invocations that functioned as guided imagery inducing the state being sought:

> I also am a Star in Space, unique and self-existent, an individual essence incorruptible. . . . I am in All, and all in me. . . . I am a God, I very God of very God; I go upon my way to work my will. I have made Matter and Motion for my mirror; I have decreed for my delight that Nothingness should figure itself in twain, that I might dream a dance of names and natures. . . .
> (Duquette, *The Magick of Thelema*: 108)

Crowley was the head of two Thelemic orders, both still in existence. Ordo Templi Orientis (OTO) was his public society. It was actually founded in 1902, by Kellner and Ruess, as yet another German occult society modeled on the Freemasons and concentrating on sexual and black magic, with centers eventually in seventeen countries. In 1912 Ruess wrote an angry letter to Crowley accusing him of somehow learning and divulging the secrets of their highest level of initiation. After Crowley convinced them that he had come to these understandings by himself, he was made head of the order, so that with the later suppression of all of these groups in Germany by Hitler, Crowley became the head of the world organization. Their's was an exoteric membership, celebrating public neo-gnostic masses and rites. In London in the 1920s Crowley attracted both followers and badly needed funds by staging theatrical versions of these rites—featuring poetry reading, music, Nietzschean evocations of the death of God, and ritualistically enacted sexual revels, which at times seem to have included quite young children (Regardie and Stephensen 1986).

Crowley's other organization, which he called A.⋆. A.⋆., was esoteric and secret. He founded it in 1907 after he left the Golden Dawn. The usual view is that it stands for Agentum Astrum, or Silver Star, but Crowley denied this to some of his followers near the end of his life, without further clarification (Wilson 1987). Conceivably it could stand for "above the abyss," because he uses that phrase a great deal in relation to A.⋆. A.⋆., or for the Ain, Ain Soph of the Kabbalah. Here the individual adept, who knows only his or her private teacher and no one else in the organization, is seeking states of consciousness and powers associated with the Sephiroth. One works alone, telling no one of one's membership, and is periodically tested by the teacher to confirm one's level of attainment.

Later students, and Crowley's correspondence students, seem to have escaped the more extreme forms of Crowley's sexual magick and drug use. In contrast to Eastern yogic practices of Tantric sexuality, where sexual arousal is held short of orgasm, so that its energies might be sublimated into numinous ecstasy (Blofeld 1973), Crowley's idea seems to have been that it was *completed* acts of sexuality, the more shocking and perverse the better, that would call forth just the energies needed to make the rituals effective. So there is promiscuity, threesomes, homosexual and heterosexual sodomy, flagellation, animal sacrifice, and bestiality, in addition to the doctrine of the scarlet woman—actually dozens of them, often badly traumatized by the experience, and lasting in the role from a few weeks to years.[1]

By 1910 and especially from the 1920s Crowley's practice centered around the use of drugs, well beyond the more obviously psychedelic hashish and opium and into heroin and cocaine. He was decades ahead of his time in using them in tandem—the practice that would destroy so many in recent years, including, as we shall see for comparison below, Jerry Garcia. Crowley died still addicted to heroin. He also used ether as a hallucinogen, during which he describes animal identification experiences similar to Grof on high dosage LSD (Crowley 1973).

In 1922, largely in order to earn money after squandering his inheritance, Crowley wrote the semifictional and deliberately notorious *Diary of a Drug Fiend*. The book does have the virtue of showing how cocaine and heroin can provide brief glimpses of essential will and power—however inevitably sliding into their false forms. It is probably one of the few sources to demonstrate the grounds for the popularity of hard drugs as inferior versions of the states sought in inner-worldly mysticism. The book describes a group of young occultists who dabble in heroin and cocaine, get in over their heads, and are rescued by the mysterious leader of an institute called Thelema, King Lamus, who is obviously supposed to be Crowley himself. King Lamus teaches them how to use these and other drugs in an intelligent and spiritually enhancing way, so that, in particular, cocaine and heroin will be nonaddictive—especially if used together or in rapid alternation!

What I may call the philosophical types of dope, of which morphine and heroin are the principle examples, are directly unfriendly to active emotion and emotional action. The normal human feelings are transmuted into what seem on the surface their spiritual equivalents. Ordinary good feeling becomes universal benevolence. A philanthropy which is infinitely tolerant because the moral code is become meaningless for it. . . . We took fresh doses of the dull soft powder—without greed, hurry or even desire. The sensation was of infinite power which could afford infinite deliberation. . . . With cocaine, one is indeed master of everything; but everything matters intensely. With heroin, the feeling of mastery increases to such a point that nothing matters at all. . . . We felt ourselves crowned with colossal calm. We were masters; we had budded from nothingness into existence! . . . Again, despite our consciousness of infinity, we maintained, concurrently, a perfect sense of proportion in respect of ordinary matters. (Crowley, *Diary of a Drug Fiend*: 60–62)

What's doubly outrageous or weirdly humorous, depending on your point of view, is that by the time he was writing this book, Crowley himself was hopelessly addicted to both heroin and cocaine, and he had acknowledged this to his closest followers. So he is writing a book describing how these things can be done in a safe fashion, and without addiction, by following his drug regimen, while his own life had by then assumed the shut in and shut down, deeply schizoid pattern of the long-term heroin addict.

His chief biographer, Symonds, describes his situation during this period:

All the time Crowley was, of course, taking drugs. Now he openly admitted his failure to resist them. Gone was the pretense of curing himself by the strength of his will or submitting to them for the sake of discovering the power of corruption. Without taking drugs he could no longer exist; he compared drug taking now to living on borrowed capital. Since he could not sleep—insomnia is one of the symptoms of drug poisoning—it did not matter when he went to bed or when he got up. A great deal of his time anyhow was spent in bed, whether asleep or awake. . . During the night he calmed his nerves with ether. If he was lucky, he fell into a light sleep by 4 a.m. but more often "I merely fade away about 7." At about 9 a.m., in a condition of half sleep, he took his breakfast. Then he dozed brokenly till mid-day or 1 p.m., by which time he more or less considered himself awake, so he pulled himself together with cocaine or heroin, "the choice depending on some self-instinctive impulse. . . . I wake (too often) depressed, anxious, and with some premonitory systems of dissociation of thoughts." . . . He . . . wondered whether a man yields himself to drugs because of an unconscious wish to destroy himself. (Symonds, *The Great Beast*: 365–66)

Crowley and Spiritual Realization

The distance between Crowley and King Lamus is not only far greater, but different in kind from the distance between Nietzsche and his Zarathustra or Thoreau and his serene self-personification in *Walden*. We will trace Crowley's disastrous childhood below, but despite his immense creativity and intuitive post-Nietzschean understanding of the dilemmas of a new inner-worldly mysticism, Crowley's own life and realizations illustrate mostly the false aspects of essence. Specifically, we see a false will in his attempts at magical control of the numinous, false love in his sexual acting out, and false power in his sadism toward his followers and his use of heroin. Crowley's Thelema stands out chiefly as a perversion of the potentials of an inner-worldly mysticism by literalizing and acting out its energies. It is a mysticism under the control of the ego, rather than an opening that comes from surrendering and letting go. This is a dilemma that all self-realization faces once past the access phases of the numinous.

FALSE WILL

With respect to false will and narcissistic inflation, which is certainly obvious in Crowley, there is a huge difference between Crowley's "Do what thou wilt" and St. Augustine's "Love, and do as thou will." The latter implies an alignment of personal will with universal will, especially if, as with Plotinus and Augustine, we understand universal will to be inseparable from divine love. The difference is emphasized in Crowley's second law: "Love, but love under will." Crowley's understanding of the will aspect of essence stays on the personal level of a non paradoxical control and direction of transpersonal states. Essential will, for Almaas, has a quality of steadfastness, but it is paradoxical in that it involves an attitude of openness, letting be, and acceptance notably absent from Crowley's rituals of sexual magick. Crowley's rituals sought to will and control states of ecstasy and revelation. Issues blocking the will aspect are related to the dynamics of early support and trust, and these were never resolved for Crowley. The core phenomenology of the numinous is the felt sense that it has you, rather than you having it in the ordinary sense of our experience. It is not ultimately open to suggestion or self-programing on its higher levels.

The risk in Crowleyn mysticism is that the experiences undergone though these various rituals must remain an unwitting projection of ego, rather than an opening out from its surrender—since each level and its various archetypal beings are largely specified in advance. This is the risk of a modern Nietzschean inner-worldly mysticism. For Nietzsche, and the early Jung, the numinous is a reflection of ourselves, albeit on the deepest unconscious layers of our being. But the attendant risk is that the sense of the wholly other, beyond all categories as a sense of absolute mystery, will be unconsciously restricted by a more superficial sense of self-identity wherever the numinous is "humanized" in its core phenomenology. Only Emerson, and the later Heidegger on the numinous as Being itself, avoid this spiritual quandary of modernity. Whatever our "rational" understanding, once we "humanize" Being, spiritual unfolding stops prematurely and is left with an unavoidable dualism— inside vs. outside, ego vs. Absolute, love vs. hate. In addition, some sort of inflation of the ego becomes inevitable, because the experience of oneness with the Absolute will mix identity as Being with more ordinary levels of self identity.

Although the Nietzschean understanding of humanity as source of the spiritual seems inescapable on a conceptual level, to act from it as spiritual practice risks reinforcing a pathology and/or metapathology of narcissistic inflation—certainly well illustrated with Crowley. Almaas (1996) suggests that at some point beyond the access levels of spiritual development, one encounters a series of choice points over whether essence assimilates and metabolizes ego, or ego comes to reown its essential openings. The latter is automatically inflating. Here enter the imageries and issues of Satan or the "Beast," as the holding onto a sense of separateness and control that is part of unassimilated hatred. We will see how Crowley's childhood, unfortunately, gave him ample warrant for such hatred. The dilemma of inflation and false will runs all through contemporary occultism and naturalistic approaches to a "science" of the transpersonal.

There are ample signs of a clinical narcissism in Crowley, which his spiritual practices could only augment. Even allowing for his stance of deliberate provocation and his immense, and ultimately cynical, self-irony, proclaiming oneself the Messiah for the next 2000 years must illustrate a false inflation—as in the following passage from his autobiography, where he writes of himself in the third person:

> This Aleister Crowley was not a man, or even a number of men; he is obviously a solar myth. Nor could he himself deny such an impeachment too brutally; for already, before he has attained the prime of life, his name is associated with fables not less fantastic than those which have thrown doubt upon the historicity of the Buddha. (Crowley, *The Confessions of Aleister Crowley*: 32)

That grandiosity was a pre-existing characterological vulnerability is seen from Crowley's account of his first meeting with W. B. Yeats, who was one of the most important and original poets of his age, while Crowley's poetry, although critically recognized, was largely derivative in style. Crowley called on him unannounced one night to show him his own poetry, clearly expecting Yeats to acclaim him as a fellow poetic genius:

> He forced himself to utter a few polite conventionalities, but I could see what the truth of the matter was. I had by this time become fairly expert in clairvoyance, clairaudience and clairsentience. But it would have been a very dull person indeed who failed to recognize the black, bilious rage that shook him to the soul. I instance this as proof that Yeats was a genuine poet at heart, for a mere charlatan would have known that he had no cause to fear an authentic poet. What hurt him was the knowledge of his own incomparable inferiority. (Symonds, *The Great Beast*: 51–52)

This is a breathtaking example of a brittle, highly inflated sense of identity.

FALSE LOVE

Crowley's "sexual magick" offers an equally compelling example of false love or merging essence. Certainly, from Plato to many Christian and Sufi mystics, the Absolute is understood as the very form of Eros, purged or not of its lower concretely sexual contents, and sexual metaphors run all though many accounts of ecstatic states. Laski (1961) also calls attention to the striking similarities in descriptions of sexual orgasm and mystical ecstasy, and offers accounts of how, especially in women, one can pass over into the other (chapter 12). So it is not surprising that controversial wings of Taoism, Tibetan Buddhism, and Hindu yoga have used actual sexual arousal, but short of orgasm and ejaculation in male Tantric practitioners, as a means to induce higher or sublimated forms of bliss. Yet even allowing for the ambiguity of sexuality in inner-worldly mystical practice, ranging from Tantric sexual yoga to the total suppression advocated by Plotinus, Crowley's version of ritualistic, deliberately perverse sexuality is, as he intended, shocking and unique—at least outside of overt Satanism. It was in the energy and thrill created by orgasm under these circumstances, often accompanied by animal sacrifice, that he sought to call forth his visionary states.

Crowley's use of ritual sexuality fits less well with Eastern Tantrism than it does with Masud R. Khan on sexual perversion in borderline and schizoid clients. Khan (1974) developed Winnicott's views on the dilemma of feeling real as the core of schizoid and borderline issues. Here it is the search for direct experiences of Being that would counteract the sense of a dead, false self. Khan comments on the search for special "happenings" or "epiphanies" in these clients, which can involve drugs, thrill-seeking behaviors, and promiscuous sexuality—ultimately a fascination with "oblivion" as unconscious spiritual search.

James (1902) had similarly understood alcoholism as an inferior mysticism. In *Alienation in Perversions* (1979) Khan extends this insight to include a cultivation of sexual adventuring and sadomasochistic perversions as a kind of mysticism—albeit unconscious, literalized, and falsely exteriorized. Khan describes a number of his clients who potentially at great risk would go in search of the "perfect sexual encounter," often in a highly ritualized and/or sado-masochistic way, with a view to quasi-magical inner transformation. Khan concludes that this kind of sexuality is very much like a private religion, with a ritualized search for a perfect transcendent moment that will bring a feeling of power and presence. This is exactly what Crowley was doing. It was not classical Tantrism, as controversial as that alone might be, but a ritualized acting out of deliberately extreme sexuality for the transformative effects of the energies called forth. Interestingly enough, Crowley himself has the same insight as Khan.

He comments that Kraft-Ebbing, in his famous nineteenth-century study, completely misunderstands sexual perversion. Crowley says that what these people are really doing are unconscious ritual acts of magic in search of a spiritual transformation.

Of course, from the perspective of an inner-worldly mysticism oriented to a full and balanced development of essence, these behaviors are literalized concretizations of sexual energy—the conflicted dynamic contents of erotic love rather than its Platonic forms.

FALSE POWER AND THE ROLE OF HATRED

Fairbairn portrays the core of the schizoid attitude in terms of isolation, withdrawal, and a false sense of omnipotence. In the schizoid character there is a characteristic transformation of values resulting from the child's experience of love as dangerous and shameful. This leads to a substitution of hate and its false sense of power for love, an "evil be my good." Fairbairn's portrait is consistent with Crowley's adult behavior and what we know of his childhood. He ends as utterly cold and separate, based on the false autonomy that can come from an early child-mother symbiosis characterized by negative merging and frustration. We will see below how true this was of Crowley's childhood. His hatred for his mother eclipses that of Maslow. As an adult Crowley substitutes the energies of hatred and domination for the energies of mergence and love that would be the classical pathway of mysticism.

What Almaas calls false power, with its inner agitation and absence of peace—except via heroin—runs all through accounts of Crowley's behavior and his fascination with the energies of evil. His followers were sadistically manipulated in the name of their own higher development, which becomes especially clear in the breakdowns and suicides among the scarlet women. One of his favorite tricks to shock those who had annoyed him, or on whom he wished to make an impression, was to enter their homes in secret, defecate on the carpet, and then leave. In regard to false power as dominance, Crowley was especially skilled at hypnosis, which he largely used to impress his followers with his uncanny control over others. He also had his teeth filed so that he could administer an unexpected "serpent's kiss," drawing blood from the unsuspecting.

Perhaps ultimately more ominous, since it was not deliberately crafted to create the impression of notoriety he later sought, was his behavior on mountain climbing expeditions, at which he excelled as one of the major climbers of his day. These unsettling incidents appeared especially at heights where lack of oxygen would have its effect. In 1905, leading an expedition up Kanchenenjunga, the third highest mountain in the world, the group replaced him as leader due to his increasingly erratic behavior and sadistic treatment of the sherpas. Soon they were pinned down by a sudden storm. He stayed alone in his tent while several of the climbers were dying, and in the morning walked past the entire group, descending on his own and leaving them to their fate, rather than helping with the difficult process of rescue. He explained later that no one had asked him to stay, so he simply left. The survivors were more inclined to incredulity. The incident effectively ended his mountain climbing career, since no one would climb with him afterwards.

It seems clear that the early stages of cocaine and heroin usage for some people will convey a brief, but direct experience of personal will and essential power. Otherwise their almost religious appeal seems incomprehensible. Especially if one is feeling a deficit of energy and purpose, or an inner agitation and longing for repose, cocaine or heroin could be very tempting. Of course, the user soon spends more and more time in states of false will and frenzied grandiosity, or in false power and near-coma, respectively, in the attempt to regain one's initial openings. It is of interest to see how Crowley's own descriptions cover this same range.

We have already considered his more positive claims, in marked contrast to his actual decline into long-term addiction. So it is also relevant to see his awareness of false will with cocaine: "The sense of our superiority to mankind was constantly present. . . . A more than Satanic pride swells in our soul" (Crowley 1992: 60, 62). There is also this chilling description of the schizoid core of advanced heroin use from the chapter titled "A Heroin Heroine." It provides a powerful illustration of false power, its coldness and dissociated hatred:

> The whole of the woman's vitality was directed to some secret interior shrine of her own soul. The only subject that interested her in this wide universe was heroin. Her voice was monotonous. . . . "It's the only thing there is," she said in a tone of extraordinary ecstatic detachment. . . . "You mustn't expect to get the result at once . . . It always takes some months before you get rid of that stupid nuisance—life. As long as you have animal passions you are an animal. How disgusting it is to think of eating and loving and all those appetites, like cattle. Breathing itself would be beastly if one knew one were doing it." (Crowley, *Diary of a Drug Fiend*: 69)

Crowley as an old man had this same strangely remote quality of the long term addict. His dying words were, "I am perplexed."

The Horrific Childhood of Aleister Crowley

Whereas we could say that Jung and Heidegger suffered narcissistic metapathologies, reinforced by early childhood dynamics, with Crowley, like Hitler, whom he admired, we are dealing with something more clinically diagnosable. Crowley presents more of a permanent split between brilliant insight and experiential capacity, on the one hand, and a schizoid aloofness and sadistic, manipulative curiosity in dealing with others, on the other. It is not surprising that his childhood and young adulthood are an object-relational disaster.

What most stands forth is his total hatred and contempt for his mother, doubtless reinforced by his idealized father's death at age eleven. The parents were Plymouth Brethren, a Quaker sect, and religious fanatics. In his *Confessions,* he describes his mother as "a brainless bigot of the most narrow, logical, and inhuman type." Her name for this already independent child, apparently meant seriously, was "666" or "the Beast." This became the conscious core of his negative identity after his father's death. Within the first weeks of life he underwent an operation for phimosis, a tightening of the foreskin. Since in those days anaesthetics were not used on babies, one of his first experiences would have been hideous pain in his genitals, which may have helped predispose him to what he himself calls "my congenital masochism." So there is some combination here of early physical traumatization and a cold and rigid maternal atmosphere.

His father he describes as his hero and only friend as a child. While there seems not to have been a real intimacy, he admired his father, the Plymouth Brethren preacher, from a distance. Young Crowley was deeply impressed by his father's oratory power over his congregation, and the careful, considerate way he exercised that power. In his *Confessions*, he said that as a young child he wanted to be like Jesus. The father dies of cancer of the tongue, one of the more cruel forms of cancer, and doubly cruel if you are a gifted orator. So we might well wonder what it is that the young Crowley learned from this about God.

He says that almost immediately after the bewildering blow of his father's death, his education and discipline were taken over by his uncle, an overt sadist. He is sent away to school at Malvern, an especially rigid Plymouth Brethren school. Within three weeks of the father's death Crowley is accused of some minor misdemeanor by another student, and thus inspired by his misfortune and isolation, other students add in rumors of something sexual, an area of life of which he had as yet no awareness. The result, as nightmarish as any schoolboy boarding school story, is that within a month of his father's death, away from home for the first time, he is sentenced to coventry —no one speaking to him, walking alone, eating alone, bread and water only. This went on for months until another uncle stopped it.

So it is not very surprising that what follows is what Harry Stack Sullivan (1953) called the "malevolent transformation." Crowley consciously turned to the practice of hatred, to a kind of Satanism, as he then understood it:

> I had accepted the theology of the Plymouth Brethren. In fact, I could hardly conceive of the existence of people who might doubt it. I simply went over to Satan's side; and to this hour I cannot tell why. But I found myself as passionately eager to serve my new master as I had been to serve the old. I was anxious to distinguish myself by committing sin. Here again my attitude was extraordinarily subtle. It never occurred to me to steal or in any other way to infringe the decalogue. Such conduct would have been petty and contemptible. I wanted a supreme spiritual sin; and I had not the smallest idea how to set about it. There was a good deal of morbid curiosity among the saints about 'the sin of the Holy Ghost' which 'could never be forgiven'. Nobody knew what it was. . . . This mysterious offence which could never forgiven might be inadvertently committed by the greatest saint alive, with the result that he be bowled out at the very gate of glory. Here was another impossibility to catch my youthful fancy; I must find out what that sin was and do it very thoroughly. For (evidently) my position was exceedingly precarious. I was opposed to an omnipotent God; and for all I knew to the contrary, He might have predestined me to be saved. . . . The only possibility of outwitting Him was to bring Him up against His own pledge that this particular sin should never be forgiven, with a certificate from the recording angel that I had duly done it. (Crowley, *The Confessions of Aleister Crowley*: 67)

By the time he is twelve he has set out to understand what evil is and then do it. He kills a cat as an experiment. He soon determines that it must have something to do with sex, and from his own account proceeds therein with admirable precocity. He also takes to solitary bare-face cliff climbing, finding, much as Khan suggests, that the constant proximity to imminent death affords him a vivid sense of being alive and alone moderates his core sense of separateness—which he also comes to see, instead of pride, as the real sin of Satan. He finds that his new sense of confidence and arrogance frightens both his schoolmates and teachers, and he begins to learn how to use this to dominate them.

At the same time, there is in Crowley, and to a lesser extent in Jung and Heidegger, a certain obtuseness to the more complex feelings of other people, which becomes of course part of his impact and dominance over them. A characteristic of narcissistic and schizoid self-involvement can include especially intense feeling states such as an immediate bliss, dread, hate, longing, envy, or shame—the emotions of the symbiotic or mirroring dyad (Searles 1965). This is coupled with an inability to feel or appreciate grief, ambivalent anger, guilt, jealousy—the more sequentially patterned feelings of what Balint (1968) terms the "three-person area of mind" and what Freud made the core of his "Oedipal politics." Crowley says he just does not understand guilt or jealousy, they do not make sense to him. Why would someone be sexually jealous? What a small-minded emotion—and certainly not something he appears to have felt. "The sentimental wrong of so-called infidelity is a symptom of the childishness of the race." (Crowley 1969: 111).

People like Crowley must block or dissociate these feelings in themselves, often by inducing them in others, since such feelings rest on the sense of a whole ambivalent object and a corresponding self-identity that would bring their extreme splitting of love and hate into dangerous proximity. They cannot understand the damage that this failure of empathy, coupled with an uncanny intuition into the states of others, must inflict on those around them. Correspondingly, as Freud (1922) pointed out, highly narcissistic persons can have a charismatic fascination for others, who find reflected, at what at first must seem a safe distance, their own innermost issues around dilemmas of being and feeling real. An idealized leader, or would-be lover, comes to embody our own unfinished search for an inner ground and support of true self.

Contrawise: The Avoidance of Essential Power and Will in Jerry Garcia

A comparison of Crowley with Jerry Garcia of the Grateful Dead, a contemporary guru of psychedelia, is instructive in terms of their similarly self-destructive turn to cocaine and especially heroin, but for precisely opposite reasons. Whereas Crowley sought some version, albeit false, of essential power and will, Garcia was seeking an escape from his own power—both from the potential social impact of the consciousness-expanding effects of his music and from his inherent charismatic effect on others. Both of these, while tied to his creativity, he found frightening and impossible to reconcile with a more personal quality of intimate contact and sweetness, widely remarked by those who knew him (Jackson 1999). The inward dynamics with which he struggled, an isolated schizoid core and self-hatred, are similar to Crowley, but Garcia's response is utterly different.

Jerry Garcia (1942–1995) belongs in our discussion of a contemporary inner-worldly mysticism both in terms of the expansive effects of his music and his own experiences with and advocacy of psychedelic drugs. Grateful Dead concerts had striking shamanic and ritual qualities that could induce a collective sense of transcendence and a luminous joyous expansion—paradoxically fused with a deep poignancy—in huge stadium audiences. At its most transcendent, the band entered a state of surrender in which the music "played itself." These effects were in large part made possible by Garcia's experiences with LSD and other psychedelic drugs, especially earlier in his musical career. He describes a contact with a "higher order of consciousness": "a huge presence that uses all of the available sensory material to express an idea" (interview with Jerry Garcia [Brown and Novick 1995]). What is sadder is the way in which Garcia's life also comes to illustrate what Weber calls the "broken humility" and "broken quality" of inner-worldly mysticism.

At the age of four, Garcia stood and watched as his idolized musician father drowned in a boating accident. Amazingly, his first conscious memory had been as a toddler being thrown into a swimming pool by a stranger and, as he blissfully sank, rescued by his father, who then punched the man (Garcia 1995). After his father's death, Garcia became resentful and emotionally distant from his mother, who soon remarried, and apart from supportive and happy periods living with his grandparents, he grew up as a tough street kid. So he was more than ready as a young adult to respond to an itinerant beatnik, soon to become hippie, lifestyle. What set him apart, however, was the minimum five hours a day spent practicing guitar and banjo. He was dedicated to his playing, and ruthless with fellow musicians who did not share his intensity, in a way that many at the time found "scary"— but which does make sense as his tie to the missing father. Early death of a parent often creates a later fascination with death and

oblivion, and an unconscious core of self-hatred. From a child's perspective, by definition fantastical, if his father had earlier saved him
from drowning, how could Garcia have failed to save him in turn?

The adult Garcia was stuck with unmetabolized issues of hatred that turned outward would become the ferocity of his dedication, which could also overwhelm and frighten, and returned
inward would become the self-destructiveness that took over his
later personal life and, to some extent, his musical career. As part
of this inwardness, however, Garcia was also known for his humility, accessibility, and kindness to other musicians. Beyond the
sphere of intensity and perfection that surrounded his own playing
and that of fellow band members, he was widely appreciated for his
generosity and gentle humor.

Garcia became an increasingly split soul. On the one hand there
was an undeniable charismatic power and force. This was conjoined
to the creative brilliancy of his instrumental playing. Also, there had
always been the tendency of others to follow his lead in social situations. This was a response he never understood and about which he
became increasingly ambivalent: "Look at David Koresh. If you start
believing any of that kind of stuff about yourself, where does it leave
you? . . . If I started to think about controlling that power, then it
would become fascism. . . . Something I learned from psychedelic experience, you don't want to be the king because then you are responsible for everybody" (Brown and Novick 1995). On the other hand,
and every bit as impactful on others, was his spontaneous generosity, quality of endless curiosity, and endearing personal sweetness.
The two sides often did not go together and Garcia had no way to
reconcile them except through the periodic abrupt withdrawals and
abandonments which those close to him, friends and wives, came to
dread. These must have exteriorized something of his own early experience of sudden and absolute loss.

His second wife described him as a "wounded soul" who avoided
all emotional pain and direct confrontation (Greenfield 1996). A close
friend said, "He hated the fame that had made him into a sacred monster" (Scully and Dalton 1996: 368). The result was a progressive detachment, at first aided and then enforced by heroin. By the late 1970s
Garcia had shifted from the more open-ended effects of psychedelics to
cocaine, to arouse and focus his energies, and heroin, as a facsimile of
the inner peace denied him by both his social role and inner dynamics.
At first he was interested in the effects of these drugs on his music,
but personal and social escape soon became the predominant motivation. The result, while it went in waves, followed by efforts at detoxifi-

cation, was an increasing remoteness and sense of inner loneliness and futility. He "lost heart" and retreated into apathy and inaccessibility (Greenfield 1996). His health deteriorated, and his drug-enforced denial led to a prolonged and nearly fatal diabetic coma in 1986 that destroyed his memory and necessitated a complete re-learning of the guitar. As he returned again to heroin in the 1990s, also overweight and ignoring all dietary considerations, there was a progressive hardening of the arteries, edema, and an enlarged heart that finally killed him at the age of fifty-three.

Perhaps testifying to the dilemmas of hatred and false power, he describes prolonged hallucinatory experiences during his recovery from coma involving insectoid forms in a continuous, furiously agitated movement—the very opposite of the peace of essential power for which he longed. Near the end of his life, he was so slowed by the heroin and had lost so much feeling in his swollen hands and fingers that he had to transform his famously intricate guitar playing into an admittedly ingenuous "guitar shorthand," which enabled him to approximate the effects he sought. Yet he continued to have a charismatic impact on his audience and periodically could still touch others with his spontaneous vulnerability and sweetness.

Heroin approximated the oblivion, in Khan's sense, that would both fascinate and frighten someone with such an early traumatic loss. The 'hole' where father qualities would otherwise have been available became filled with a more abstract brilliancy and power, but suffused with unresolved hatred and destructiveness. A deep unconscious guilt is all but inevitable under such circumstances, and his genuine humility would also cover a self-hatred and sense of shame to be "solved," but mostly deepened, by his drug use. In late interviews, he responds, "If you were me, you'd be modest too" (Brown and Novick 1995) and then says that he wished he could be more forthcoming, in an obvious allusion to the addiction that so embarrassed him and which he worried would influence his worshipful fans to follow suit.

With Garcia the false will and power afforded by his later drug use actually served to avoid the kind of dominating, grandiose power sought by Crowley by means of the same substances. Garcia found the narcissistic grandiosity of a Crowley (and Hitler) repugnant and personally threatening. He handled a similar inner dynamic struggle by directing it more at himself and tempering, as he could, its impact on others. Like Crowley, however, his creative brilliancy continued to manifest itself, suppressed but not eliminated by the heroin. Essential will, in contrast to the false omnipotent control of cocaine, involves a personal surrender, rather than mere passivity. But to Garcia that would also have an inner connotation of death as annihilation—both longed for as a rejoining with the idealized father and feared as traumatic abandonment. Similarly, the stillness of essential power would call forth the longed for but dreaded "oblivion." Thus the more radically transforming and healing states of the formless dimensions would be blocked.

The conscious grandiosity of Crowley's self-image made him overtly abusive, whereas Garcia's negative sense of self meant that he both sought to protect others from his power and periodically abandoned them to avoid emotional confrontation, in a way that unconsciously duplicated his own trauma. Side by side with this carefully segregated pain, there was a joy, kindness, capacity for contact, and poignancy—all qualities of personal essence and utterly absent in Crowley. Yet the sense of separateness and unmetabolized hatred from the aftermath of his father's death meant that this personalness could not include his more impersonal charismatic power.

Crowley and the Dilemmas of Contemporary Spirituality

Fearing the grandiosity to which he was inevitably tempted, Jerry Garcia sought to control and direct his power issues with cocaine and heroin. Aleister Crowley explicitly sought what he could not see as a false will and false power by these same means. Crowley's profound schizoid separateness, and the intensity of his actual hatred, could not allow a true autonomy of personal essence, since that would also entail an openness to genuine interpersonal contact. Instead there could only be a grandiosity, explicitly cultivated in competition with God, and ultimately seeking vengeance for his father's death. Correspondingly, there would be no real potential for developing the actual formless or higher dimensions of Kabbalah because these involve letting go of that very separateness. Crowley must resist the experiences of mergence and surrender of ego which would open to formlessness. His identity is one of inherent separateness, which he sees as the core attribute of Satan. He is not overtly a Satanist, but rather a practitioner of a "lefthanded" magical path. Yet the dynamics of using the energies of hatred are similar, as is the dualism of good and evil. His magical practices are in the service of ego, so will, power, and love are all acted out concretely. They are literalized. They lack the paradoxicality and openness of true forms of essence.

Crowley offers a perversion of inner-worldly mysticism. Yet his life and work also show the dilemmas and vulnerabilities within a contemporary naturalistic inner-worldly mysticism. These are the temptations inherent within it. With Jung and Heidegger we see slippages, mistakes, and periods when a false will turns to true, but in Crowley we find mainly an unmitigated slide from beginning to end.

CHAPTER **12**

Feminist Spirituality: The Return of Sophia

There are psychological, socio-cultural, and historical reasons why women tend to have a greater openness to the experience of essential states than men. So it is not surprising that a major form of inner-worldly mysticism in the past 150 years might properly be regarded as variations on a feminist spirituality. Yet as we have seen with all other metaphoric forms that can be embodied in numinous experience, specifically maternal and feminine imageries for essential states can serve simultaneously as both a spiritual opening for many women and a potential limitation on later development—depending on individual dynamics and stages of realization.

Psychology, Gender, and Transpersonal Experience

There does seem to be some agreement in terms of empirical research on openness to altered and transpersonal states of consciousness that women tend to have more of these experiences than men. Obviously this tendency is only statistical, but individual difference research on measures of imaginative absorption/openness to experience finds women scoring typically a little higher than men (Gackenbach and Bosveld 1989; Hunt 2000). More specifically, in research on states such as out-of-body experience, lucid dreaming, spontaneous mystical experience, nightmares, and response to meditation in a laboratory setting, women, on average, show higher levels of response. Women also tend to report more synesthetic experience, or to be more aware of it, and respond more immediately to aesthetics.

Although it verges on stereotype, statistically, women do seem more experientially and men more pragmatically oriented.

Laski's *Ecstasy* reports that women prone to numinous experience sometimes describe states of specifically sexual orgasm passing over into a sense of numinous ecstasy that is felt as transcendentally spiritual, beyond the sexual experience that was its trigger. This phenomenon seems absent or rare in men. Laski also found that women make more spontaneous comparisons of their essential states to sexual orgasm than do men. I found this same phenomenon, to my surprised and somewhat embarrassed edification, in my dissertation research, based on interviewing subjects who were being instructed in a meditative technique. Several women, but no men, in trying to convey the qualities of expansion and inner liquidity in their ecstatic states, likened them to a diffuse nonlocalized orgasm. An example of such a report from this my very first experimental research was given already in chapter 1.

There are several, potentially related, levels of analysis that might help explain these gender differences in transpersonal experience.

From the present perspective on psychoanalytic object-relations theory, early structures from the first three years of life are being reused as a metaphoric medium for the emergence of later spiritual experiences, and unassimilated issues from these stages seem to have a highly distortive effect on essential states. Now it is true that these stages are usually regarded as coming before gender identity, since the young child's self-image is not yet differentiated in terms of "boy" or "girl." It is these object-relations structures that get internalized as the inner mirroring processes of consciousness. Yet it is also true that these earliest interpersonal patterns unfold in terms of the dyadic relation with the mothering one and/or in terms of a "mothering" function—in terms of a holding and mirroring—rather than a "fathering" one. There does indeed seem to be an intrinsic lean towards the imagery of the feminine and maternal in essential states, especially in approaching the formless dimensions of mysticism. Thus, the soul is "held," "mirrored," and "nurtured" by the Absolute. The One in most traditions is pictured as loving out of pure outflowing generosity, again a reflection of Winnicott's portrayal of the mothering function.

So it is not surprising that the more formless and developed levels of mysticism have this maternal flavor rather than the more paternal flavor of the prophetical religions and their theistic version of God's will. The formless dimensions are usually discussed in terms of an absolute love reflected in themes of mergence, compassion, and giving. While both young girls and boys experience a primary identification with the mothering one, girls maintain this into adulthood, while the development of gender identity in boys typically necessitates a shift to the father and hence an unconscious sense of loss of the earlier mergence with the mother (Washburn 1994). Accordingly, it may be that the less disrupted identification of girls with their mothers, however ambivalent that often is, helps women to be more open to experiences for which these early maternal functions are primary metaphors. So a way is open for women in certain stages of later essential self-realization that is often more problematic for men. It may be similarly significant that in many cultures the soul is considered as feminine or as having feminine connotations. This notion was central to Jung and Hillman on the anima and the Gnostic Valentinians on the soul as angelic bride.

A related conclusion comes from the neuropsychology of brain laterality in men and women (Kolb and Whishaw 1990)—albeit an often debated research area (Efron 1990). In men the left hemisphere, usually more specialized for sequential analytic activities, is typically more activated than the right hemisphere. In women the tendency is towards more equality in hemispheric arousal and a wider corpus colossum linking the two hemispheres, in principle allowing more access to right-hemisphere functions. Right-hemisphere functions include the felt meaning or "gist" side of symbolic meaning, aesthetic and metaphor appreciation, and experience of the body image (Geschwind 1982). The body image and its transformations, so important in essential states, is centered in the right parietal area of the neocortex, which is especially activated in vivid dreaming and altered states (Maquet et al. 1996). There is also some indication that the right hemisphere has more to do with our overall state of consciousness, in that nonspecific right-hemisphere damage is associated with delirium syndromes and confusional states, while an increased clarity of consciousness is apparent in lucid dreaming and meditative states (Hunt 1995a). Accordingly, women, at least statistically, will have more access to the felt phenomenology of immediate consciousness and will be more open to the transformations of consciousness in spiritual development.

In my own research on forms of dreaming (Spadafora and Hunt 1990) and transpersonal states (Hunt, Gervais, Shearing-Johns, and Travis 1992) and in Gackenbach's studies of lucid dreaming (Gackenbach and Bosveld 1989), it is much easier to locate robust correlations of these states with other predictor variables in samples of women subjects in contrast to male subjects. Relationships between these states and the trait of imagination absorption, and with the spatial skills and physical balance capacities which seem to be re-used in their metaphor-based genesis, are present in both sexes, but much easier to locate and less confounded with other variables in female samples. Twice as many male subjects are often needed to locate statistical significance for the same relationships. Accordingly, it may be that when high levels of essential experience are present in men they will also tend to be more conflicted, and less consistent with stereotypical gender identity. This may also fit with the frequency of various New Age spiritual movements and cults being developed by men while having predominantly women members (Dawson 1998; Oakes 1997). An early example was Jung's own circle. These male founders may often be responding to a deeper "challenge" in coming to terms with their own high proclivity to transpersonal experience—and so with an increased likelihood of either pathology *or* major breakthrough.

Some research on gender identity helps to explain further why many men might experience more conflict with respect to intense states of consciousness. Hood and Hall (1980) provided men and women with adjective checklists to describe both their mystical and sexual experiences. Women tended statistically to use more words related to receptivity and passivity for both sexual and mystical experience. Not surprisingly, men used more agentive words, implying more active initiation for their sexual experiences, but then used a mixture of agentive and receptive synonyms for mystical experience. For Rudolph Otto, numinous experience entails a "creature feeling," or sense of absolute dependency and helplessness in the face of the power of a sensed "wholly other." So stereotypically, men, with their agentive bias, will have more difficulty than women in fully accepting or allowing these states to develop. They will be a little more resistant to the connotations and implications of an experience that has you rather than you having it. Women's typical mode of experiencing sexual orgasm will be more suited and open to the phenomenal properties of mystical experience, as also reflected in Laski's observations.

Almaas (1986b) has his own psychodynamic version of this distinction, with what he terms the "genital hole" in essential development. As we have seen, Almaas identifies several different "holes" or felt deficiencies that are specific to the unfolding of essential aspects. The genital hole is the blockage that often stops the development of essential will as surrender. The quasi physical aspects of ecstasy, as specifically seen in yogic Kundalini experience, Tibetan Dumo heat states, and Taoist circulation of the light, often include a sense of energy beginning at the base of the spine that rises to the top of the head, culminating in states of luminosity. Phenomenologically these experiences can involve an awareness of a hollow column or empty space that goes through the center of the body from top of the head to perineum. This means that someone having such experiences can be aware of a sensed opening in the body and/or a corresponding lack of sensation in the general area of the genitals. Almaas suggests that this genital hole experience will stir up anxiety in both men and women, because of emotional associations with the vagina, but this will be less resisted in women to the extent that they are comfortable with their female identity. For many men, however, and also for the many women without a secure self-image as a woman, the experience of the genital hole will stir up what Freud would understand as classical castration anxiety—or more conservatively, a sense of gender inadequacy.

A striking example of this defensive sexualization of mystical experience as genital hole is seen in the famous case of the psychotic judge Schreber (chapter 5), with Freud (1911) basing one of his major case history analyses on Schreber's *Memoirs of My Nervous Illness* (1903). After hallucinations of being sexually assaulted, Schreber began to have ecstatic experiences of God, who he came to believe was turning him into a woman in order to procreate a new human race. Here we have a delusional distortion of the phenomenology of surrender in numinous experience, doubtless conditioned by the crushing of young Schreber's will by the famously brutal educational regime of his pedagogue father. Freud's exclusive interpretation of Schreber's experience in terms of castration anxiety misses its more general basis in the phenomenology of body image in ecstatic states, which will then induce and/or reactivate traumatic fantasies related to sexuality and gender identity.

Socio-Cultural Bases of a Feminist Shamanism

Anthropologist Barbara Tedlock (1997) suggests that ur-shamanism, the earliest form of shamanism we can infer as the common religiosity of hunter-gatherer peoples, was predominantly a female activity, and centered around maternal imagery. The myths of historical female shamanism in South America and Siberia portray the creation of the world by a primal goddess, who generates matter and world out of withheld menstrual blood. Interestingly, this would make the Gnostic Sophia, and her abortive creation of the demiurge, a return to earlier shamanic beliefs. Tedlock points out that the earliest gravesites of shamans in Europe and Mongolia, identifiable because they were buried by themselves with ritual implements, contain the bones of women. In addition, the first Roman contacts with Mongol shamanism and Buddhist contacts with Asian shamanism describe women shamans as the most powerful, with male shamans often wearing women's dress. Both groups were shocked by the overt eroticism that was part of ecstasy in female shamans, and tended to suppress female shamanism over that of the males, who in contrast to the predominance of healing and herbal knowledge in the women, tended to emphasize a more familiar warrior imagery. Tedlock also calls attention to the "sacred androgeny" in shamanism, such that shamans of both genders partially adopt the dress of the other—also Jung's observation with the cross gender anima-animus identities of individuation. Yet the accent, in Jung's terms, is on the anima, with the core of shamanism as the opening of a feminine soul, in both sexes.

In the oral mythic narratives of Central American shamanism, in which Tedlock specializes, there is widespread agreement that the first shamans were women, and that their shamanic powers were then stolen by the men. She also finds that in contemporary Central America, wherever traditional shamanism has been the most preserved, most of the shamans are women, and that male shamans are commonly taught by their female relatives. Much of this has been missed by earlier male anthropologists because they are usually only allowed to work closely with the male members of these societies. In more warrior oriented groups, men will have taken over shamanic functions in a more activist and hence visible fashion, and it would certainly make sense from the preceding discussion that their initiatory crises would be more conflicted and extreme—thereby further biasing our overall understanding of native shamanism.

This brings us to the earlier much debated theories of a Great Goddess mysticism as not only the original form of human religiosity but as evidence for matriarchy as the first form of socio-economic organization. In 1861 Johann Bachofen wrote a widely influential book called *The Law of the Mothers*, arguing that the predominantly male imagery of the mythologies of the great civilizations was actually layered over an earlier form of goddess imagery, which he felt established a suppressed matriarchy as the first social order of an agricultural, family centered age. Bachofen was of interest to Jung and occultists seeking a return to pagan roots (Noll 1994). Engels, colleague of Karl Marx, gave Bachofen a distinctly socialist interpretation, and not surprisingly Bachofen had a huge influence on the early Suffragette movement (Ellenberger 1970).

Certainly there is a chthonian level under the more patriarchal mythologies of Greece, Babylon, and Egypt, as in the legends of earlier female powers of Moira (fate) and the Furies. The Dionysius figure of such cross-cultural fascination also implies earlier shamanic properties of immersion in nature, with his exclusively women followers who dismember him in their ecstasy. However, what we know of contemporary hunter-gatherer societies shows that, while often egalitarian, with both men and women having equally important functions, they are hardly matriarchal. Historically, it may well be that it would be population and crowding pressures that put a later premium on male warriorship, thereby shifting predominant mythologies, rituals, and shamanic practices. It would seem that what Bachofen discovered was an overstated and overgeneralized version of Tedlock's conclusion about an earliest female shamanism, with Bachofen rightly detecting this as a layer beneath the more male-centered mythologies and rituals of the great civilizations, but misapplying it to socio-economic organization.

More recent restatements of Great Goddess mythology as the historical core of Western religiosity are found in *The Great Cosmic Mother* (1987) by Sjöö and Mor, a major work of contemporary feminist spirituality, and *The Great Goddess and the Aistian Mythical World* (1990), by Vincent Vycinas, a Heideggerian view of a primal religion of the earth in prehistoric Europe. Both books, using some of the same sources as Bachofen, argue that the original object of primary worship was the Great Goddess, as the most all-inclusive symbol of a sacred totality. In Egypt and arguably in European prehistory, the sky was seen as female, and as giving birth to the earth. Only with the shift to patriarchy does the earth become passive and the male gods ascend to take over the sky. Similarly, the early European marsh dwellers, with presumably considerable preservation of an earlier hunter-gatherer shamanism, held the water serpent as a major sacred symbol. Each hearth had a water serpent as a sacred house pet, to be tended by the eldest woman. This remained true in some rural areas until modern historical times, and was remarked on in Roman accounts of pagan communities. The Great Goddess image is also part of this serpent imagery. Early sculptures of the Goddess from prehistoric Europe often show her with the head of a serpent. The Egyptian Isis and Babylonian Ishtar are both serpent goddesses. It is only later in the Old Testament and Greek traditions that the serpent becomes a symbol of evil. Again, Gnosticism, as an aristocratic shamanism, appears here as a revival of something earlier. The serpent becomes the wisdom of Sophia or the being into which the higher Eve can escape from Yaldabaoth. The carnal Eve then has her own secret whispered back into her by the serpent, the symbol of a specifically feminine wisdom.

Common to South American shamanism, ancient Europe, and the later alchemical imagery of the Renaissance is the imagery of the cosmic serpent coiled at the foot of the World Tree, sometimes around an egg at its base, with a bird depicted at the top of the tree. As the snake ascends the bird flies. Again, we have an iconic depiction of the Kundalini experience and/or out-of-body experience, emerging from the matrix of a primary goddess imagery. Vycinas sees the sacredness of such animal imagery as coming from the sensed incompleteness of human experience compared to the totality symbols offered by animals and nature in general—the true language of the self-reflective soul as afforded by a maternal nature.

The Feminist Roots of Nineteenth-Century Spiritualism and Theosophy

It is difficult to appreciate today the extent and impact of mediumistic spiritualism in the second half of the nineteenth century, because it was later so discredited. The New Age rebirth of "trance channeling" is a much more limited phenomenon. Spiritualism, with its way prepared by the spirit dictated lectures of Andrew Jackson Davis, springs up literally overnight in the house of the Fox sisters in the small town of Acadia, New York (Isaacs 1983). Margaret and Kate Fox, on one night in 1848, with their sister Leah joining them later, started hearing mysterious rappings. They question the rappings and realize that they can be interpreted as spelling out letters, apparently conveying messages from the spirits of the dead. It may not be accidental that in that same year in the nearby town of Seneca Falls, there was the first world feminist conference, a precursor to the Suffragette movement.

In Weber's terms, spiritualism, with the vast majority of its mediums being women, was to become the mystical wing of the more prophetical women's liberation movement, with, as we will see, several key figures switching between the two perspectives—a phenomenon continuing into contemporary feminist circles. The ground had been laid by the popular fascination with traveling mesmerists, a healing movement with most of its followers being women and which taught trance induction on a wide scale. There were also the more esoteric uses of mesmerism to explore metaphysical issues experientially, often based on Swedenborgian notions (Ellenberger 1970). The inner-worldly aspect of these tendencies rested on the induction of "trance" as a new empirical means to study spirituality, soon to become inseparable from a nineteenth-century science of "unconscious mind."

Thus primed, spiritualism spread with unprecedented rapidity, undoubtedly, along with the theosophical movement that followed, the most striking spiritual revolution of modernity. By 1851 there were hundreds of mediums in each of the major cities in the Western world. This was a truly astonishing phenomenon. Some mediums continued with rapping, others were clairvoyant, and some did spirit speaking or channeling—as we saw with Enesee in touch with the dead pirate Thomas Veal. In 1855 there were one million people who were in some sense adherents of spiritualism in the United States alone. Most of the mediums were initially sincere, suddenly discovering in themselves capacities whose unconscious bases they did not understand, but inevitably many would encounter times when their powers were not available, and so would increasingly learn to fake their performances. Margaret and Kate Fox traveled worldwide, famous, but increasingly accused of fakery.

As various scientists began to study these phenomena, one after another of the major mediums were caught generating their effects. In 1888 Margaret Fox confessed her fakery publicly and then demonstrated, on later equally well-paid lecture tours, how the rappings were done by putting her toes in and out of joint. Both Margaret and Kate finally died alcoholic and destitute (Webb 1974). By the 1890s the major newspapers were full of such exposures, although William James bravely continued to study his Mrs. Piper, with his conviction of her genuineness doubtless also motivated by the painful loss of a young son and his wife's overwhelming grief (Simon 1998). Many of the mediums were extraordinarily sensitive women who had a capacity for deep trance and a resulting heightened intuition that allowed them to tell people some of the things that a very good therapist might see today.

The major historical significance of spiritualism, however, in terms of the development of an explicit inner-worldly mysticism, was in setting the stage for Helena Blavatsky (1831–1891) and Theosophy. She took the mediumship phenomenon, of which by all accounts she was a master, and integrated it with the more experiential attitude and philosophies of Gnostic Hermeticism and later of Eastern spirituality. She and her followers and feminist colleagues in the theosophical movement created the first widespread, though often inaccurate, popularization of Vedantic and Buddhist ideas in the West, which gradually helped in the translation of major works and created an audience for the Eastern gurus who began to visit the United States in the 1920s (Taylor 1999). Before her exposure for fraud in the mid 1880s, Theosophy had a huge and worldwide membership, and her successors continued to be the heads of large splinter organizations until a succession of sexual scandals narrowed their appeal in the 1920s. Krishnamurti, until he declared his own independence, had been reared from childhood as their Avatar (Washington 1995).

Blavatsky herself is a fascinating figure, her own background showing this crossover between feminist politics and its mystical counterpart in a feminist spirituality. Her mother and her great-aunt were both well-known feminist novelists, widely read all through Europe. They actually had a considerable influence on the political consciousness of nineteenth-century women. Meanwhile Blavatsky's own major followers, Annie Besant, Anna Kingsford, and Katharine Tingley, began as radical socialists and suffragettes before being won over to theosophical mysticism by Blavatsky. Helena herself was the picture of a high absorption, high fantasy-proneness child. Even then she had a charismatic impact on other children through her extraordinary openness to imagistic states. Her sister later described both her terrifying visions from which she would flee screaming and hide in corners for hours, and her captivating imagination:

> I well remember when stretched to full length on the ground her chin reclining on her two palms, and her two elbows buried deep in the soft sand, Helen used to dream aloud, tell us of her visions, evidently clear, vivid and palpable as life to her! . . . It was her delight to gather around herself a party of us younger children, at twilight, and after taking us into the large, dark museum, to hold us there, spellbound, with her weird stories. Then she narrated to us the most inconceivable tales about herself; the most unheard of adventures of which she was the heroine, every night, as she explained. Each of the stuffed animals in the museum had taken her in turn into its confidence, had divulged to her the history of its life in previous incarnations or existences. Where had she heard of reincarnation, or who could have taught her any-

thing of the superstitious mysteries of metempsychosis, in a Christian family? (Kingsland, *The Real H. P. Blavatsky*: 34)

She was forced by her family into an unwanted marriage at eighteen in circumstances that become an emblem of her entire life. The governess of the family had told her that her wild uncontrollable temper tantrums would mean that no one would ever marry her. So she bet the governess that she could get a much older semi-retired state official, a friend of the family, to propose marriage, which he did three days later. She was very proud of herself until her family, clearly hopeful of curbing her tempestuousness, insisted she go through with the marriage, and this despite her anguished pleadings. Soon after the marriage she began running away from home. Brought back twice by her very influential aristocratic family, her third escape was successful, and she commenced years of world travel, largely on her own, and finally aided financially by relatives, through Egypt, India, and more doubtfully Tibet, despite her later claims.

She does appear to have crossed the Rockies in a wagon train, and then traveled down into Mexico (Cranston 1993). Throughout, she studied a diversity of occult practices, especially in the Masonic and Rosicrucian groups that were the precursors to the Golden Dawn Society of Yeats. For many years she traveled with an artist, Albert Rawson, with whom she had a child who died at the age of six. She was present during the Greek revolution, where she was shot at, and later barely survived a shipwreck in the Mediterranean. In 1860 she was back for a Russian visit with her sister Vera, who describes her considerable trance abilities:

All those who were living in the house remarked that strange things were taking place in it. Raps and whisperings, sounds, mysterious and unexplained, were now being constantly heard wherever [she] went. That such raps could be increased or diminished, and at times even made to cease altogether by the mere force of her will, she acknowledged, proving her assertion generally on the spot. The sounds were not simple raps as they showed extraordinary intelligence, disclosing the past as well as the future. . . . More than that, for they showed the gift of disclosing unexpressed thoughts, a penetrating freely into the most secret recesses of the human mind, and divulging past deeds and present intentions. (Cranston, *HPB*: 65–66)

In 1875 she was again in the United States, where with Henry
Alcott she founded the Theosophical Society, her work now based on
using her mediumship to channel telepathic messages from hidden
masters of ancient wisdom, initially Hermetic Egyptian priests,
later shifting to Tibetan Mahatmas, living in the Himalayas. The
messages she received were often written as personal letters, some
explicitly channeled and others delivered more miraculously, being
thrown by hands unseen at the heads of visitors she sought to influence. A few contemporary theosophists later claimed, amazingly
enough, that it could not have been Helena who wrote them because
the handwriting in the letters was so various, although Alcott described her spontaneous shifts between five or six handwriting
styles while writing her first book *Isis Unveiled*. In other words, she
was very much a multiple personality, with some measure of control
over her shifts in consciousness and an access to hypnotic techniques
that would remain mysterious until the more recent studies of the
hypnotic abilities of Milton Erickson (Erickson and Rossi 1981). Alcott describes some of these behaviors, complexing mixing magical
illusion, hypnotic induction, and control over the attention of others:

> I have seen her cause objects in the room to move without
> aid from anyone. Once a silver spoon came from the furthest
> room through two walls and three rooms into her hands be-
> fore our eyes, at her simple silent will. . . . At another time a
> letter was taken by her unopened, sealed, and in a moment
> the letter lay in her hand, while the envelope was unbroken;
> again the same letter was taken in the fingers and instantly
> its duplicate was lifted off it, thus leaving in her hands two
> letters, facsimiles of each other. (In Cranston, *HPB*: 175)

In short, in Blavatsky we find an idiosyncratic mix of fraudu-
lence and sincerity, a usually benign trickery designed to support
syncretic ideas that would have a considerable influence on turn-of-
the-century culture. *Isis Unveiled* (1877) was intended as a fusion of
modern science and the ancient hermetic and neoplatonic mysticisms, very much in the spirit of Capra's contemporary transpersonal
linkage of Eastern mysticism and quantum mechanics in his widely
read *Tao of Physics* (1975). Blavatsky took Hermetic Gnosticism and
linked it with what was then understood about x-rays, atomic structure, and vibrational levels of matter. It was a thousand-page hodge-
podge that nonetheless fascinated several generations of spiritual
seekers, including quite obviously, Gurdjieff (Webb 1987).

In 1878 she relocated herself and the headquarters of the Theosophical Society to India, first becoming a U.S. citizen and thereby enjoying the consular protection she would soon need in the face of British outrage over her vocal support for Indian nationalism. Her widely publicized interest in Vedantic and Buddhist classical texts was largely responsible for the revival of their importance to colonialized India. Like Gurdjieff some years later, she was suspected of being a secret agent for the Czarist secret police, intent on lessening British control over the region. In both cases there seems to have been some basis in reality. So, in 1884, when the major exposes began, initiated by a devastating investigation by the British Society for Psychical Research, she was finally forced to leave India. The story goes that one of her followers, protesting against the accusation of former helpers that there was false back to the cabinet between an outer room and Helena's bedroom, and within which many of the Mahatma letters materialized, hit it with his hand as indignant proof of her innocence, only to have the secret door spring open into her bedroom—a clear demonstration to everyone of what had been going on. On leaving India she bitterly announced that there would be no more "miracles," and that she had only done them for her followers because they kept begging for them, while she had grown tired of the whole thing. Terminally ill, she resettled in Germany and then England, somehow finishing her second massive book, *The Secret Doctrine*, based more explicitly on her somewhat idiosyncratic understanding of Eastern thought, in 1888. In conversation with W. B. Yeats she said, "Beware of mediumship; it is a kind of madness; I know, for I have been through it" (Wilson 2000: 88).

Obviously Blavatsky had a huge impact, leaving an impression of quiet power and expansive, alive strength on people all through her life. Her idiosyncratic intellectual synthesis clearly speaks of an essential brilliancy. Hers was primarily a mysticism of knowledge. Very much like Gurdjieff, she taught by emotional shocks and challenges, finding the student's emotional weak point and overtly challenging it. But while there is ample evidence of her essential openings, and of her conviction of the compassionate basis of her teachings, the degree of manipulative control she exercised over her followers, however well intended, must also bespeak a false form of will. What is also lacking from an Almaas perspective is personal essence, since her mediumistic trances, conscious trickery aside, entailed a somewhat dissociated state where ordinary personality was split off and other non ordinary identities (spiritual guidance figures) entered instead. Accordingly there could not be the development of a personalness and contactfulness. She remained a more impersonal and mysterious being, with much the same temper tantrums that had originally occasioned the challenge from her governess. Still, as cults go, Blavatsky's seems to have done more good than harm to those close to her, and some of the women who succeeded her as head of later splinter groups within Theosophy were among the most remarkable and politically aware of their generation. The sexual and pedophilic scandals that still later overtook the remaining segments of her Society can hardly be blamed on Blavatsky herself.

Contemporary Feminist Spiritualities

Contemporary feminist mysticism is obviously this-worldly in that it is centered around the primacy of gender imagery as an opening to the numinous. There is much variation among these groups. Some meet in small circles, others are more individually centered, sometimes there are utopian communes where property is shared, some include men, some not, others are predominantly lesbian. There is much controversy over whether there is an inherent tension between a feminist spirituality and feminist politics, with concern that a primary experiential emphasis can detract from the larger need for social action (Eller 1993).

There have been two major forms of this feminist spirituality over the past thirty years. The first is more neo-pagan in origin, covering the witchcraft or wicca organizations. These, typified by Starhawk's *The Spiral Dance* (1979) and Viviane Crowley's *Wicca* (1989), tend to use magic and ritual for raising energy, buttressing self esteem, guided meditation, and at times hexing spells of various kinds. Many give allegiance to an earlier book by Margaret Murray, *The God of the Witches* (1933), which argues that medieval witchcraft was really a pagan European female shamanism suppressed by the church, and not devil worship. Controversial though it is, Murray's work fits loosely with both Bachofen and more recently Tedlock. These neo-pagan groups are very much like the Society of the Golden Dawn, and so raise similar issues about false will in seeking to control and manage the surrender, or essential will, inherent to any opening to the full experience of the numinous.

The other form of contemporary feminist inner-worldly mysticism is so-called "New Age" feminist spirituality, of which we will consider Jean Houston a major exemplar. Here there is a division over what is considered to be the originating cultural source. Some adopt a Native American woman-centered shamanism—best represented by the books of Lynne Andrews, an associate of Carlos Casteneda and so with the same kind of controversy over whether her accounts are partially fictionalized. The other side of this new age spirituality involves a direct cultivation of the goddess imagery or goddess archetypes of ancient Greece and Egypt, as in Sjöö and Mor, and the more Jungian perspectives of the Woolgers (1989), and Jean Houston. The view of this goddess literature is that both traditional Western and Eastern religiosities are as inherently patriarchal as the civilizations from which they emerged. They do not offer women their own numinous image of wholeness and healing. Making contact with goddesses rather than gods becomes especially important in a modern era where mothers and daughters tend to have highly ambivalent relationships, and daughters and mothers both suffer chronically low self esteem. So the argument follows that Great Goddess imagery, schematizing the numinous by means of feminine imagery, will operate on a healing level, both personally and collectively (Carlson 1990). We have already seen how essential states can lend themselves to a maternal metaphorization.

The goddess literature overlaps with Almaas on multiple aspects of essence and their felt deficits or "holes." The Jungians Jennifer and Roger Woolger in *The Goddess Within* (1989) use the Greek goddesses to distinguish multiple archetypes of feminine identity. An original Great Mother Goddess would have encompassed all aspects of the feminine, but in a patriarchal world history this gets fragmented into the multiple goddesses, each of whom is a different archetypal identity for women and a different essential aspect. Thus, there is Hera, the Greek goddess of family and marriage, whose determination to protect and support the values of family reflects something of essential will. Persephone, the goddess of the underworld and night, death, and occult powers, reflects the inner power of the essential black. Aphrodite, the goddess of love and sensuality, becomes the essential aspect of joy and golden mergence. Demeter, with her emphasis on childbearing and nurturance, fits with Almaas's characterization of compassion, or the green, while Artemis, the huntress and goddess of the wilderness, lady of the beasts, reflects something of the essential strength and vitality of the red. Finally, Athena, the goddess of wisdom, civilization, and the arts, and Jean Houston's own totem goddess and central identity, corresponds to the blue of essential intelligence and awareness.

Both the Woolgers and Jean Houston (1996) develop their own version of Almaas on the holes of felt deficiency, with each image of female identity having its characteristic woundedness and vulnerability.

It is only through accepting this characteristic hole of suffering that the positive aspect of the goddess can be embodied. Thus, the incipient Aphrodites of this world are ashamed of their sexuality and sensuality, Athena doubts her intelligence, Hera feels an absence of social power and will, Demeter distrusts her fertility, Persephone denies her visions, and Artemis misunderstands her bodily wisdom. Each feels a deficiency that, fully accepted, becomes precisely the point of their potential realization.

Maternal and feminine imagery on the goddess level can allow women an opening and extending of ordinary ego identity, and so mediate a consciousness expansion and sense of transcendence. Yet as much as such imagery can expand experience, it must also restrict a more complete opening to the totality of the numinous, especially and obviously in its formless dimensions. Feminist spirituality must by definition remain a dualism, however empowering it is initially in essential development. As a further limitation, Michael Washburn (1994), echoing Engler's (1984) reservations about many Western students who learn Eastern meditational practices, suggests that low self-esteem, a predominant issue for many women in modern society, means that some development of a sense of self may be necessary before it can be safely let go in essential states.

The surrender inherent in essential experience will keep women with issues of self-esteem from fully opening toward formlessness, their own gender counterpoint to the difficulty we saw in many men of surrendering an agentive identity. Cynthia Eller, in *Living in the Lap of the Goddess*, comments that many women in feminist spiritualist groups, New Age or neo-pagan, do not really seek direct ecstatic experience to the degree one might expect. For them, a feminist spirituality is part of a taking control of one's life, personally and politically, so that creature feeling, vulnerability, and the full acceptance of the pain of felt inadequacy will seem opposed to the personal empowerment and control sought by membership in a feminist group. For Eller this becomes an irony of modern feminist spirituality, which would further slow its development and hold it short of the formless dimensions.

The Autobiography of Jean Houston

Jean Houston began her professional career as an LSD researcher, and with her husband, Robert Masters, wrote *The Varieties of Psychedelic Experience* (1966), still one of the most complete overviews of psychedelic drug research. When this work became more problematic legally, she shifted to guided imagery, inducing the same kinds of states that would occur with psychedelics, and which she came to conceptualize in terms of Joseph Campbell's Jungian approach to comparative mythology (Masters and Houston 1972). Later she developed her own "mystery school," rather like Almaas's Diamond-Heart groups, based on a mixture of guided imagery, meditation, psychodynamics, and mythology, and taught in a retreat format.

Houston has a similar insight to Almaas on the importance of entering the holes or felt deficiencies in one's experience as the only genuine way for opening to a fuller sense of archetypal expansion.

> The challenge is to take one's woundings and open them to the treasures they contain without becoming fixated. . . . Our woundings then seen in their fullness can be doorways leading us into a richer and more complex universe . . . in which the usual bounded perceptions of space and time are stretched. (Houston, *A Mythic Life*: 277)

Our characteristic agonies contain the inner spiritual potentials specific to them. Thus, for Houston (1996), people who are angry all the time really have a potential emotional brilliance that has been frustrated, a passion held back, while fearfulness covers an adventurous spirit that has scared the person as a child into pulling back from their own promise, and jealousy actually implies a potential for the generous appreciation of others. Houston identifies her own wound as a hypersensitivity to criticism that when accepted allows her a sensitivity and deep empathy to the pain of others. She identifies her own sense of expanded identity as an Athena consciousness, centered on wisdom and healing. Her account of her early development makes clear the level of suffering from which it emerged—most especially in her ambivalent relation with her father.

Like Madame Blavatsky, there is early indication of a high childhood fantasy proneness and capacity for absorption. In her powerful autobiography, *A Mythic Life*, she recalls a unitive mystical experience at the age of six, which became a life-long influence on her. The impact of her father is huge, pushing her towards a precocity of total efforts, while her own spiritual development went directly against his extreme materialist and success-oriented values. What supported her inner development was a series of mentors and mentor-like encounters from early childhood. One of the most eye opening was with her screenwriter father's friend, Edgar Bergen, who apparently also used his famed puppet Charlie McCarthy for a kind of philosophical trance channeling. There is a brief school visit encounter with Helen Keller, during which Houston dares to ask her, "Why are you so happy?" and is answered "Because I live my life each day as if it were my last. And life in all its moments is so full of glory" (Houston 1996: 117). In the painful wake of her parents' divorce at fourteen, she forms a long-lasting mentor relation, through a chance encounter in Central Park, with Teilhard de Chardin, one of the major spiritual thinkers of the twentieth century. She did not understand who he was until after his death, but she would seem to have internalized his gentle guidance as a key support for her own essential development. Later she is directly influenced by a long association with Joseph Campbell. Her final mentor is Margaret Mead, which adds feminist and ecological values to her fundamentally Jungian perspective. It is interesting that with both Campbell and Mead her chief function seems to have been one of offering them a mirroring support, with Mead later becoming angry when Houston's insights went beyond her own.

Her relation to her utterly charming and funny, but overwhelming father, the mother being less mentioned, involves a similar supporting role. This is consistent with Kohut's discussion of the child being used as a narcissistic self-object, with the pressure to mirror the parent rather than the other way around. The inevitable result is what she herself sees as some curtailment of her own autonomy and strength, also reflected in what Almaas might term a false compassion that seeks primarily to alleviate the pain of others and thereby avoid one's own vulnerability. Houston is brilliant at mediating others' experience through evoked imagistic states, while conceding that her own capacity for imagery is relatively weak, and that she does not experience to the same degree the states that she so readily mediates in others.

For Winnicott one of the ways the core sense of self can be attenuated is through enforced emotional accommodation to and mirroring of parental issues—and it becomes clear that in turn her dynamic father did not receive mirroring from his own mother. Thus in college, in the midst of a crisis of identity, she writes:

> That's right, I say to myself, constantly celebrate the joy and opportunity of being alive. And if you don't feel that way at least try to act as if you do. . . . Then always have friends, relatives, and projects that I check up on, following their progress, being part of their lives. Be open to their hurts and

pains, their enemies from within and without, and be ready
if called to do something about it. Take some part of the universe as my special care, some chronic evil I will regularly
try to redress. . . . This early fractile of . . . always being fran-
tically busy has rarely left me, and I fully expect that at my
deathbed many people will surround me, insisting that I
hold on for a few minutes more so I can write prefaces for
their books, get them a bibliography off the top of my head,
and offer the name and telephone number of a suitable
mate. (Houston, *A Mythic Life*: 259–61)

While the tone is admirably jaunty, the space and openness afforded
so empathically to others seems not available to herself. This is a
common dilemma in those called to the spiritual and therapeutic
guidance of others.

As her father's narcissistic self-object, Houston's own sense of
adequacy was largely defined by him. She was told that her father
had wanted her aborted, but her mother refused to terminate the
pregnancy, following a dream of Athena who forbade it. Later her father treats this dedicated student's schoolwork as a comedy routine,
doing it for her despite her protests, and overwhelming her with his
persistent charm. At the same time he pushes her to an emotional
precocity in which fear is unacceptable, teaching her to swim by the
proverbial throwing of the child into water, leaving her outside with
a barking neighborhood dog until she is no longer afraid, and teaching her to ride a bicycle by sending her down a steep hill. She responds with the desired courage and resourcefulness, but says with
some irony that her father regarded her "as one of his better produc-
tions." She is devastated when, shortly before her father dies, he rejects in a final letter her now internationally recognized lifework on
mythology, telling her to concentrate more on science—ostensibly because she had declined a car ride he wished her to share because of
other commitments:

my dad, my greatest friend and ally, had concluded while
nearing his conclusion that my life had been in vain. At that
moment something very palpable began to die in me as well.
Perhaps one would have to call it self-value. (Houston, *A
Mythic Life*: 256)

As with Washburn's analysis of feminist spirituality, a vulnerability in an autonomous sense of self, even in the face of her
widely recognized objective accomplishments, leaves her with an

extreme attunement to others that makes the space for her own experience problematic. Houston's complex self-portrait thus includes what Antonia Wolff, Jung's early muse and paramour, termed the "medial woman"—operating primarily as a mediator or medium for others. Wolff helped Jung and later others in their circle to develop visionary capacities that she sacrificed in herself, and ended somewhat bitter about this in old age (Stern 1976). In Jean Houston, the centrality of compassion and brilliancy coexists with an inner division and uncertainty in her own sense of self, a vulnerability around personal essence. "My hypersensitive availability to others' wounding makes for a constancy of inner pain that belies the outer merry face that I present to the world." (Houston 1996: 268). So again we see in Jean Houston something of the broken humility that Weber made the personal mark and price of a this-worldly mysticism.

Limitations of a Feminist Inner-Worldly Mysticism

Contemporary feminist spirituality is a return to the Gnostic Sophia, herself a late modification of the Great Goddess. This goddess imagery clearly does open and empower certain essential aspects, but, as in all partial forms of inner-worldly mysticism, the use of gender as the most inclusive level of metaphor must also be limiting. In inner-worldly mysticism the numinous is always schematized or categorized in terms of particular forms that both expand consciousness and yet hold it short of the more inclusive dimensions. Certainly feminine and maternal imagery is closer to the formless levels of realization than paternal and masculine imagery. The One of Plotinus is inseparable from a pure overflowing love that has many of the attributes of the primal mothering one for Winnicott. Erik Erikson (1962) similarly found the deeper experiential level of mysticism linked with maternal imagery, in contrast to the patriarchal imagery of theistic propheticism, but deeper still was an all-inclusive genderless oneness.

There are two further limitations of feminist spirituality, the one political, the other experiential. Janet Biehl (1989), in an analysis similar to Max Weber on the intrinsic separation of spirituality and politics, sees a danger in mixing goddess imagery with the politics of liberation and equality in modern feminism. Goddess imageries are primarily therapeutic, and personally empowering. They appeal to the emotional needs of an individual, which are not necessarily the same as economic and political issues. She cites Sorel's *Reflections on Violence* to the effect that the mythologies of social movements must be based only on political effectiveness and not on personal truth. Georges Sorel (1908) argued for a cynical manipulation of myth and symbol in the service of social revolution. The risk then, from a feminist political perspective, is that the personally satisfying maternal goddess imagery will lead away from political action. Carlson (1990) makes a similar point, that the personal healing involved in experiencing oneself as a wounded daughter in relation to a particular or generic mother, may offer solace for a personal wound while actually making a feminist social stance more difficult. In addition, there can be a resultant infantalizing of the practitioners of these spiritualities by keeping them on the level of the child—more specifically the daughter. For Almaas (1988), while it is necessary in spiritual development to re-experience one's inner child, which includes the relation to a primal mother image, ultimately both men and women will fail to achieve spiritual enlightenment to the extent that they remain inwardly and unconsciously tied to their mother. Accordingly, feminist inner-worldly mysticism enshrines a level of experience that while initially opening must in the end create its own deeper blockage.

Finally, it is interesting to note that these limitations of goddess imagery in essential realization should not exist on the literal model of Freud, as updated by the object-relations case study analyses of Rizzuto (1979), where the concept of God and mystical experience itself is considered primarily a projection, however therapeutic, of early mother-infant structures. If the projection explanation were literally true and complete, then the development of a Great Goddess spirituality should be the final breakthrough into a naturalistically grounded this-worldly mysticism—into a truly objective spirituality—because its imageries and metaphors would finally reflect the true origins of the spiritual in the reconstitution of the maternal holding environment. Demonstrably this is not true. Feminist spirituality suffers from the same dualisms and limitations of all form-based mysticisms and has an appeal much more specific to women than men. The unitive One of the more complete mysticisms transcends and so reconciles the object-relations of gender and infancy, along with other this-worldly forms and issues. That is why it is sought.

PART **VI**

Transpersonal Psychology, New Age
Spirituality, and the Human Sciences

CHAPTER 13

Concluding Reflections

Reconciling Transpersonal Approaches
and the Human Sciences

An exaggerated split has grown up between transpersonal-humanistic psychologies, largely developed outside universities in special institutes, and the more mainstream psychology and socio-anthropologies of consciousness. The former often tend to view the latter as falsely reductionistic, while the latter see transpersonal studies as outside science. However, if we do understand spirituality as an inherent frame of human intelligence, mediated by an intuitive, metaphor-based capacity for synthesis, then we can understand cognitive-developmental, psychoanalytic, and socio-cultural approaches to the numinous as showing the contingent matrices through which this capacity will express itself—rather than as its reductive or even eliminative "explanation." In turn, the more mainstream social-scientific perspectives can be challenged and deepened by the phenomena of higher states of consciousness, indicating the potentials for personal development that transpersonalists like Maslow and Jung originally saw as neglected within the academies.

There are, in fact, legitimate debates as to whether the human sciences actually explain in the manner of the traditional physical sciences, or instead offer higher-order descriptions that contextualize problematic human phenomena by locating variations in their deep structures or patterns. Both William James (1902) and the philosopher Wittgenstein (1979) saw the core of methodology in the human sciences as a "placing of things in their series" and the

303

location of prototypes or key exemplars, similar in some ways to
Max Weber on "ideal types." For Wittgenstein "perspicuous" dis-
plays of basic phenomena can do the "work" of traditional explanations, without a reductionism that must remain false if we cannot
ultimately know ourselves outside the circle of our own being.
Even the new technologies and developments within neuroscience
remain within this hermeneutic circle of our humanity, since the
potential significance of their specifically discovered neural
"causalities" depends ultimately on our cognitive, personal, cultural, and historical understandings of our nature and purpose as
self-sentient beings.

Along these lines, we have been able to highlight certain parallels between basic forms and varieties of essential states, the cognitive psychology of naturalistic metaphors that mediate these states,
basic conflicts in early relating and sense of self that can both energize and distort spiritual development, *and* the social and anthropological forms of spirituality. These phenomonological, cognitive,
personality, and sociocultural perspectives, brought together in our
paradigmatic life histories, do not so much "explain" the existence
of human spirituality, which arguably is inherent to our species, as
show the patterns that condition, encourage, and block its manifestation. These multilevel perspectives of understanding, applied to
the this-worldly spirituality of modernity, often support the more
immediate intuitions of transpersonal and spiritual psychologies.
Namely, it does appear that essential states show the higher development of a form of intelligence. Yet this does not require that a non
reductive transpersonal psychology must succumb to the temptations of ideological "over belief." For James this was the opposite
danger from reductionism in approaching spiritual experience, according to which ostensible psychologies of spirituality slide into
crypto-religions. Transpersonal psychology has often risked this
grandiose donning of priestly robes. Although Noll (1994) and others
think Jung succumbed here, he was at least critically aware of the
danger—insisting his psychology was primarily a phenomenology of
"psychic reality."

Approaching spirituality as "psychic reality" and "form of intelligence" may yet seem reductive to those who would insist, consistent
with its phenomenology, that the numinous is "real" and not "subjective." Yet if we study the form of intelligence developed in higher
mathematics and/or theoretical physics as also a human faculty, that
is surely not to deny it an objective reference. William James (1912)
emphasized the primary insight of phenomenology that all forms of

knowledge come to us only through our experience, which is ultimately all we have. As I have argued elsewhere (Hunt 1995a, 2001), I know of no criterion by which we might distinguish *among* the forms of symbolic intelligence which organize that experience in terms of some objective, closer proximity to truth—i.e., Einstein deals in pure objectivity, while Van Gogh, by contrast, is somehow . . . lying? An approach—ultimately epistemological—to the reality open to us by focusing on the separate frames of intelligence that would know it is hardly a denial or a reductionism. It simply starts with where we are and what we can know of the "categories" we embody as a species—including the numinous. This is something to which the human sciences can make a genuine contribution.

We have seen in the terms of Weber and Troeltsch how an inner-worldly mysticism in the modern West, exemplified by our paradigmatic figures and traceable into the current "New Age" spiritualities they have influenced, will emerge in the context of an increasingly educated middle class disenchanted with the more prophetical emphasis of the Judeo-Christian tradition. Inner-worldly mysticism would be an inevitable consequence of modernity, evoking the very sense of felt presence and aliveness needed to make our hyper-autonomous individuality more bearable. Yet openness to the immediate experience that is inherent to a mystical spirituality, when manifested in the context of living within a complex, secular, and materialistic society—with its continuous pressures towards role differentiation, competition, and endless accountability—must also open individuals to more intense levels of emotional pain and sensitivity than they might otherwise face.

The question then becomes what to do with the fears, despair, grief, and hatreds that must be part of an openness to being in the felt here and now in such socially demanding circumstances? In the more inner-worldly propheticisms and theisms, the practical dualism separating God and humanity may at least allow one to "hate the infidels." However, the non-theistic mysticisms of direct experience move towards the all-one of a spiritual Absolute, Void, Tao, or Being-as-such, which in practical terms may fit ill with the painful dualisms of everyday life. How is the suitably autonomous and independent modern individual supposed to live in this complex world from the perspective of a oneness—at least without either emotional withdrawal or overwhelming feelings of rage and dread and sadness? Again, we see how very premature was the separation of a transpersonal psychology of higher states from the object-relational psychoanalysis that alone could make its frustrations and confusions more comprehensible.

We would expect accordingly that those most responsive to the tendency toward an inner-worldly spirituality would be both pushed forward in their search for meaning, and at times specifically blocked and conflicted, by the presence of early-childhood trauma and deficit as understood by object-relations psychoanalysis. We have seen how the very diffuseness of these basic issues of early development will become confused with later more genuinely abstract forms of spiritual experience, and at the same time push towards their realization. This is exactly what we found within our paradigmatic precursor figures, where early encounters with loss, death, and inadequate or cold mothering left a kind of "hole" in their experience that encouraged a precocious orientation toward the spiritual realizations that might also resolve these early emotional deficits. The anthropologist D'Andrade (1961) has similarly noted that the death or loss of a parent in childhood was often considered a precursor to later shamanistic abilities in hunter-gatherer societies. Yet this is hardly a necessity. The same deep levels of feeling will be stirred up anyway as spiritual "metapathologies" in the wake of essential states.

Still, the link with childhood loss is striking within the figures we have studied. Most of our major precursors of inner-worldly spirituality and/or transpersonal psychology had deeply conflicted relations with their mothers, with indications of her emotional coldness and distance, or a smothering, negative-merging quality. This certainly includes Nietzsche, Thoreau, Jung, Maslow, Heidegger, Crowley, and Garcia, and by implication, Hiram Marble. We could also add Jean Houston in terms of her father as the opposite gendered parent. In terms of traumatic loss, Nietzsche, Emerson, Crowley, and Garcia all suffered the early death of their fathers, leaving the "hole" of the absent father and the pull for its later "filling" with an analogously all-powerful spiritual source. Within this impact of early encounters with death in establishing a precocious spiritual orientation, we might also add Gurdjieff's account of the powerful effect of his grandmother's death.

Further, in several of our figures, we see the actual beginnings of direct experience of the numinous being mediated or triggered by death and painful loss suffered in early adulthood. This is true of Thoreau, with the death of his beloved brother, Emerson, looking into the coffin of his first wife, Marble and the impact of his son's death on his turn to spiritualism, and perhaps in the death of Jung's father when he was twenty. Again, on more marginal grounds, we could add the divorce of Jean Houston's parents, and the subsequent death of her saving mentor, Teilhard de Chardin. Arguably only

Blavatsky had a genuinely supportive early childhood, here in fact considerably indulged.

Two methodological concerns might arise here in terms of the generalizability of these observations, given such a small number of paradigmatic life histories: First, might it not be, especially in terms of my own early loss of my father and its orienting me towards spiritual questioning, that I have unwittingly selected just those precursors of contemporary inner-worldly mysticism who mirror my own experience? This does not seem a conclusive criticism. In fact, I looked only for figures who had reasonably extensive biographical and/or autobiographical information available on their childhoods and/or adulthoods, to fill out my pre-existing work on Gurdjieff, Jung, and Heidegger. I did not know when I began collecting these comparative lives anything of early loss and/or maternal ambivalence in Emerson, Thoreau, Crowley, Maslow, or Garcia. Indeed, it came as something of a surprise. Of the two other lives I might also have included, Wilhelm Reich and John Lilly, the first suffered the traumatic death of his mother in late childhood and the second exemplifies many of the object-relational themes discussed above. Finally, although on more reductionist grounds, Capps (1997) independently observed the role of childhood melancholia and maternal alienation in the lives of Jung, William James, Rudolf Otto, and Erik Erikson, and traced this forward into their later explorations of spirituality.

Second, some readers might be concerned with my cheerful application of contemporary object-relations theory to historical figures outside the era of the development of psychodynamics, such as Nietzsche, Emerson, and Thoreau. Yet it was precisely the earlier nineteenth-century understanding of mesmerism and spiritualism in terms of the dynamics of an unconscious mind and multiple personality that would lead directly into Freud's own further development of this perspective. But of course I do go further in locating object-relational issues in Plotinus, the Socratic philosophers, and the Gnostics—as offering us the root forms of a specifically Western inner-worldly mysticism. Here arise all the debates about the validity and limitations of psycho-history—the application of contemporary life-history methodology to historical figures. I will not rehearse these issues past reference to treatments such as those of Elms (1994) and Runyon (1982). However, it is worth noting that more recent studies of the historical roots of New Age spirituality (Hanegraaff 1998), do demonstrate a form of inner-worldly mysticism specific to the West and surfacing with recognizable similarities and continuity in the Hellenistic era, Medieval Kabbalah,

Renaissance hermeticism and visionary practices, Romanticism and nature mysticism, mesmerism, spiritualism, and theosophy, as well as in the psychedelic and Eastern meditational movements of the 1960s.

To the extent that we can locate herein the unfolding of a common culture, then there is every reason to hope that its different components and stages may usefully cross-reference and illuminate each other. After all, the unconscious complexes of contemporary psychoanalysis still divide their terrain between the Greek myths of Oedipus and Narcissus, and we have seen the relevance of Narcissus both as an organizing template and a surprisingly contemporary characterological critique, respectively, in the Gnostics and Plotinus. The object-relations psychoanalysts primarily developed differentiations within what Freud had more loosely termed the narcissistic layers of early personality development. It was these basic forms that Almaas found so useful in understanding the distortions and metapathologies in the development of essential states in contemporary individuals.

Contemporary Societal Implications

INNER-WORLDLY MYSTICISM AND DEEP ECOLOGY: THE WEBERIAN DILEMMA REVISITED

The significance of abstract physical metaphor and a related "nature mysticism" in the ecstatic states of inner-worldly mysticism is especially clear in Nietzsche, Emerson, Thoreau, Jung, the later Heidegger, and the Gaia imageries of feminist spiritualities. It also suggests a potential congruence with contemporary ecological consciousness. The luminosities, spaces, flows, and dark densities of these states are readily experienced in non humanized natural settings. These are not merely convenient metaphors for transpersonal experiences but, in cognitive terms, are directly involved in their actual constitution and self-referential recognition. Even when not directly triggered by contact and empathy with nature, these same physiognomies seem to appear on a more abstract and interior level in spontaneous essential states as described by Laski and Almaas.

The loss of access to natural settings with urbanization and ecological decay would make nature-mediated experience less available to the majority of people for the spontaneous mirroring and support of nascent essential states. At the same time, the contemporary pressure towards a this-worldly mysticism means that as long as the socio-economic support for a large, educated middle-class continues, many of its members will respond to ecological crisis with a deeply felt, intuitive grief over a loss of the sacred. Certainly one concludes from the writings of current ecological theorists (Roszak 1992) and the self-reports of activists (Hollis-Walker 2000) that their ecstatic times alone in the presence of nature, from childhood on, are a major source of their commitment to ecology as a social and political movement— also manifested in a re-sacralization of physical nature and its non human life forms. Zimmerman (1994) and Fox (1995) have already linked transpersonal psychology and the ecological movement on very similar grounds.

There are also limitations in this interface of ecology and spirituality. On the side of spirituality, Wilber (1995) and other transpersonal psychologists of the formless levels of mysticism ("without seed") have been less aware of the implicit metaphors of light, darkness, and spaciousness still central to their descriptions. Accordingly they, along with traditional Christian theology (Zaehner 1961), tend to see "nature mysticism" as a lower, more concrete "animism" that risks a mere romanticism and regression. Yet the view of Yoga and Taoism as abstract shamanisms (Eliade 1964; Izutsu 1984) implies the presence of the same nature metaphors in meditative states, but more interiorized and abstracted—as in the very notion of an "enlightenment." Whatever the degree of felt ineffability and cessation in advanced states of formlessness, they seem unapproachable without the abstract form of open spaciousness. At the same time, the classical "other-worldly" mysticisms remain outwardly, at least, just that—in their world-rejecting radicalism.

On the side of ecology, its radical and activist forms constitute a more obviously prophetical, non mystical political movement. Although radical ecology tends to reject the more inevitably "quietest" cultivation of a nature mysticism, perhaps its activist forms can be seen as the prophetical wing of a future more globalized inner-worldly mysticism, and vice versa—an ethic of inner-worldly ecological commitment to mirror an aesthetic of nature. It is precisely here that we must re-encounter Weber's strictures on the necessary separation between the felt inner mandate of spiritual movements and the ethics of competition and compromise that are central to the political form of intelligence in a complex society. These are two very different forms of symbolic intelligence, the one inherently interior and personal, and the other practical and activist. Whatever effects ecological activism hopefully has on pulling us back from the destruction of our planet will depend on its intersections with the rather different orders of economics and politics. Yet, of course, any such impact will also depend on the extent to which an ecological love of nature can also help to inspire enough of us to the kinds of sacrifice needed. Such inspiration or "re-enchantment" is necessary to call forth the powerful mythologies needed for revolutionary change, which returns us to the inevitable crossing of politics and spirituality that Weber found so potentially dangerous.

A radically prophetical version of ecological consciousness faces the same Weberian dilemma that Janet Biehl (1989) locates in the debate between those who center on the goddess imageries of feminist mysticism and those who focus on the political and economic realities of a feminist movement. As we saw in relation to the flirtations with political fascism in Heidegger and Jung, the issues of "personal essence" that must arise within the inner-worldly mysticisms will entail for many the sense that their personal being in the world, in its feelings of fullness and contactfulness, directs them to social and political involvement. That in itself can only be admirable. The "category mistake" to which Weber and Biehl alert us comes only when the *specifics* of a spiritual realization or charismatic group seem to dictate the *specifics* of a political ideology and action. It is then that violence and death can seem to become mandates of the sacred. However significant these "true believer" movements may be for social change, they also inevitably corrupt and compromise the inner balance of any this-worldly spiritual realization. What is personally redeeming and what is politically effective may not be the same, and may often conflict. The same is presumably true of an experiential ecological consciousness and a political ecological movement.

However, since very different forms of symbolic intelligences *are* involved in politics and spirituality, and whatever the dangers in their crossovers, differently talented people *will* be pulled in their respective directions. One group already moves towards a more aesthetic mysticism of nature—with its danger of a relative political withdrawal but with the simultaneous potential to sanctify the natural environment. The other moves towards a more extraverted political intelligence, necessary for any ecological progress, but with its own danger of a prophetical mythologizing that can sanction violence and authoritarianism—now on the left in contrast to the *volkische* fascisms of the 1930s. Both these tendencies are already present, along with the potential for at least some mutually constructive linkages, in the mid-range of each movement, between the aesthetics of nature and the ethics of global survival. Meanwhile, the extremes of mysticism and deep ecology will continue to pass each other by, and probably should—based both on Weber's cautionary analysis *and* on the very different intelligences actually involved.

CONSCIOUSNESS EVOLUTION VS. CULTURAL GLOBALIZATION

Weber and Troeltsch, combined with the anthropological research of Bourguignon, provide an empirical understanding of the cyclic socio-economic conditions that would make inner-worldly mysticism an inescapable tendency among the educated middle classes of a globalizing, sensate culture. In contrast, much of contemporary transpersonal psychology and "New Age" spirituality have been drawn to more speculative views that would understand the same tendency in terms of a linear and inherent evolution of consciousness itself. Linear evolution models include Teilhard de Chardin's (1959) quasi-biological evolution towards a collective "Omega-Point" of world consciousness, and Gebser's (1985) and Wilber's (1995, 2000) view of an inherent progression in stages of world culture, moving from magic and myth into an "aperspectival" or "integral" consciousness that would make the formless mysticisms more available as a mode of ordinary experience.

Teilhard de Chardin's *The Phenomenon of Man*, written by this Jesuit priest and palaeontologist in 1938 and only published after his death owing to church opposition, posits a future "planetization" of consciousness. This anticipation of what is now termed "globalization" would so pressure and confront the diversity of humanity that it would have the potential to push evolution to a further development and then integration of spiritual love and personal individuality. De Chardin's Omega Point is very much like Hegel's notion of a World Spirit, or a Plotinian Logos, working its way through human history, but here understood in terms of evolution. For many drawn to the optimism of "New Age" spiritualities, some such notion of a potential biological evolution of the species towards an expanded awareness seems needed to sustain hope in the face of a steadily increasing cultural materialism. However, it is utterly inconsistent with a contemporary evolutionary biology that finds no indication of any further human neural evolution since the dawn of *Homo Sapiens*.

Gebser's view of the development of consciousness growing more abstract through successive ages of man, in his influential *The Ever-Present Origin* (1985), akin to earlier attempts to posit progressive stages of world culture by Rank (1941) and Wundt (1916), is similarly inconsistent with contemporary anthropology. It falsely simplifies the demonstrated subtleties of shamantic cultures (Lévi-Strauss 1966) and contradicts Bourguignon's (1973) statistical demonstration of an inverse relationship between societal complexity and widespread direct cultivation of numinous experience. It does not fit either with Weber's tracing of the later cyclical conditions favoring mystical or prophetical radical salvation groups on the level of the urban civilizations, or Sorokin and Weber on eras of secularization vs. sacralization. Gebser's "ever-present" spirituality of the future, and Wilber's (1995) related forecast of a linear social evolution that would integrate the path of mystical "ascent" with an in-the-world path of "descent," seem more parsimoneously addressed in the historical and social context of Weber on inner-worldly mysticism—also more consistent with the self-understanding of Nietzsche, Emerson, Thoreau, Jung, Gurdjieff, and feminist mysticism.

From a human sciences perspective the tendency to align the meditative traditions with linear notions of world-historical development— whether that of Hegel, Gebser, or de Chardin—is a kind of category mistake—a slide into James's "over belief." Mystical spirituality, whether systematically developed in meditative techniques or unfolding more spontaneously, rests on an attunement to the immediacy of a moment by moment consciousness. Normally we see through and with our self-referential consciousness, and do not step back enough from our immersion in the contents of everyday life to allow that awareness to sense itself fully and as such. It is clear from the meditative accounts of Buddhism (Guenther 1984), Sufism and Taoism (Izutsu 1984), as well from the transformations of consciousness described in Western introspectionist psychology (Hunt 1985, 1986), that sustained attentiveness to moment by moment experiencing opens and unfolds consciousness into essential states. It is their schematic reification that creates the various categories and systems of "meta physics," all of which for Emerson and Heidegger emerge from felt realizations nascent within the immediate moment.

In this sense spirituality *is* a kind of extended or radical phenomenology—the development and exploration of a first-person perspective increasingly decoupled from its ordinary intersection with a third-person or behavioral perspective. Of course, this decoupling is never complete, as in the charismatic and empowering impact on others of highly realized spiritual figures. In that sense presence is catching. But just as there is an inherent tilt to validation through the third person "taking the role of the other" in everyday social life, so there is a tilt to first-person immediacy in mystical spirituality.

Heidegger saw this link between a fully experiential phenomenology and spirituality, as did Emerson and William James, whereas for the secular Husserl, its originator, phenomenology remained an exclusively conceptual exercise.

A realization common to the Eastern meditative traditions, as well as to Emerson, Nietzsche, Heidegger, Crowley, and Gurdjieff, is that the experiential attunement to immediacy reveals a moment by moment alternation between cognitive processes that are arising and those that are perishing. Buddhist meditators describe this cyclicity of immediate consciousness as the ultra brief "mind moments" revealed at deeper levels of meditation (Goleman 1972; Walsh 1977), while psychedelic drug researchers described the "flashing" or "scintillation" of momentary consciousness (Fischer 1975), and the introspectionists a rapid, ordinarily masked "microgenesis" of experience (Hunt 1986). Fully realized, this awareness becomes one of a continuous cycle of moment by moment arising, annihilation, and re-birth. The result can be a felt sense of a continuous welling forth of Being out of a simultaneously present and paradoxically full emptiness or void.

However, such a sustained enlightenment is infrequent, and especially so within a more this-worldly mystical perspective. Accordingly, the more accessible middle level of sensitization to this continuously renewed pulsing of consciousness is often associated with what the Tibetan Buddhist Trungpa (1984) termed the contrasting attitudes of "sunrise" or "sunset." In other words, the realizations more characteristic of the complex inner-worldly mystical reconciliation of content and form, will at least initially push the individual toward either a more optimistic sense of a continuous creation and emergence, "sunrise," or a more pessimistic sense of a continual destruction and decay, "sunset." Individuals will tend to align with moments "up" or moments "down." Emerson shows the former, wherein we continuously participate in an ever-renewed divine creation. The later Thoreau and Crowley, in their very different ways, cannot take their eyes off the latter. There can also be the sense of a continuous tension between the two, when the seamlessness of creation-destruction is not yet sensed continuously. We seem to see this in Nietzsche, Heidegger, and possibly Gurdjieff (1975, 1978) in some of his autobiographical descriptions.

However, it is not the physical universe of our uniquely developed modern science that appears and disappears moment by moment, whatever the partial analogies on the quantum level and/or temptations to "syncretism" (Hunt 2001). Instead it is the full development of consciousness that cross-culturally has revealed this "universal" creation and annihilation—with its own validity as an intelligence of spirituality. Its function becomes to make each lived moment not just bearable, but precisely fulfilled with a sense of totality, emergence, completion, wonder, and gratitude.

This brings us back to the various attempts, within the inner-worldly mysticisms, and necessarily in the more prophetical religiosities, to link their direct experiential realizations to history and politics. Some will then see only a continuous historical decline and decay, an inherent falling off from an originating golden age, and either despair, or seek with thinly masked grandiosity to save the world—much as Heidegger and Jung in responding to Hitler's Aryan apocalypse. Others, such as Gebser and de Chardin, will see world history in terms of a positive effluence, a divine Logos or Hegelian world spirit, moving toward some variant of "Omega Point."

From this place we can see the category mistake involved. "Omega Point" notions confuse the perspectives of history and spirituality, however inevitable and well meaning. Here the more objectified third-person perspective of history and politics becomes imbued with what is actually a radically first-person perspective. The realized meditator does experience a Logos, as the temporal dynamism of the Absolute, but it is as a *moment by moment* welling forth, with a *felt sense* of eternity. Any link to the longer "moments" or "eras" of world history, whether in optimism or pessimism, can never be clear. They are inherently different levels of understanding, although it would be the sensed eternity and timelessness of endlessly recurring mind moments that makes the linkage to "similarly" vast periods of history so tempting.

Of course, the immediate first-person realization of Logos can be a genuine support for the individual living in the midst of these larger historical and ecological trends, which for all we can know may be globally and irrevocably destructive. In that sense, inner-worldly mysticism could become a source of strength and personal renewal for those who do choose to become committed to a struggle for social and environmental betterment. But first-person realization cannot be adduced as evidence for speculative schemes of world historical development, which must rest instead on inevitably controversial integrations of economic, political, historical, ecological, biological, and cultural disciplines, not to mention the sheer contingency, even on a planetary level, that no discipline could anticipate in any lawful fashion. What we can say is that the globalizing of the individual values of an educated middle class will, for whatever time frame it comes to include, favor and encourage the forms of inner-worldly mysticism that have been our focus.

The range of contemporary inner-worldly mysticisms seems to fit best with the complexities, role differentiations, and need for purpose and meaning of contemporary society. We have also seen that it is inner-worldly mysticism that comes the closest among Weber's forms to being an abstract re-constitution of a generic shamanism—described by Eliade (1964), Bourguignon (1973), and Winkelman (2000) as the very archetype of human spirituality. Given the widespread openness to cultivating transpersonal states in these hunter-gatherer societies, it would be a very optimistic future "Omega Point" indeed, before a similar "average level" of consciousness development could be re-constituted in larger scale societies. Parallels of native shamanism with contemporary New Age spiritualities include the individualized basis of an experiential visionary quest, higher states of consciousness and archetypal dreaming, hands-on-healing, androgyny and gender mergence, extreme physical tests and conditions, and the use of consciousness-transforming psychedelics and meditation. Less like the classical accounts of yogis or Buddhist sages, our individual precursor figures seem more like contemporary shamans—each on some version of their own highly original vision quest—driven, often faltering, but deeply courageous.

From the more linear approaches of the classical other-worldly mysticisms, culminating in the rare establishment of a non dual unitive awareness as one's predominant state, it has been tempting to see the inner-worldly mysticisms—Taoism, Sufism, Hellenistic mysticism, Gurdjieff, and various New Age spiritualities—as less developed. They would remain at the "with seed" stages of mysticism that Wilber terms the lower "psychic" and "subtle" stages of spiritual realization. However, this ignores the increase in range of essential realizations sought in these traditions—extending in Almaas' terminology from the formless levels of Plotinus to the felt presence of "personal essence." Inner-worldly mysticism is also guided by the template of an all-encompassing unitive consciousness, but from the beginning it seeks a contactful fullness and sense of autonomy in personal being within the everyday social order—Gurdjieff's "self remembering"—which is clearly visible in our precursor figures and by implication also part of the more realized hunter-gatherer shamans. They are all similarly "in the world but not of it."

A Closing Word from Kierkegaard

It may be helpful here to turn to the humility of Kierkegaard on the generational relativity of all spiritual development:

> Whatever the one generation may learn from the other, that which is genuinely human no generation learns from the foregoing. In this respect every generation begins primitively, has no different task from that of every previous generation. . . . Thus no generation has learned from another to love. . . . But the highest passion . . . is faith, and here no generation begins at any other point than did the preceding generation, every generation begins all over again, the subsequent generation gets no further than the foregoing—in so far as this remained faithful to its task and did not leave it in the lurch. . . . There are perhaps many in every generation who do not even reach it, but no one gets further. . . . But he who reached faith . . . without reducing it to an insignificance, to an ailment of childhood which one must wish to get over as soon as possible . . . does not remain standing at faith, yea, he would be offended if anyone were to say this of him, just as the lover would be indignant if one said that he remained standing at love, for he would reply, "I do not remain standing by any means, my whole life is in this." (Kierkegaard, *Fear and Trembling*: 130–31)

The value of our paradigmatic figures and precursors becomes more apparent. Perhaps reflected already in the solitary vision quest of the shaman, it seems to be individuals who best exemplify the potentialities of the spiritual frame. Buddha, Laotzu, Jesus, Mohammed, and later Eckhart, Dogen, and Ibn-Arabi, remain the inspiration of our deepest spiritualities. Yet if the present analysis is correct, Nietzsche, Emerson, Thoreau, Jung, Maslow, Heidegger, Crowley, Gurdjieff, Blavatsky, Houston, and Almaas are the exemplary figures of our era and the one to come. It is their struggles, relative successes, and often conspicuous failures, that best reflect both the dilemmas and the promise of a renewed mystical spirituality in a globalizing society so otherwise lacking in any sense of inner purpose and ground. For good or ill, it is in Nietzsche's ecstasy and dementia, Emerson's euphoria, Thoreau's schizoidness and detachment, Jung and Heidegger's periodic grandiosities, Crowley's strange drug-induced dissipations, Gurdjieff's and Blavatsky's drivenness, and the more balanced inner cartographies of Houston and Almaas that we find the mirror of contemporary dynamic conflicts and some promise of their potential transformation.

While the conditions of a mass, hyper-individualized, materialist society do encourage an inner-worldly spirituality, and one with an unprecedented historical uniqueness mixed into this Weberian cyclicity, they as surely present complexities and issues that the founding visionaries of an earlier "axial age" (Jaspers 1953) could not have imagined. Rather than hold ourselves to the highest forms of an earlier other-worldly mysticism, developed in monasteries, ashrams, and prolonged isolation, we need to recall that we have no idea what the response of a Buddha, Jesus, or Laotzu would be to the prospect of a potential humanity-generated destruction of environment and life forms on a planetary level. We alone face that. It is impossible to know what forms their astonishing personal realization and radical openness of consciousness might take in our very material circumstances. Yet if spirituality is a core and constant human capacity, we may see some of how these earlier figures might respond to modernity by at least considering Emerson, Nietzsche, Heidegger, Jung, Gurdjieff, Houston, and Almaas. We have seen the continuity between these figures and the earlier foundational forms of spiritual realization, but their relative triumphs, mistakes, and pain are more recognizably our own. More than precursors, they exemplify where we still find ourselves.

Notes

Chapter 2. A.H. Almaas and the Synthesis of Spiritual Development and Psychoanalytic Object-Relations Theory

1. This account of Wilber's system deliberately omits his more recent attempt (Wilber 2000) to include a spiritual intelligence, as one among the multiple symbolic frames of Gardner (1983), within his original concept of a general post-formal cognition. The problem is that higher states of consciousness are now located in multiple places (post-formal intelligence, a separate spiritual line, and related side streams in the development of Self), in a system so complex that, with classical Freud and Marx, it manages to "explain everything." The dilemma of such over-inclusive systems is that they go too far past any potential criteria for more specific empirical verification. Accordingly, it seemed preferable here to stay with the more perspicuous contrast between Wilber's post-formal cognition, Washburn's positive regression, and my own view of spiritual intelligence as formal operations in the affective schemata, without entering into the possible over intricacies of Wilber's own recent mediations of these views.

2. The closest parallel to Almaas's descriptive physiognomy of the *lataif* or essential aspects is James Hillman's (1978, 1980, 1989, 1993) development of Jung's later psychology of alchemy as a metaphoric depiction of spiritual individuation. Hillman's phenomenology of the states of the *nigredo* (blackening), contrasting the dissolution and decay of self at the initiation of the alchemical process with its perfection as the "luminous night," echoes Almaas on essential power. The *albedo* (whitening) corresponds to essential will, again with its disintegrative and positive aspects, the alchemical blue (the "peacock's tail") to essential awareness, and the alchemical yellow to essential joy. The final goal of Renaissance alchemy is the *rubedo* (reddening) of the "philosopher's stone." This corresponds to Almaas on the essential aspect of

strength and vitality, which in its side of personal autonomy also underlines the in-the-world quality of Jung's individuation of the Self.

Chapter 3. The Sociology of Inner-Worldly Mysticism in Max Weber and Ernst Troeltsch

1. There is some ambiguity in Weber's vocabulary and classification of radical salvation movements, in that at times he uses the simpler distinction between ethical vs. exemplary prophecy, considering Old Testament prophets as the former and Buddha as the latter. Yet his more detailed typology of asceticism vs. mysticism, inner- vs. other-worldly, is introduced in the later sections of his 1922 master work, and loosely coexists with earlier discussions of the two types of prophecy. Since there seems something profoundly misleading in referring to Buddha as a prophet, let alone Meister Eckhart, I will follow the more complex usage, which also has the virtue of being echoed in Bourguignon's (1973) anthropology of types of trance states in native societies. Yet I have also taken some liberties with Weber by often renaming his "asceticism" dimension as a "prophetical" one, which is then more aligned with Troeltsch's sect-mysticism distinction and with the phenomenology of the relatively distinct experiences of prophet and mystic (Van der Leeuw 1933).

2. Stark (1999) has suggested that the contemporary rise of Islamic fundamentalism, including among the more educated classes of the Arab nations, contradicts Troeltsch's claim that the educated classes tend toward mysticism. However, Islamic fundamentalism is part of the more general turn to propheticism in the political liberation of oppressed nations and peoples, similar to the Christian fundamentalism taught in church schools that then paved the way for a more secularized but prophetical Marxism in African colonies (Lanternari 1963). We might still predict that over time, with a greater economic development renewing an overall sense of identity in the Arab nations, their more educated classes would eventually turn (again) toward a more individualized Sufism—in contrast to the current recasting of some Sufi groups as militant secret societies.

3. In addition to replicating Bourguignon's (1973) distinction between vision and possession trance, Shaara and Strathern's (1992) more detailed statistical analyses confirm the suggestion that possession trance societies are more overtly conflicted and their trance experiences closer to what Almaas terms "negative merging" than is true of shamanic, vision-trance societies. Possession-trance societies were significantly more likely to see altered states of consciousness as manifestations of illness, to be cured by a possession based healing trance, i.e. sorcery as "institutionalized paranoia." There is typically less emphasis in shamanic societies on the alien intrusions of sorcery, with the exception of the elaborate charades sometimes used by shamans to extract "poison" objects from the bodies of the physically ill.

4. I thank Nathan Hunt for this insight and image.

Chapter 5. Gnosticism

1. The ground for the widespread Hermetic and Gnostic notions of a second hypostasis, as a feminine principle of forethought or pure awareness, would have been well prepared by the ancient Egyptian mythology of Nut, the maternal sky goddess, extended over and generating a masculine earth—a theme similarly re-emerging from archaic shamanism in contemporary feminist spirituality (chapter 12). In Tibetan Buddhism "blue sky awareness" is similarly understood as the cultivation of a state of pure consciousness, as a second principle emerging out of a primordial void as originating first principle (Gampopa).

2. On the one hand, it is hard to imagine such a derisive, mocking, and intricately detailed satire of *Genesis* being done by anyone not Jewish, also consistent with the bitter dissension among multiple Jewish sects after 70 A.D. and a powerful Hellenizing influence among Jewish intellectuals. On the other hand, Jonas (1963) makes the simple but powerful point that there are just no Hebrew names among this group, except for Simon (Magus), who was Samarian. The denunciations of the church fathers are directed, after all, at dissident Christian groups, and there was much opposition among some early Christians to Paul's careful linkage of the life of Jesus to the Hebrew prophetical tradition. What better way to create an alternative mystical-contemplative Jesus than to systematically turn *Genesis* on its head on the way to inserting it underneath a more primary Platonic cosmology? The complexities of syncretism among Hellenistic Christians, Jews, and Pagans may mean that there was actually no single explanatory scenario.

3. There are a few hints in the *Enneads* (5.1.5; 5.4.2) that Plotinus was tempted toward inserting a similar second principle between the pure repose of the Absolute and the Platonic Forms of the *Nous*, which he called Dyad. He saw this Dyad as the first positive "emanation" of the One, such that their interaction would then generate *Nous*, although Dyad is never sufficiently elaborated to be more than implicitly feminine. A reason why he might have avoided formalizing this Dyad would stem from his putatively Christian training. If the spiritual dimensions are to be organized into triads, then Plotinus's primary Trinity would include Absolute, Nous, and All-Soul, with the highest level of the individual human soul included within the All-Soul, and so binding spiritual humanity and the Absolute. If Plotinus had formally inserted this implied second principle of pure awareness, then humanity would be irrevocably separated from the Divine Trinity in the dualistic manner of the Gnostics, whom he attacks.

4. Any curse from the inferior Yahweh could only be from His envy of what is higher—namely humanity. The spirit of the Cainites may have been nicely captured in some lyrics by Robert Hunter with Jerry Garcia and the Grateful Dead:

> They say that Cain caught Abel
>   rolling loaded dice,

Ace of spades behind his ear,
and him not thinking twice.
(Robert Hunter and Jerry Garcia, "Mississippi
Half-Step Uptown Toodleloo," 1973)

Chapter 6. Nietzsche

1. Nietzsche's eternal recurrence, as infinitely repeating versions and variations of each person's life, followed from his assumption of a finite space but infinite time. It bears some similarity to Everett's interpretation of modern quantum theory in terms of infinite parallel universes (Chalmers 1996), in which it seems to be space that has become infinite. Yet it could be argued that both are projections of the repeating and varying features of consciousness into a quasi-scientific metaphysics (Hunt 2001). The difference between them would be that Nietzsche pictures a sequential infinity of possible universes and Everett a simultaneous one. Both can evoke in us analogous attitudes of quasi-meditative detachment and creature feeling in the face of such "wholly other" immensity—as partly reflected in the popularity of the "multiple universes" notion in New Age spiritual thought. Nietzsche's vision evoked a similar "creature feeling" at the turn of the century in the Russian mystic and associate of Gurdjieff, P. D. Ouspensky, who, supported by the impact of his own experiences of déja vu, gave it a fictional treatment in his *Strange Life of Ivan Osokin*. Experiences of déja vu could also be taken as direct intuitions of eternal recurrence, perhaps a major source of its plausibility to many (Klossowski 1997).

2. Köhler's (2002) "Gay Studies" reading of Nietzsche seems as reductionistic and simplifying as any other exclusive account of this complex thinker. It may well be that "Zarathustras's Secret" is, in part, that this ideal self-figure is inwardly a woman, especially given his often strident and over-compensated false strength, but it is necessary to recall that contra gender identity is also a definite aspect of spiritual development in both shamanism, Jung's anima/animus configuration, and the Valentinian Christians. It seems impossible to determine from the letters and materials assembled by Köhler, what of Nietzsche's homoeroticism was acted out and what sublimated into his Dionysian over-man. Especially since part of the blatantly vindictive character assassination of Wagner and his circle after Nietzsche's defection/awakening included deliberately circulated rumors about Nietzsche's mannered effeminacy, masturbation-engendered poor health (and this from his physician!), and sly hints of pederasty. While Freud knew of these rumors, and respected Nietzsche's own intuitions about human bisexuality, he, of all people, preferred to regard Nietzsche's actual sexuality as an "enigma." It is a bit of a paradox of our postmodern "culture wars" to have to dip quite so low to render a reductionist reading of a major philosopher as a would-be compliment.

3. The neurologist Richard Schain (2001) has offered a critical re-assessment of this same material. He argues for a diagnosis of schizophrenia, citing the lack of any autopsy, and selectively questioning the majority medical diagnosis of the day, while giving maximum credence to one or two dissenting voices *and* to Nietzsche's mother's rather transparent attempts to maintain the already romanticized Nietzsche legend by hiding his complete dementia. Yet Schain largely concedes the original diagnosis of syphilis, and downplays the long established release of schizophrenic and/or manic-depressive symptomatology as a common feature of the initial phase of general paresis (White 1956). That remains far the most likely diagnosis, still well supported by the overall picture Schain presents.

Chapter 7. Emerson, Thoreau, and Hiram Marble

1. Emerson's personal openings are roughly contemporaneous with the Great American Revival, sweeping New York and New England starting from 1832, and leading to the Gnostic-like doctrines of Perfectionism. This was the view that a perfection of humanity was possible within this life through the sublimation of sexuality and the taking of multiple "spiritual" wives and husbands (Wilson 2000). John Noyes, in founding his Oneida community, literalized Perfectionism as a communal sexuality, on the understanding that the Second Coming had already occurred and sin was now impossible. This reflects the characteristic antinomianism of inner-worldly mysticism, of which Emerson emerges as the more sublimated reflection.

2. Some of the flavor of this local resentment against Thoreau is illustrated in townspeople being interviewed years after his death insisting that his actual name was not Henry David, but David Henry, "and he knows that." Thoreau was in fact christened David Henry but was referred to as Henry David by his family and started signing his name in that manner in young adulthood (Harding 1965). It seems testimony to the depth of local dislike, certainly reciprocated, that this should have been such a widespread concern.

3. Much as with Nietzsche's figure of Zarathustra, it is important to realize that *Walden* is very much a portrait of an ideal self, and while based on his exquisitely detailed journals is also very much their further spiritual sublimation. His actual isolation during the time at Walden Pond, for instance, was quite variable. Sundays usually saw the arrival of his mother and sister with a picnic lunch, and he had suppers with the Emersons and others, often several times a week, returning to his hut late at night through the darkened fields and woods (Le Beaux 1977).

The relation between Thoreau's and Nietzsche's ordinary identities and their guidance or wisdom imagos goes in opposite directions. The power and strength of Nietzsche's Zarathustra figure compensated for and balanced his actual gentleness, while Thoreau's *Walden* portrays a calm detachment often lacking in his daily life.

4. My own way to these figures of the New England countryside in which I grew up has been surprising to me. As a Harvard college student I resented the self-congratulatory and pompous treatments of Emerson and Thoreau, and so refused to read in them—and this despite my many hours alone as a youth in my own local woods. And, although I had often visited the strange tunnel dug in Lynn Woods by Hiram Marble, and been entertained by his mediumistic search for pirate gold, I did not then see that episode as relevant to my intellectual interests. In short, as an undergraduate I read only in sources Germanic—in Jung, Nietzsche, Heidegger, Wittgenstein, Weber, Freud, and Klein. Heidegger says something interesting about this common disregard for the near, while journeying to the far, only to finally return home again by that distanced route:

> One's own is what is most remote. . . . Becoming homelike demands a going away into the foreign. . . . to find, in an encounter with the foreign, whatever is fitting for the return to the hearth. For history is nothing other than such return. . . . (Heidegger, *Hölderlin's Hymn "The Ister"*: 125, 142, 143).

So it was that after twenty-seven years teaching in Canada, I returned via Jung and Weber and Nietzsche and Kierkegaard to these closer sources— and finally began to understand them and see how much I had by then unwittingly lived their very New England perspective.

Chapter 8. Jung, Visionary Racial Occultism, and Hitler

1. These two sides of Jung's "collective unconscious" are already present in Plato, with, on the one hand, his resort to mythological imagery when discursive reason fails, along with his fascination with creativity (*Phaedrus*), and, on the other, his notion that the Forms are ultimately memories—that our deepest knowledge comes with a felt sense of it being somehow familiar and already known (*Meno*). Both sides are still present without contradiction in the ascent of the soul into the *Nous* in Plotinus, which is both a recollection of its Divine origin and the fullest expression of its aesthetic intelligence. However, when we add in the Darwinian evolutionary framework of modernity, the "forms" can now be seen as "ancestral" and so "primitive" rather than "abstract." Origin and goal are no longer identical. Jung's attempt to adapt a Hellenistic spirituality into a naturalistic psychology becomes self-contradictory at precisely this point—and with his characteristic eclecticism Jung allows both versions their loose co-existence.

2. The works of Richard Noll (1994, 1997) are important sources for the cultural context of Jung's early work and the group that grew up around him after his split from Freud, but curiously marred by several paragraphs in each book of gratuitous character assassination. Material that more balanced

accounts, such as Ellenberger's (1970), deal with as controversial but legitimate expressions of Jung's complex, conflicted personality and his post-Nietzschean focus on spirituality, periodically for Noll become indications of near villainy (Shamdasani 1998).

Chapter 9. "Triumph of the Will": Heidegger's Nazism as Spiritual Pathology

1. For many scholars it is this shift that begins Heidegger II—the "turn" or reversal of the later Heidegger (Richardson 1963). Of course, Heidegger continued to offer careful analyses of classical metaphysical philosophers, but his most significant writings came to have a more experiential, explicitly metaphoric or poetic, and evocative quality. He is now explicitly trying to unconceal the "felt sense" of Being as the holy, hitherto lost within the categories of Western metaphysics. In their analyses of Heidegger's lecture courses beginning in 1919, Kisiel (1993) and Van Buren (1994) have argued that there is really no "later" Heidegger, since by the late 1930s he had actually returned to those earlier lectures to develop their concepts of clearing, unconcealment, and event. While this is true on a purely conceptual level, it is precisely the more directly experiential element, the physiognomy and metaphor in the later Heidegger's evocation of "primordial Being experiences," that is lacking in what Kisiel (1992) himself terms these "very unpoetic" earlier conceptual analyses, and which Heidegger himself saw as "scientific."

2. There are debates about Heidegger's relation to the Eastern meditative traditions. One view (Guenther 1976; Hunt 1995a) is that his inner development of phenomenology is the first genuine bridge from West to East that simplifies neither. On the other hand, although his first roots are undeniably in Eckhart and the medieval scholastics, Heidegger was also exposed to sophisticated presentations of Taoism and Buddhism by visiting Japanese scholars in the early 1920s (May 1996). Accordingly, these parallels with Eastern thought may not be as spontaneously emergent but instead informed his major works from the beginning.

3. This "turn" in Heidegger's thought is also reflected in his *Contributions to Philosophy*, his mantra-like repetitive notebooks, only recently published and translated. The bulk of the *Contributions* was written in 1936 and 1937. Its "being-historical thinking" represents a sublimation of Heidegger's grandiosity around his personal hopes within National Socialism. Here he announces a "new beginning" for Western thought itself, but one now independent of politics.

Chapter 10. George Ivanovitch Gurdjieff

1. Some of Gurdjieff's early talks, based on pupil notes, are collected in *Views from the Real World* (1973). A somewhat confusing pamphlet, *Herald of*

Coming of Good (1933), was quickly withdrawn from circulation by Gurdjieff. In addition, there is the debated authenticity of *Secret Talks with Mr. G.*, purportedly based on talks given to a small group in New York and transcribed from memory. While later books in this series are clearly contemporaneous and not consistent with Gurdjieff's teachings and writings, the discussions in *Secret Talks* do have a quality of authenticity.

2. Gurdjieff's "chemical factory" and the related pictorial Enneagram depict cycles of transformation for the octaves of food, air, and impressions in terms of "hydrogen" densities. On the level of the impressions octave, the "discontinuity in vibrations" between Mi and Fa is bridged by self-remembering and that between Si and Do by work on negative emotions. Yet in terms of his hypothetical levels of density this more advanced work on experience leads from positive into minus density numbers, although this is never explicitly pointed out. One implication would be that the shift into "objective consciousness" is indeed understood by Gurdjieff as occurring either after death and/or on levels of consciousness that move beyond anything Gurdjieff himself taught. His discussion of four levels of being-body, with the fourth immortal, do amount to a Gurdjieffian version of a post-death *bardo* state (Ouspensky 1949).

3. The Kabbalah also posits a primordial space of creation based on an original constriction, withdrawal, or "shrinkage" within the Absolute, and into which a light of cosmological creation would enter (Scholem 1946). Some influence on Gurdjieff seems obvious but his immediate source is unknown.

4. To Gurdjieff's personally expressed regret, Ouspensky maintained his separation. Although he taught the system to thousands of students over the rest of his life in England and America, and was responsible for its most coherent written presentations, Ouspensky died an alcoholic and in despair (Webb 1987).

5. For many in the 1920s, the Gurdjieff teaching would be seen, as with Jung's psychology, as a kind of Nietzschean mysticism. Ouspensky (1931) made this linkage explicit, adding in his own fascination with the doctrine of eternal recurrence.

Chapter 11. Aleister Crowley, Sexual Magick, and Drugs

1. Crowley and Gurdjieff met each other briefly. In 1924 Crowley arrived uninvited at the Institute at Fontainebleau, posturing as a black magus and apparently hoping for a "struggle of the magicians," a major theme of Gurdjieff's early ballets. Gurdjieff refused to play along, ignored him, and then, as he was leaving, denounced him as "dirty inside" and forbade Crowley to return (Nott 1961; Webb 1987). It would appear Gurdjieff won.

References

Albrow, M. 1990. *Max Weber's Construction of Social Theory*. New York: St. Martin's Press.

Almaas, A. H. 1996. *The Point of Existence*. Berkeley, Calif.: Diamond Books.

———. 1995. *Luminous Night's Journey: An Autobiographical Fragment*. Berkeley, Calif.: Diamond Books.

———. 1988. *The Pearl Beyond Price—Integration of Personality into Being: An Object-Relations Approach*. Berkeley, Calif.: Diamond Books.

———. 1986a. *Essence—The Diamond Approach to Inner Realization*. York Beach, Maine: Samuel Weiser.

———. 1986b. *The Void: A Psychodynamic Investigation of the Relationship Between Mind and Space*. Berkeley, Calif.: Diamond Books.

———. 1984. *The Elixir of Enlightenment*. York Beach, Maine: Samuel Weiser.

Angyal, A. 1936. The experience of the body-self in schizophrenia. *Archives of Neurology and Psychiatry* 35: 1029–53.

Arnheim, R. 1969. *Visual Thinking*. Berkeley: University of California Press.

Baehr, P. 2001. "The iron cage" and the "Shell as hard as steel": Parson's Weber and the *Stahlhartes Gehause*. *The Protestant Ethic and the Spirit of Capitalism, History and Theory* 40: 153–69.

Balint, M. 1968. *The Basic Fault*. New York: Brunner/Mazel.

Bellah, R., R. Madsen, W. Sullivan, A. Swidler, and S. Tipton. 1985. *Habits of the Heart: Individualism and Commitment in American Life*. New York: Harper and Row.

Bendix, R. 1960. *Max Weber: An Intellectual Portrait*. Berkeley: University of California Press.

Bennett, J. G. 1973. *Gurdjieff: Making of a New World*. New York: Harper Colophon Books.

———. 1962. *Witness: The Story of a Search*. London: Hodder and Stroughton.

Bickman, M. 1988. *American Romantic Psychology*. Dallas: Spring Publications.

Biehl, J. 1989. Goddess mythology in ecological politics. *New Politics* 2: 84–105.

Bion, W. R. 1970. *Attention and Interpretation*. New York: Basic Books.

———. 1965. *Transformations*. New York: Basic Books.

———. 1962. *Learning from Experience*. London: Heineman.

Blavatsky, H. P. 1888. *The Secret Doctrine*, 2 vols. London: Theosophical Publishing House.

———. 1877. *Isis Unveiled*, 2 vols. London: W. J. Bouton.

Blofeld, J. 1973. *The Secret and Sublime: Taoist Mysteries and Magic*. London: George Allen and Unwin.

Bloom, H. 1996. *Omens of Millennium: The Gnosis of Angels, Dreams, and Resurrection*. New York: Riverhead Books.

Bode, C., ed. 1982. Introduction and epilogue to *The Portable Thoreau*. New York: Penguin.

Boisen, A. 1936. *The Exploration of the Inner World*. New York: Harper.

Boss, M. 1988. Martin Heidegger's Zollikon seminars. In *Heidegger and Psychology*, ed. K. Hoeller. Special issue of *Review of Existential Psychology and Psychiatry* 16: 7–20.

Bourguignon, E. 1973. A framework for the comparative study of altered states of consciousness. In *Religion, Altered States of Consciousness, and Social Change*, ed. E.Bourguignon, 3–35. Columbus: Ohio State University Press.

Bower, T. 1977. *A Primer of Infant Development*. San Francisco: W. H. Freeman.

Bridgman, R. 1981. *Dark Thoreau*. Lincoln: University of Nebraska Press.

Bromberg, N. and V. Small. 1983. *Hitler's Psychopathology*. New York: International Universities Press.

Brown, D. and R. Novick. 1995. Interview with Jerry Garcia. *Relix* 22 (4): 12–19.

Buchholz, E. 1999. Neonatal temperment, maternal interaction, and the need for "alonetime." *American Journal of Orthopsychiatry* 69: 9–18.

Bucke, R. 1901. *Cosmic Consciousness*. New York: University Books.

Campbell, C. 1978. The secret religion of the educated classes. *Sociological Analysis* 39: 146–56.

Capps, D. 1997. *Men, Religion, and Melancholia: James, Otto, Jung, and Erikson*. New Haven: Yale University Press.

Capra, F. 1975. *The Tao of Physics*. Berkeley, Calif.: Shambhala.

Caputo, J. 1986. *The Mystical Element in Heidegger's Thought*. New York: Fordham University Press.

Carlson, K. 1990. *In Her Image: The Unhealed Daughter's Search for Her Mother*. Boston: Shambhala.

Chalmers, D. 1996. *The Conscious Mind*. Oxford: Oxford University Press.

Charlesworth, J. H., ed. 1983. *The Old Testament Pseudepigrapha*. New York: Doubleday.

Cohn, N. 1993. *Cosmos, Chaos, and the World to Come: The Ancient Roots of Apocalyptic Faith*. New Haven: Yale University Press.

Copenhaver, B., ed. and trans. 1992. *Hermetica*. Cambridge: Cambridge University Press.

Corbin, H. 1978. *The Man of Light in Iranian Sufism*. Boulder and London: Shambhala.

Craig, E. 1988. An encounter with Medard Boss. *The Humanistic Psychologist* 16: 24–55.

Cranston, S. 1993. *HPB: The Extraordinary Life and Influence of Helena Blavatsky, Founder of the Modern Theosophical Movement*. New York: Jeremy Tarcher/Putnam.

Crowley, A. 1973. *Magick Without Tears*. Tempe, Ariz.: New Falcon Publications.

———. 1969. *The Confessions of Aleister Crowley: An Autohagiography*. London: Jonathan Cape.

———. 1922. *Diary of a Drug Fiend*. York Beach, Maine: Samuel Weiser.

Crowley, V. 1989. *Wicca: The Old Religion in the New Millennium*. London: Thorsons.

D'Andrade, R. 1961. Anthropological studies of dreams. In *Psychological Anthropology*, ed. F. Hsu, 296–332. Homewood, Ill.: Dorsey Press.

Dawson, L. 1998. *Comprehending Cults: The Sociology of New Religious Movements*. Toronto: Oxford University Press.

De Chardin, T. 1959. *The Phenomenon of Man*. New York: Harper Torchbooks.

De Hartmann, T. 1964. *Our Life with Mr. Gurdjieff*. New York: Cooper Square Publishers.

De Vilaine-Cambessedes, A. 1997. No conscious effort is ever lost. In *Gurdjieff*, ed. J. Needleman and G. Baker. New York: Continuum.

Diamond, S. 1996. *Anger, Madness, and the Daimonic: The Psychological Genesis of Violence, Evil, and Creativity*. Albany: State University of New York Press.

Dick, P. K. 1981. *Valis*. New York: Bantam Books.

Diogenes Laertius. third century. *Lives of the Eminent Philosophers*, vol. 1. Trans. R. Hicks. Cambridge: Harvard University Press, 1925.

Duquette, L. M. 1993. *The Magick of Thelema: A Handbook of the Rituals of Aleister Crowley*. York Beach, Maine: Samuel Weiser.

Durkheim, E. 1912. *The Elementary Forms of the Religious Life* Trans. J. Swain. New York: Collier Books, 1961.

Efron, R. 1990. *The Decline and Fall of Hemispheric Specialization*. Hillsdale, N.J.: Erlbaum.

Eigen, M. 1998. *The Psychoanalytic Mystic*. Binghamton, N.Y.: Esf Publishers.

Eliade, M. 1964. *Shamanism*. New York: Pantheon.

———. 1958. *Yoga: Immortality and Freedom*. New York: Pantheon Books.

Ellenberger, H. 1970. *The Discovery of the Unconscious*. New York: Basic Books.

Eller, C. 1993. *Living in the Lap of the Goddess: The Feminist Spirituality Movement in America*. New York: Crossroad.

Elms, A. 1994. *Uncovering Lives*. New York: Oxford University Press.

Emerson, R. W. 1862. Thoreau. In R. W. Emerson, *Representative Men*, 135–51. London: Ward, Lock, and Co., 1912.

———. 1850. Swedenborg. In R. W. Emerson, *Representative Men*, 46–71. London: Ward, Lock, and Co., 1912.

———. 1844. Experience. In R. W. Emerson, *Selections*, ed. S. Whicher, 254–74. Cambridge, Mass.: Riverside Press.

———. 1841a. The over-soul. In *The Selected Writings of Ralph Waldo Emerson*, ed. B. Atkinson, 261–78. New York: Modern Library, 1940a.

———. 1841b. Compensation. In *The Selected Writings of Ralph Waldo Emerson*, ed. B. Atkinson, 170–89. New York: Modern Library, 1940b.

———. 1836. Nature. In *Nature, the Conduct of Life, and Other Essays*, 1–38. London: Dent, 1963.

————. 1819–1882. *The Journals and Miscellaneous Notebooks of Ralph Waldo Emerson*, 16 vols. Ed. R. Bosco and G. Johnson. Cambridge, Mass.: Belknap Press, 1982.

Enesee. 1856. *The History of Dungeon Rock*. Boston: Bela Marsh.

Engler, J. 1984. Therapeutic aims in psychotherapy and meditation: Developmental stages in the representation of self. *Journal of Transpersonal Psychology* 16: 25–61.

Epictetus. first cent. *The Discourses*. Vols. 1 and 2, Trans. W. Oldfather. Cambridge: Harvard University Press, 1925.

Epstein, M. 1998. *Going to Pieces Without Falling Apart: A Buddhist Perspective on Wholeness*. New York: Broadway Books.

Erikson, E. 1969. *Gandhi's Truth*. New York: Norton.

————. 1963. *Childhood and Society*. New York: Norton.

————. 1962. *Young Man Luther*. New York: Norton.

Erikson, E., J. Erikson, and H. Rivnick. 1986. *Vital Involvement in Old Age*. New York: Norton.

Erickson, M., and E. Rossi. 1981. *Experiencing Hypnosis*. New York: Irvington.

Ettinger, E. 1995. *Hannah Arendt / Martin Heidegger*. New Haven: Yale University Press.

Fairbairn, W. R. D. 1954. *An Object-Relations Theory of the Personality*. New York: Basic Books.

Farias, V. 1989. *Heidegger and Nazism*. Philadelphia: Temple University Press.

Feldman, B. 1992. Jung's infancy and childhood and its influence upon the development of analytical psychology. *Journal of Analytical Psychology* 37: 255–74.

Feuerstein, G. 1990. *Holy Madness*. New York: Paragon House.

Filoramo, G. 1990. *A History of Gnosticism*. Oxford: Basil Blackwell.

Fischer, R. 1975. Cartography of inner space. In *Hallucinations: Behavior, Experience, and Theory*, ed. R. Siegel and L. West, 197–239. New York: Wiley.

Fordham, M. 1958. *The Objective Psyche*. London: Routledge and Kegan Paul.

————. 1957. *New Developments in Analytical Psychology*. London: Routledge and Kegan Paul.

Forman, R. K. C. 1999. *Mysticism, Mind, Consciousness*. Albany: State University of New York Press.

Fox, W. 1995. *Toward a Transpersonal Ecology*. Albany: State University of New York Press.

Freud, S. 1930. *Civilization and its discontents*. New York: Norton, 1961.

———. 1923. *The Ego and the Id*. London: Hogarth.

———. 1922. Certain neurotic mechanisms in jealousy, paranoia, and homosexuality. In *Collected Papers*, vol. 2, trans. J. Riviere, 232–43. New York: Basic Books, 1959.

———. 1919. *Beyond the Pleasure Principle*. London: Hogarth, 1950.

———. 1911. Psycho-analytic notes upon an autobiographical account of a case of paranoia. In *Collected Papers*, vol. 3, trans. A. and J. Strachery, 387–470. New York: Basic Books, 1959.

Fromm, E. 1963. C. G. Jung: Prophet of the unconscious. *Scientific American* 209 (3): 283–90.

Gackenbach, J., and J. Bosveld. 1989. *Control Your Dreams*. New York: Harper and Row.

Gampopa. 12th cent. *The Jewel Ornament of Liberation*. Trans. H. Guenther. Berkeley: Shambhala, 1971.

Garcia, J. 1995. *Harrington Street*. New York: Delacorte Press.

Gardner, H. 1993. *Creating Minds*. New York: Basic Books.

———. 1983. *Frames of Mind*. New York: Basic Books.

Garrett, W. 1975. Maligned mysticism: The maledicted career of Troeltsch's third type. *Sociological Analysis* 36: 205–23.

Gebser, J. 1985. *The Ever-Present Origin*. Trans. N. Barstad and A. Mickunas. Athens: Ohio University Press.

Gendlin, E. 1978. *Focusing*. New York: Bantam.

Geschwind, N. 1982. Disorders of attention: A frontier in neuropsychology. *Philosophical Transactions of the Royal Society of London* B298: 173–85.

Gibson, J. J. 1979. *The Ecological Approach to Visual Perception*. Boston: Houghton Mifflin.

Gifford-May, D., and Thompson, N. 1994. "Deep states" of meditation: Phenomenological reports of experience. *Journal of Transpersonal Psychology* 26: 117–38.

Gilman, S., ed. 1987. *Conversations with Nietzsche: A Life in the Words of His Contemporaries*. New York: Oxford University Press.

Glover, E. 1956. *Freud or Jung*. New York: Meridian Books.

Goleman, D. 1972. The Buddha on meditation and states of consciousness. *Journal of Transpersonal Psychology* 4 (1): 1–44.

Goodheart, W. 1984. C. G. Jung's first "patient": On the seminal emergence of Jung's thought. *Journal of Analytical Psychology* 29: 1–35.

Goodrick-Clarke, N. 1985. *The Occult Roots of Nazism*. New York: New York University Press.

Green, C. 1968a. *Lucid Dreams*. London: Hamish Hamilton.

———. 1968b. *Out-of-Body Experiences*. New York: Ballantine.

Greenfield, R. 1996. *Dark Star: An Oral Biography of Jerry Garcia*. New York: William Morrow and Company.

Grof, S. 1988. *The Adventure of Self-Discovery*. Albany: State University of New York Press.

———. 1980. *LSD Psychotherapy*. Pomona, California: Hunter House.

Guenther, H. 1984. *Matrix of Mystery: Scientific and Humanistic Aspects of rDzogs-chen Thought*. Boulder: Shambhala.

Guenther, H., trans. 1976. *Longchenpa's "Kindly Bent to Ease Us,"* vols. 1–3. Emeryville, California: Dharma.

Guntrip, H. 1968. *Schizoid Phenomena, Object Relations, and the Self*. New York: International Universities Press.

Gurdjieff, G. 1978. *Secret Talks with Mr. G*. New York: IDHAB.

———. 1975. *Life is Real Only Then, When "I Am."* New York: E. P. Dutton.

———. 1973. *Gurdjieff: Views from the Real World*. New York: E. P. Dutton.

———. 1963. *Meetings with Remarkable Men*. New York: E. P. Dutton.

———. 1950. *All and Everything: Beelzebub's Tales to His Grandson*. London: Routledge and Kegan Paul.

———. 1933. *The Herald of the Coming Good*. Paris: G. Gurdjieff.

Hadot, P. 1995. *Philosophy as a Way of Life*. Oxford: Blackwell.

———. 1993. *Plotinus, or the Simplicity of Vision*. Chicago: University of Chicago Press.

Hanegraaff, W. 1998. *New Age Religion and Western Culture: Esotericism in the Mirror of Secular Thought*. Albany: State University of New York Press.

Hannah, B. 1976. *Jung: His Life and Work*. G. P. Putnam's Sons.

Happold, F. 1963. *Mysticism: A Study and an Anthology*. Baltimore: Penguin Books.

Harding, W. 1965. *The Days of Henry David Thoreau*. New York: Alfred A. Knopf.

Hayman, R. 2001. *A Life of Jung*. New York: W.W. Norton.

Hebb, D.O. 1980. *Essay on Mind*. Hillsdale, N.J.: Erlbaum.

Heidegger, M. 1962. *On Time and Being*, trans. J. Stambaugh. New York: Harper and Row, 1972.

———. 1959. *On the Way to Language*. Trans. P. Hertz. New York: Harper and Row, 1971.

———. 1956. *The Question of Being*. Trans. W. Kluback and J. Wilde. New York: Twayne Publishers, 1958.

———. 1954. *What is Called Thinking?* Trans. F. Wieck and J. Gray. New York: Harper and Row, 1968.

———. 1947a. The thinker as poet. In *Poetry, Language, Truth*, trans. A. Hofstadter, 1–14. New York: Harper and Row, 1971.

———. 1947b. The pathway. In *Heidegger: The Man and the Thinker*, ed. and trans. T. Sheehan, 69–72. Chicago: Precedent Publishing, 1981.

———. 1947c. Letter on humanism. In *Philosophy in the Twentieth Century*, vol. 3, ed. W. Barrett and H. Aiken, trans. E. Lohner, 270–302. New York: Random House, 1962.

———. 1946. What are poets for? In *Poetry, Language, Thought*, trans. A. Hofstadter, 91–142. New York: Harper and Row, 1971.

———. 1944–45. Conversation on a country path. In *Discourse on Thinking*, trans. J. Anderson and E. Freund, 58–90. New York: Harper and Row, 1966.

———. 1944. Logos (Heraclitus, Fragment B50). In *Early Greek Thinking*, trans. D. Krell and F. Capuzzi, 59–78. New York: Harper and Row, 1975.

———. 1943a. Remembrance of the poet. In *Existence and Being*, trans. D. Scott, 233–69. Chicago: Henry Regnery, 1949.

———. 1943b. Aletheia (Heraclitus, Fragment B16). In *Early Greek Thinking*, trans. D. Krell and F. Capuzzi, 102–23. New York: Harper and Row, 1975.

———. 1942–43. *Parmenides*. Trans. A. Schuwer and R. Rojcewicz. Bloomington: Indiana University Press, 1992.

———. 1942. *Hölderlin's Hymn "The Ister."* Trans. W. McNeill and J. Davis. Bloomington: Indiana University Press, 1996.

———. 1941. *Basic Concepts*. Trans.G. Aylesworth. Bloomington: Indiana University Press, 1993.

References 335

———. 1938. *Basic Questions of Philosophy*. Trans. R. Rojcewicz and A. Schuwer. Bloomington: Indiana University Press, 1994.

———. 1936-8. *Contributions to Philosophy (from Enowning)*. Trans. P. Emad and K. Maly. Bloomington: Indiana University Press, 1999.

———. 1935a. *An Introduction to Metaphysics*. Trans. R. Manheim. New York: Doubleday, 1961.

———. 1935b. *The Origin of the Work of Art*. In *Poetry, Language, Thought*, trans. A. Hofstadter, 17–87. New York: Harper and Row.

———. 1936a. Hölderlin and the essence of poetry. In *Existence and Being*, trans. D. Scott, 270–91. Chicago: Henry Regnery.

———. 1936b. *Schelling's Treatise on the Essence of Human Freedom*. Trans. J. Stambaugh. Athens: Ohio University Press, 1985.

———. 1931. *Hegel's Phenomenology of Spirit*. Trans. P. Emad and K. Maly. Bloomington: Indiana University Press, 1988.

———. 1930. On the essence of truth. In *Existence and Being*, trans. R. F. C. Hull and A. Crick, 325–61. Chicago: Henry Regnery, 1949.

———. 1929–30. *The Fundamental Concepts of Metaphysics: World, Finitude, Solitude*. Trans. W. McNeill and N. Walker. Bloomington: Indiana University Press, 2001.

———. 1929. *The Essence of Ground* [also translated as *The essence of reasons*]. Trans. T. Malick. Evanston, Ill.: Northwestern University Press, 1969.

———. 1928. What is metaphysics? In *Existence and Being*, trans. R. F. C. Hull and A. Crick, 325–61. Chicago: Henry Regnery, 1949.

———. 1927. *Being and Time*. Trans. J. Macquarrie and E. Robinson. New York: Harper and Row, 1962.

Hennis, W. 1988. *Max Weber: Essays in Reconstruction*. Trans. K. Tribe. London: Allen and Unwin.

Hillman, J. 1996. *The Soul's Code: In Search of Character and Calling*. New York: Random House.

———. 1993. Alchemical blue and the unio mentalis. *Spring 54*: 132–48.

———. 1989. The yellowing of the work. *Eranos 56*, 77–96. Frankfort: Insel-Verlag.

———. 1981. Silver and the white earth (Part Two). *Spring*: 21–66.

———. 1980. Silver and the white earth (Part One). *Spring*: 21–48.

———. 1978. The therapeutic value of alchemical language. *Dragonflies* 33–42.

————. 1975. *Revisioning Psychology*. New York: Harper and Row.

Hillman, J., and M. Ventura. 1992. *We've Had a Hundred Years of Psychotherapy—And the World's Getting Worse*. San Francisco: Harper.

Hoffman, E. 1988. *The Right to be Human: A Biography of Abraham Maslow*. Los Angeles: Jeremy Tarcher.

Hollis-Walker, L. 2000. Environmental and social activism: Group members from a non-violent civil disobedience in Temagami, Ontario. Honors thesis, Dept. of Psychology, Brock University, St. Catharines, Ontario.

Homans, P. 1989. *The Ability to Mourn*. Chicago: University of Chicago Press.

Hood, R. W. and Hall, J. 1980. Gender differences in the description of erotic and mystical experiences. *Review of Religious Research* 21: 195–207.

Houston, J. 1996. *A Mythic Life*. San Francisco: Harper.

Hulme, K. 1966. *Undiscovered Country: In Search of Gurdjieff*. Boston: Little Brown.

Hunt, H. 2001. Some perils of quantum consciousness: Epistemological pan-experientialism and the emergence-submergence of consciousness. *Journal of Consciousness Studies* 8: 35–45.

————. 2000. Experiences of radical personal transformation in mysticism, religious conversion, and psychosis: A review of the varieties, processes, and consequences of the numinous. *Journal of Mind and Behavior* 21: 353–98.

————. 1999. Transpersonal and cognitive psychologies of consciousness: A necessary and reciprocal dialogue. In *Toward a Science of Consciousness III*, ed. S. Hameroff, A. Kaszniak, and D. Chalmers, 449–58. Cambridge: MIT Press.

————. 1998. "Triumph of the Will": Heidegger's Nazism as spiritual pathology. *Journal of Mind and Behavior* 19: 379–414.

————. 1995a. *On the Nature of Consciousness: Cognitive, Phenomenological, and Transpersonal Perspectives*. New Haven: Yale University Press.

————. 1995b. Some developmental issues in transpersonal psychology. *Journal of Mind and Behavior* 16: 115–34.

————. 1992. Dreams of Freud and Jung: Reciprocal relationships between social relations and archetypal/transpersonal psychology. *Psychiatry* 55: 28–47.

————. 1989. *The Multiplicity of Dreams: Memory, Imagination, and Consciousness*. New Haven: Yale University Press.

————. 1986. A cognitive reinterpretation of classical introspectionism: The relation between introspection and altered states of consciousness and their mutual relevance for a cognitive psychology of metaphor and felt meaning, with commentaries by D. Bakan, R. Evans, and P. Swartz, and response. *Annals of Theoretical Psychology* 4(245): 245–313.

———. 1985. Relations between the phenomena of religious mysticism and the psychology of thought: A cognitive psychology of states of consciousness and the necessity of subjective states for cognitive theory. *Perceptual and Motor Skills* 61: 911–61.

———. 1984. A cognitive psychology of mystical and altered state experience. *Perceptual and Motor Skills* 58: 467–513.

Hunt, H., Gervais, A., Shearing-Johns, S., and Travis, F. 1992. Transpersonal experiences in childhood: An exploratory empirical study of selected adult groups. *Perceptual and Motor Skills* 75: 1135–53.

Hunt, N. 1994. Non-politics as a vocation: Martin Heidegger and National Socialism. Honors thesis, Dept. of Social Studies, Harvard College.

Isaacs, E. 1983. The Fox sisters and American spiritualism. In *The Occult in America: New Historical Perspectives*, ed. H. Kerr and C. Crow, 79–110. Chicago: University of Illinois Press.

Izutsu, T. 1984. *Sufism and Taoism: A Comparative Study of Key Philosophical Concepts*. Berkeley: University of California Press.

Jackson, B. 1999. *Garcia: An American Life*. New York: Viking.

Jacobson, E. 1964. *The Self and the Object World*. New York: International Universities Press.

Jacoby, M. 1994. *Shame and the Origins of Self-Esteem*. London: Routledge.

Jaffe, A. 1971. *From the Life and Work of C. G. Jung*. New York: Harper.

James, W. 1912. *Essays in Radical Empiricism*. New York: Longmans, Green.

———. 1902. *The Varieties of Religious Experience*. Garden City, N.J.: Dolphin Books.

———. 1897. *The Will to Believe*. New York: Dover Publications.

Jaspers, K. 1953. *The Origin and Goal of History*. New Haven: Yale University Press.

———. 1936. *Nietzsche: An Introduction to the Understanding of His Philosophical Activity*. Trans. C. Wallraff and F. Schmitz. Baltimore: Johns Hopkins University Press, 1997.

———. 1922. *Strindberg and VanGogh: An Attempt at a Pathographic Analysis with Reference to Parallel Cases of Swedenborg and Hölderlin*, trans. O. Grunow and D. Woloshin. Tucson: University of Arizona Press, 1977.

Johnson, M. 1987. *The Body in the Mind: The Bodily Bases of Meaning, Imagination, and Reason.* Chicago: University of Chicago Press.

Jonas, H. 1996. *The Phenomenon of Life: Toward a Philosophical Biology.* New York: Harper and Row.

———. 1963. *The Gnostic Religion.* Boston: Beacon Press.

Joyce, J. 1934. *Ulysses.* New York: Modern Library.

Jung, C. G. 1988. *Nietzsche's Zarathustra: Notes of the Seminar Given in 1934–1939.* Princeton: Princeton University Press.

———. 1975. *Letters*, vol. 2. ed. G. Adler, trans. R. F. C. Hull. Princeton: Princeton University Press.

———. 1961. *Memories, Dreams, Reflections.* ed. A. Jaffe, trans. R. C. Winston. New York: Pantheon Books.

———. 1959. *Aion: Researches into the Phenomenology of the Self.* Vol. 9(2), *Collected Works of C. G. Jung.* ed. G. Adler and trans. R. F. C. Hull. Princeton: Princeton University Press.

———. 1958. *Flying Saucers: A Modern Myth of Things Seen in the Skies.* In vol. 10, *Collected Works of C. G. Jung*, ed. G. Adler and trans. R. F. C. Hull, 307–433. Princeton: Princeton University Press, 1964.

———. 1955. *Mysterium Coniunctionis.* Vol. 14, *Collected Works of C. G. Jung.* Ed. G. Adler and trans. R. F. C. Hull. Princeton: Princeton University Press, 1963.

———. 1950. A study in the process of individuation. In vol. 9(1), *Collected Works of C. G. Jung*, ed. G. Adler and trans. R. F. C. Hull, 290–354. Princeton: Princeton University Press, 1960.

———. 1946. Epilogue to "Essays on Contemporary Events." In vol. 10, *Collected Works of C. G. Jung*, ed. G. Adler and trans. R. F. C. Hull, 227–43. Princeton: Princeton University Press, 1964.

———. 1944. *Psychology and Alchemy.* Vol. 12, *Collected Works of C. G. Jung.* Ed. G. Adler and trans. R. F. C. Hull. Princeton: Princeton University Press, 1953.

———. 1939. Psychological commentary on "The Tibetan Book of the Great Liberation." In vol. 11, *Collected Works of C. G. Jung*, ed. G. Adler and trans. R. F. C. Hull, 479–508. Princeton: Princeton University Press, 1958.

———. 1938. *Psychology and Religion.* In vol. 11, *Collected Works of C. G. Jung*, ed. G. Adler and trans. R. F. C. Hul, 3–105. Princeton: Princeton University Press, 1958.

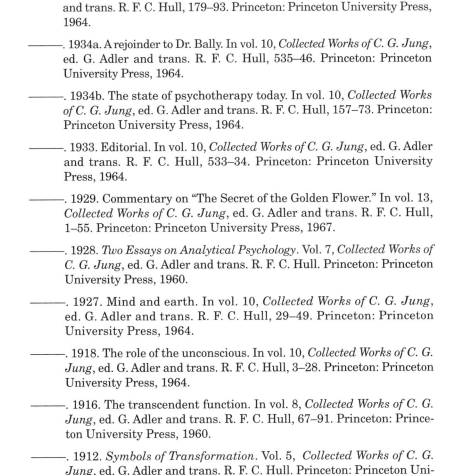

———. 1936. Wotan. In vol. 10, *Collected Works of C. G. Jung*, ed. G. Adler and trans. R. F. C. Hull, 179–93. Princeton: Princeton University Press, 1964.

———. 1934a. A rejoinder to Dr. Bally. In vol. 10, *Collected Works of C. G. Jung*, ed. G. Adler and trans. R. F. C. Hull, 535–46. Princeton: Princeton University Press, 1964.

———. 1934b. The state of psychotherapy today. In vol. 10, *Collected Works of C. G. Jung*, ed. G. Adler and trans. R. F. C. Hull, 157–73. Princeton: Princeton University Press, 1964.

———. 1933. Editorial. In vol. 10, *Collected Works of C. G. Jung*, ed. G. Adler and trans. R. F. C. Hull, 533–34. Princeton: Princeton University Press, 1964.

———. 1929. Commentary on "The Secret of the Golden Flower." In vol. 13, *Collected Works of C. G. Jung*, ed. G. Adler and trans. R. F. C. Hull, 1–55. Princeton: Princeton University Press, 1967.

———. 1928. *Two Essays on Analytical Psychology*. Vol. 7, *Collected Works of C. G. Jung*, ed. G. Adler and trans. R. F. C. Hull. Princeton: Princeton University Press, 1960.

———. 1927. Mind and earth. In vol. 10, *Collected Works of C. G. Jung*, ed. G. Adler and trans. R. F. C. Hull, 29–49. Princeton: Princeton University Press, 1964.

———. 1918. The role of the unconscious. In vol. 10, *Collected Works of C. G. Jung*, ed. G. Adler and trans. R. F. C. Hull, 3–28. Princeton: Princeton University Press, 1964.

———. 1916. The transcendent function. In vol. 8, *Collected Works of C. G. Jung*, ed. G. Adler and trans. R. F. C. Hull, 67–91. Princeton: Princeton University Press, 1960.

———. 1912. *Symbols of Transformation*. Vol. 5, *Collected Works of C. G. Jung*, ed. G. Adler and trans. R. F. C. Hull. Princeton: Princeton University Press, 1956.

———. 1902. On the psychology and pathology of so-called occult phenomena. In vol. 1, *Collected Works of C. G. Jung*, ed. G. Adler and trans. R. F. C. Hull, 3–88. Princeton: Princeton University Press, 1957.

Käsler, D. 1988. *Max Weber: An Introduction to His Life and Work*. Trans. P. Hurd. Chicago: University of Chicago Press.

Kaufmann, W. 1980. *Discovering the Mind: Nietzsche, Heidegger, and Buber*, vol. 2. New York: McGraw-Hill.

———. 1956. *Nietzsche: Philosopher, Psychologist, Antichrist*. New York: Meridian Books.

Keniston, K. 1966. *The Uncommitted: Alienated Youth in American Society.* New York: Harcourt Brace Jovanovich.

Kernberg, O. 1984. *Object-Relations Theory and Clinical Psychoanalysis.* Northvale, N.J.: Jason Aronson.

Kerr, J. 1993. *A Most Dangerous Method: The Story of Jung, Freud, and Sabrina Spielrein.* New York: Alfred A. Knopf.

Khan, M. R. 1979. *Alienation in Perversions.* New York: International Universities Press.

———. 1974. *The Privacy of the Self.* New York: International Universities Press.

Kierkegaard, S. 1844. *The Concept of Dread.* Trans. W. Lowrie. Princeton: Princeton University Press, 1967.

———. 1844. *Philosophical Fragments.* Trans. H. Hong and E. Hong. Princeton: Princeton University Press, 1985.

———. 1843. *Fear and Trembling.* Garden City, N.Y.: Doubleday, 1954.

King James Bible. Boston: Massachusetts Bible Society.

Kingsland, W. 1928. *The Real H. P. Blavatsky.* London: Theosophical Publishing House.

Kirsch, J. 1991. Carl Gustav Jung and the Jews: The real story. In *Lingering Shadows: Jungians, Freudians, and Anti-Semitism,* ed. A. Maidenbaum and S. Martin. Boston: Shambhala.

Kisiel, T. 1993. *The Genesis of Heidegger's Being and Time.* Berkeley: University of California Press.

———. 1992. Heidegger's apology: Biography as philosophy and ideology. In *The Heidegger Case: On Philosophy and Politics,* ed. T. Rockmore and J. Margolis, 11–51. Philadelphia: Temple University Press.

Klein, M., Heimann, P., Isaacs, S., and Rivere, J. 1952. *Developments in Psycho-analysis.* London: Hogarth Press.

Klossowski, P. 1997. *Nietzsche and the Vicious Circle.* Trans. D. Smith. Chicago: University of Chicago Press.

Köhler, J. 2002. *Zarathustra's Secret: The Interior Life of Friedrich Nietzsche.* Trans. R. Taylor. New Haven: Yale University Press.

Kohler, L., and Saner, H., eds. 1992. *Hannah Arendt / Karl Jaspers Correspondence 1926–1969.* New York: Harcourt Brace Jovanovich.

Kohut, H. 1984. *How Does Analysis Cure?* Chicago: University of Chicago Press.

———. 1977. *The Restoration of the Self*. New York: International Universities Press.

———. 1971. *The Analysis of the Self*. New York: International Universities Press.

Kolb, B. and Whishaw, I. 1990. *Fundamentals of Human Neuropsychology*. New York: W. H. Freeman.

Krell, D. 1996. *Nietzsche: A Novel*. Albany: State University of New York Press.

———. 1992. *Daimon Life: Heidegger and Life-Philosophy*. Bloomington: Indiana University Press.

Kugler, P. 1993. Alchemy. Paper presented at the Analytical Psychology Society of Western New York, Buffalo, November.

LaCarriere, J. 1989. *The Gnostics*. San Francisco: City Lights Books.

Lacoue-Labarthe, P. 1990. *Heidegger, Art and Politics*. Trans.C. Turner. Oxford: Basil Blackwell.

Lakoff, G. 1987. *Women, Fire, and Dangerous Things*. Chicago: University of Chicago Press.

Lakoff, G. and Johnson, M. 1999. *Philosophy in the Flesh*. New York: Basic Books.

Landau, R. 1964. *God is My Adventure*. London: Unwin Books.

Lanternari, V. 1963. *The Religions of the Oppressed*. New York: Alfred A. Knopf.

Lasch, C. 1978. *The Culture of Narcissism*. New York: Norton.

Laski, M. 1961. *Ecstasy*. Bloomington: Indiana University Press.

Layton, B., ed. and trans. 1987. *The Gnostic Scriptures*. New York: Doubleday.

LeBeaux, R. 1984. *Thoreau's Seasons*. Amherst: University of Massachusetts Press.

———. 1977. *Young Man Thoreau*. Amherst: University of Massachusetts Press.

Lévi-Strauss, C. 1966. *The Savage Mind*. Chicago: University of Chicago Press.

Levenda, P. 2002. *Unholy Alliance: A History of Nazi Involvement with the Occult*. New York: Continuum.

Levinson, D. 1978. *The Seasons of a Man's Life*. New York: Ballantine Books.

Lewis, A. and Newhall, J. 1865. *History of Lynn, Essex County, Massachusetts*. Boston: John H. Shorey.

Locwenberg, P. 1988. Psychoanalytic models of history: Freud and after. In *Psychology and Historical Interpretations*, ed. W. M. Runyan. New York: Oxford University Press.

Lowith, K. 1997. *Nietzsche's Philosophy of the Eternal Recurrence of the Same*. Trans. J. Lomax. Berkeley: University of California Press.

Lowry, R., ed. 1982. *The Journals of Abraham Maslow*. Lexington, Mass.: Lewis Publishing Company.

Mahler, M., Pine, F., and Bergman, A. 1975. *The Psychological Birth of the Human Infant*. London: Maresfield Library.

Maidenbaum, A., and Martin, S., eds. 1991. *Lingering Shadows: Jungians, Freudians, and Anti-Semitism*. Boston: Shambhala.

Maquet, P., Peters, J., Aerts, J., Delfiore, G., Dequeldre, C., Luxen, A., and Franck, G. 1996. Functional neuroanatomy of human rapid-eye movement sleep and dreaming. *Nature* 383: 163–166.

Maslow, A. 1971. *The Farther Reaches of Human Nature*. New York: Viking.

———. 1966. *The Psychology of Science*. New York: Harper and Row.

———. 1962. *Toward a Psychology of Being*. Princeton, N.J.: Van Nostrand.

———. 1942. Self-esteem (dominance-feeling) and sexuality in women. *Journal of Social Psychology* 16: 259–94.

———. 1939. Dominance, personality, and social behavior in women. *Journal of Social Psychology* 10: 3–39.

———. 1936. The role of dominance in the social and sexual behavior of infra-human primates. *Journal of Genetic Psychology* 49: 161–98.

Masters, R. and Houston, J. 1972. *Mind Games*. New York: Viking Press.

———. 1966. *The Varieties of Psychedelic Experience*. New York: Delta.

Mathers, S. and MacGregor, L., trans. 1900. *The Book of the Sacred Magic of Abramelin the Mage*. New York: Dover Publications, 1975.

May, R. 1996. *Heidegger's Hidden Sources*. London: Routledge.

McCrae, R. 1994. Openness to experience as a basic dimension of personality. *Imagination, Cognition, and Personality* 13: 39–55.

McKenna, S. 1991. Introduction to Plotinus, *The Enneads*. New York: Penguin Books.

McPherran, M. 1996. *The Religion of Socrates*. University Park: Pennsylvania State University Press.

Mead, G. H. 1934. *Mind, Self, and Society*. Chicago: University of Chicago Press.

Meister Eckhart. 14th cent. *Meister Eckhart: A Modern Translation*. Trans. R. Blakney. New York: Harper and Row.

Meltzoff, A., and Moore, M. 1992. Early imitation within a functional framework. The importance of person identity, movement, and development. *Infant Behavior and Development* 15: 479–505.

Middleton, C., ed. and trans. 1969. *Selected Letters of Friedrich Nietzsche*. Chicago: University of Chicago Press.

Miller, A. 1990. *The Untouched Key*. New York: Doubleday.

Monroe, R. 1985. *Far Journeys*. Garden City, N.Y.: Doubleday.

Moody, R. 1975. *Life After life*. Atlanta: Mockingbird Books.

Moore, J. 1991. *Gurdjieff: The Anatomy of a Myth*. Rockport, Mass.: Element.

Murray, H. A. 1938. *Explorations in Personality*. New York: Wiley.

Murray, M. 1933. *The God of the Witches*. Garden City, N.Y.: Doubleday, 1960.

Neske, E., and Kettering, E., eds. 1990. *Martin Heidegger and National Socialism*. New York: Paragon House.

Niederland, W. 1974. *The Schreber Case: Psychoanalytic Profile of a Paranoid Personality*. New York: Quadrangle.

Nietzsche, F. 1888a. *Ecce Homo*. In *The Philosophy of Nietzsche*, trans. C. Fadiman. New York: Modern Library, 1954.

———. 1888b. *The Antichrist*. In *The Portable Nietzsche*, ed. and trans. W. Kaufmann. New York: Viking Press, 1954.

———. 1888c. *Nietzsche contra Wagner*. *The Portable Nietzsche*, ed. and trans. W. Kaufmann. New York: Viking Press, 1954.

———. 1888d. *The will to power*. Trans. W. Kaufmann and R. J. Hollingdale. New York: Random House, 1967.

———. 1888e. *Twilight of the idols*. In *The Portable Nietzsche*, ed. and trans. W. Kaufmann. New York, Viking Press, 1954.

———. 1887. *The Genealogy of Morals*. In *The Philosophy of Nietzsche*, trans. H. Samuel. New York: Modern Library, 1954.

———. 1886. *Beyond Good and Evil*. In *The Philosophy of Nietzsche*, trans. H. Zimmern. New York: Modern Library, 1954.

———. 1885. *Thus Spoke Zarathustra*. In *The Portable Nietzsche*, ed. and trans. W. Kaufmann. New York: Viking Press, 1954.

———. 1882. *Joyful wisdom*. Trans. T. Common. New York: Frederick Ungar Publishing, 1960.

————. 1878. *Human, All Too Human*. Trans. R. J. Hollingdale. Cambridge: Cambridge University Press, 1986.

Nock, A. D. 1972. Gnosticism. In *Arthur Darby Nock: Essays on Religion and the Ancient World*, ed. Z. Steward, 940–59. Cambridge: Harvard University Press.

Noll, R. 1997. *The Aryan Christ: The Secret Life of Carl Jung*. New York: Random House.

————. 1994. *The Jung cult: Origins of a charismatic Movement*. Princeton: Princeton University Press.

Nott, C. S. 1961. *Teachings of Gurdjieff: A Pupil's Journal*. London: Routledge and Kegan Paul.

Oakes, L. 1997. *Prophetic Charisma: The Psychology of Revolutionary Religious Personalities*. Syracuse, N.Y.: Syracuse University Press.

Oliver, H. 1994. The psychological dimension in Jaspers' relationship with Heidegger. In *Heidegger and Jaspers*, ed. A. Olson, 65–76. Philadelphia: Temple University Press.

Onians, R. B. 1951. *The Origins of European Thought about the Body, the Mind, the Soul, the World, Time, and Fate*. Cambridge: Cambridge University Press.

Ott, H. 1993. *Martin Heidegger: A Political Life*. New York: Basic Books.

Otto, R. 1932. *Mysticism East and West*. Trans. B. Bracey and R. Payne. New York: Collier Books, 1962.

————. 1917. *The Idea of the Holy*. Trans. J. Harvey. New York: Oxford University Press, 1958.

Ouspensky, P. D. 1987. *Strange Life of Ivan Osokin*. London and New York: Arkana.

————. 1957. *The Fourth Way*. New York: Alfred A. Knopf.

————. 1949. *In Search of the Miraculous: Fragments of an Unknown Teaching*. New York: Harcourt, Brace.

————. 1931. *A New Model of the Universe*. New York: Alfred A. Knopf.

Pagels, E. 1995. *The Origin of Satan*. New York: Random House.

————. 1979. *The Gnostic Gospels*. New York: Random House.

Parkes, G. 1999. Nietzsche and Jung: Ambivalent appreciation. In *Nietzsche and Depth Psychology*, ed. J. Golomb, W. Santaniello, and R. Lehrer, 205–27. Albany: State University of New York Press.

Patterson, W. P. 2000. *Voices in the Dark: Esoteric, Occult, and Secular Voices in Nazi-Occupied Paris 1940–44*. Fairfax, Calif.: Arete Communications.

References

References 345

Pauwels, L. 1964. *Gurdjieff.* Douglas, Isle of Man: Times Press.

Persinger, M. 1987. *Neuropsychological Bases of God Beliefs.* New York: Praeger.

Peters, F. 1965. *Gurdjieff Remembered.* London: Victor Gollancz.

———. 1964. *Boyhood with Gurdjieff.* New York: E. P. Dutton.

Petzet, H. 1993. *Encounters and Dialogues with Martin Heidegger, 1929–1976.* Trans. P. Emad and K. Maly. Chicago: University of Chicago Press.

Piaget, J. 1962. *Play, Dreams, and Imitation in Childhood.* New York: W. W. Norton.

Plato. 4th cent. B.C. *The Collected Dialogues.* ed. E. Hamilton and H. Cairns. Princeton: Bollingen.

Pletsch, C. 1991. *Young Nietzsche: Becoming a Genius.* New York: Free Press.

Plotinus. 3rd cent. *The Enneads.* Trans. S. MacKenna. New York: Penguin Books, 1991.

Podach, E. 1931. *The Madness of Nietzsche.* Trans. F. Voight. New York: Gordon Press, 1974.

Popoff, I. 1973. *Gurdjieff: His Work on Myself, with Others, for the Work.* New York: Samuel Weiser.

Provenzano, R. 1987. *Pirates Glen and Dungeon Rock: The Evolution of a Legend.* Saugus, Mass.: Saugus Historical Society.

Rank, O. 1941. *Beyond Psychology.* New York: Dover Publications.

———. 1932. *Art and Artist.* New York: Agathon Press.

Raschke, C. 1980. *The Interruption of Eternity: Modern Gnosticism and the Origins of the New Religious Consciousness.* Chicago: Nelson-Hall.

Redlich, F. 1998. *Hitler: Diagnosis of a Destructive Prophet.* Oxford: Oxford University Press.

Regardie, I. and Stephensen, P. 1986. *The Legend of Aleister Crowley.* Las Vegas: New Falcon Publications.

Reich, W. 1976. *People in Trouble.* Trans P. Schmitz. New York: Farrar, Straus and Giroux.

———. 1949. *Character Analysis.* New York: Noonday Press.

Ribble, M. 1943. *The Rights of Infants: Early Psychological Needs and Their Satisfaction.* New York: Columbia University Press.

Richardson, R. 1995. *Emerson: The Mind on Fire.* Berkeley, University of California Press.

Richardson, W. 1963. *Heidegger: Through Phenomenology to Thought*. The Hague: Martinus Nijhoff.

Ring, K. 1989. Near death and UFO encounters as shamanic initiations. *Revision* 11, no. 3: 14–22.

Rizzuto, A. 1979. *The Birth of the Living God*. Chicago: University of Chicago Press.

Roberts, T. 1998. *Contesting Spirit: Nietzsche's Affirmation Religion*. Princeton: Princeton University Press.

Rockmore, T. 1992. *On Heidegger's Nazism and Philosophy*. Berkeley: University of California Press.

Rosenfeld, H. 1965. *Psychotic States*. New York: International Universities Press.

Roszak, T. 1992. *The Voice of the Earth*. New York: Simon and Schuster.

Rothberg, D. 1996. How straight is the spiritual path? Conversations with Buddhist teachers Joseph Goldstein, Jack Kornfield, and Michele McDonald-Smith. *Revision* 19: 25–40.

Rudolph, K. 1987. *Gnosis; The Nature and History of Gnosticism*. San Francisco: Harper and Row.

Runes, D., ed. and trans. 1965. *Martin Heidegger: German Existentialism*. New York: Philosophical Library.

Runyan, W. 1982. *Life Histories and Psychobiography*. Oxford: Oxford University Press.

Safranski, R. 1998. *Martin Heidegger: Between Good and Evil*. Cambridge: Harvard University Press.

Samuels, A. 1992. National psychology, national socialism, and analytical psychology: Reflections on Jung and anti-semitism. *Journal of Analytical Psychology* 37: 3–28, 127–48.

Sanders, E. 1971. *The Family: The Story of Charles Manson's Dune Buggy Attack Battalion*. New York: E. P. Dutton.

Schain, R. 2001. *The Legend of Nietzsche's Syphilis*. Westport, Conn.: Greenwood Press.

Schleiermacher, F. 1821. *On Religion: Speeches to Its Cultured Despisers*. Trans. R. Crouter. Cambridge: Cambridge University Press, 1988.

Scholem, G. 1946. *Major Trends in Jewish Mysticism*. New York: Schocken Books.

Schreber, D. P. 1903. *Memoirs of My Nervous Illness*. London: Dawson.

Schwartz-Salint, N. 1989. *The Borderline Personality: Vision and Healing.* Wilmette, Illinois: Chiron Publications.

Scully, R. and Dalton, D. 1996. *Living with the Dead: Twenty Years on the Bus with Garcia and the Grateful Dead.* Boston: Little, Brown.

Searles, H. 1979. *Countertransference and Related Subjects.* New York: International Universities Press.

———. 1965. *Collected Papers on Schizophrenia and Related Subjects.* New York: International Universities Press.

Sereny, G. 1995. *Albert Speer: His Battle with Truth.* New York: Alfred A. Knopf.

Shaara, L. and Strathern, A. 1992. A preliminary analysis of the relationship between altered states of consciousness, healing, and social structure. *American Anthropologist* 94: 145–60.

Shamdasani, S. 1998. *Cult Fictions: C. G. Jung and the Founding of Analytical Psychology.* London: Routledge.

———. 1995. Memories, dreams, omissions. *Spring* 57: 115–37.

Sharaf, M. 1983. *Fury on Earth: A Biography of Wilhelm Reich.* New York: St. Martin's.

Silberer, H. 1914. *Hidden symbolism of Alchemy and the Occult Arts.* Trans. S. E. Jelliffe. New York: Dover, 1971.

———. 1912. On symbol formation. In *Organization and Pathology of Thought*, ed. and trans. D. Rapaport, 208–33. New York: Columbia University Press, 1951.

———. 1909. Report on a method of eliciting and observing certain symbolic hallucination-phenomena. In *Organization and Pathology of Thought*, ed. and trans. D. Rapaport, 195–207. New York: Columbia University Press, 1951.

Simon, L. 1998. *Genuine Reality: A Life of William James.* New York: Harcourt Brace.

Sjöö, M. and Mor, B. 1987. *The Great Cosmic Mother: Rediscovering the Religion of the Earth.* San Francisco: Harper and Row.

Sluga, H. 1993. *Heidegger's Crisis: Philosophy and Politics in Nazi Germany.* Cambridge: Harvard University Press.

Snow, E.R. 1944. *Pirates and Buccaneers of the Atlantic Coast.* Boston: The Yankee Publishing House.

Sorel, G. 1908. *Reflections on Violence.* Trans. T. Hulme and J. Roth. Glencoe, Ill.: The Free Press, 1950.

Sorokin, P. 1957. *Social and Cultural Dynamics*. Boston: Porter Sargent.

————. 1937–41. *Social and Cultural Dynamics*, 4 vols. New York: Bedminster Press.

Spadafora, A., and Hunt, H. 1990. The multiplicity of dreams: Cognitive-affective correlates of lucid, archetypal, and nightmare dreaming. *Perceptual and Motor Skills*,71: 627–44.

Spilka, B., Hood, R., and Gorsuch, R. 1985. *The Psychology of Religion: An Empirical Approach*. Englewood Cliffs, N.J.: Prentice-Hall.

Spranger, E. 1928. *Types of men*. Trans. P. Pigors. New York: Johnson Reprint Corporation, 1966.

Starbuck, E. 1899. *The Psychology of Religion*. London: Walter Scott.

Starhawk 1979. *The Spiral Dance: A Rebirth of the Ancient Religion of the Great Goddess*. San Francisco: Harper.

Stark, R. 1999. Secularization, R.I.P. *Sociology of Religion* 60: 249–73.

Stark, R. and Bainbridge, W. 1985. *The Future of Religion: Secularization, Revival, and Cult Formation*. Berkeley: University of California Press.

Stavely, A. 1978. *Memories of Gurdjieff*. Aurora, Ore.: Two Rivers Press.

Steiner, G. 1999. The magician in love: Heidegger's correspondence with Hannah Arendt. *The Times Literary Supplement* (29 January): 3–4.

Stern, P. 1976. *C. G. Jung: The Haunted Prophet*. New York: George Braziller.

Stevens, A. 1982. *Archetypes: A Natural History of the Self*. London: Routledge and Kegan.

Stone, D. 1978. New religious consciousness and personal religious experience. *Sociological Analysis* 39: 123–34.

Stone, I. F. 1988. *The Trial of Socrates*. New York: Anchor Books.

Storr, A. 1996. *Feet of clay: Saints, sinners, and Madmen: A Study of Gurus*. New York: Free Press.

Sullivan, H. S. 1953. *The Interpersonal Theory of Psychiatry*. New York: W. W. Norton.

Symonds, J. 1973. *The Great Beast: The Life and Magick of Aleister Crowley*. St. Albans, U.K.: Mayflower Books.

Tart, C. 1994. *Living the Mindful Life*. Boston: Shambhala.

Taylor, E. 1999. *Shadow Culture: Psychology and Spirituality in America*. Washington, D.C.: Counterpoint.

References 349

349

Tedlock, B. 1997. Sacred androgeny in shamanism. Paper presented at the Analytical Psychology Society of Western New York, 24 September.

Tellegen, A., and Atkinson, G. 1974. Openness to absorbing and self altering experiences ("absorption"), a trait related to hypnotic susceptibility. *Journal of Abnormal Psychology* 83: 268–77.

Thoreau, H. D. 1865. *Cape Cod*. New York: Bramhill House, 1951.

———. 1862. Walking. In *The Portable Thoreau*, ed. C. Bode, 592–630. New York: Penguin, 1982.

———. 1854. *Walden; or, Life in the Woods*. In *The Portable Thoreau*, ed. C. Bode, 258–572. New York: Penguin, 1982.

———. 1849. *A Week on the Concord and Merrimack Rivers*. In *The Portable Thoreau*, ed. C. Bode, 138–227. New York: Penguin, 1982.

———. 1849. Civil disobedience. In *The Portable Thoreau*, ed. C. Bode, 109–137. New York: Penguin, 1982.

———. 1837–1861. *The Journal of Henry David Thoreau*, 2 vols., ed. B. Torrey and F. Allen. New York: Dover Publications, 1962.

Tiryakian, E. 1981. The sociological import of a metaphor: Tracking the source of Max Weber's "iron cage." *Sociological Inquiry* 51: 27–33.

Troeltsch, E. 1931. *The Social Teachings of the Christian Churches*, vols. 1 and 2. Trans. O. Wyon. New York: Harper Torchbooks, 1960.

Trungpa, C. 1984. *Shambhala; The Sacred Path of the Warrior*. Boston: Shambhala.

Tylor, E. 1871. *Primitive Culture*, vol. 1. New York: Gordon Press.

Underhill, E. 1955. *Mysticism*. New York: Meridian.

Van Buren, J. 1994. *The Young Heidegger: Rumor of the Hidden King*. Bloomington: Indiana University Press.

Van der Leeuw, G. 1933. *Religion in Essence and Manifestation: A Study in Phenomenology*, 2 vols. Trans. J. Turner. New York: Harper & Row, 1963.

Vico, G. 1744. *The New Science*. Trans. T. Bergin and M. Fisch. Ithaca, N.Y.: Cornell University Press, 1970.

Vycinas, V. 1990. *The Great Goddess and the Aistian Mythical World*. New York: Peter Lang.

Waite, R. 1993. *The Psychopathic God: Adolf Hitler*. New York: Da Capo Press.

Walker, K. 1957. *A Study of Gurdjieff's Teaching*. London: Jonathan Cape.

Walsh, R. 1977. Initial meditative experiences. *Journal of Transpersonal Psychology* 9: 151–92.

Washburn, M. 1994. *Transpersonal Psychology in Psychoanalytic Perspective*. Albany: State University of New York Press.

———. 1988. *The Ego and the Dynamic Ground*. Albany: State University of New York Press.

Washington, P. 1995. *Madame Blavatsky's Baboon: A History of the Mystics, Mediums, and Misfits Who Brought Spiritualism to America*. New York: Schocken Books.

Webb, J. 1987. *The Harmonious Circle: The Lives and Work of G. I. Gurdjieff, P. D. Ouspensky, and Their Followers*. Boston: Shambhala.

———. 1976. *The Occult establishment*. Lasalle, Ill.: Open Court.

———. 1974. *The Occult Underground*. Lasalle, Ill.: Open Court.

Weber, M. 1967. *The Religion of India*. ed. and trans. H. Gerth and D. Martindale. New York: Free Press.

———. 1964. *The Religion of China*. ed. and trans. H. Gerth. New York: Collier and Macmillan.

———. 1952. *Ancient Judaism*. ed. and trans. H. Gerth and D. Martindale. Glencoe, Ill.: Free Press.

———. 1922a. The social psychology of the world religions. In *From Max Weber: Essays in Sociology*, ed. and trans. H. Gerth and C. W. Mills, 267–301. New York: Oxford University Press, 1946.

———. 1922b. *The Sociology of Religion*. Trans. E. Fischoff. Boston: Beacon Press, 1963.

———. 1918a. Politics as a vocation. In *From Max Weber: Essays in Sociology*, ed. and trans. H. Gerth and C. W. Mills, 77–127. New York: Oxford University Press, 1946.

———. 1918b. Science as a vocation. In *From Max Weber: Essays in Sociology*, ed. and trans. H. Gerth and C. W. Mills, 129–56. New York: Oxford University Press, 1946.

———. 1915. Religious rejections of the world and their directions. In *From Max Weber: Essays in Sociology*, ed. and trans. H. Gerth and C. W. Mills, 323–59. New York: Oxford University Press, 1946.

———. 1906. The Protestant sects and the spirit of capitalism. In *From Max Weber: Essays in Sociology*, ed. and trans. H. Gerth and C. W. Mills, 302–22. New York: Oxford University Press, 1946.

———. 1905. *The Protestant Ethic and the Spirit of Capitalism*. Trans. T. Parsons. New York: Charles Schribner's Sons, 1958.

White, R. W. 1975. *Lives in Progress*. New York: Holt, Rinehart, Winston.

———. 1956. *The Abnormal Personality*. New York: Ronald Press.

Whiteman, J. 1961. *The mystical Life*. London: Faber and Faber.

Wilber, K. 2000. *Integral Psychology*. Boston: Shambhala.

———. 1997. *The Eye of Spirit*. Boston: Shambhala.

———. 1995. *Sex, Ecology, Spirituality*. Boston: Shambhala.

———. 1984. The developmental spectrum and psychopathology. *Journal of Transpersonal Psychology* 16: 75–118; 137–66.

Williams, M. 1996. *Rethinking "Gnosticism": An Argument for Dismantling a Dubious Category*. Princeton: Princeton University Press.

Wilson, C. 2000. *The Devil's Party: A History of Charlatan Messiahs*. London: Virgin Publishing.

———. 1987. *Aleister Crowley: The Nature of the Beast*. Wellingborough, Northamptonshire, U.K.: Aquarian Press.

Winkelman, M. 2000. *Shamanism: The Neural Ecology of Consciousness and Healing*. Westport, Conn.: Bergin and Garvey.

Winnicott, D.W. 1971. *Playing and Reality*. New York: Basic Books.

———. 1964. Review of *Memories, dreams, reflections*. *International Journal of Psychoanalysis* 45: 450–55.

———. 1963a. Communicating and not communicating leading to the study of certain opposites. In *The Maturational Processes and the Facilitating Environment*, ed. D. W. Winnicott, 179–92. New York: International Universities Press.

———. 1963b. The development of the capacity for concern. In *The Maturational Processes and the Facilitating Environment*, ed. D. W. Winnicott, 73–82. New York: International Universities Press.

———. 1960. Ego distortion in terms of true and false self. In *The Maturational Processes and the Facilitating Environment*, ed. D. W. Winnicott, 140–52. New York: International Universities Press.

Wittgenstein, L. 1979. *Remarks on Frazer's "Golden Bough."* Atlantic Highlands, N.Y.: Humanities Press.

———. 1953. *Philosophical Investigations*. New York: Macmillan.

Wolin, R. 1990. *The Politics of Being: The Political Thought of Martin Heidegger*. New York: Columbia University Press.

Woolger, J. and Woolger, R. 1989. *The Goddess Within: A Guide to the Eternal Myths That Shape Women's Lives*. New York: Fawcett/Columbine.

Wundt, W. 1916. *Elements of Folk Psychology*. Trans. E. Schaub. London: George Allen and Unwin.

Young-Bruehl, E. 1982. *Hannah Arendt: For Love of the World*. New Haven: Yale University Press.

Zaehner, R.C. 1961. *Mysticism: Sacred and Profane*. New York: Oxford University Press.

Zimmerman, M. 1994. *Contesting Earth's Future: Radical Ecology and Postmodernity*. Berkeley: University of California Press.

Index

Underhill, E., 25, 204

Valentinus, 111–114
Van Buren, J., 14, 325
Van der Leeuw, G., 320
Vico, G., 54, 150
Volkische movements, 186–87,
  189–193

Waite, R., 191, 193, 194
Walsh, R., 34, 313
Washburn, M., 37, 281
Washington, P., 288
Webb, J., 190, 226, 227, 228, 287,
  326
Weber, M., 4, 57–59, 61–65,
  195–97, 221, 308–11; on mysticism, 61: inner-worldly, 63,
  65–67, 69–71, 72–78, 81–82,
  105–06, 153, 221, 305, 308–09,
  314–15; other-worldly, 63; on

propheticism/asceticism, 61–63,
  193, 195: inner-worldly, 63–65,
  309–10, 320; other-worldly, 63;
  on Protestant Reformation,
  63–65, 66, 146; on radical salvation movements, 57–58, 104–05,
  116; on secularization, 58–59
White, R. W., 3, 323
Wilber, K., 23, 25, 35–37, 38, 309,
  311, 312, 319
Williams, M., 101
Winkelman, M., 72, 175, 315
Winnicott, D.W., 2, 26, 29–31,
  32–33, 42, 74, 94, 95, 121, 157,
  181–82, 183, 211, 212, 213,
  232–33, 241, 296
Wittgenstein, L., 102, 303–04
Wolin, R., 203, 221
Woolger, J., 293

Zimmerman, M., 309